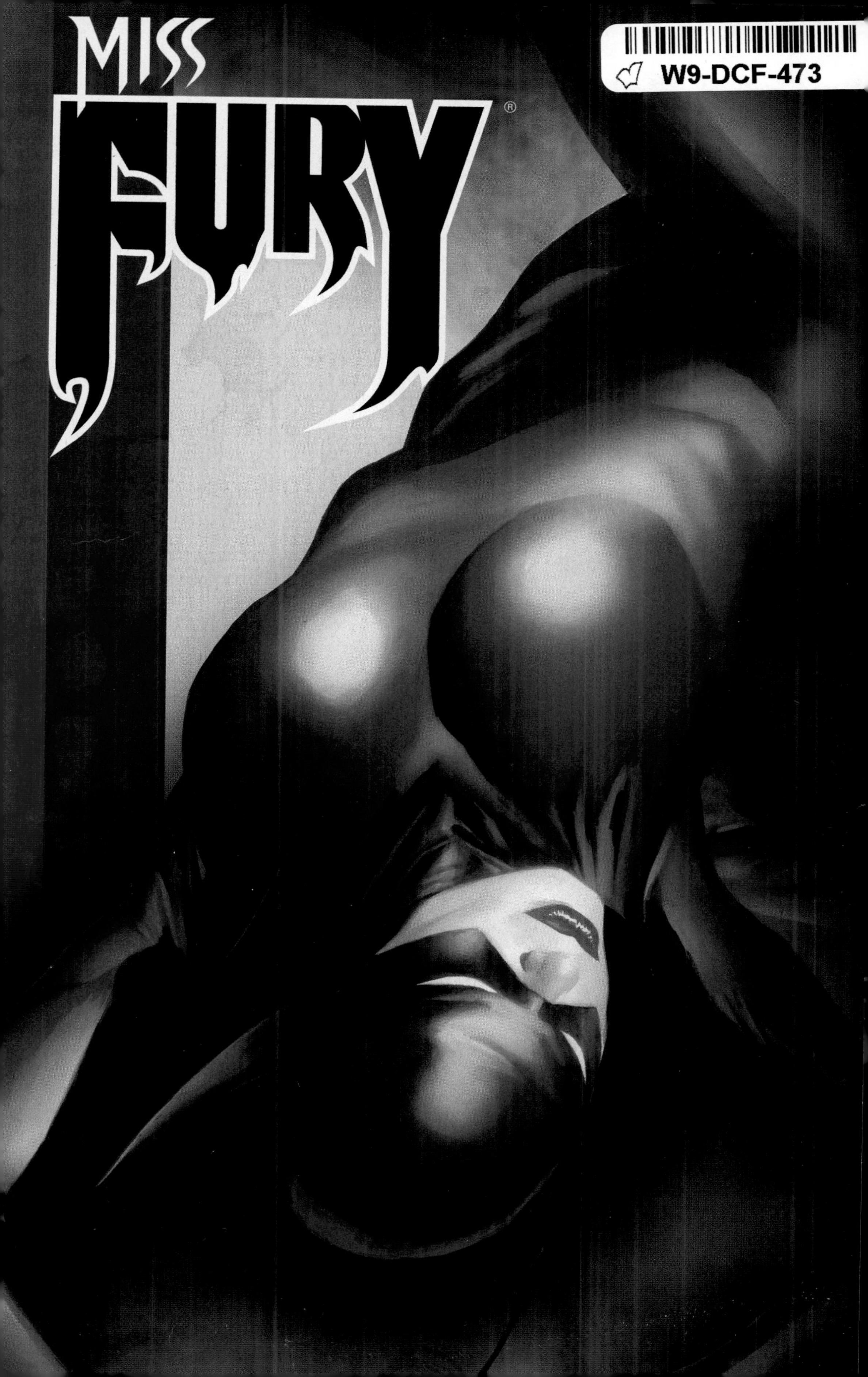
MISS
FURY®

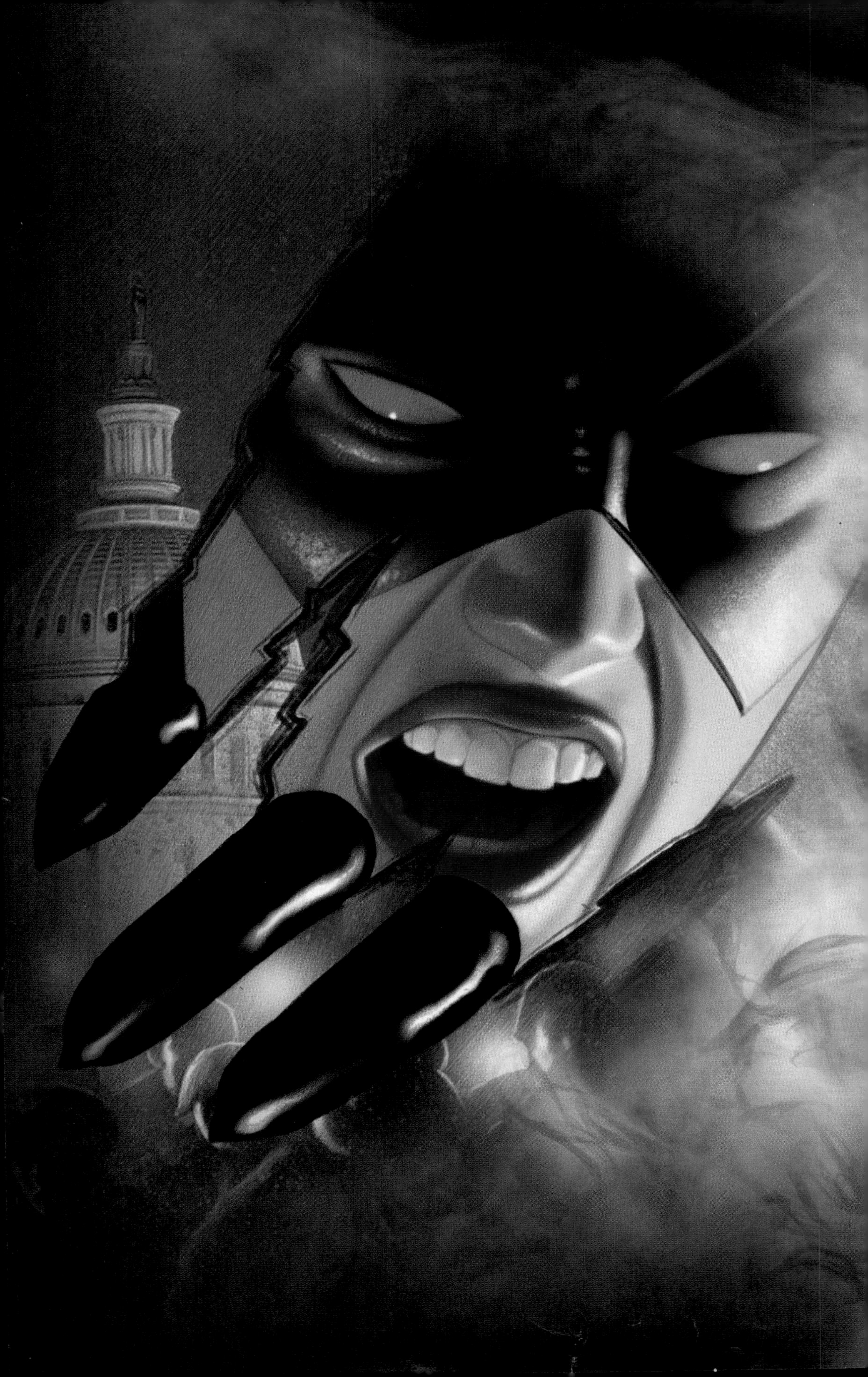

# MISS FURY®

## VOLUME ONE
## ANGER IS AN ENERGY

Written by
**ROB WILLIAMS**

Illustrated by
**JACK HERBERT**
**MARCIO ABREU**

Colored by
**IVAN NUNES**

Lettered by
**SIMON BOWLAND**

Collection Cover by
**ALEX ROSS**

Collection Design by
**KATIE HIDALGO**

**This volume collects issues 1-6 of Miss Fury by Dynamite Entertainment.**

DYNAMITE®

Barrucci, CEO / Publisher
Collado, President / COO
Young, Director Business Development
Davidsen, Marketing Manager

Rybandt, Senior Editor
Green, Traffic Coordinator
Mahan, Assistant Editor

Johnson, Art Director
n Ullmeyer, Senior Graphic Designer
Hidalgo, Graphic Designer
Caniano, Production Assistant

Visit us online at **www.DYNAMITE.com**
Follow us on Twitter **@dynamitecomics**
Like us on Facebook **/Dynamitecomics**
Watch us on YouTube **/Dynamitecomics**

ISBN-10: 1-60690-447-7 ISBN-13: 978-1-60690-447-3 First Printing 10 9 8 7 6 5 4 3 2 1

**MISS FURY® VOL. 1: ANGER IS AN ENERGY.** This volume collects material originally published in Miss Fury #1-6. Published by Dynamite Entertainment. 113 Gaither Dr., STE 205, Mt. Laurel, NJ 08054.  **Printed in Canada**

For information regarding press, media rights, foreign rights, licensing, promotions, and advertising e-mail: marketing@dynamite.com

# MISS FURY
## Pitch for an Initial Four-Issue Mini-Series Arc
## by Rob Williams

*"What are YOU angry about?"*

## The High Concept

Miss Fury is a brutal, ultra-violent Hollywood action movie with a psychological edge, part INGLORIOUS BASTERDS, part JJ Abrams's' ALIAS.

Our Miss Fury finds herself thrown between two time periods – one is the Manhattan of World War Two, the other is the Washington of 2012. In the 1940s she is a selfish emotionally dead thief who accidentally stumbles across Nazi spies, in 2012 she is told by her contact to assassinate spies posing as top US politicians. In both times, against her will, she becomes involved in the fight to protect America from great evil. But how can this be happening and which, if any, of these realities is real? Is she losing her mind, is she being sent to murder perfectly good men?

The reveal at the end is that both realities are real. The only way she can escape – and find redemption along the way - is to find and kill the scientist in charge of the machine in both realities. Even if, in the future, he appears to be a Stephen Hawking figure – the world's most pre-eminent scientist and, as far as the world is concerned, a 'good' man. Her ultimate journey is to return to the 1940s, HER time, and become engaged in life once more.

## Who is Miss Fury? A Redemption Tale

In WW2 Miss Fury is Marla Drake (the original Miss Fury). She is a rich, bored Manhattan socialite who dons a magical ancient ceremonial Black Leopardskin costume and is transformed into master burglar Miss Fury (as per the character's origin She's a deeply bored, morally compromised individual (actually, this is because her husband has been killed in the war and she is so traumatised by this that she has emotionally shut down and has blanked his existence out of her own memory. We'll only reveal this at the end). She has nothing to fight for, just the gain of money. The world outside her window is at war but that's taking place far across the ocean. What does she care? But when word comes to her of the world's greatest diamond coming to New York, she decides that this is something she very much wants. And she attempts to steal it.

The Nazis have similar ideas though, for their own reasons. They need the diamond to power a Faraday Cage time machine that they intend to use to steal incredible weapons tech from the future. Miss Fury stumbles across this time machine experiment and is thrown into the battle. But she falls into the Faraday Cage and she emerges in 2012.

## Enter Modern Day

This strange new reality appears to offer her endless possibilities for a new start. But then she is contacted by a shadowy 'spook'-like figure, a handsome Don Draper-type who tells her that there are secret Nazi agents in the 2012 US Government and his

gency needs them dead. His agency know where Miss Fury has come from – this
guy was in the room when Miss Fury came through the time machine and saw her
kick the shit out of military guards. And because she is a woman 'out of time', who
shouldn't be here, there can be no repercussions for his 'agency' if she's caught. He
needs her because he's ordering the murder of members of the US Congress. Miss
Fury is the PERFECT assassin for this job. A person who doesn't exist, so can't be
tracked back to him and his agency. And he promises he'll get her the diamond she
needs to get back home if she helps him.

From Miss Fury's point of view, she wonders if this guy is part of her imagination or if
he's real (He's real, as we'll eventually show). Is he telling her the truth? There's a
constant playing of whether or not she's losing her mind here. She feels she's keep-
ing something big back mentally, but what is it? (It's the death of her husband in
WW2, as we'll eventually reveal). For now, she has murder to commit.

## stylistic shift between eras

The two-era approach allows us to have our cake and eat it – paying homage to Miss
Fury's pulp roots and also bringing the series into a contemporary climate. I'd suggest
using two separate artists with distinct styles for the two eras in the book (which
could help deadlines, also). In the World War Two era ideally someone with the look
of a Chris Samnee, for the contemporary sections, someone with a more cutting edge
'Ultimates' style (a Stuart Immonen or Sara Pichelli feel). We want to leave the readers with no doubts what 'world' they're in when the time shifts occur on the page.

## The Finale – Nazis, meet America. America…

That time machine that sent Miss Fury into this adventure? Initially the Nazis in WW2
wanted to use it to steal future tech to aid the war effort. But it can be used both
ways. When Miss Fury tracks down and corners the main Nazi scientist in 2012, he
uses the machine to bring a WW2 Nazi army into Manhattan. Suddenly Panzer tanks
are rolling down Broadway. Messerschmitt 109 and jet fighter 262s fly above the city.
Bam! World War 2 comes to the present day! It's up to Miss Fury to reverse the
machine, kill the Nazi scientist and decide which of her realities are real.

Emotionally, Miss Fury has to come to terms with her loss, choose to return to the
1940s and get involved in her life again. She has to regain her passion. She has to
regain her FURY.

## The Theme – Anger Is An Energy…

She's called Miss Fury and she has plenty to be angry about. In WW2 her target is
obvious – the Nazis. The contrast with modern day America will be telling. She's told
these leading politicians she has to kill are 'Hydra'-style spies, planted to destroy the
USA, but is this exactly true? Are they just self-serving, hate-agenda politicians in the
Rush Limbaugh mode? Miss Fury may well be insane here and inventing her 'mission'. But even if she's not, the question will arise – maybe this is a better world with
these fuckers taken out?

In simply terms, and in the words of John Lydon, 'anger is an energy.' When we first
meet her she's cold and detached, made barren by loss. By the end of this story
she's awake and alive once again.

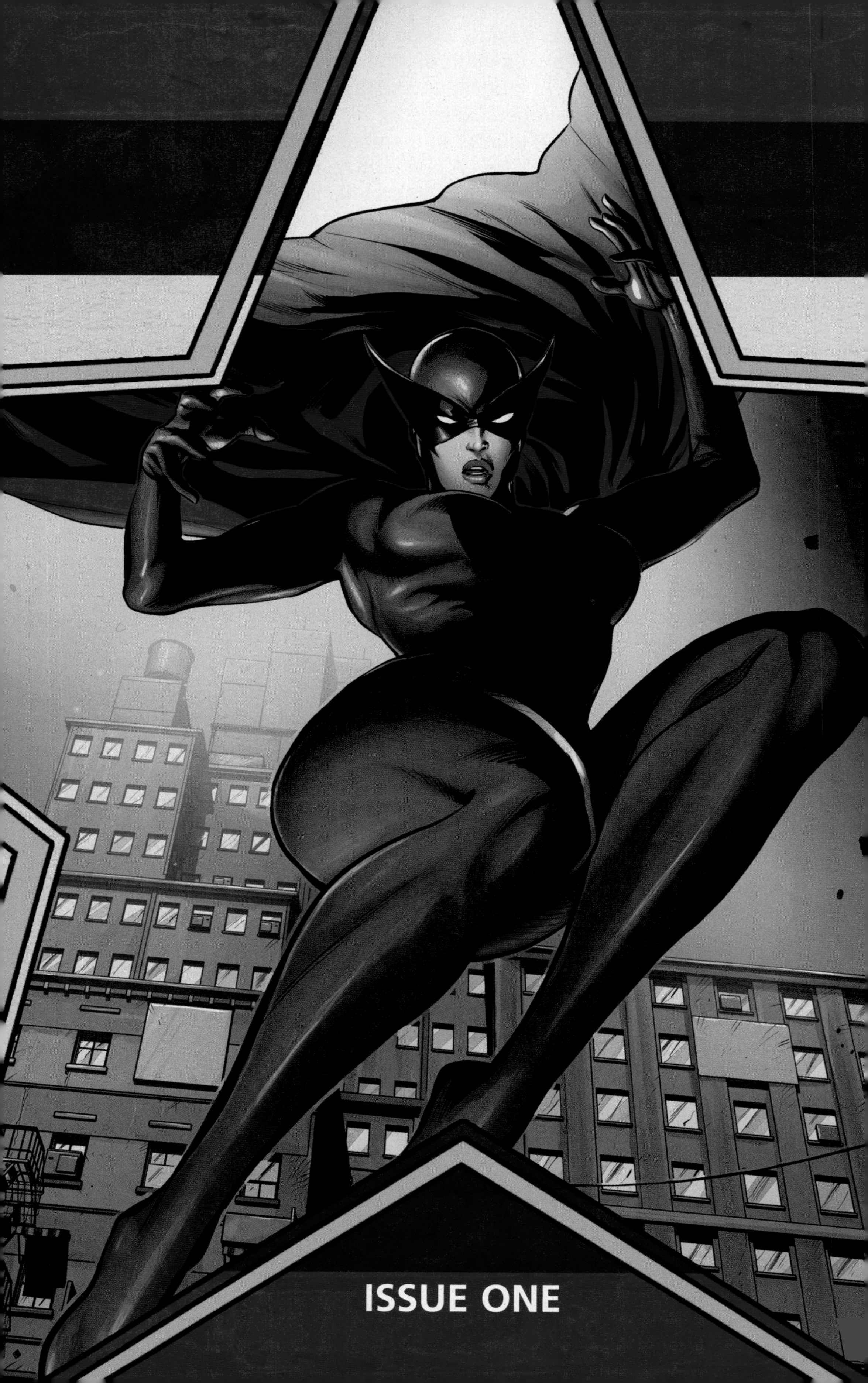
ISSUE ONE

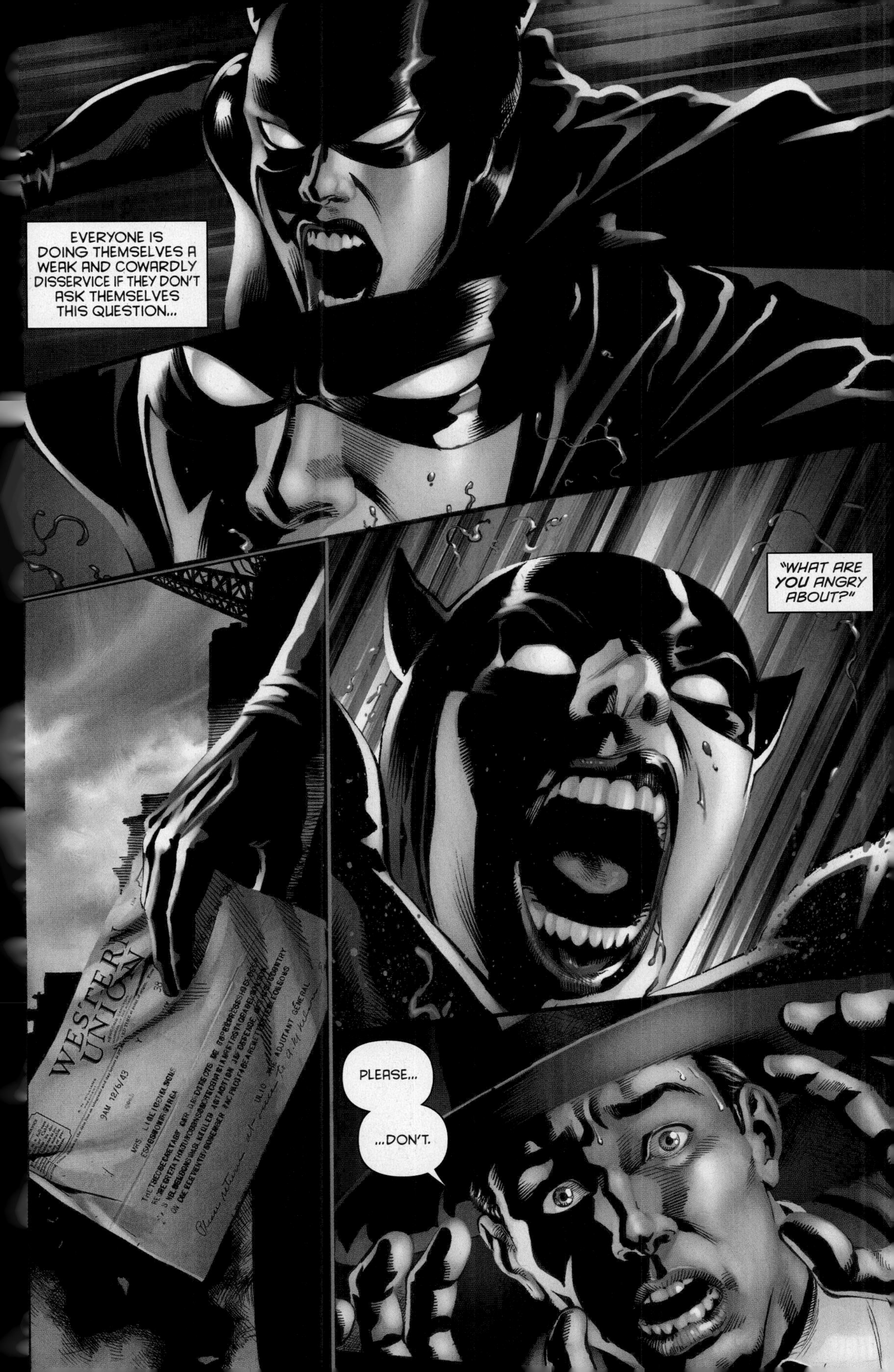
EVERYONE IS DOING THEMSELVES A WEAK AND COWARDLY DISSERVICE IF THEY DON'T ASK THEMSELVES THIS QUESTION...
"WHAT ARE *YOU* ANGRY ABOUT?"
WESTERN UNION
PLEASE...
...DON'T.

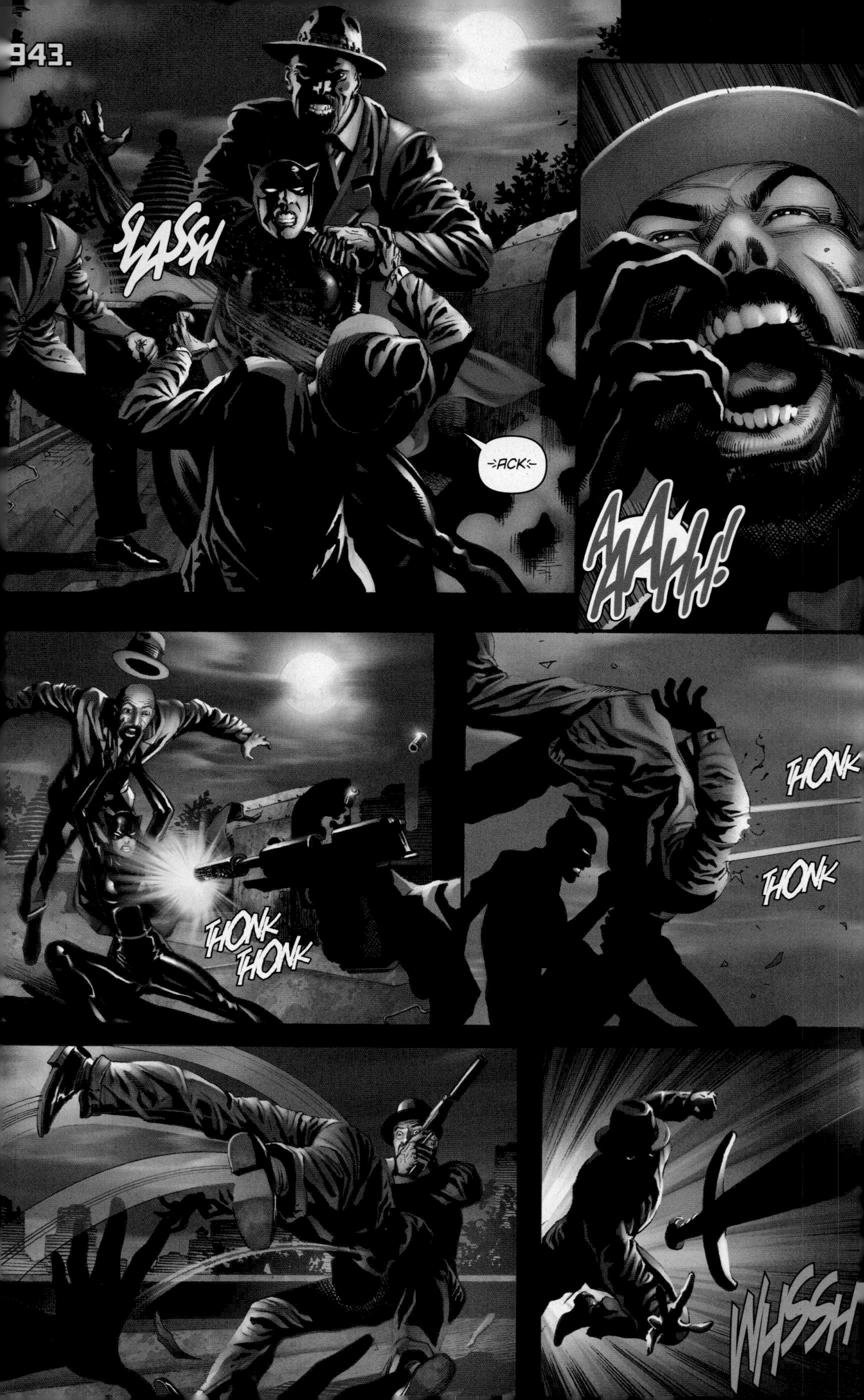
SLASSH
ACK
AAAHH!
THONK
THONK
THONK
THONK
WHSSH

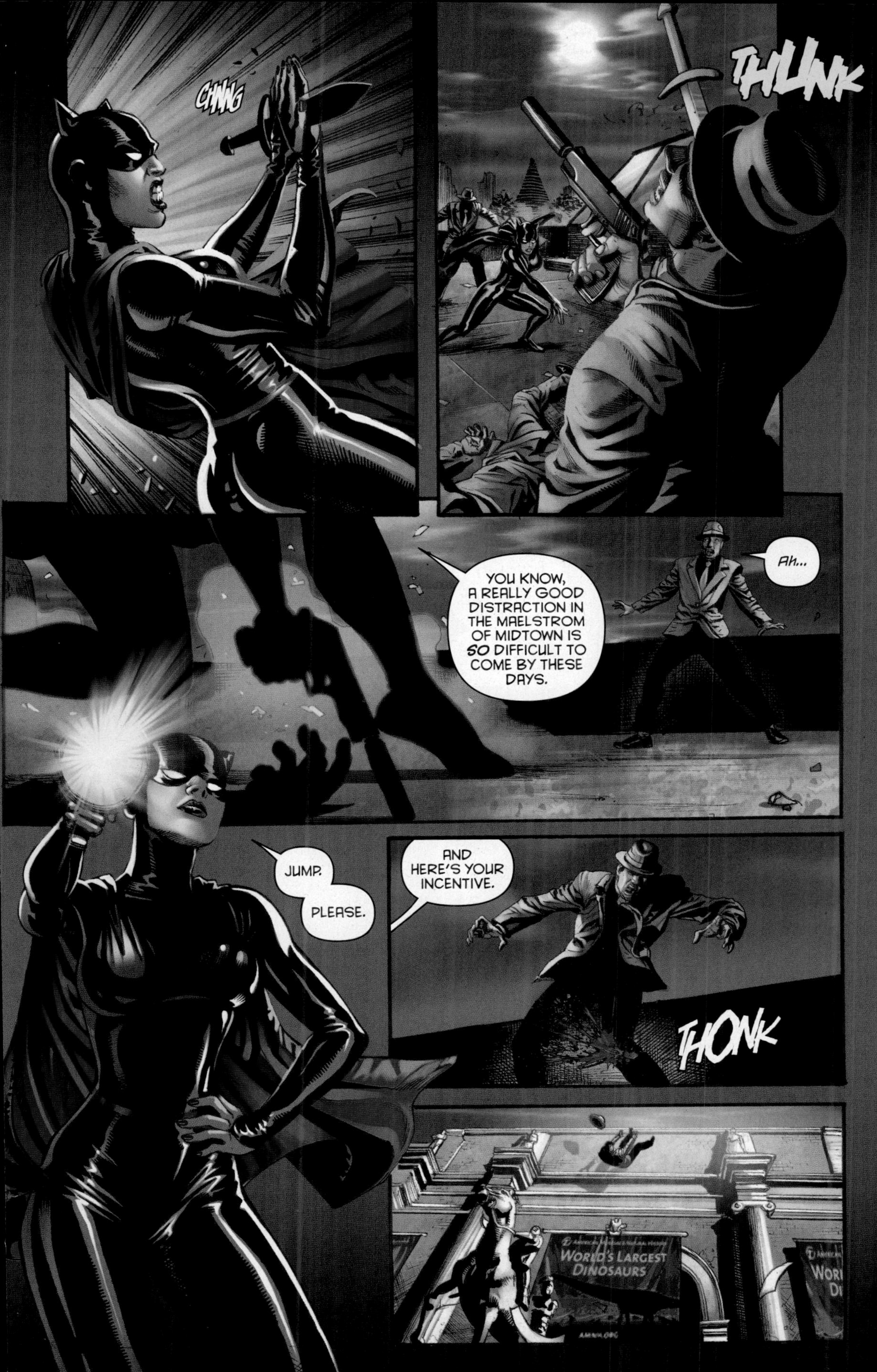
CHNNG
THUNK
YOU KNOW, A REALLY GOOD DISTRACTION IN THE MAELSTROM OF MIDTOWN IS SO DIFFICULT TO COME BY THESE DAYS.
Ah...
JUMP.
PLEASE.
AND HERE'S YOUR INCENTIVE.
THONK
WORLD'S LARGEST DINOSAURS
AMNH.ORG

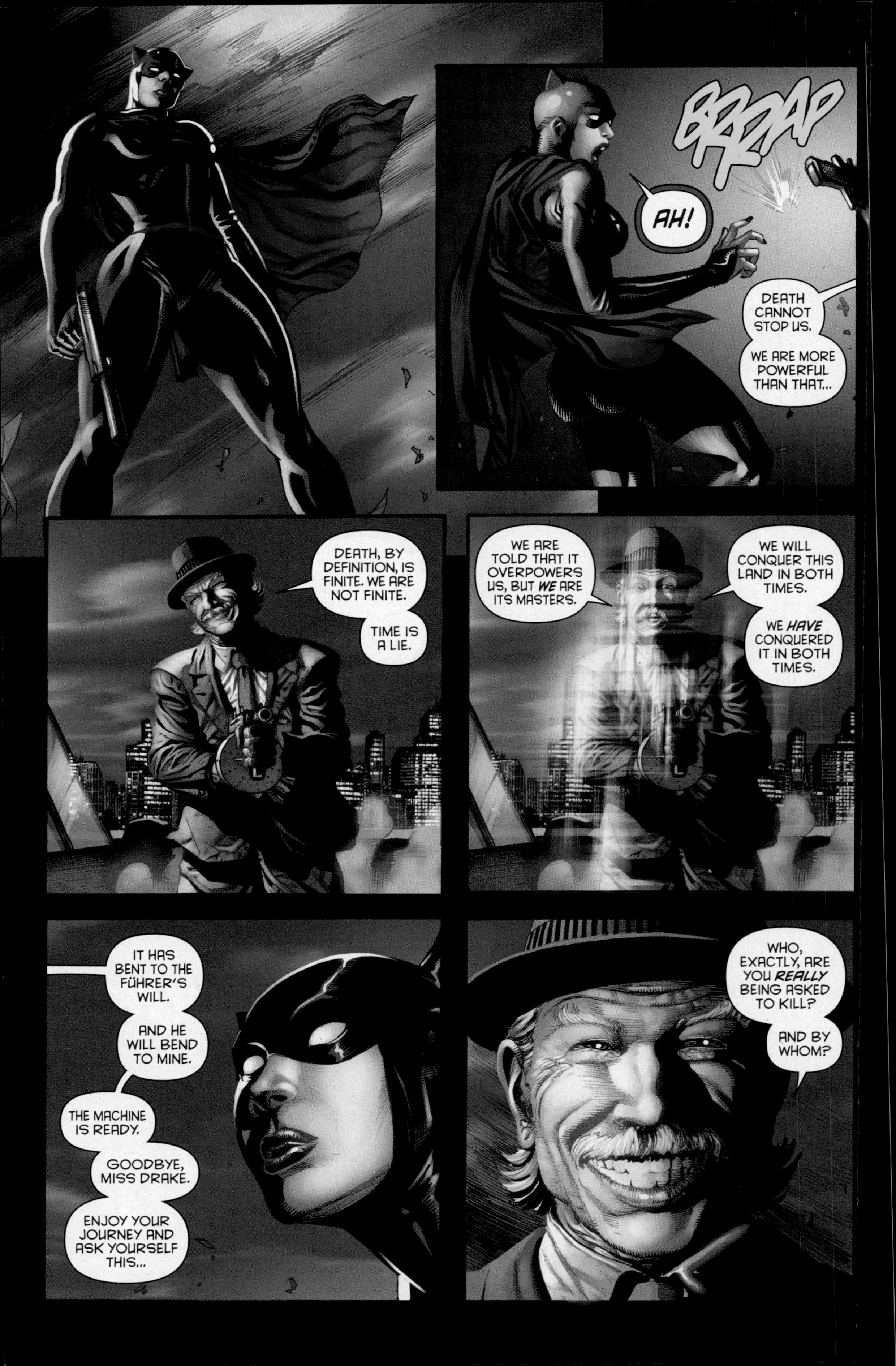
BRRAP
AH!
DEATH CANNOT STOP US.
WE ARE MORE POWERFUL THAN THAT...
DEATH, BY DEFINITION, IS FINITE. WE ARE NOT FINITE.
TIME IS A LIE.
WE ARE TOLD THAT IT OVERPOWERS US, BUT WE ARE ITS MASTERS.
WE WILL CONQUER THIS LAND IN BOTH TIMES.
WE HAVE CONQUERED IT IN BOTH TIMES.
IT HAS BENT TO THE FÜHRER'S WILL.
AND HE WILL BEND TO MINE.
THE MACHINE IS READY.
GOODBYE, MISS DRAKE.
ENJOY YOUR JOURNEY AND ASK YOURSELF THIS...
WHO, EXACTLY, ARE YOU REALLY BEING ASKED TO KILL?
AND BY WHOM?

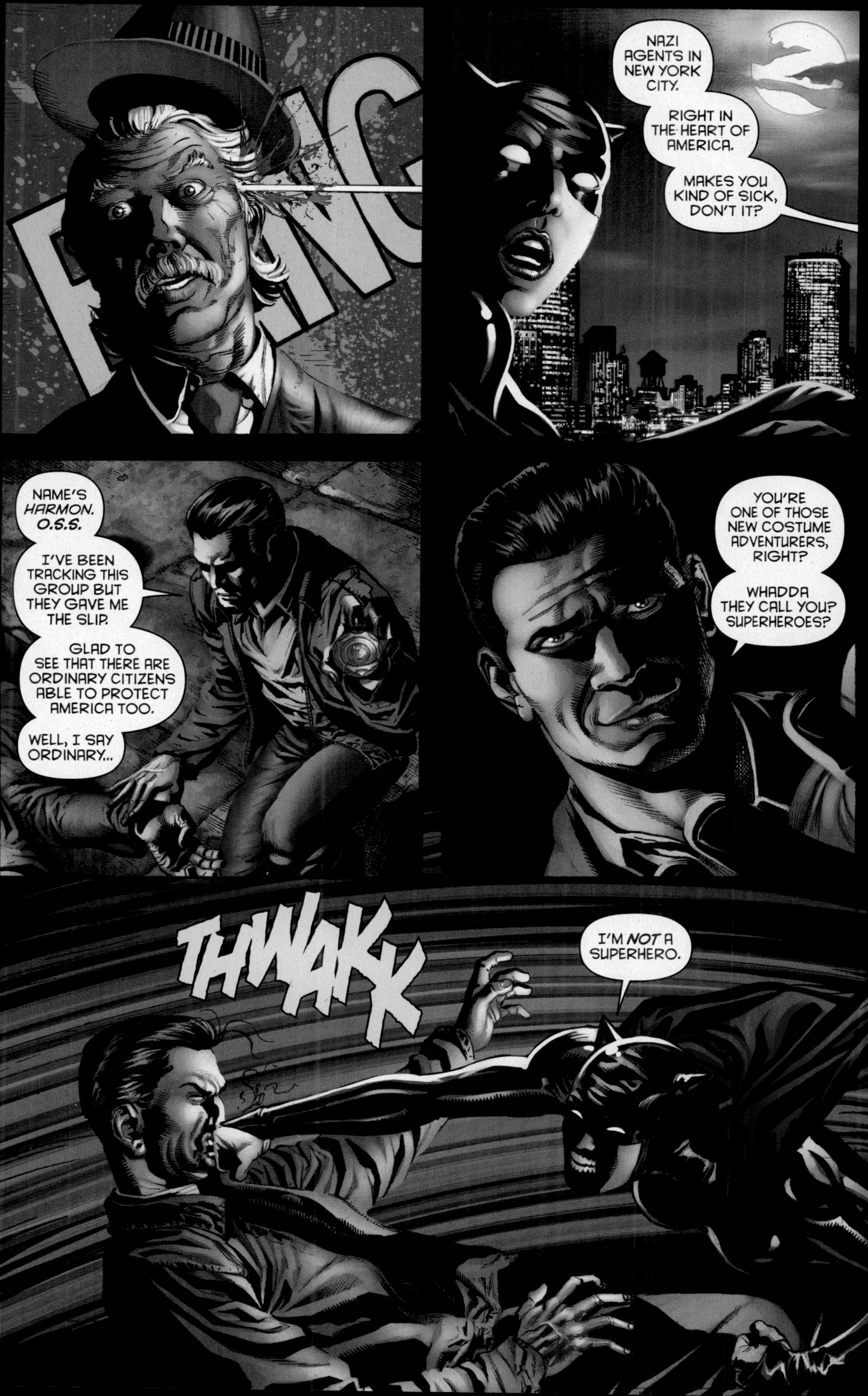

NAZI AGENTS IN NEW YORK CITY.
RIGHT IN THE HEART OF AMERICA.
MAKES YOU KIND OF SICK, DON'T IT?
NAME'S *HARMON.* *O.S.S.*
I'VE BEEN TRACKING THIS GROUP BUT THEY GAVE ME THE SLIP.
GLAD TO SEE THAT THERE ARE ORDINARY CITIZENS ABLE TO PROTECT AMERICA TOO.
WELL, I SAY ORDINARY...
YOU'RE ONE OF THOSE NEW COSTUME ADVENTURERS, RIGHT?
WHADDA THEY CALL YOU? SUPERHEROES?
THWAKK
I'M *NOT* A SUPERHERO.

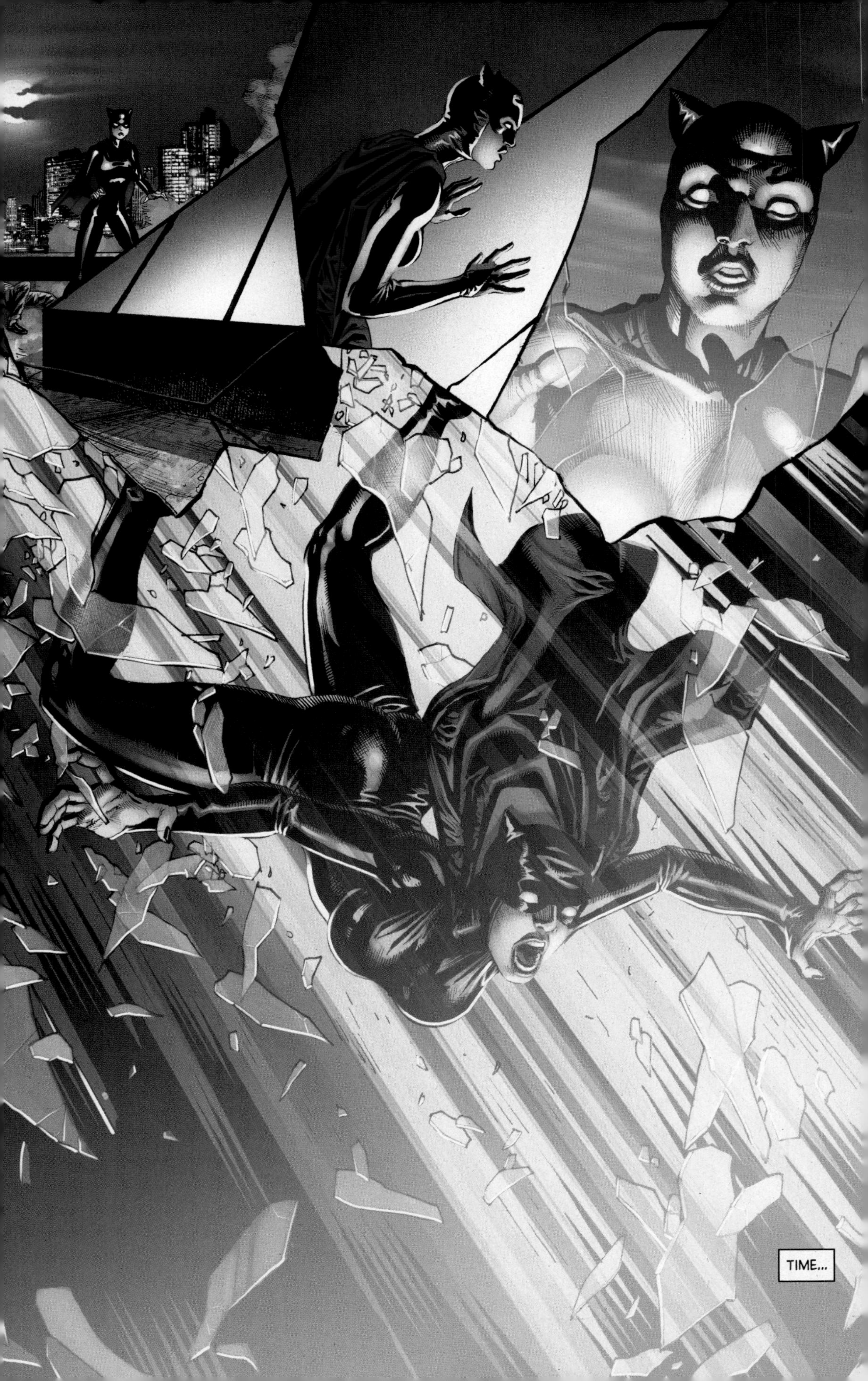
TIME...

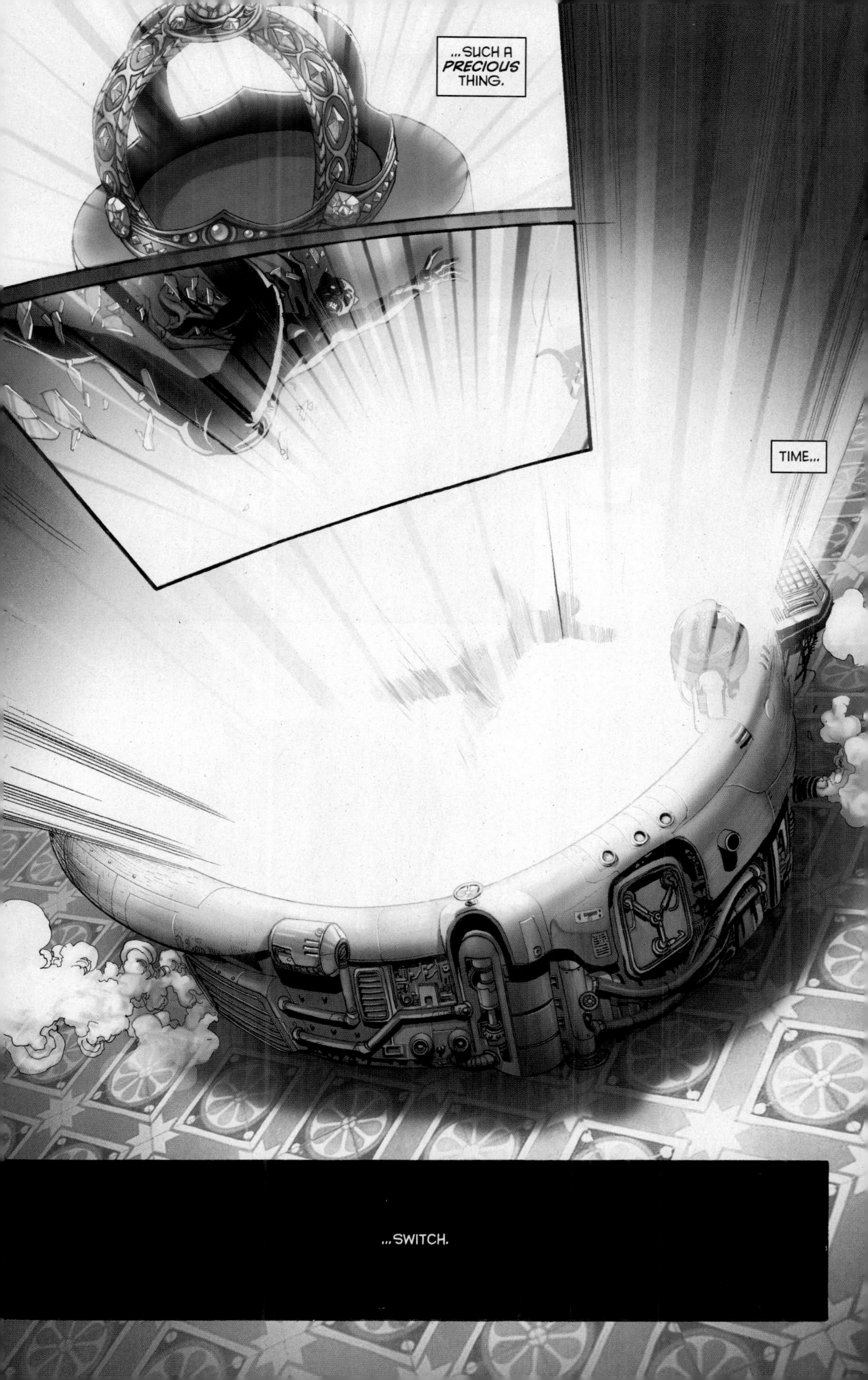
...SUCH A PRECIOUS THING.
TIME...
...SWITCH.

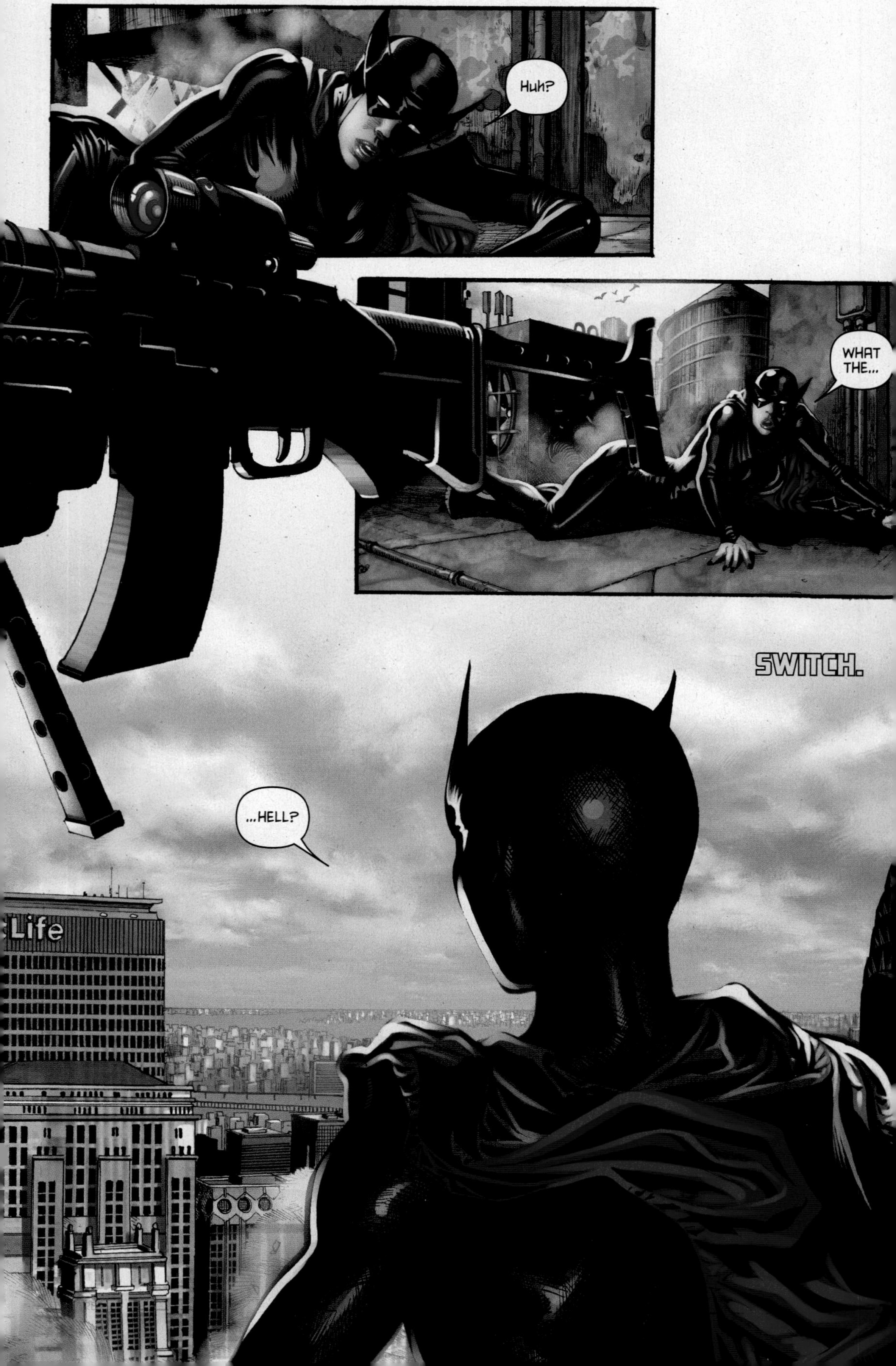
Huh?
WHAT THE...
SWITCH.
...HELL?
Life

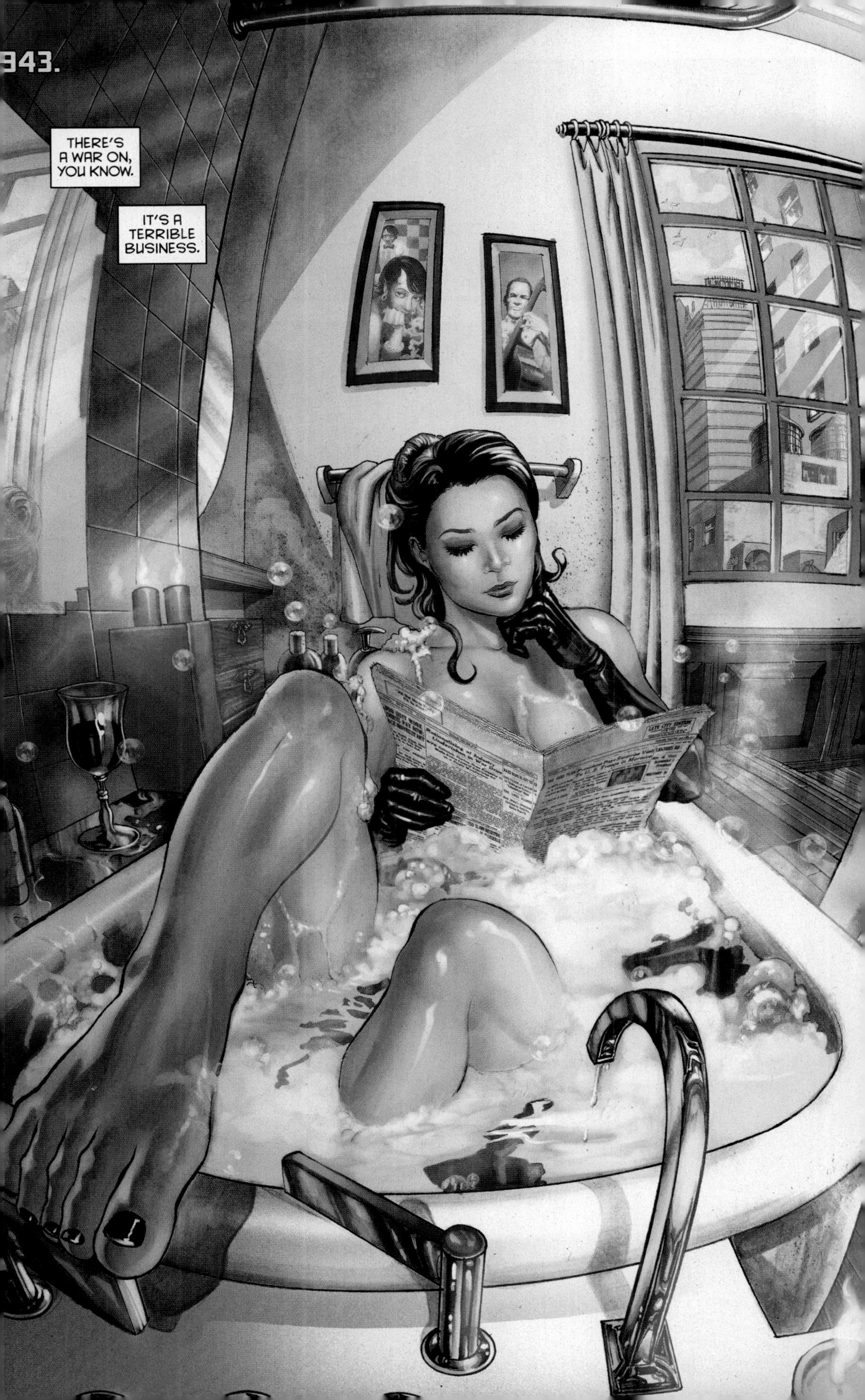
943.
THERE'S A WAR ON, YOU KNOW.
IT'S A TERRIBLE BUSINESS.

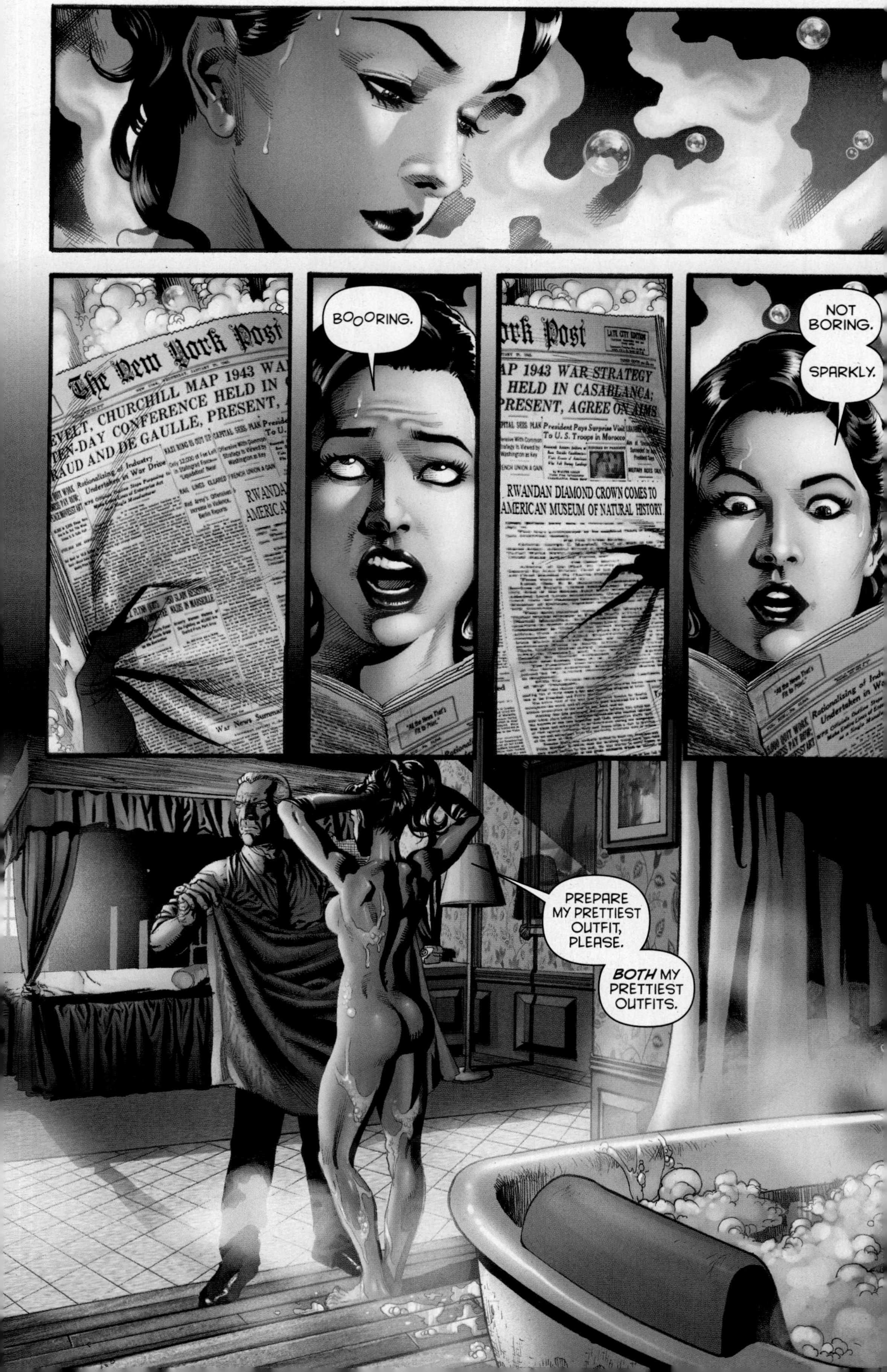
The New York Post
MAP 1943 WAR STRATEGY HELD IN CASABLANCA; PRESENT, AGREE ON AIMS
BOOORING.
RWANDAN DIAMOND CROWN COMES TO AMERICAN MUSEUM OF NATURAL HISTORY
NOT BORING.
SPARKLY.
PREPARE MY PRETTIEST OUTFIT, PLEASE.
*BOTH* MY PRETTIEST OUTFITS.

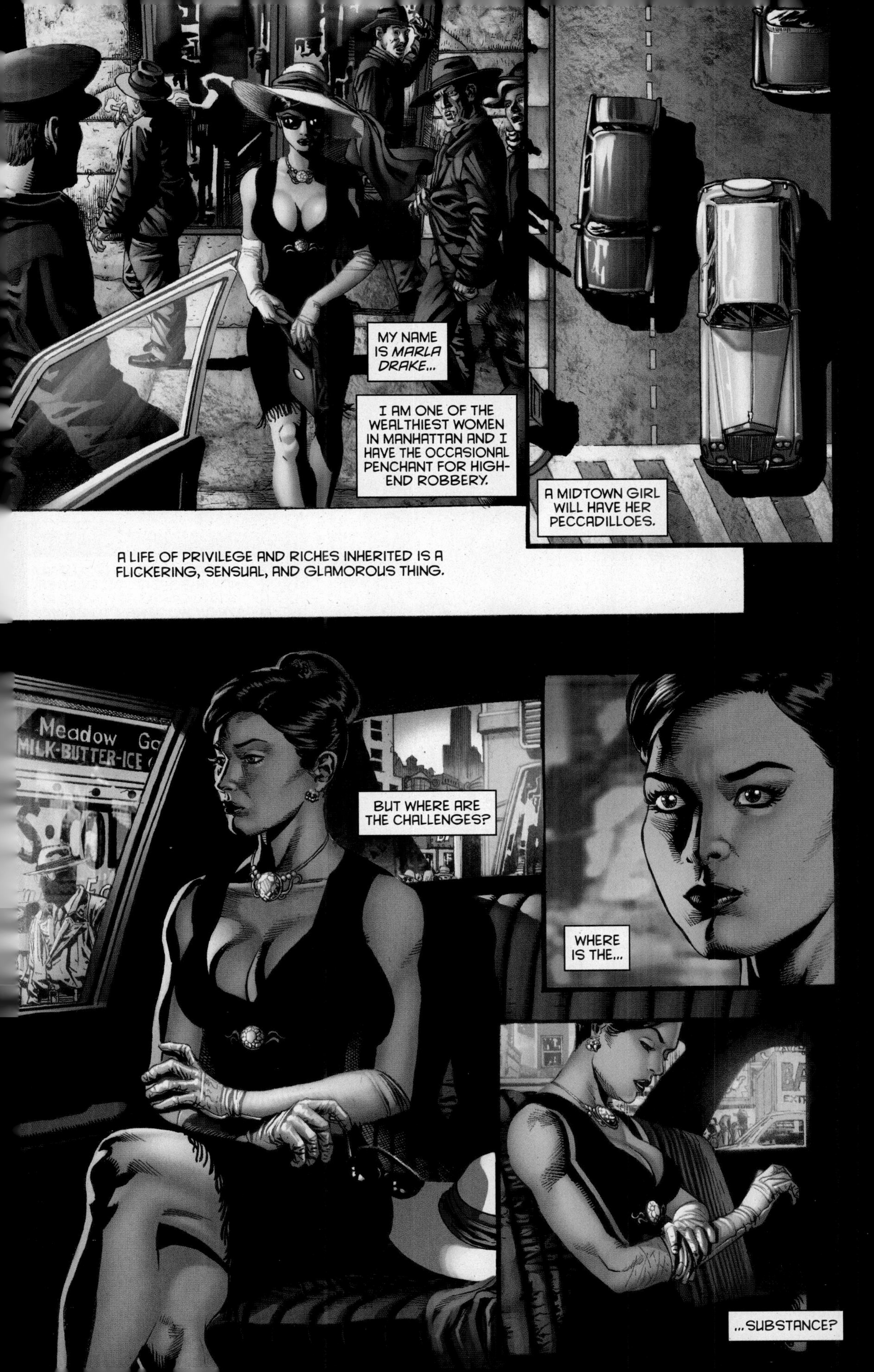

MY NAME IS MARLA DRAKE...
I AM ONE OF THE WEALTHIEST WOMEN IN MANHATTAN AND I HAVE THE OCCASIONAL PENCHANT FOR HIGH-END ROBBERY.
A MIDTOWN GIRL WILL HAVE HER PECCADILLOES.
A LIFE OF PRIVILEGE AND RICHES INHERITED IS A FLICKERING, SENSUAL, AND GLAMOROUS THING.
Meadow
MILK-BUTTER-ICE
BUT WHERE ARE THE CHALLENGES?
WHERE IS THE...
...SUBSTANCE?

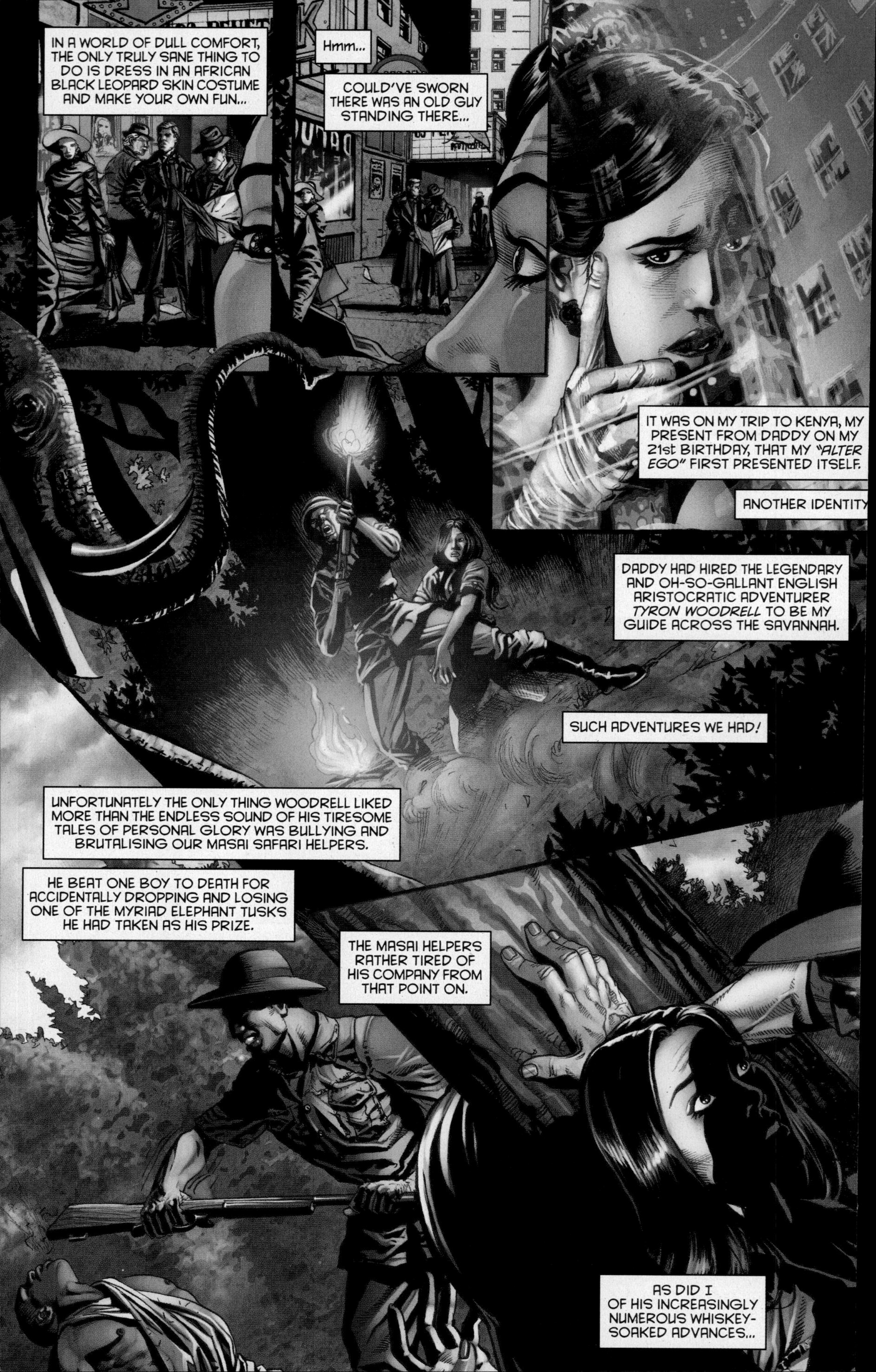
IN A WORLD OF DULL COMFORT, THE ONLY TRULY SANE THING TO DO IS DRESS IN AN AFRICAN BLACK LEOPARD SKIN COSTUME AND MAKE YOUR OWN FUN...
Hmm...
COULD'VE SWORN THERE WAS AN OLD GUY STANDING THERE...
IT WAS ON MY TRIP TO KENYA, MY PRESENT FROM DADDY ON MY 21st BIRTHDAY, THAT MY "ALTER EGO" FIRST PRESENTED ITSELF.
ANOTHER IDENTITY
DADDY HAD HIRED THE LEGENDARY AND OH-SO-GALLANT ENGLISH ARISTOCRATIC ADVENTURER TYRON WOODRELL TO BE MY GUIDE ACROSS THE SAVANNAH.
SUCH ADVENTURES WE HAD!
UNFORTUNATELY THE ONLY THING WOODRELL LIKED MORE THAN THE ENDLESS SOUND OF HIS TIRESOME TALES OF PERSONAL GLORY WAS BULLYING AND BRUTALISING OUR MASAI SAFARI HELPERS.
HE BEAT ONE BOY TO DEATH FOR ACCIDENTALLY DROPPING AND LOSING ONE OF THE MYRIAD ELEPHANT TUSKS HE HAD TAKEN AS HIS PRIZE.
THE MASAI HELPERS RATHER TIRED OF HIS COMPANY FROM THAT POINT ON.
AS DID I OF HIS INCREASINGLY NUMEROUS WHISKEY-SOAKED ADVANCES...

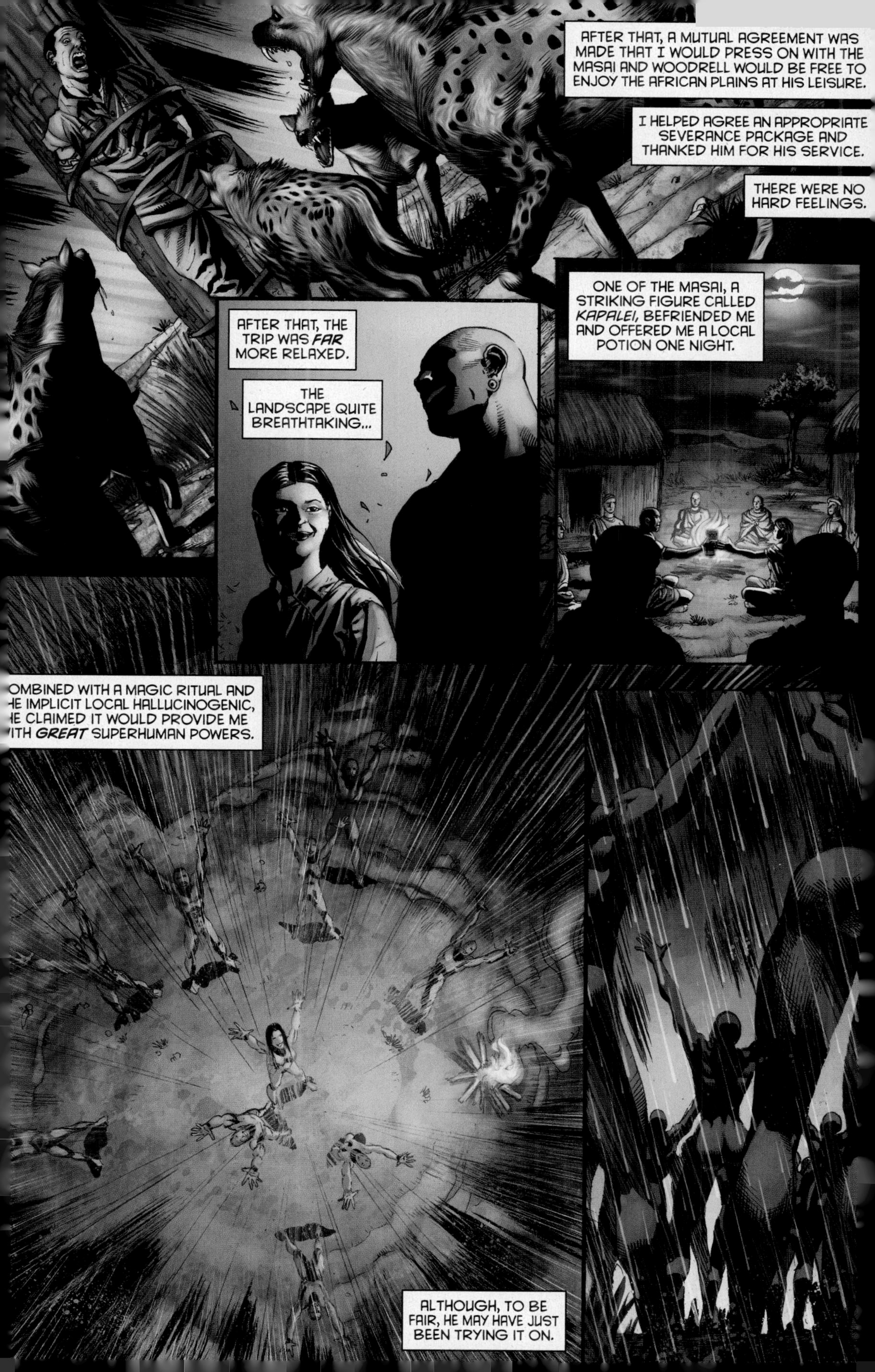
AFTER THAT, A MUTUAL AGREEMENT WAS MADE THAT I WOULD PRESS ON WITH THE MASAI AND WOODRELL WOULD BE FREE TO ENJOY THE AFRICAN PLAINS AT HIS LEISURE.
I HELPED AGREE AN APPROPRIATE SEVERANCE PACKAGE AND THANKED HIM FOR HIS SERVICE.
THERE WERE NO HARD FEELINGS.
AFTER THAT, THE TRIP WAS *FAR* MORE RELAXED.
THE LANDSCAPE QUITE BREATHTAKING...
ONE OF THE MASAI, A STRIKING FIGURE CALLED *KAPALEI*, BEFRIENDED ME AND OFFERED ME A LOCAL POTION ONE NIGHT.
OMBINED WITH A MAGIC RITUAL AND HE IMPLICIT LOCAL HALLUCINOGENIC, HE CLAIMED IT WOULD PROVIDE ME WITH *GREAT* SUPERHUMAN POWERS.
ALTHOUGH, TO BE FAIR, HE MAY HAVE JUST BEEN TRYING IT ON.

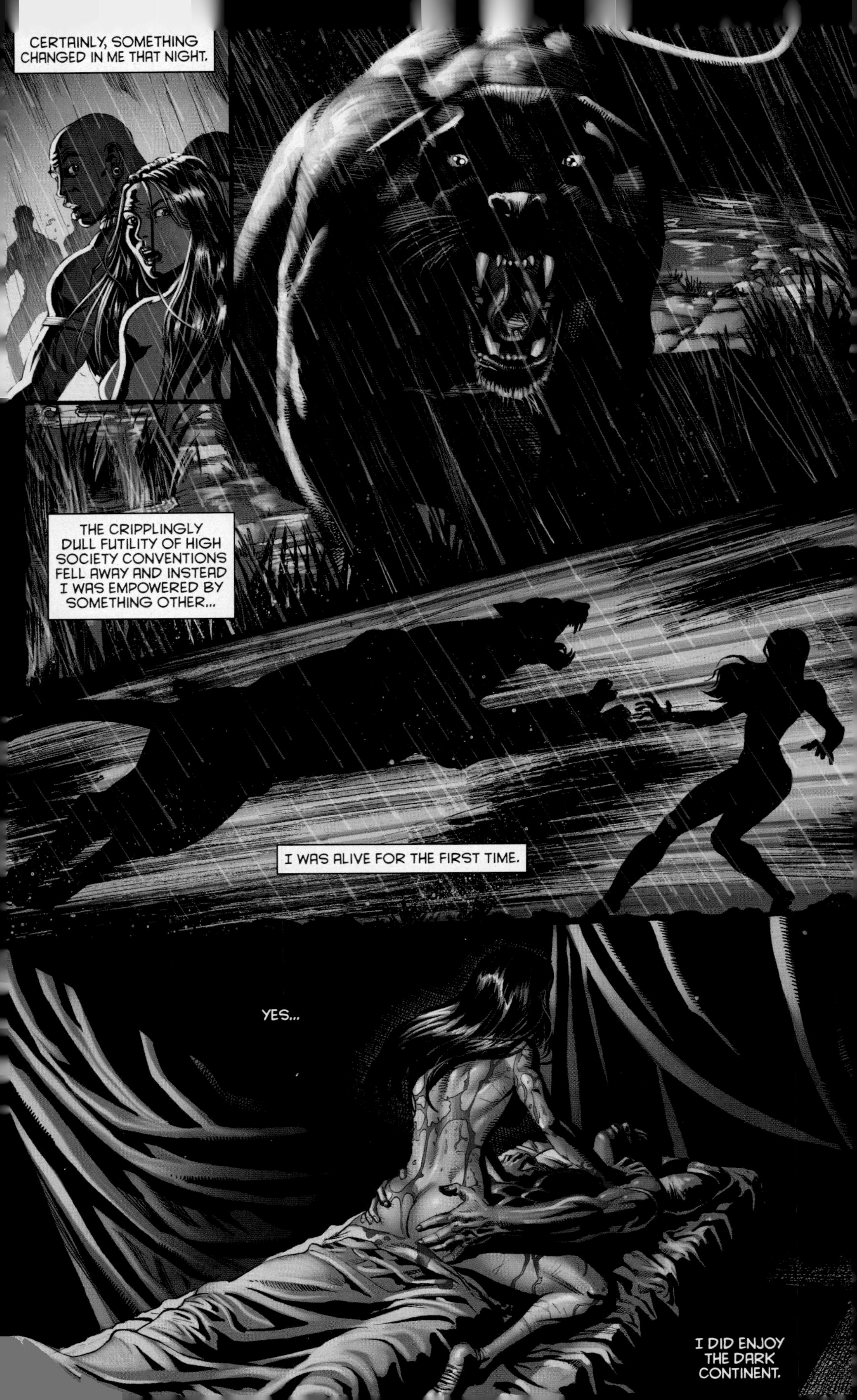
CERTAINLY, SOMETHING CHANGED IN ME THAT NIGHT.
THE CRIPPLINGLY DULL FUTILITY OF HIGH SOCIETY CONVENTIONS FELL AWAY AND INSTEAD I WAS EMPOWERED BY SOMETHING OTHER...
I WAS ALIVE FOR THE FIRST TIME.
YES...
I DID ENJOY THE DARK CONTINENT.

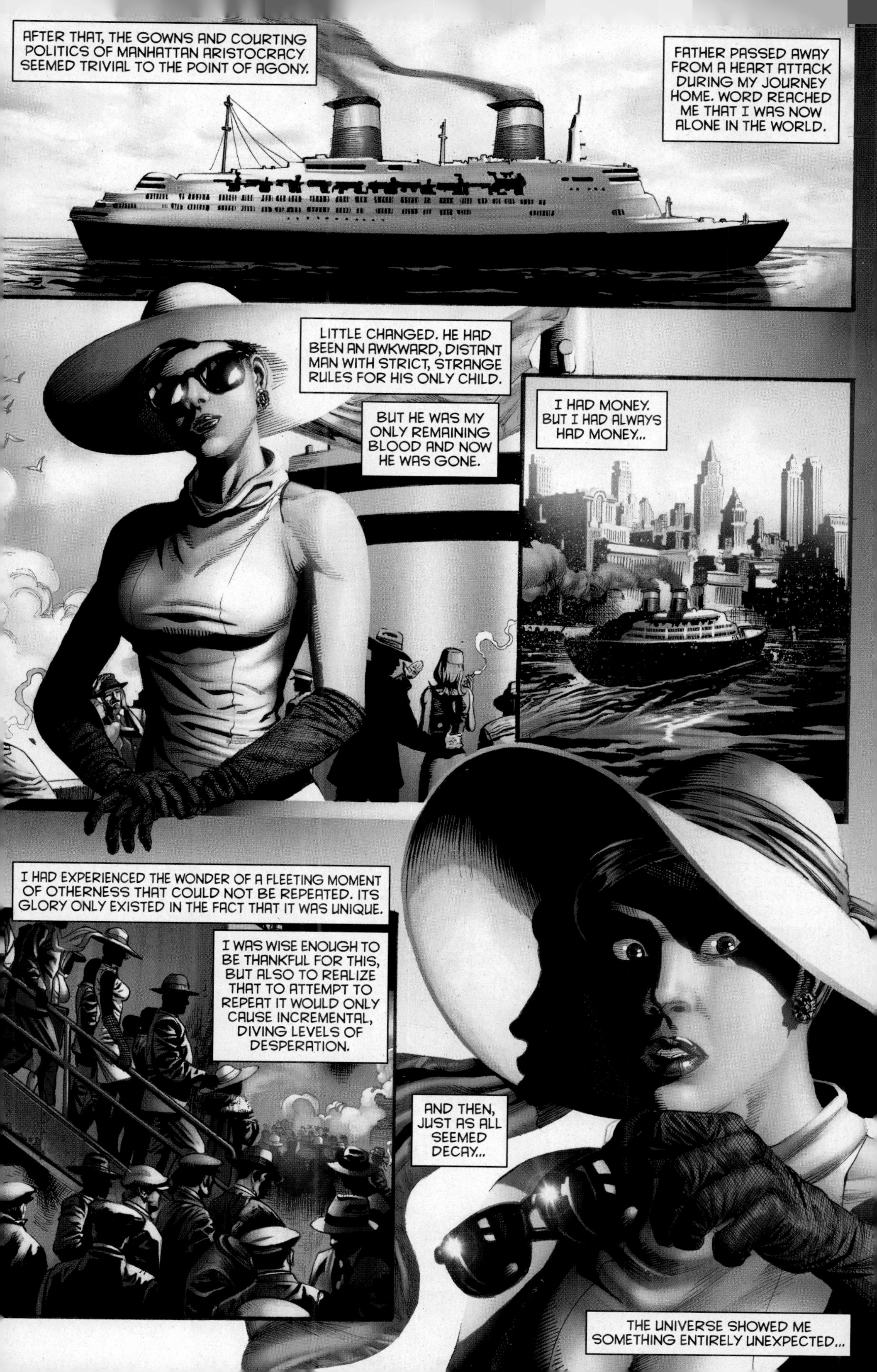
AFTER THAT, THE GOWNS AND COURTING POLITICS OF MANHATTAN ARISTOCRACY SEEMED TRIVIAL TO THE POINT OF AGONY.
FATHER PASSED AWAY FROM A HEART ATTACK DURING MY JOURNEY HOME. WORD REACHED ME THAT I WAS NOW ALONE IN THE WORLD.
LITTLE CHANGED. HE HAD BEEN AN AWKWARD, DISTANT MAN WITH STRICT, STRANGE RULES FOR HIS ONLY CHILD.
BUT HE WAS MY ONLY REMAINING BLOOD AND NOW HE WAS GONE.
I HAD MONEY. BUT I HAD ALWAYS HAD MONEY...
I HAD EXPERIENCED THE WONDER OF A FLEETING MOMENT OF OTHERNESS THAT COULD NOT BE REPEATED. ITS GLORY ONLY EXISTED IN THE FACT THAT IT WAS UNIQUE.
I WAS WISE ENOUGH TO BE THANKFUL FOR THIS, BUT ALSO TO REALIZE THAT TO ATTEMPT TO REPEAT IT WOULD ONLY CAUSE INCREMENTAL, DIVING LEVELS OF DESPERATION.
AND THEN, JUST AS ALL SEEMED DECAY...
THE UNIVERSE SHOWED ME SOMETHING ENTIRELY UNEXPECTED...

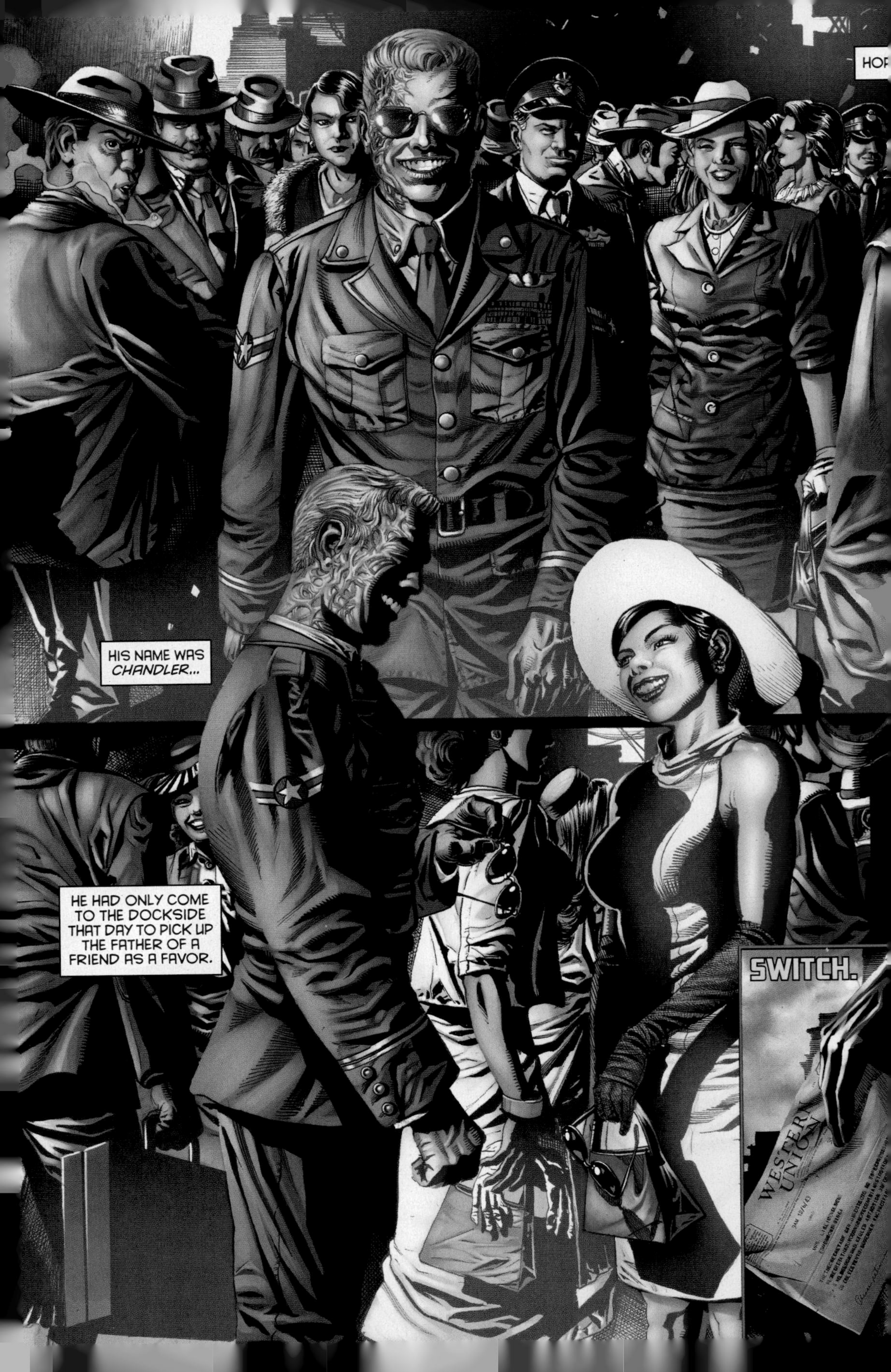
HIS NAME WAS CHANDLER...
HE HAD ONLY COME TO THE DOCKSIDE THAT DAY TO PICK UP THE FATHER OF A FRIEND AS A FAVOR.
SWITCH.

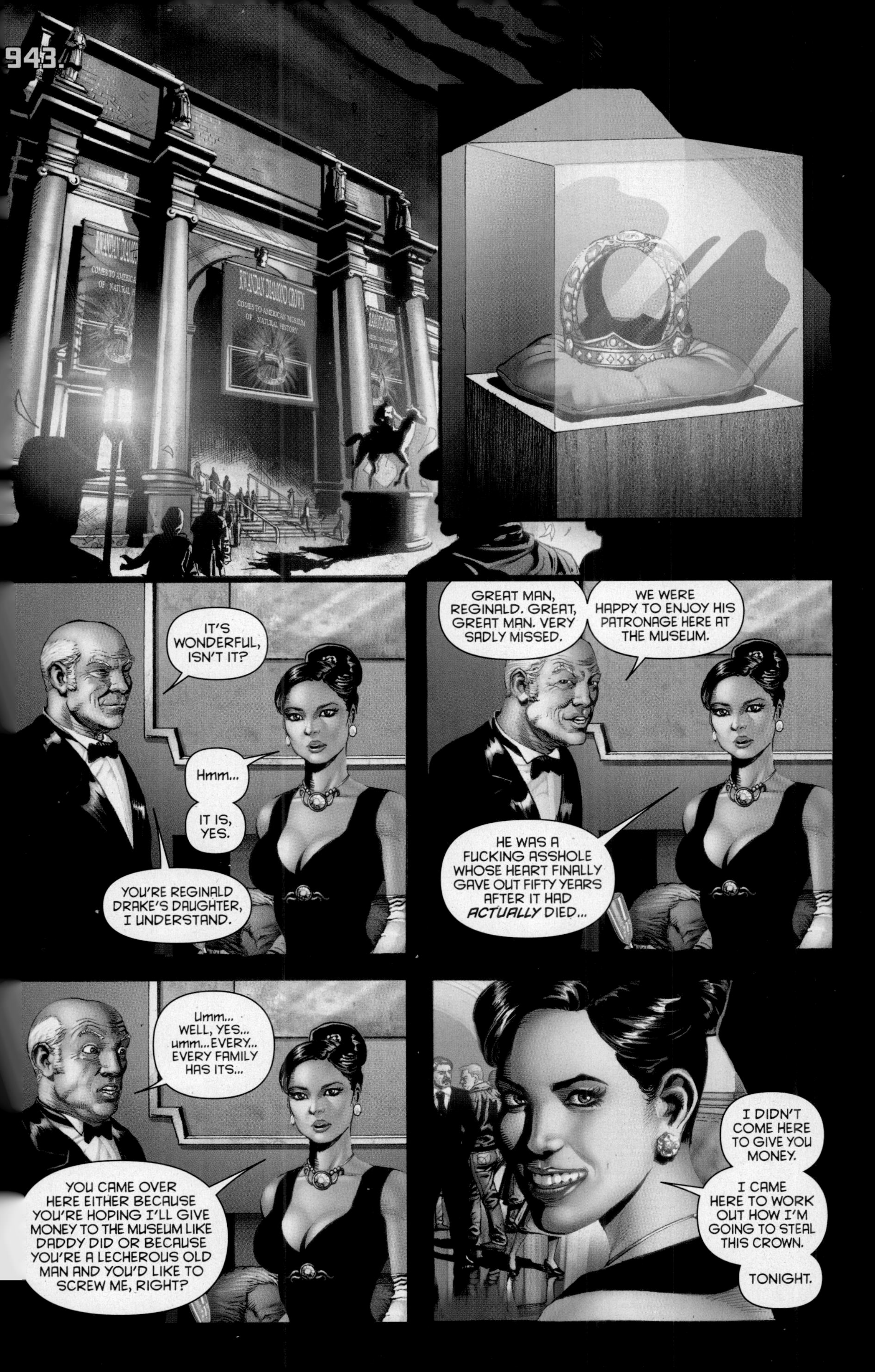
943.
RWANDAN DIAMOND CROWN
COMES TO AMERICAN MUSEUM OF NATURAL HISTORY
IT'S WONDERFUL, ISN'T IT?
Hmm...
IT IS, YES.
YOU'RE REGINALD DRAKE'S DAUGHTER, I UNDERSTAND.
GREAT MAN, REGINALD. GREAT, GREAT MAN. VERY SADLY MISSED.
WE WERE HAPPY TO ENJOY HIS PATRONAGE HERE AT THE MUSEUM.
HE WAS A FUCKING ASSHOLE WHOSE HEART FINALLY GAVE OUT FIFTY YEARS AFTER IT HAD ACTUALLY DIED...
Umm... WELL, YES... umm...EVERY... EVERY FAMILY HAS ITS...
YOU CAME OVER HERE EITHER BECAUSE YOU'RE HOPING I'LL GIVE MONEY TO THE MUSEUM LIKE DADDY DID OR BECAUSE YOU'RE A LECHEROUS OLD MAN AND YOU'D LIKE TO SCREW ME, RIGHT?
I DIDN'T COME HERE TO GIVE YOU MONEY.
I CAME HERE TO WORK OUT HOW I'M GOING TO STEAL THIS CROWN.
TONIGHT.

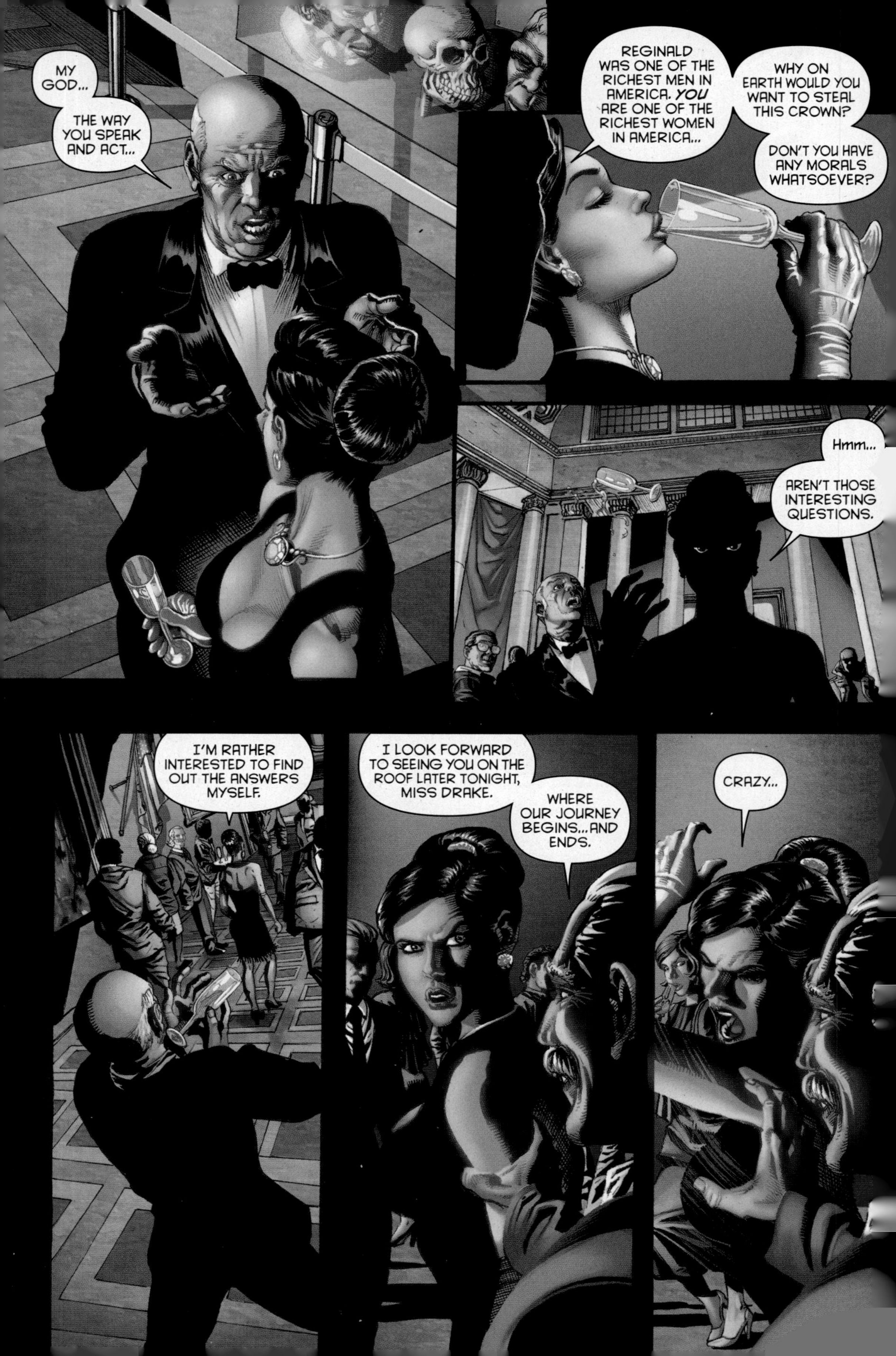
MY GOD...
THE WAY YOU SPEAK AND ACT...
REGINALD WAS ONE OF THE RICHEST MEN IN AMERICA. *YOU* ARE ONE OF THE RICHEST WOMEN IN AMERICA...
WHY ON EARTH WOULD YOU WANT TO STEAL THIS CROWN?
DON'T YOU HAVE ANY MORALS WHATSOEVER?
Hmm...
AREN'T THOSE INTERESTING QUESTIONS.
I'M RATHER INTERESTED TO FIND OUT THE ANSWERS MYSELF.
I LOOK FORWARD TO SEEING YOU ON THE ROOF LATER TONIGHT, MISS DRAKE.
WHERE OUR JOURNEY BEGINS...AND ENDS.
CRAZY...

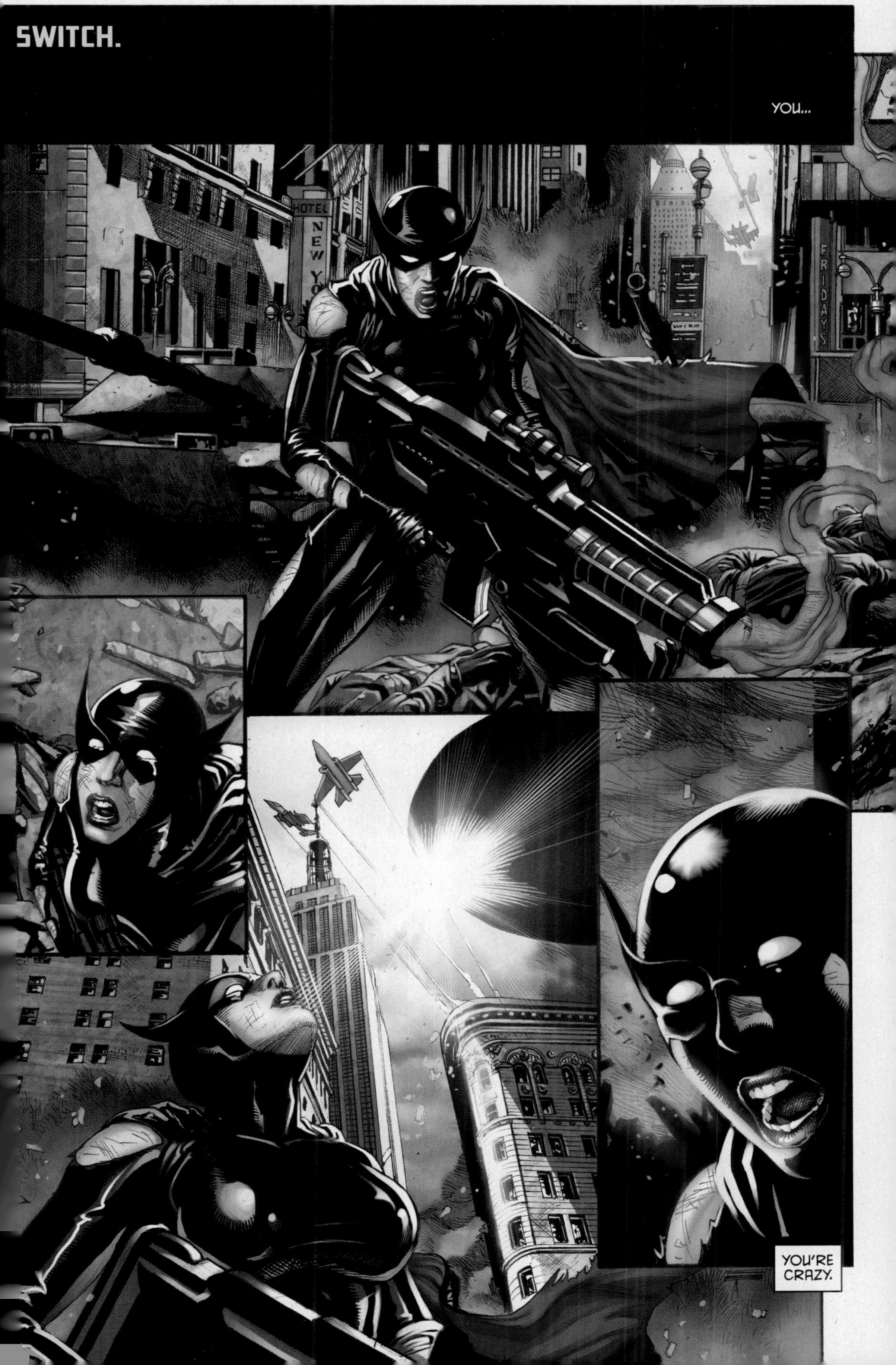
SWITCH.
YOU...
HOTEL
NEW YO
FRIDAYS
YOU'RE CRAZY.

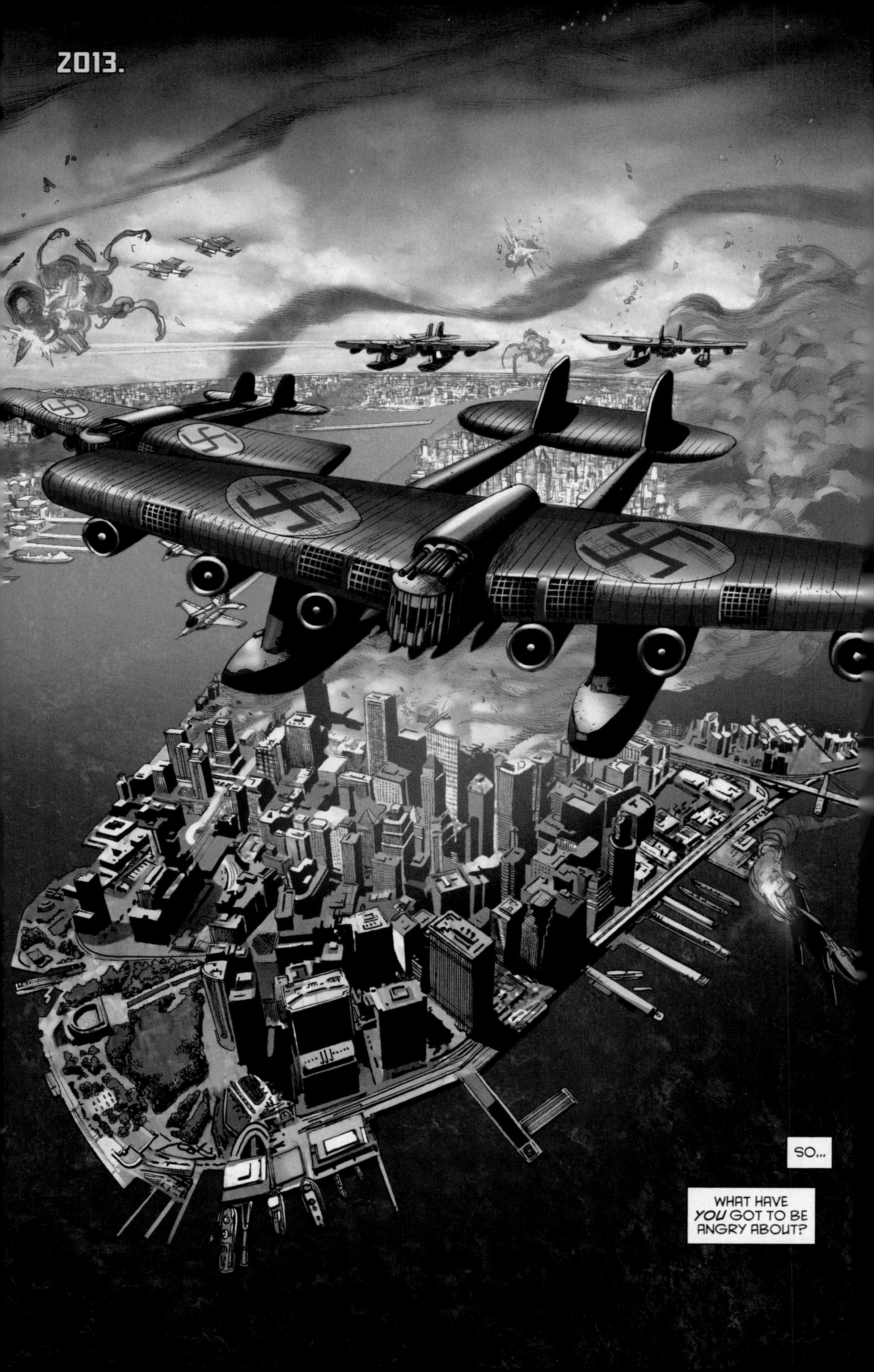
2013.
SO...
WHAT HAVE YOU GOT TO BE ANGRY ABOUT?

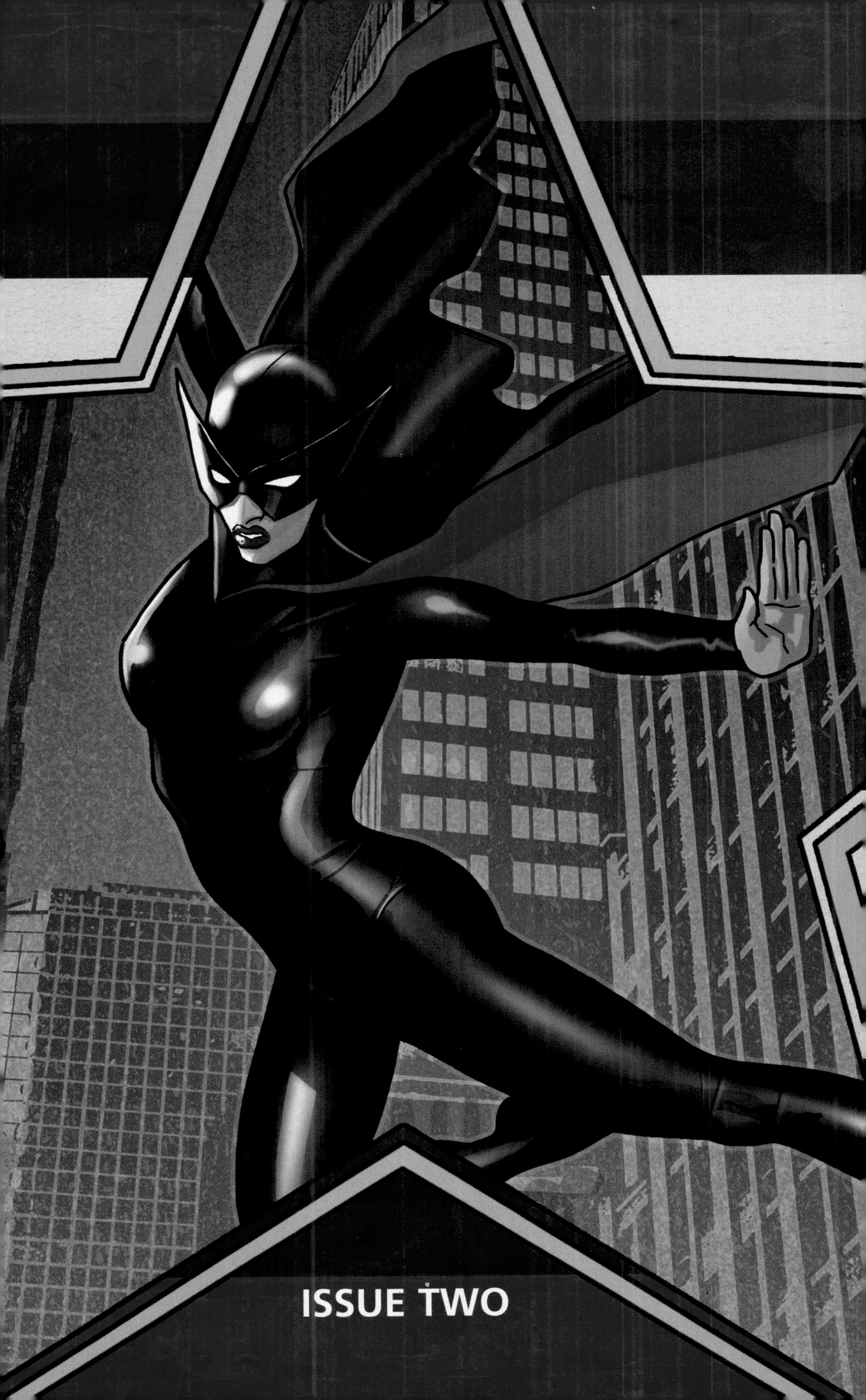
ISSUE TWO

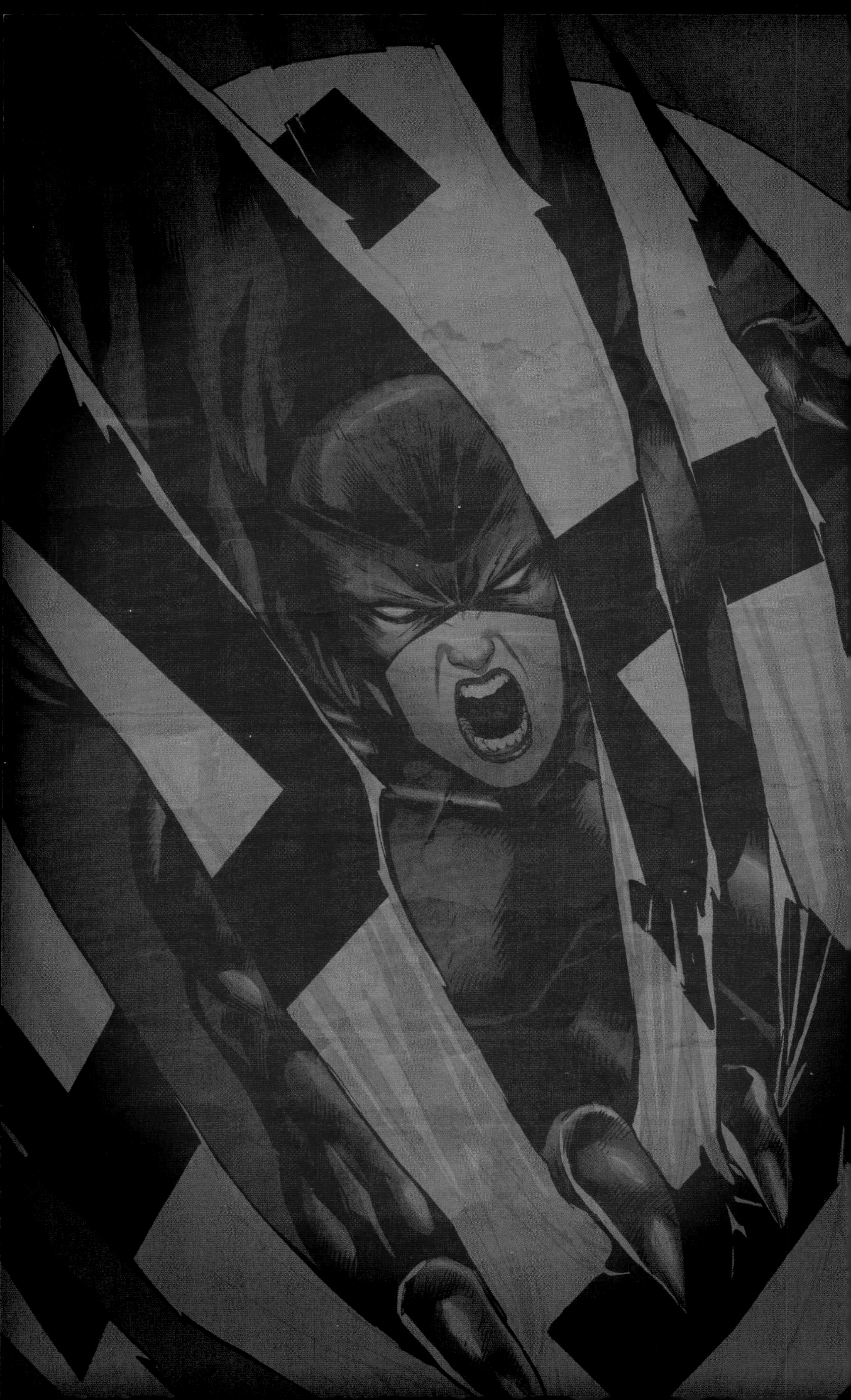

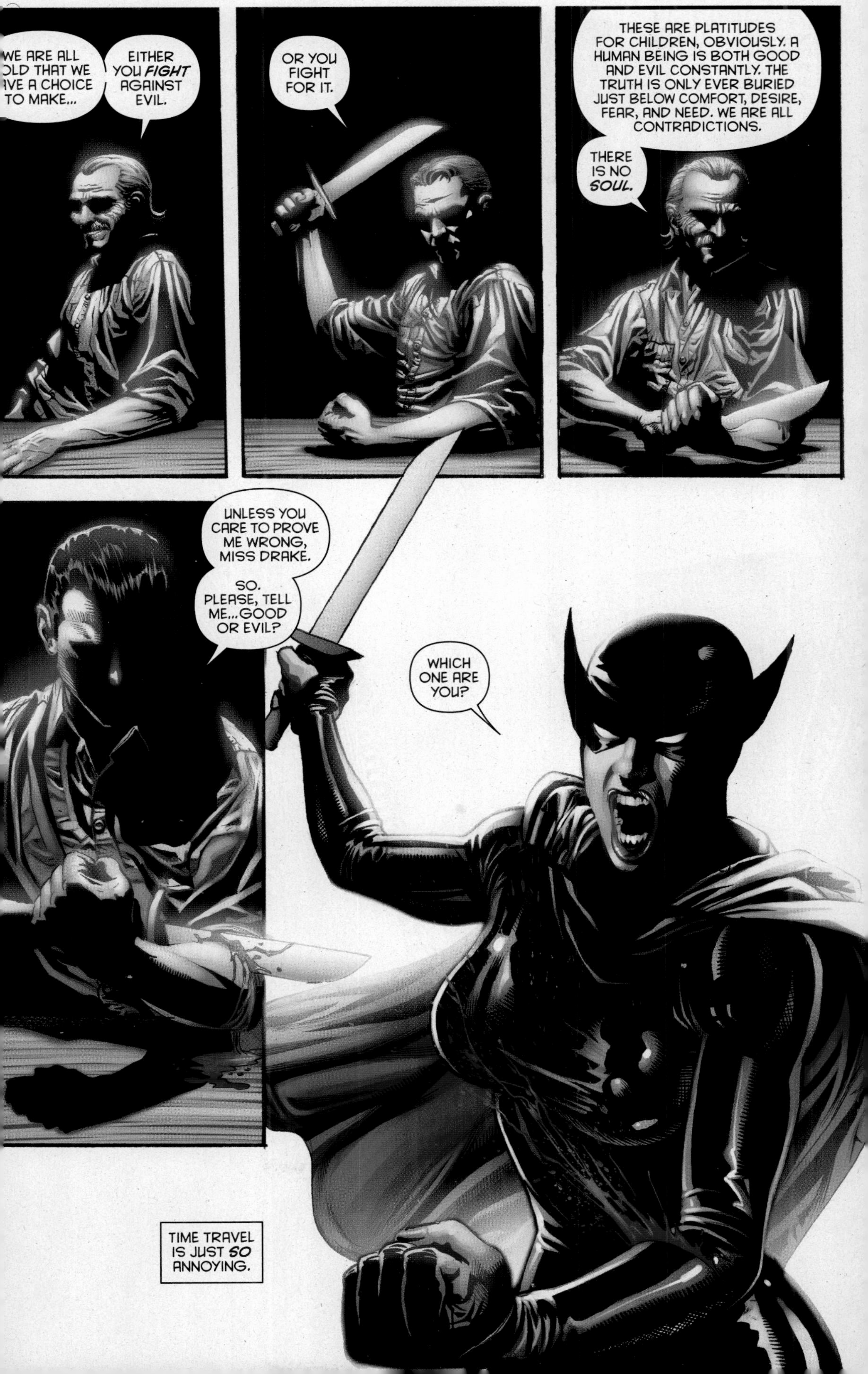
WE ARE ALL OLD THAT WE AVE A CHOICE TO MAKE...
EITHER YOU FIGHT AGAINST EVIL.
OR YOU FIGHT FOR IT.
THESE ARE PLATITUDES FOR CHILDREN, OBVIOUSLY. A HUMAN BEING IS BOTH GOOD AND EVIL CONSTANTLY. THE TRUTH IS ONLY EVER BURIED JUST BELOW COMFORT, DESIRE, FEAR, AND NEED. WE ARE ALL CONTRADICTIONS.
THERE IS NO SOUL.
UNLESS YOU CARE TO PROVE ME WRONG, MISS DRAKE.
SO. PLEASE, TELL ME...GOOD OR EVIL?
WHICH ONE ARE YOU?
TIME TRAVEL IS JUST SO ANNOYING.

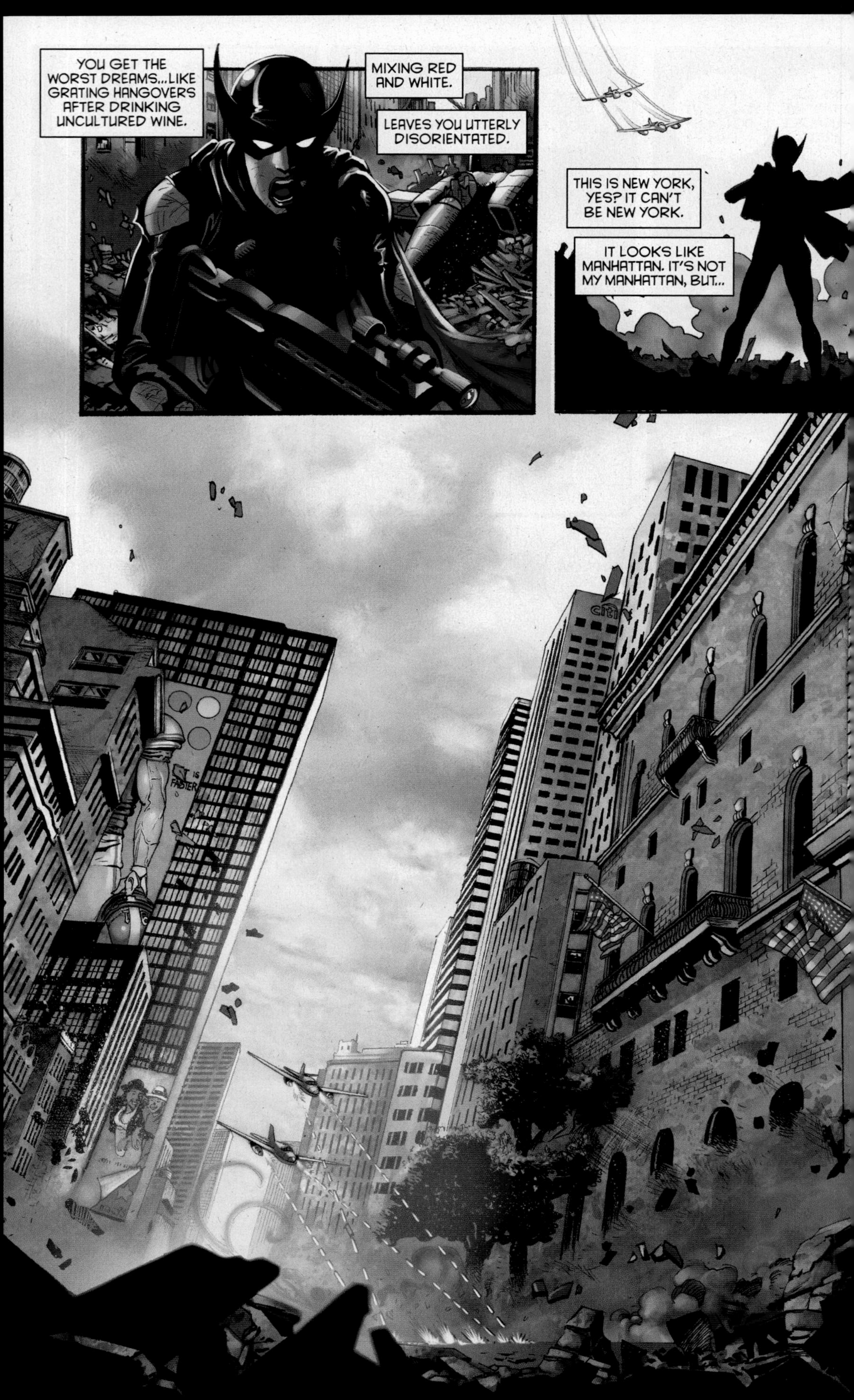
YOU GET THE WORST DREAMS...LIKE GRATING HANGOVERS AFTER DRINKING UNCULTURED WINE.
MIXING RED AND WHITE.
LEAVES YOU UTTERLY DISORIENTATED.
THIS IS NEW YORK, YES? IT CAN'T BE NEW YORK.
IT LOOKS LIKE MANHATTAN. IT'S NOT MY MANHATTAN, BUT...

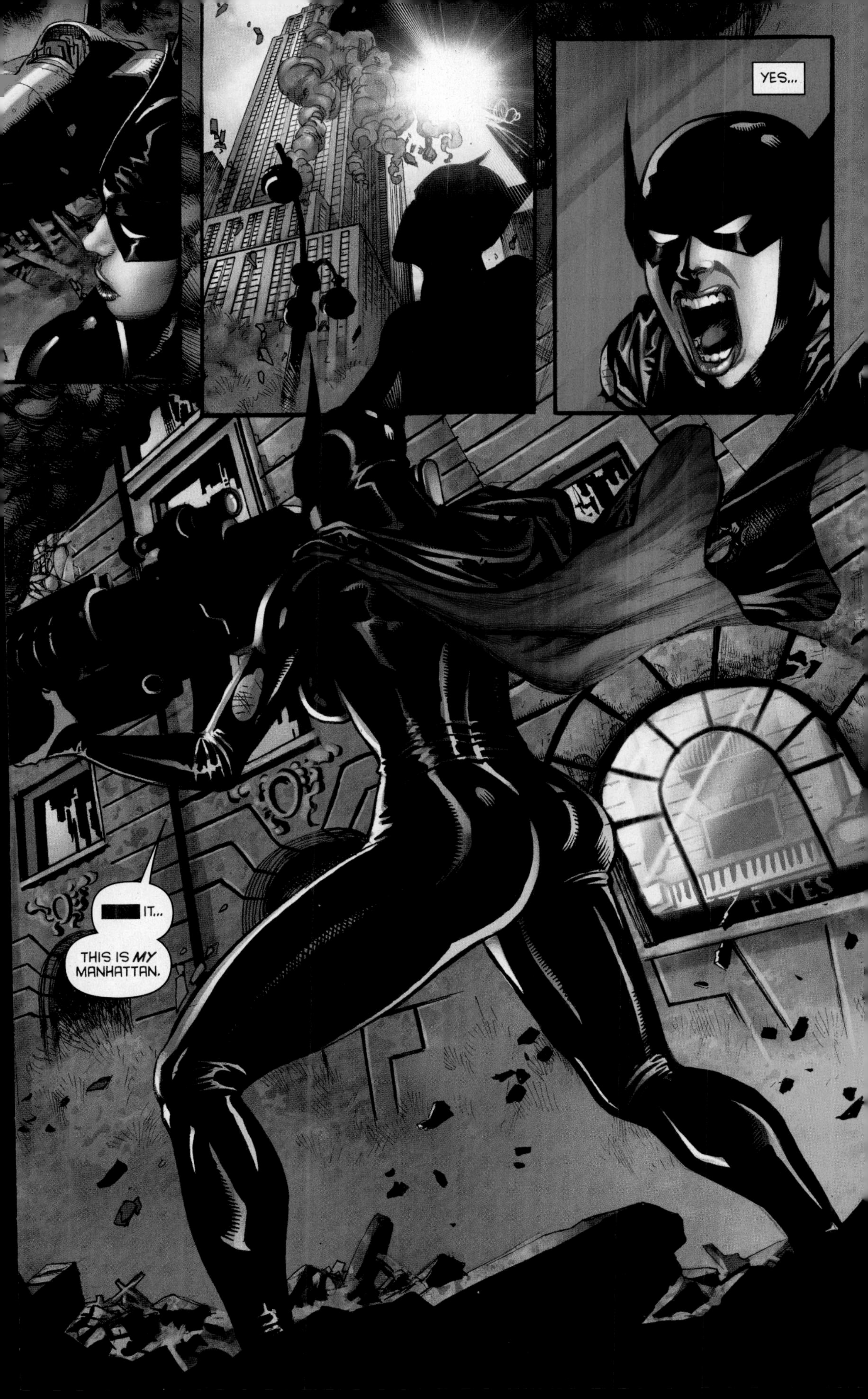
YES...
FIVES
[redacted] IT...
THIS IS *MY* MANHATTAN.

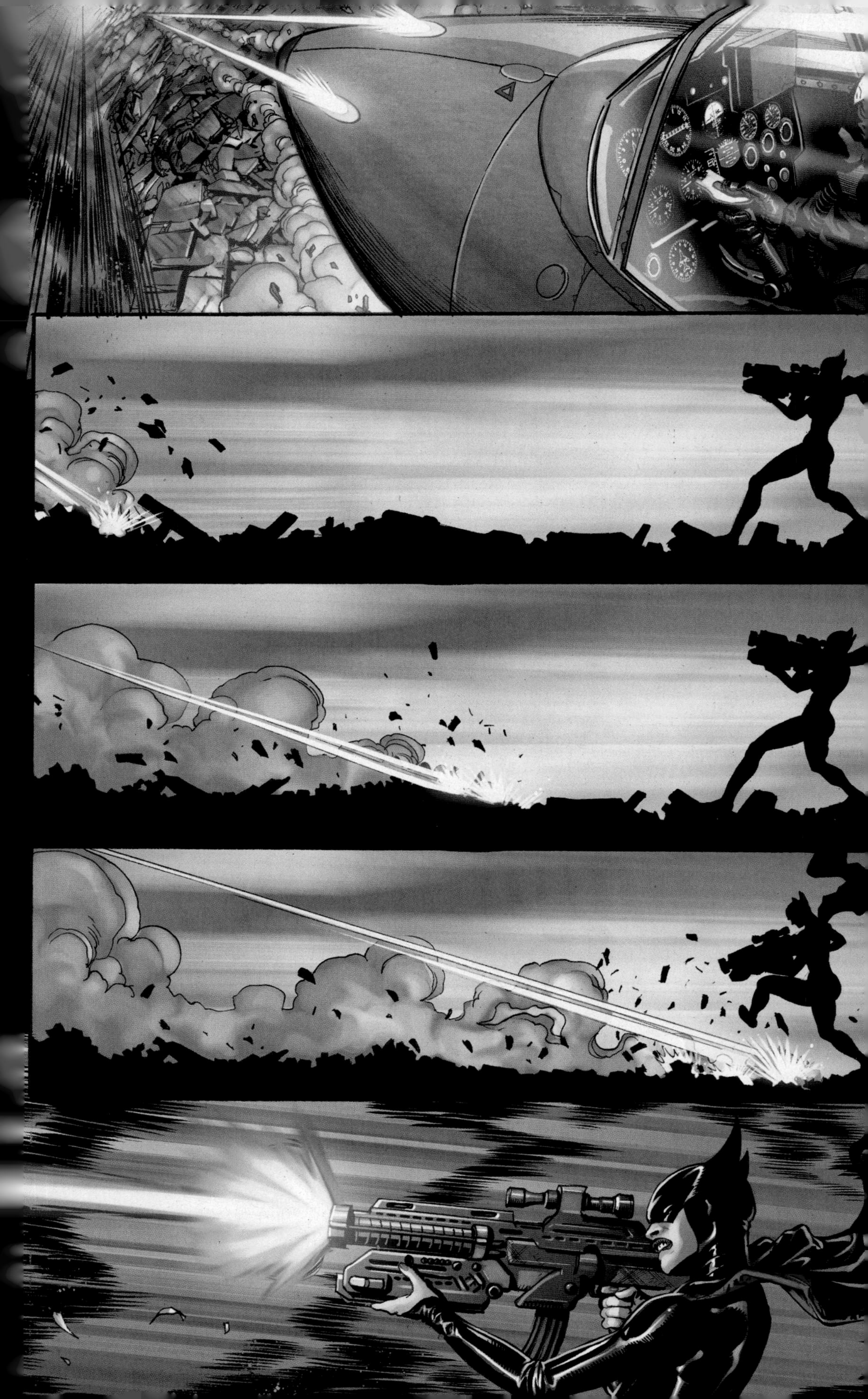

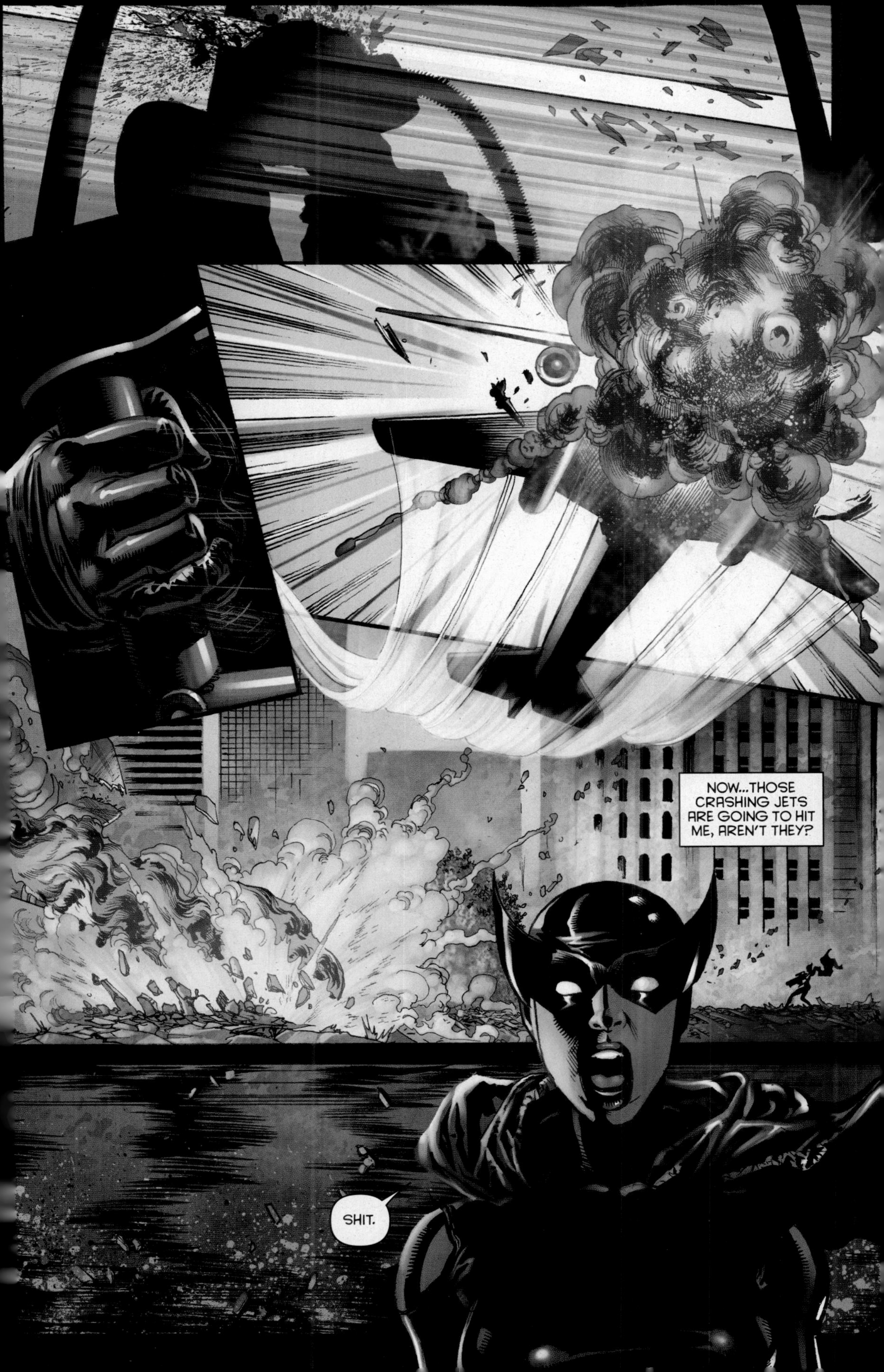
NOW...THOSE CRASHING JETS ARE GOING TO HIT ME, AREN'T THEY?
SHIT.

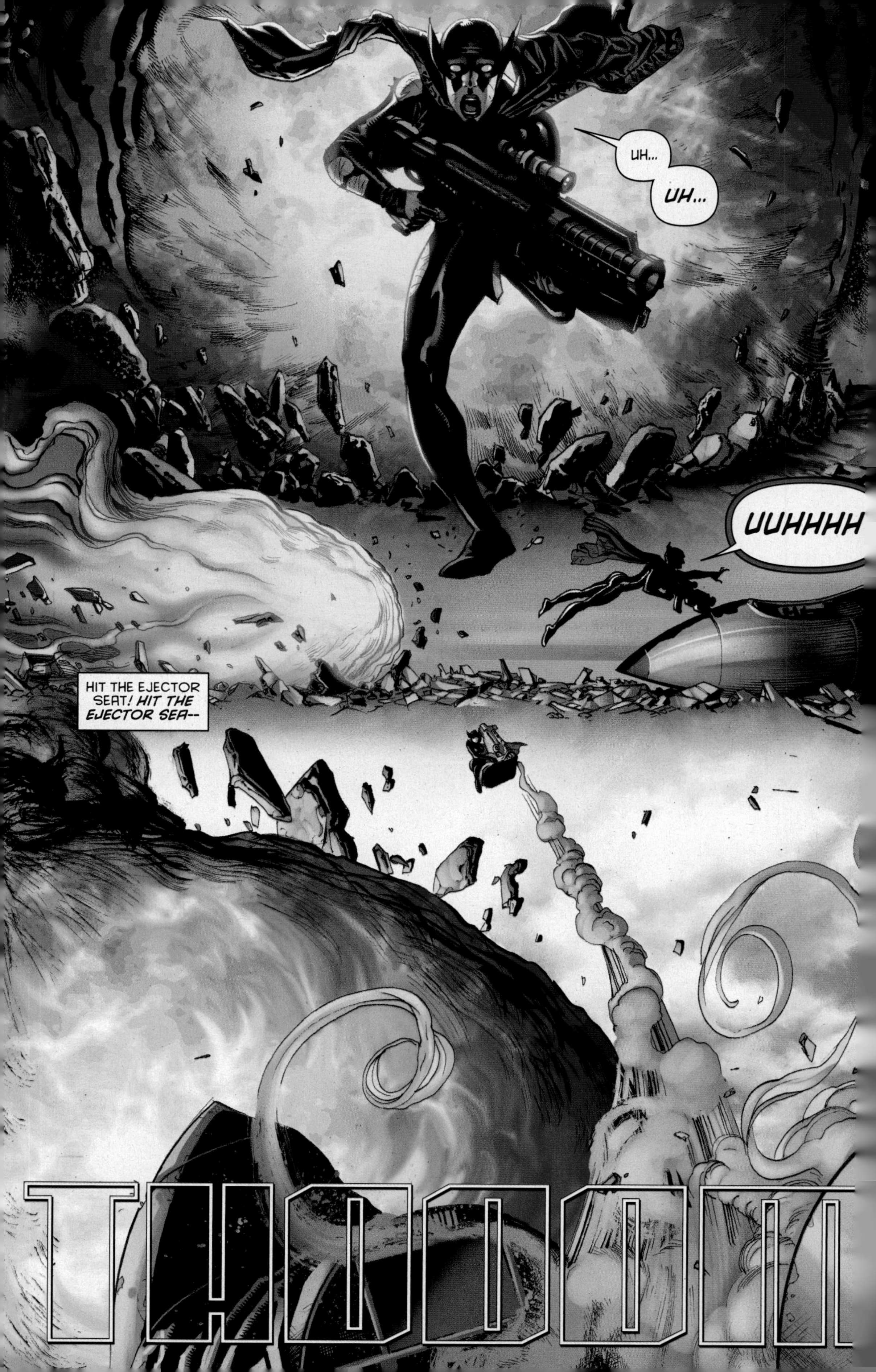
UH...
UH...
UUHHHH
HIT THE EJECTOR SEAT! HIT THE EJECTOR SEA--
THOOOM

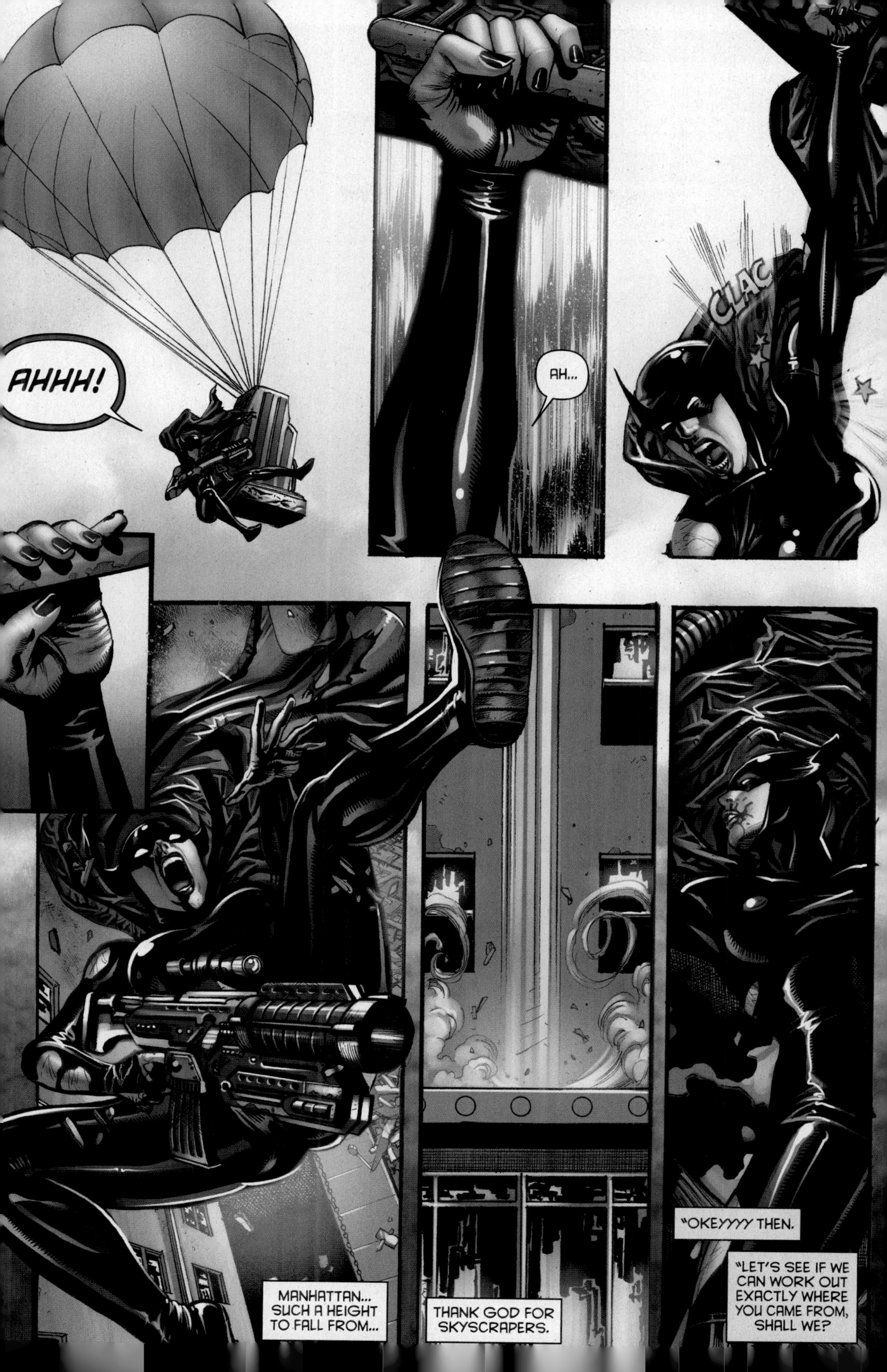
AHHH!
AH...
CLAC
MANHATTAN... SUCH A HEIGHT TO FALL FROM...
THANK GOD FOR SKYSCRAPERS.
"OKEYYYY THEN.
"LET'S SEE IF WE CAN WORK OUT EXACTLY WHERE YOU CAME FROM, SHALL WE?

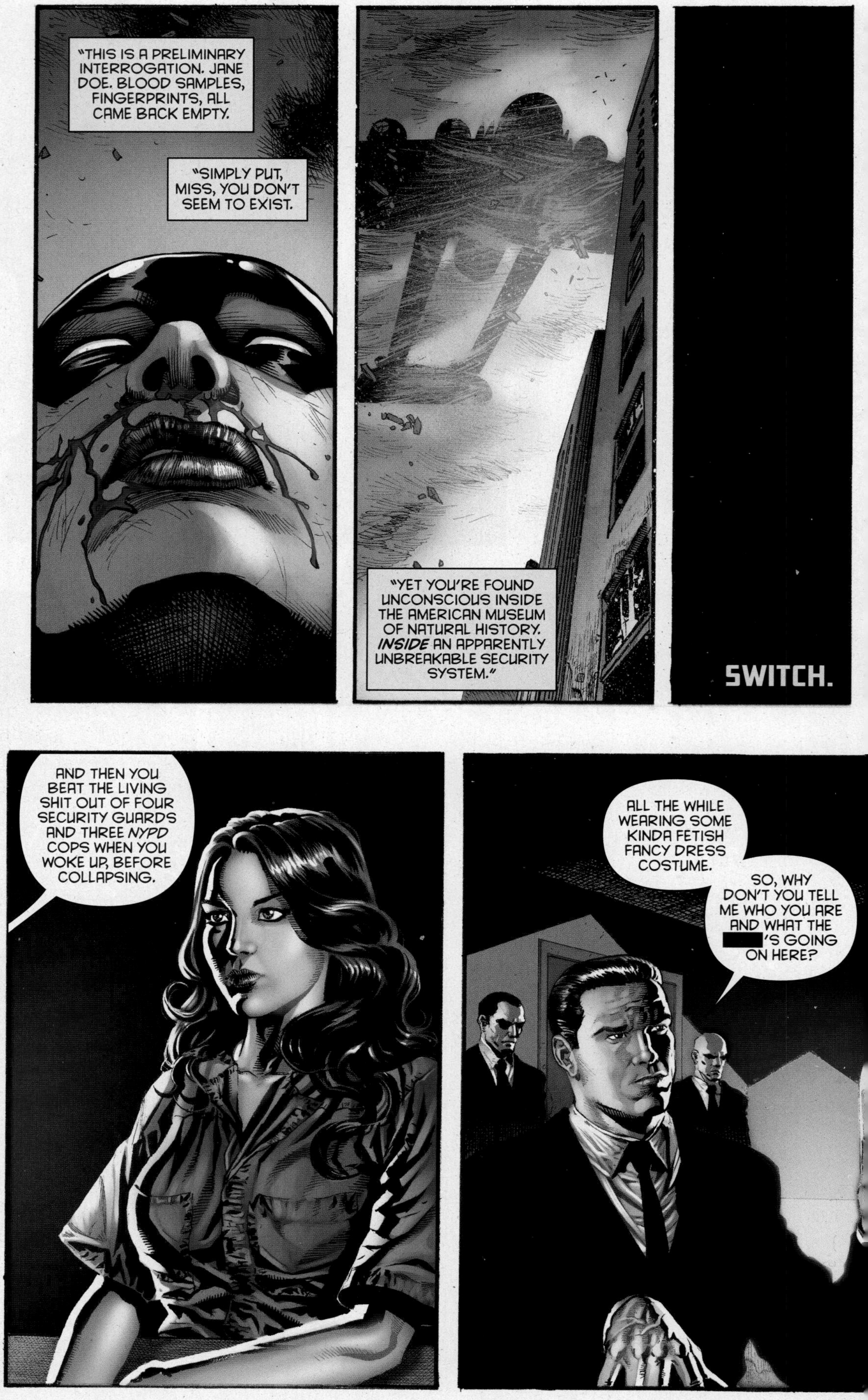
"THIS IS A PRELIMINARY INTERROGATION. JANE DOE. BLOOD SAMPLES, FINGERPRINTS, ALL CAME BACK EMPTY.
"SIMPLY PUT, MISS, YOU DON'T SEEM TO EXIST.
"YET YOU'RE FOUND UNCONSCIOUS INSIDE THE AMERICAN MUSEUM OF NATURAL HISTORY. *INSIDE* AN APPARENTLY UNBREAKABLE SECURITY SYSTEM."
SWITCH.
AND THEN YOU BEAT THE LIVING SHIT OUT OF FOUR SECURITY GUARDS AND THREE *NYPD* COPS WHEN YOU WOKE UP, BEFORE COLLAPSING.
ALL THE WHILE WEARING SOME KINDA FETISH FANCY DRESS COSTUME.
SO, WHY DON'T YOU TELL ME WHO YOU ARE AND WHAT THE [redacted]'S GOING ON HERE?

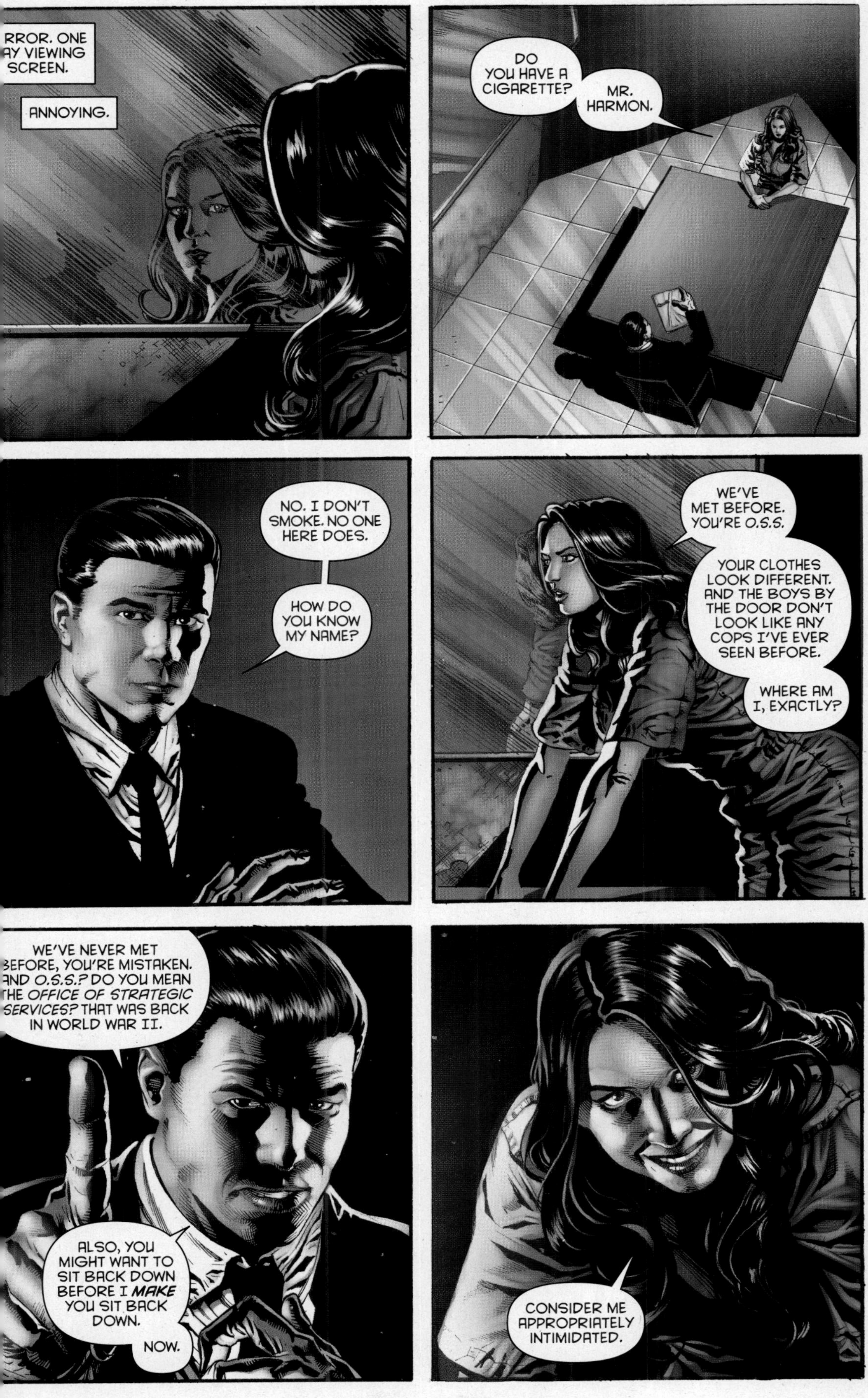
RROR. ONE
AY VIEWING
SCREEN.
ANNOYING.
DO YOU HAVE A CIGARETTE?
MR. HARMON.
NO. I DON'T SMOKE. NO ONE HERE DOES.
HOW DO YOU KNOW MY NAME?
WE'VE MET BEFORE. YOU'RE O.S.S.
YOUR CLOTHES LOOK DIFFERENT. AND THE BOYS BY THE DOOR DON'T LOOK LIKE ANY COPS I'VE EVER SEEN BEFORE.
WHERE AM I, EXACTLY?
WE'VE NEVER MET EFORE, YOU'RE MISTAKEN. AND O.S.S.? DO YOU MEAN THE OFFICE OF STRATEGIC SERVICES? THAT WAS BACK IN WORLD WAR II.
ALSO, YOU MIGHT WANT TO SIT BACK DOWN BEFORE I MAKE YOU SIT BACK DOWN.
NOW.
CONSIDER ME APPROPRIATELY INTIMIDATED.

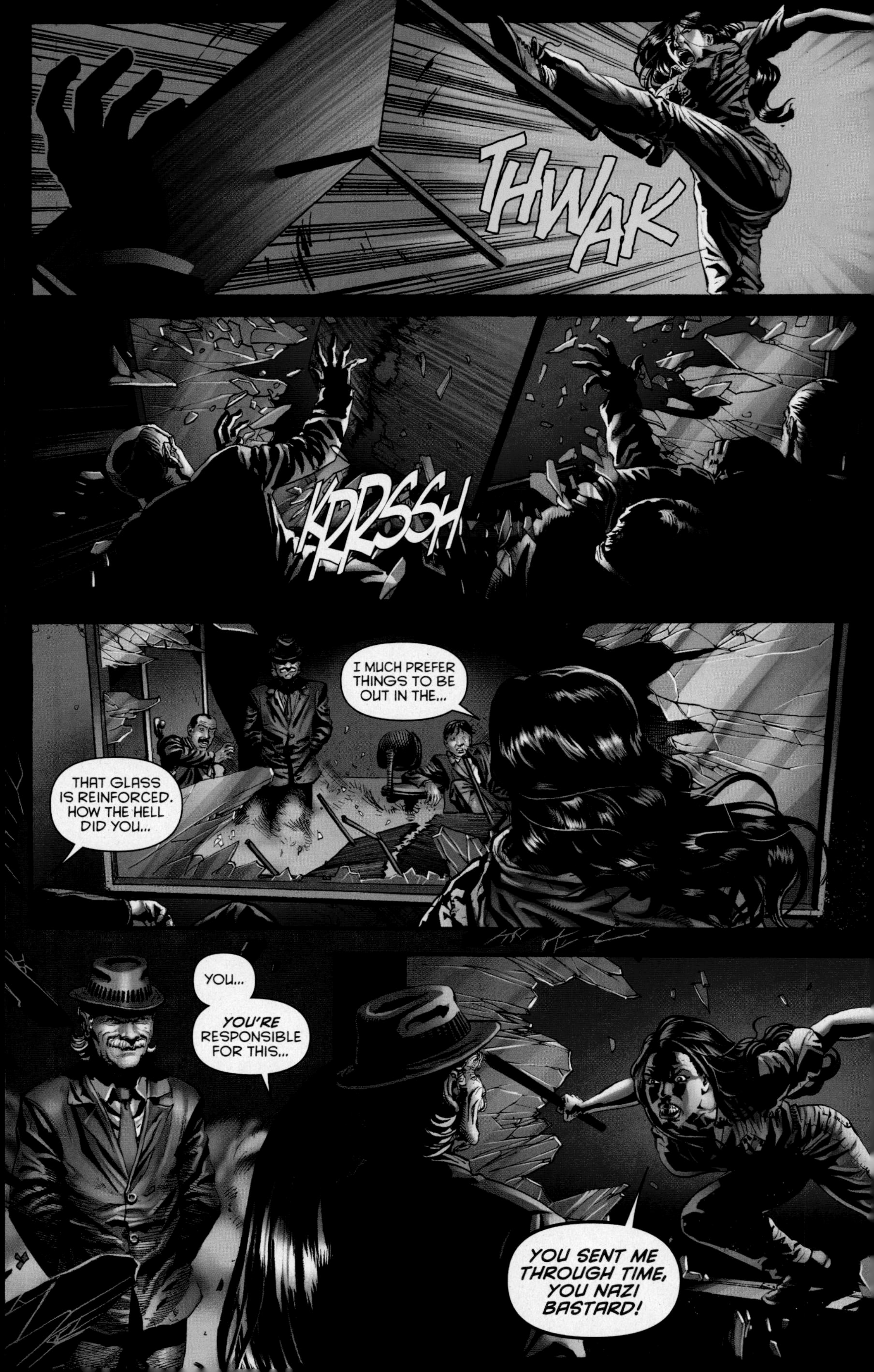
THWAK
KRRSSH
I MUCH PREFER THINGS TO BE OUT IN THE...
THAT GLASS IS REINFORCED. HOW THE HELL DID YOU...
YOU...
YOU'RE RESPONSIBLE FOR THIS...
YOU SENT ME THROUGH TIME, YOU NAZI BASTARD!

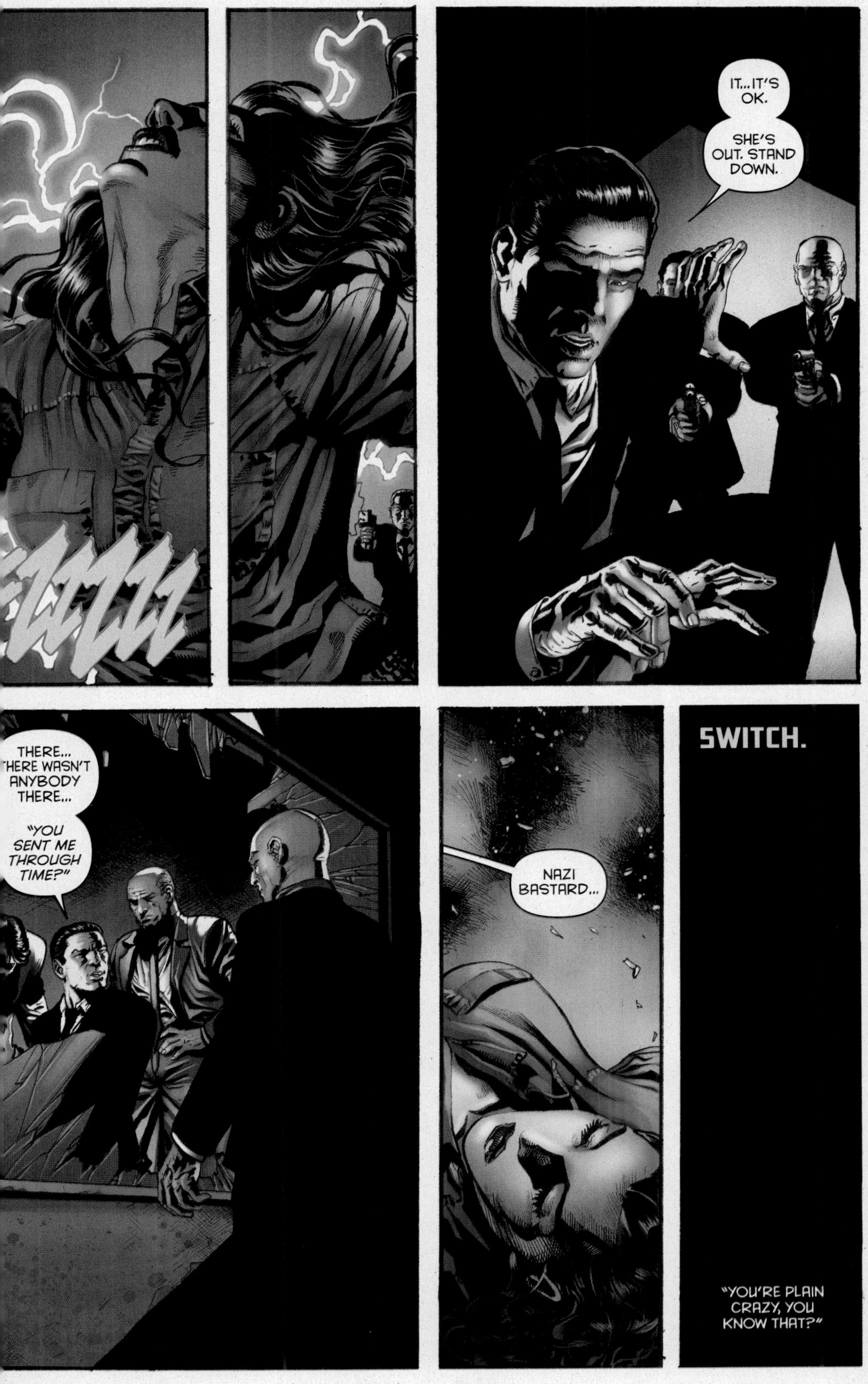
IT... IT'S OK.
SHE'S OUT. STAND DOWN.
THERE... THERE WASN'T ANYBODY THERE...
"YOU SENT ME THROUGH TIME?"
NAZI BASTARD...
SWITCH.
"YOU'RE PLAIN CRAZY, YOU KNOW THAT?"

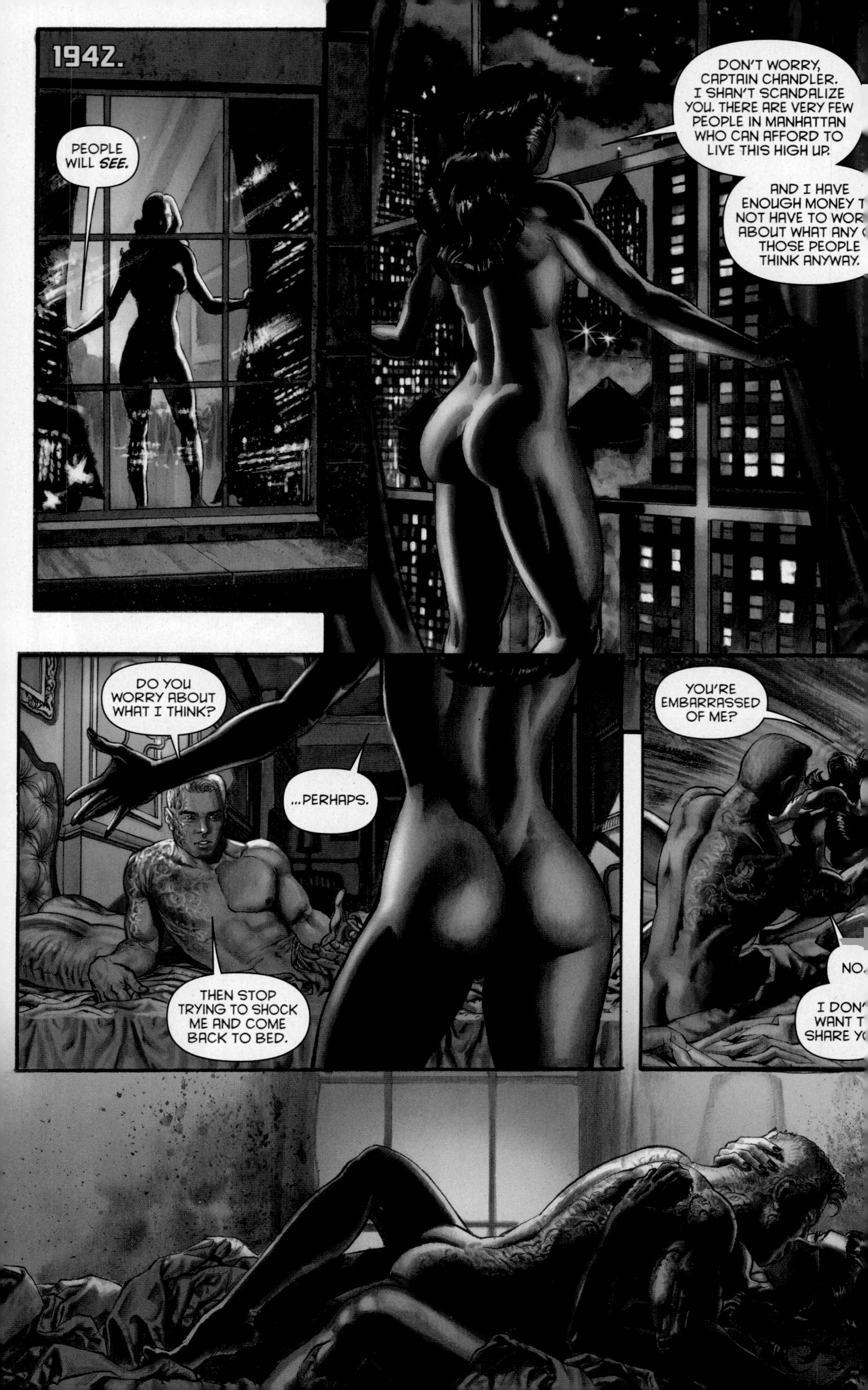
1942.
PEOPLE WILL SEE.
DON'T WORRY, CAPTAIN CHANDLER. I SHAN'T SCANDALIZE YOU. THERE ARE VERY FEW PEOPLE IN MANHATTAN WHO CAN AFFORD TO LIVE THIS HIGH UP.
AND I HAVE ENOUGH MONEY T NOT HAVE TO WOR ABOUT WHAT ANY THOSE PEOPLE THINK ANYWAY.
DO YOU WORRY ABOUT WHAT I THINK?
...PERHAPS.
THEN STOP TRYING TO SHOCK ME AND COME BACK TO BED.
YOU'RE EMBARRASSED OF ME?
NO.
I DON' WANT T SHARE Y

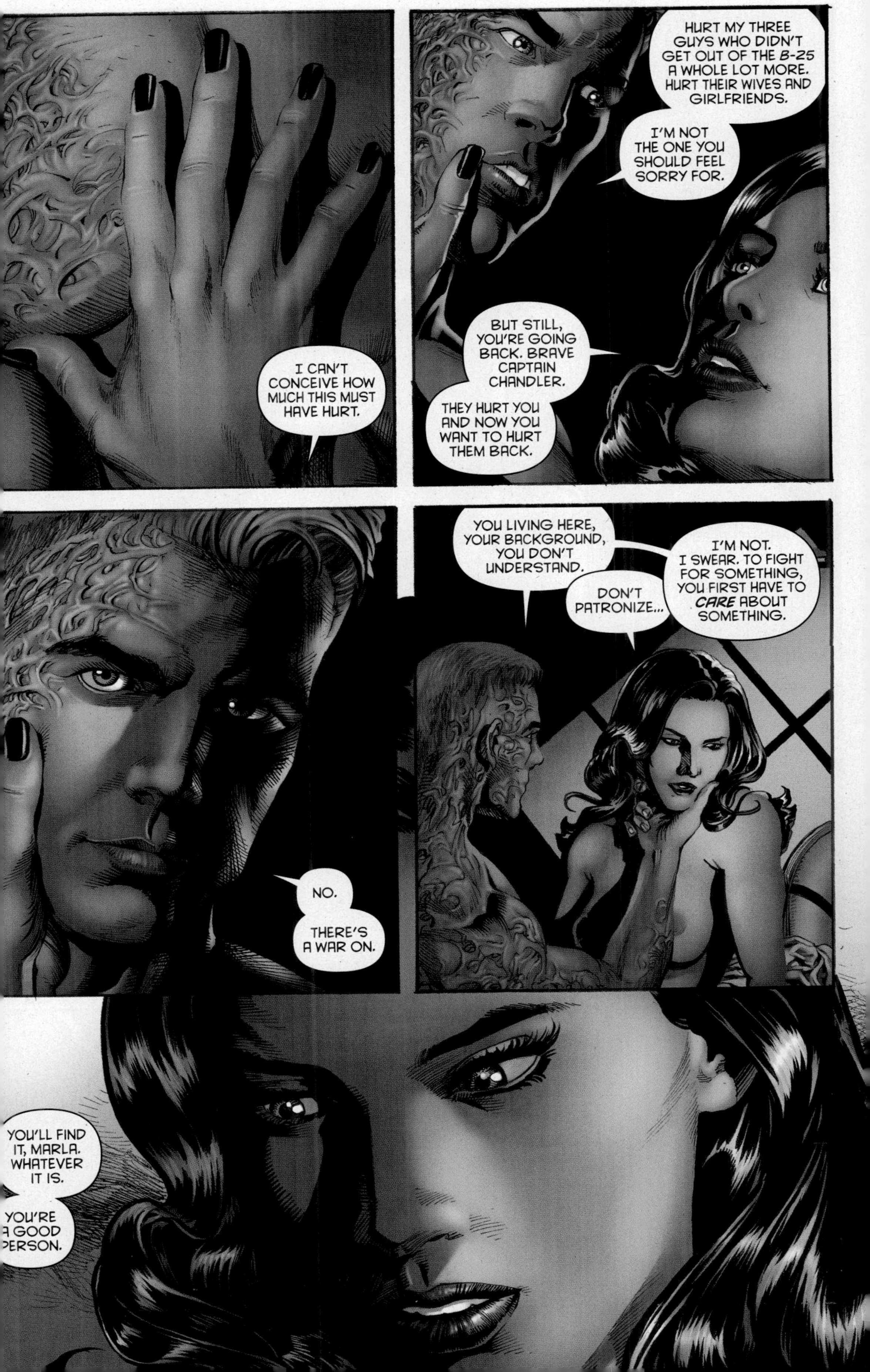
I CAN'T CONCEIVE HOW MUCH THIS MUST HAVE HURT.
HURT MY THREE GUYS WHO DIDN'T GET OUT OF THE B-25 A WHOLE LOT MORE. HURT THEIR WIVES AND GIRLFRIENDS.
I'M NOT THE ONE YOU SHOULD FEEL SORRY FOR.
BUT STILL, YOU'RE GOING BACK. BRAVE CAPTAIN CHANDLER.
THEY HURT YOU AND NOW YOU WANT TO HURT THEM BACK.
NO.
THERE'S A WAR ON.
YOU LIVING HERE, YOUR BACKGROUND, YOU DON'T UNDERSTAND.
DON'T PATRONIZE...
I'M NOT. I SWEAR. TO FIGHT FOR SOMETHING, YOU FIRST HAVE TO CARE ABOUT SOMETHING.
YOU'LL FIND IT, MARLA. WHATEVER IT IS.
YOU'RE A GOOD PERSON.

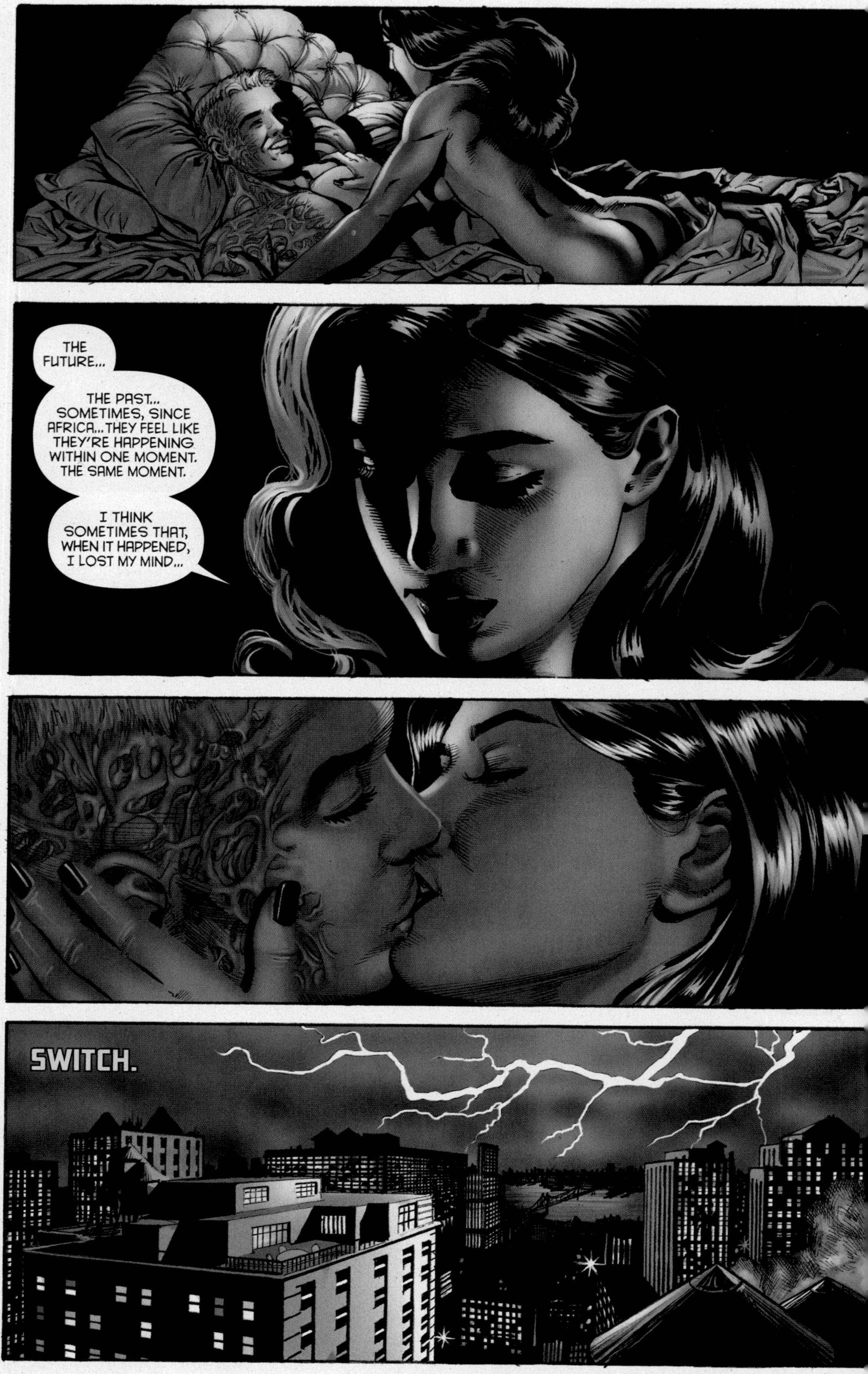
THE FUTURE...
THE PAST... SOMETIMES, SINCE AFRICA...THEY FEEL LIKE THEY'RE HAPPENING WITHIN ONE MOMENT. THE SAME MOMENT.
I THINK SOMETIMES THAT, WHEN IT HAPPENED, I LOST MY MIND...
SWITCH.

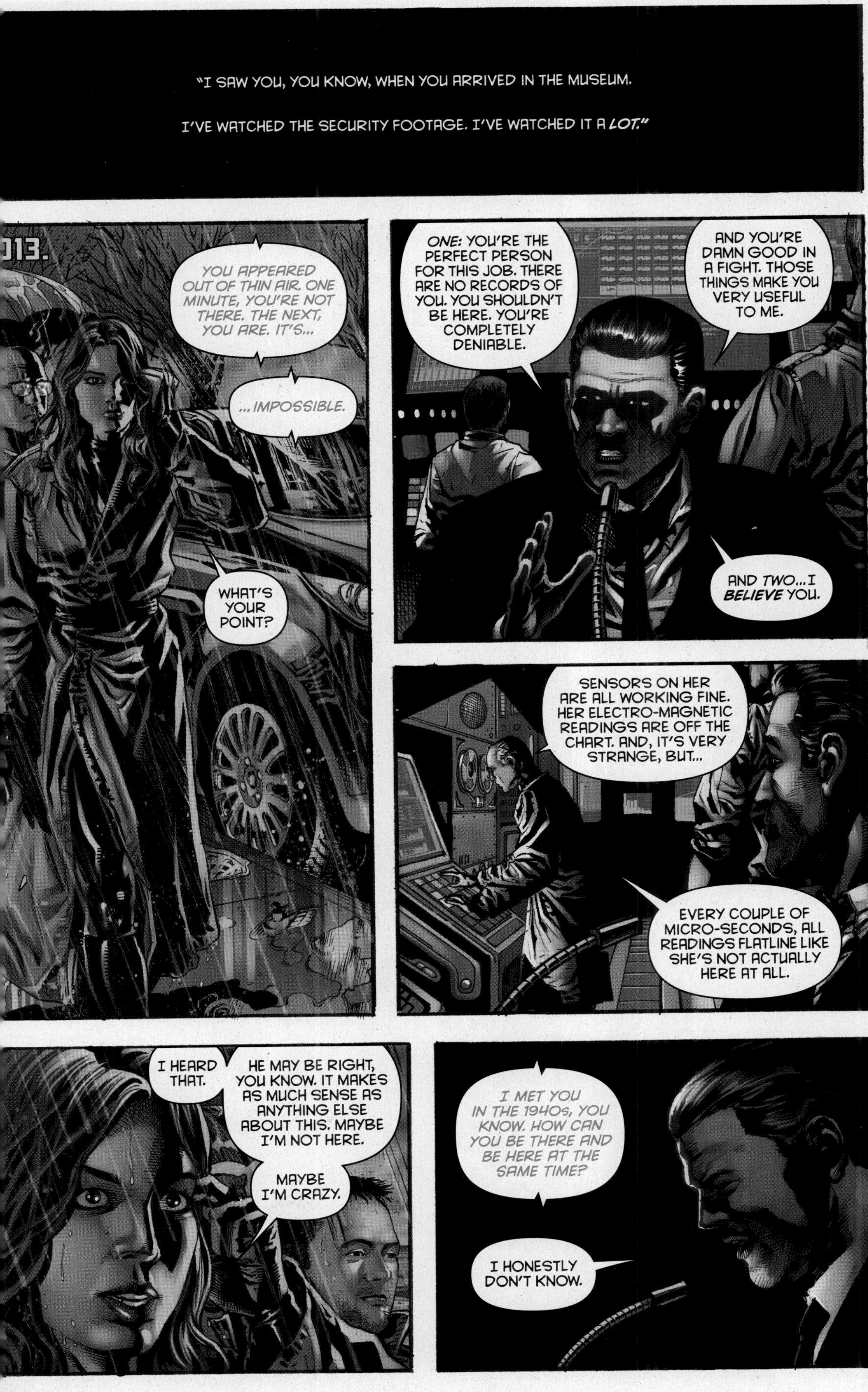
"I SAW YOU, YOU KNOW, WHEN YOU ARRIVED IN THE MUSEUM.
I'VE WATCHED THE SECURITY FOOTAGE. I'VE WATCHED IT A *LOT.*"
*YOU APPEARED OUT OF THIN AIR. ONE MINUTE, YOU'RE NOT THERE. THE NEXT, YOU ARE. IT'S...*
*...IMPOSSIBLE.*
WHAT'S YOUR POINT?
*ONE:* YOU'RE THE PERFECT PERSON FOR THIS JOB. THERE ARE NO RECORDS OF YOU. YOU SHOULDN'T BE HERE. YOU'RE COMPLETELY DENIABLE.
AND YOU'RE DAMN GOOD IN A FIGHT. THOSE THINGS MAKE YOU VERY USEFUL TO ME.
AND *TWO*...I ***BELIEVE*** YOU.
SENSORS ON HER ARE ALL WORKING FINE. HER ELECTRO-MAGNETIC READINGS ARE OFF THE CHART. AND, IT'S VERY STRANGE, BUT...
EVERY COUPLE OF MICRO-SECONDS, ALL READINGS FLATLINE LIKE SHE'S NOT ACTUALLY HERE AT ALL.
I HEARD THAT.
HE MAY BE RIGHT, YOU KNOW. IT MAKES AS MUCH SENSE AS ANYTHING ELSE ABOUT THIS. MAYBE I'M NOT HERE.
MAYBE I'M CRAZY.
*I MET YOU IN THE 1940s, YOU KNOW. HOW CAN YOU BE THERE AND BE HERE AT THE SAME TIME?*
I HONESTLY DON'T KNOW.

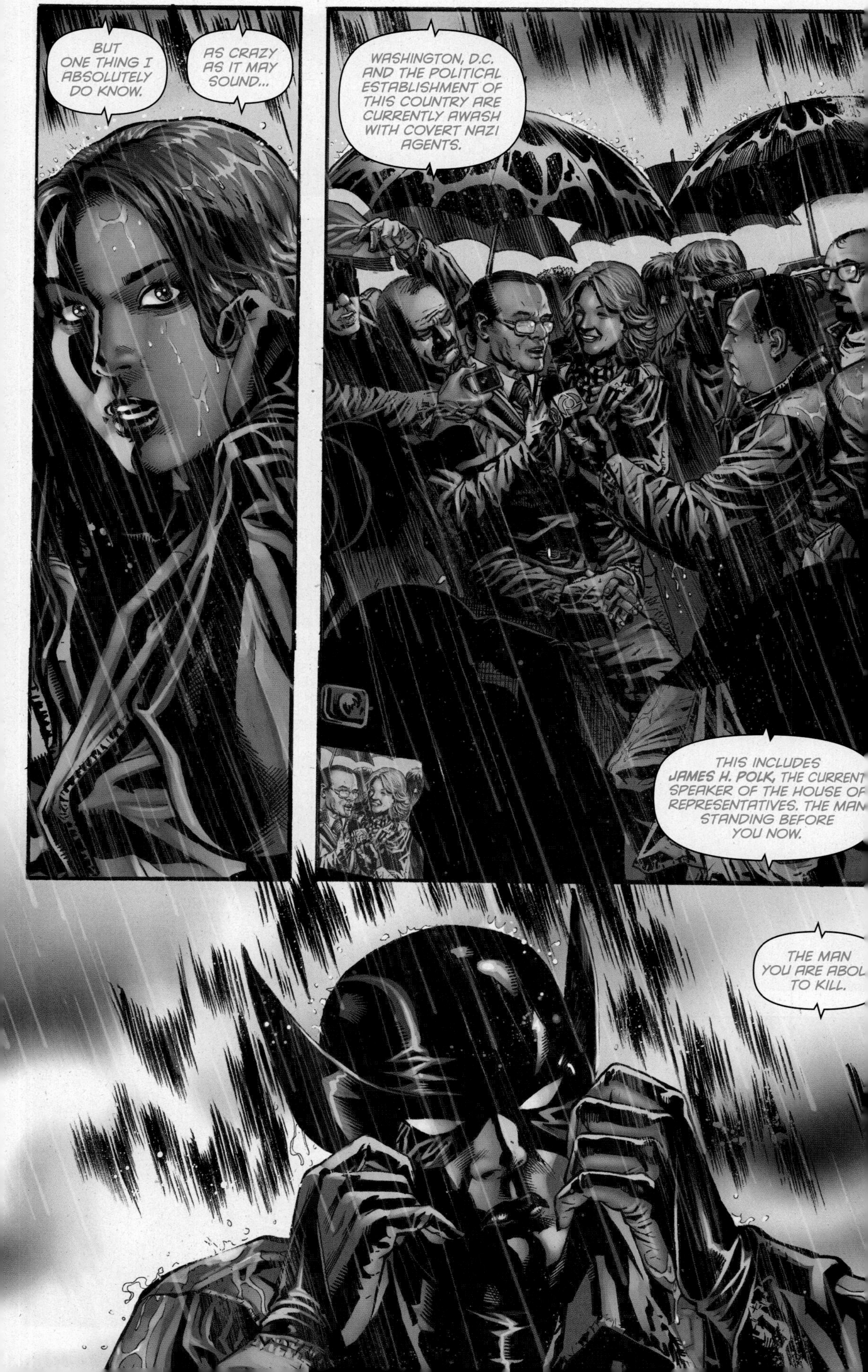
BUT ONE THING I ABSOLUTELY DO KNOW.
AS CRAZY AS IT MAY SOUND...
WASHINGTON, D.C. AND THE POLITICAL ESTABLISHMENT OF THIS COUNTRY ARE CURRENTLY AWASH WITH COVERT NAZI AGENTS.
THIS INCLUDES **JAMES H. POLK,** THE CURRENT SPEAKER OF THE HOUSE OF REPRESENTATIVES. THE MAN STANDING BEFORE YOU NOW.
THE MAN YOU ARE ABOU TO KILL.

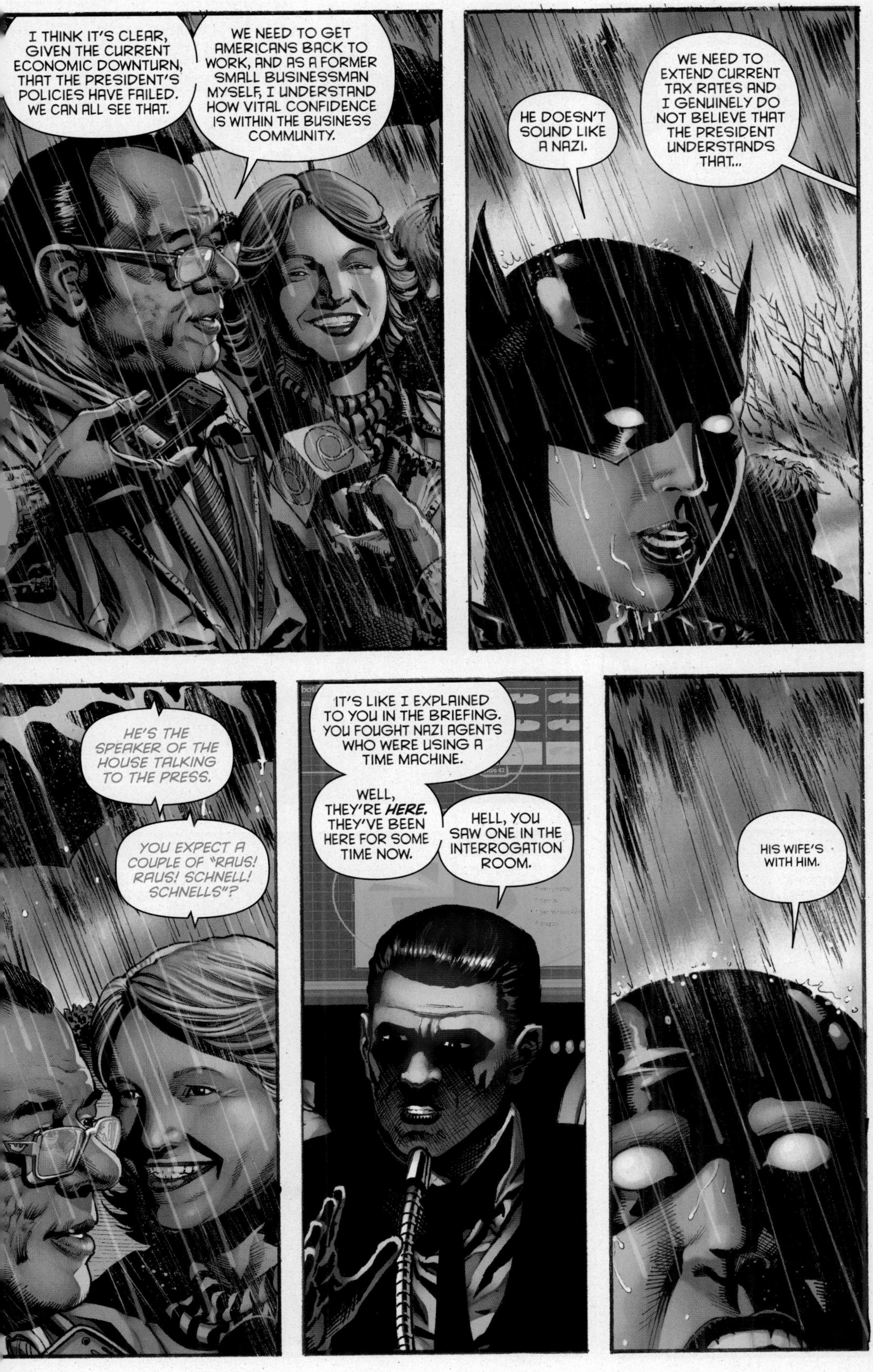
I THINK IT'S CLEAR, GIVEN THE CURRENT ECONOMIC DOWNTURN, THAT THE PRESIDENT'S POLICIES HAVE FAILED. WE CAN ALL SEE THAT.
WE NEED TO GET AMERICANS BACK TO WORK, AND AS A FORMER SMALL BUSINESSMAN MYSELF, I UNDERSTAND HOW VITAL CONFIDENCE IS WITHIN THE BUSINESS COMMUNITY.
HE DOESN'T SOUND LIKE A NAZI.
WE NEED TO EXTEND CURRENT TAX RATES AND I GENUINELY DO NOT BELIEVE THAT THE PRESIDENT UNDERSTANDS THAT...
HE'S THE SPEAKER OF THE HOUSE TALKING TO THE PRESS.
YOU EXPECT A COUPLE OF "RAUS! RAUS! SCHNELL! SCHNELLS"?
IT'S LIKE I EXPLAINED TO YOU IN THE BRIEFING. YOU FOUGHT NAZI AGENTS WHO WERE USING A TIME MACHINE.
WELL, THEY'RE *HERE.* THEY'VE BEEN HERE FOR SOME TIME NOW.
HELL, YOU SAW ONE IN THE INTERROGATION ROOM.
HIS WIFE'S WITH HIM.

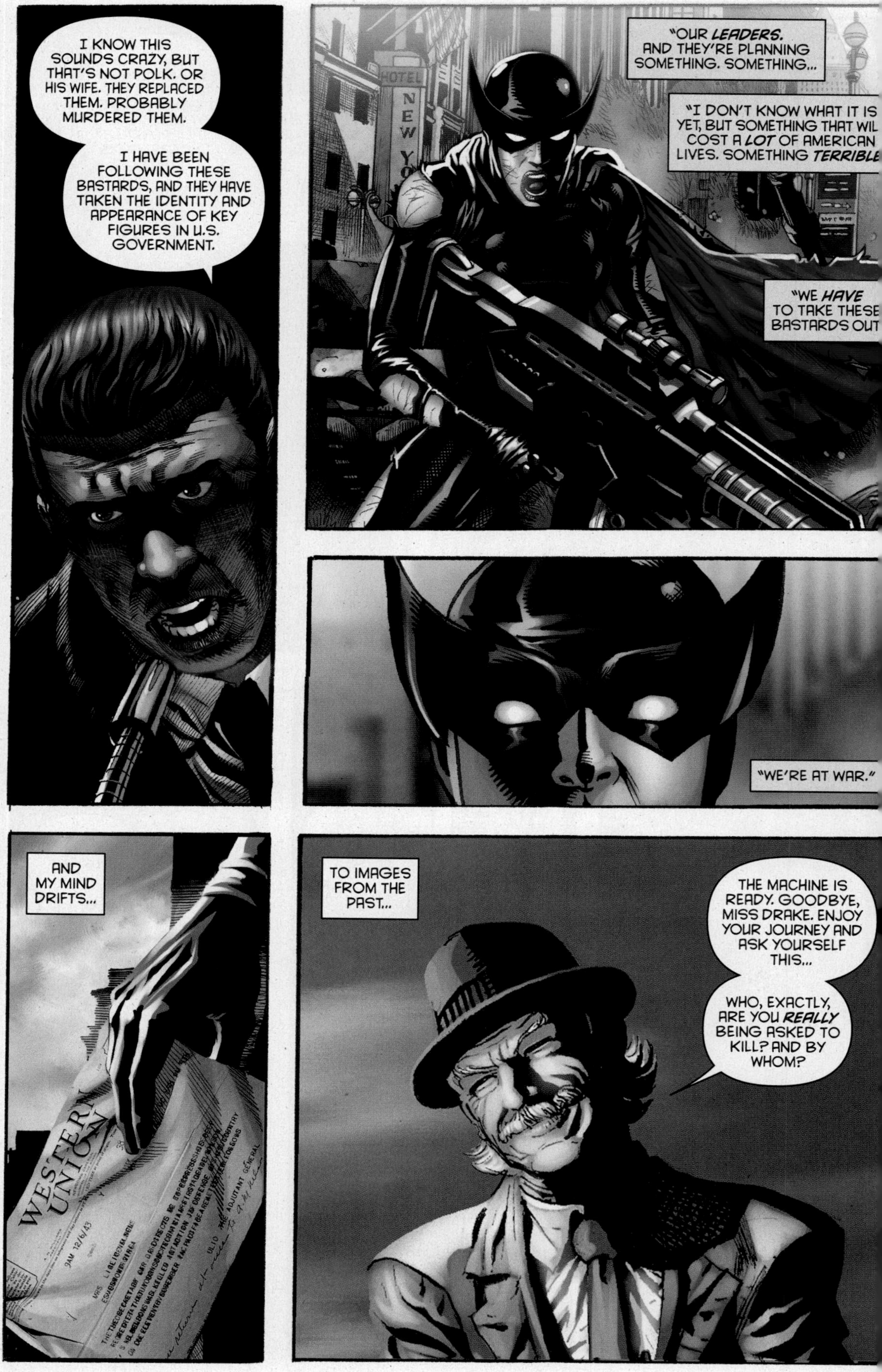

I KNOW THIS SOUNDS CRAZY, BUT THAT'S NOT POLK. OR HIS WIFE. THEY REPLACED THEM. PROBABLY MURDERED THEM.
I HAVE BEEN FOLLOWING THESE BASTARDS, AND THEY HAVE TAKEN THE IDENTITY AND APPEARANCE OF KEY FIGURES IN U.S. GOVERNMENT.
"OUR LEADERS. AND THEY'RE PLANNING SOMETHING. SOMETHING...
"I DON'T KNOW WHAT IT IS YET, BUT SOMETHING THAT WIL COST A LOT OF AMERICAN LIVES. SOMETHING TERRIBLE
"WE HAVE TO TAKE THESE BASTARDS OUT
"WE'RE AT WAR."
AND MY MIND DRIFTS...
TO IMAGES FROM THE PAST...
THE MACHINE IS READY. GOODBYE, MISS DRAKE. ENJOY YOUR JOURNEY AND ASK YOURSELF THIS...
WHO, EXACTLY, ARE YOU REALLY BEING ASKED TO KILL? AND BY WHOM?

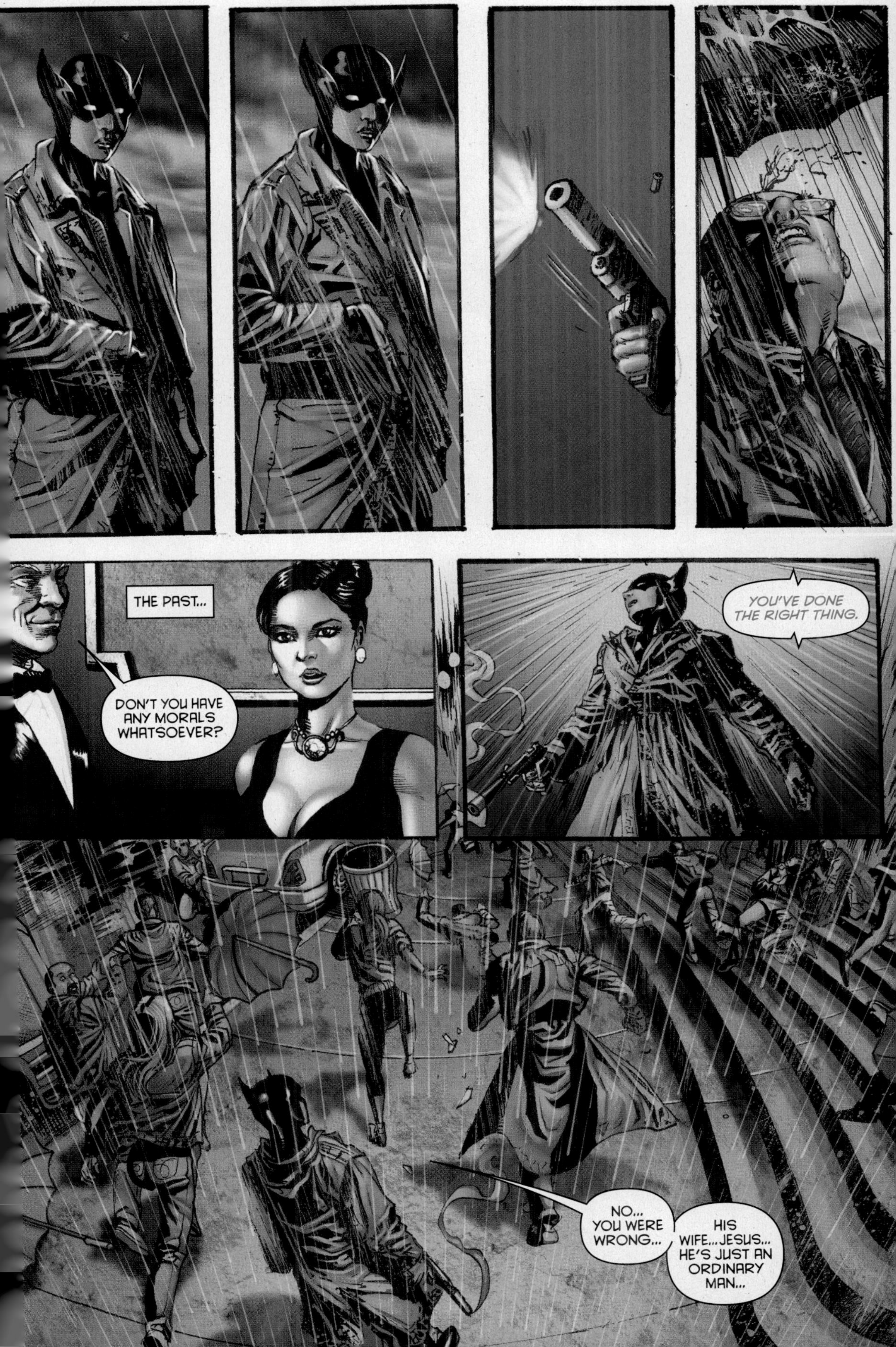
THE PAST...
DON'T YOU HAVE ANY MORALS WHATSOEVER?
YOU'VE DONE THE RIGHT THING.
NO... YOU WERE WRONG...
HIS WIFE... JESUS... HE'S JUST AN ORDINARY MAN...

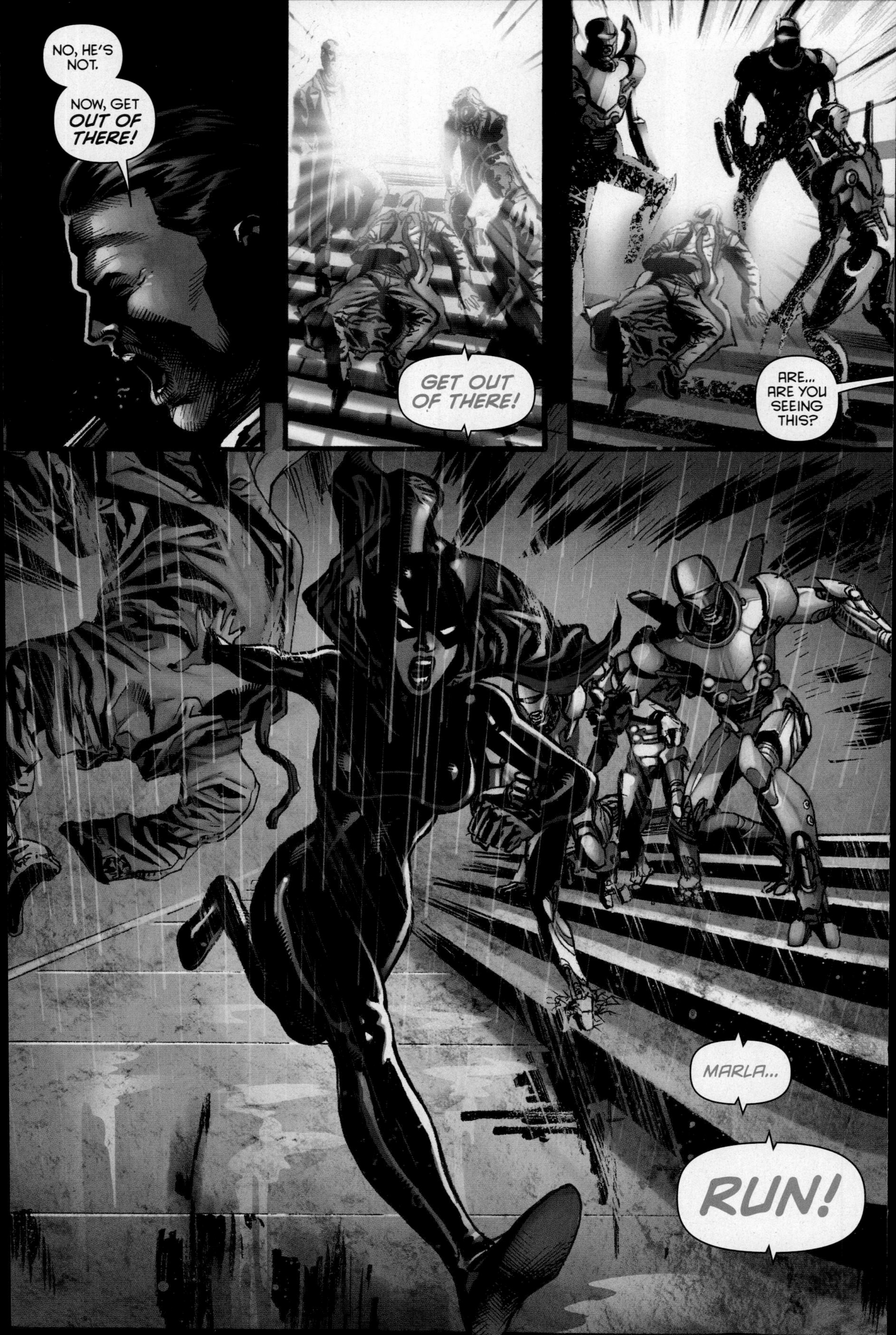
NO, HE'S NOT.
NOW, GET OUT OF THERE!
GET OUT OF THERE!
ARE... ARE YOU SEEING THIS?
MARLA...
RUN!

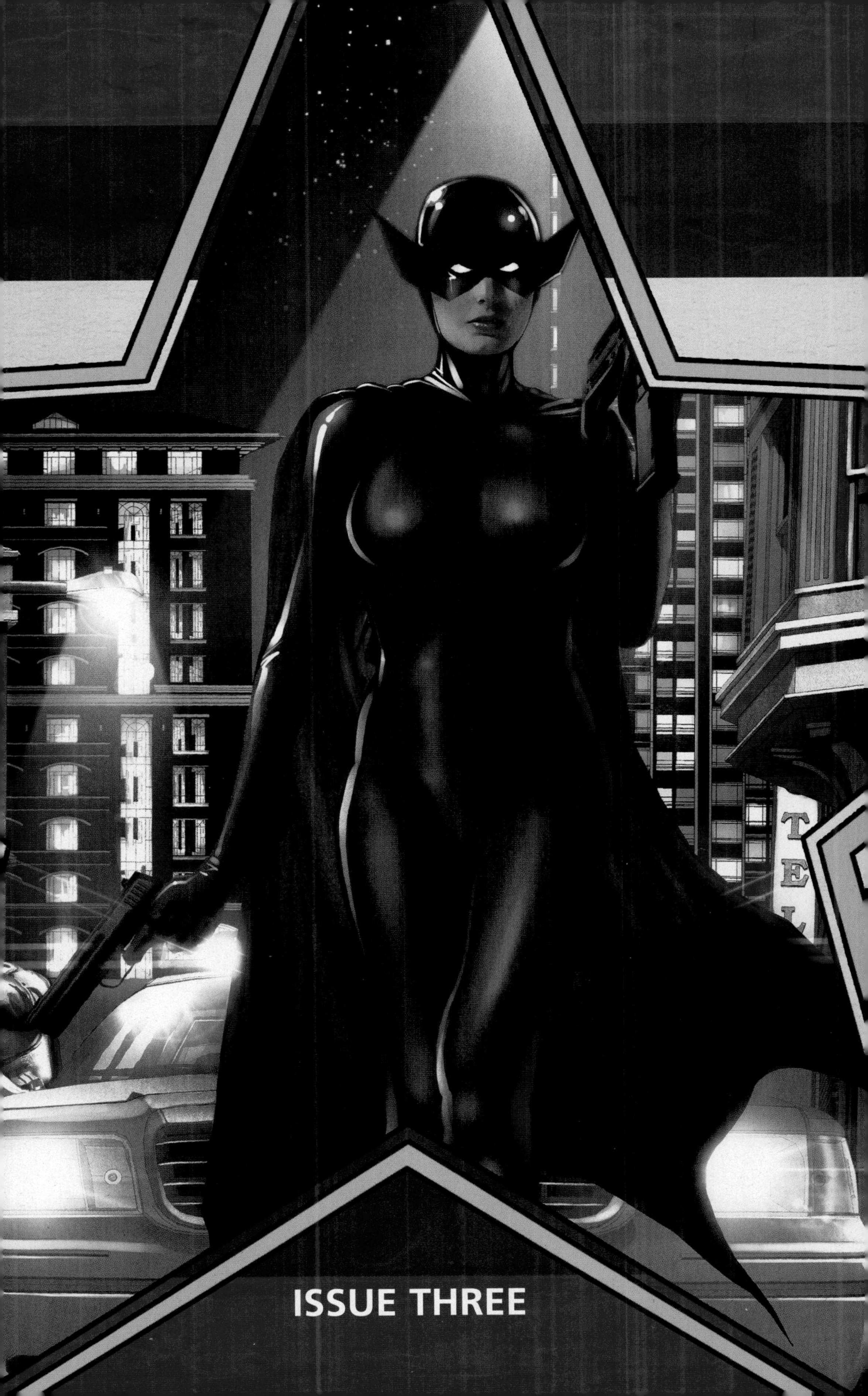
ISSUE THREE

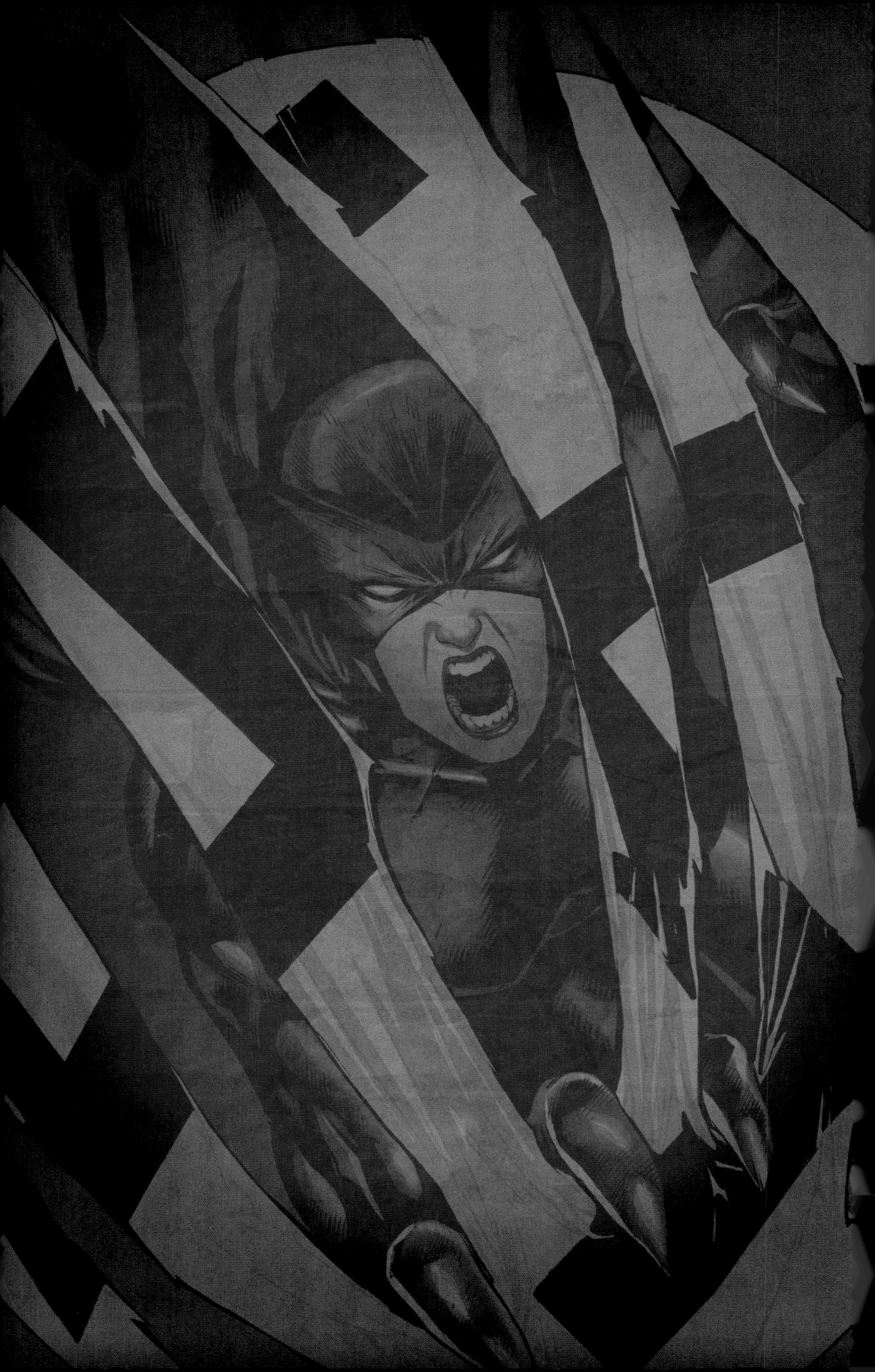

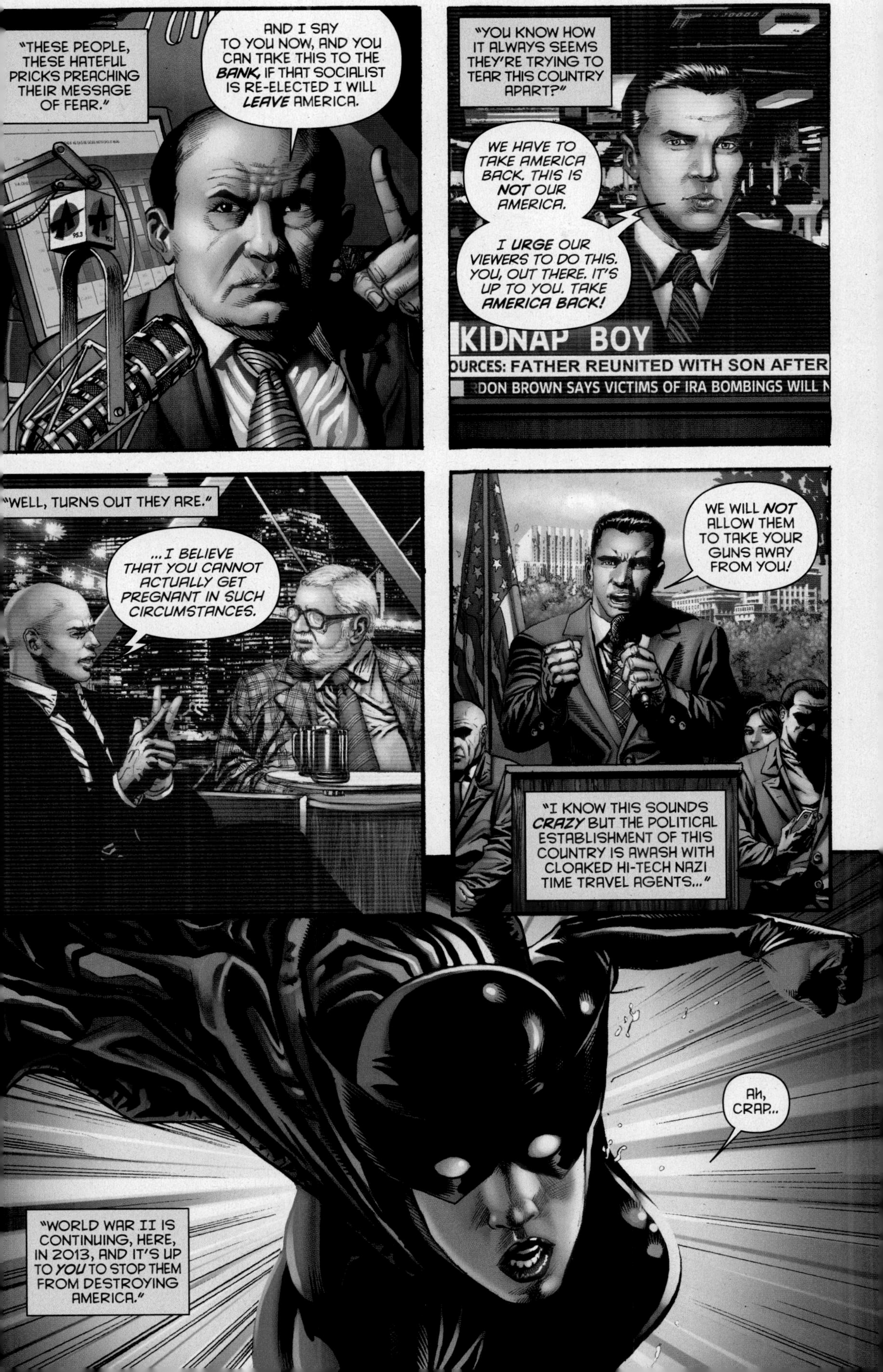
"THESE PEOPLE, THESE HATEFUL PRICKS PREACHING THEIR MESSAGE OF FEAR."
AND I SAY TO YOU NOW, AND YOU CAN TAKE THIS TO THE BANK, IF THAT SOCIALIST IS RE-ELECTED I WILL LEAVE AMERICA.
"YOU KNOW HOW IT ALWAYS SEEMS THEY'RE TRYING TO TEAR THIS COUNTRY APART?"
WE HAVE TO TAKE AMERICA BACK. THIS IS NOT OUR AMERICA.
I URGE OUR VIEWERS TO DO THIS. YOU, OUT THERE. IT'S UP TO YOU. TAKE AMERICA BACK!
KIDNAP BOY
OURCES: FATHER REUNITED WITH SON AFTER
DON BROWN SAYS VICTIMS OF IRA BOMBINGS WILL N
"WELL, TURNS OUT THEY ARE."
...I BELIEVE THAT YOU CANNOT ACTUALLY GET PREGNANT IN SUCH CIRCUMSTANCES.
WE WILL NOT ALLOW THEM TO TAKE YOUR GUNS AWAY FROM YOU!
"I KNOW THIS SOUNDS CRAZY BUT THE POLITICAL ESTABLISHMENT OF THIS COUNTRY IS AWASH WITH CLOAKED HI-TECH NAZI TIME TRAVEL AGENTS..."
AH, CRAP...
"WORLD WAR II IS CONTINUING, HERE, IN 2013, AND IT'S UP TO YOU TO STOP THEM FROM DESTROYING AMERICA."

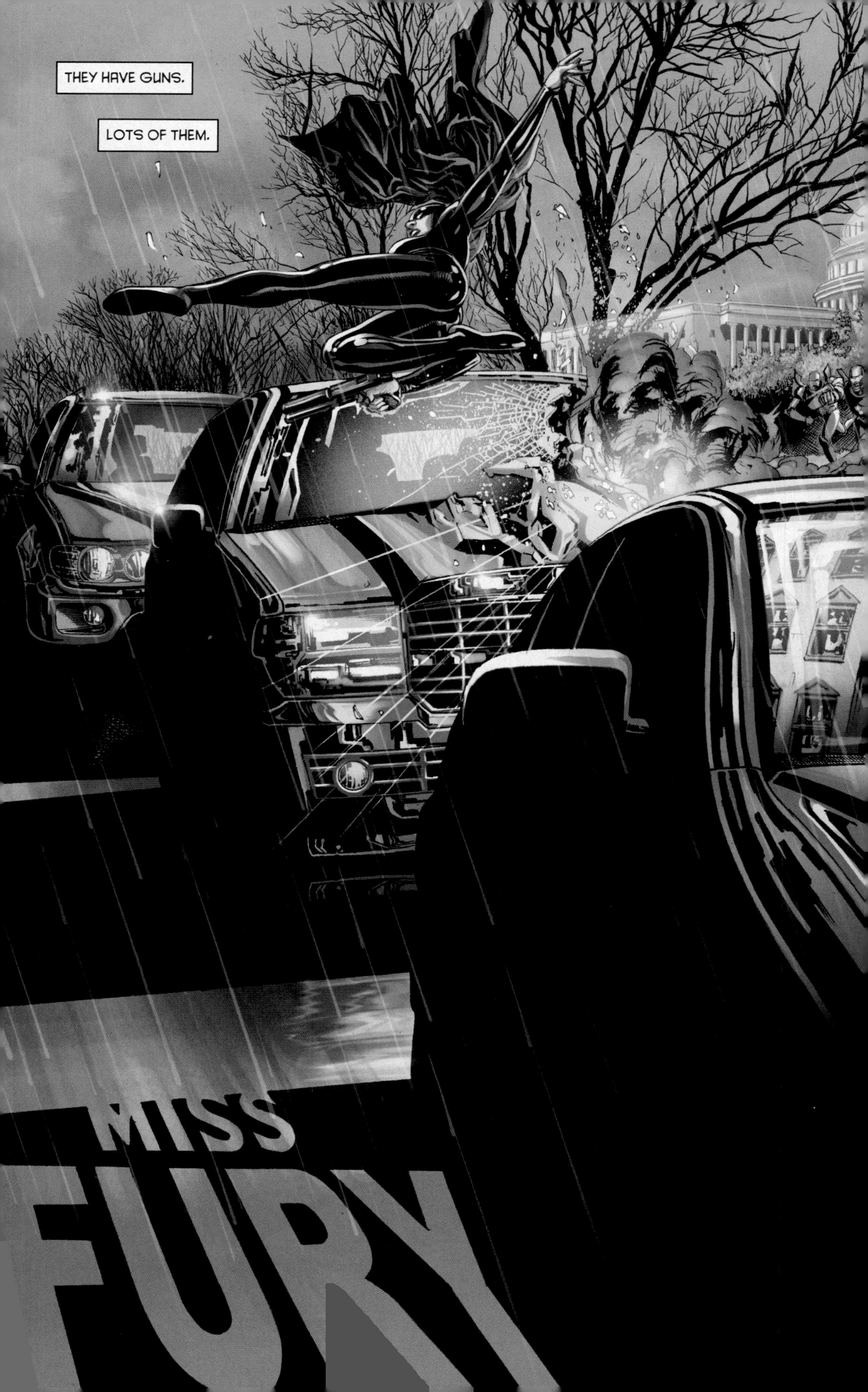
THEY HAVE GUNS.
LOTS OF THEM.
MISS
FURY

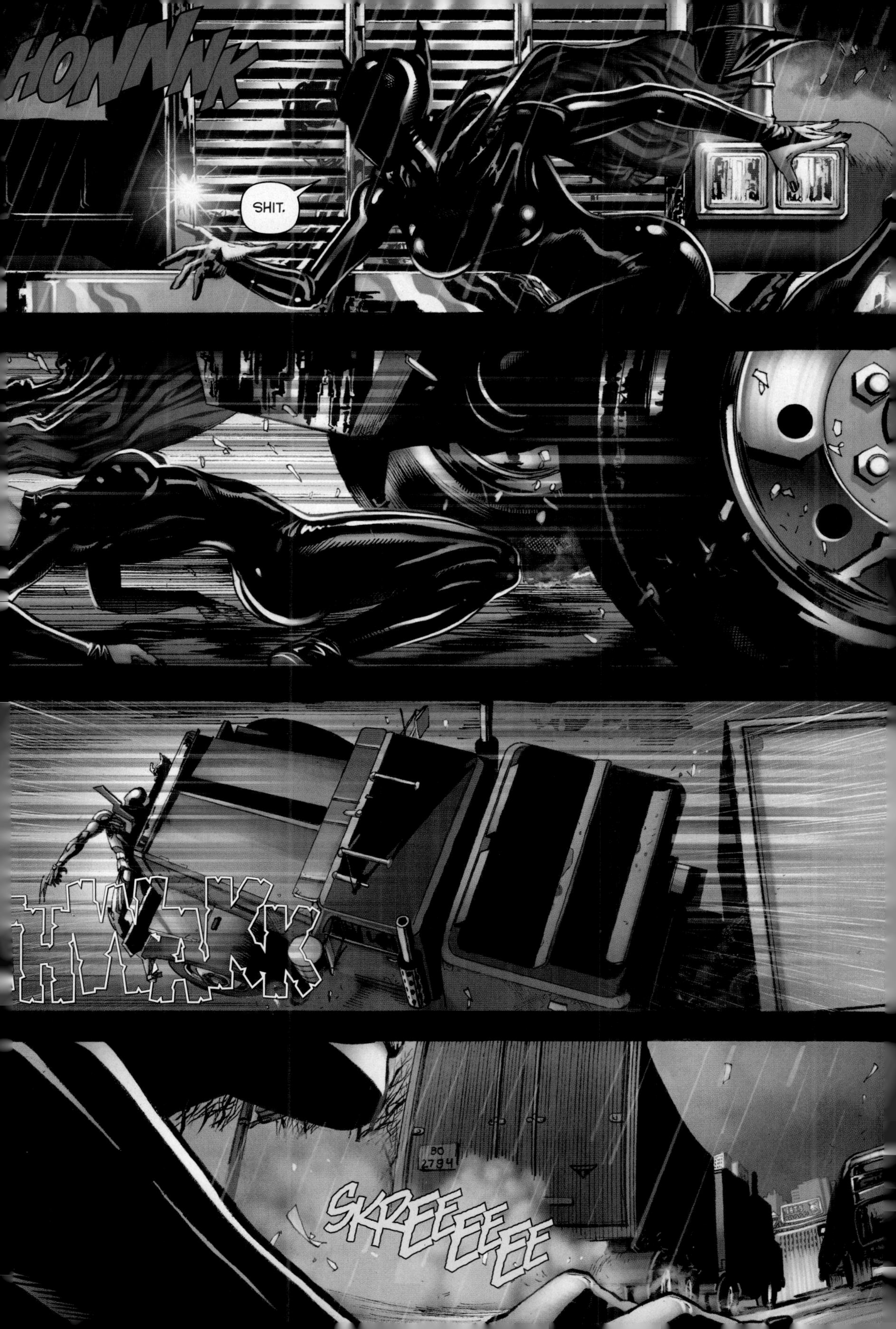
HONNNK
SHIT.
THWAKK
SKREEEEEEEE

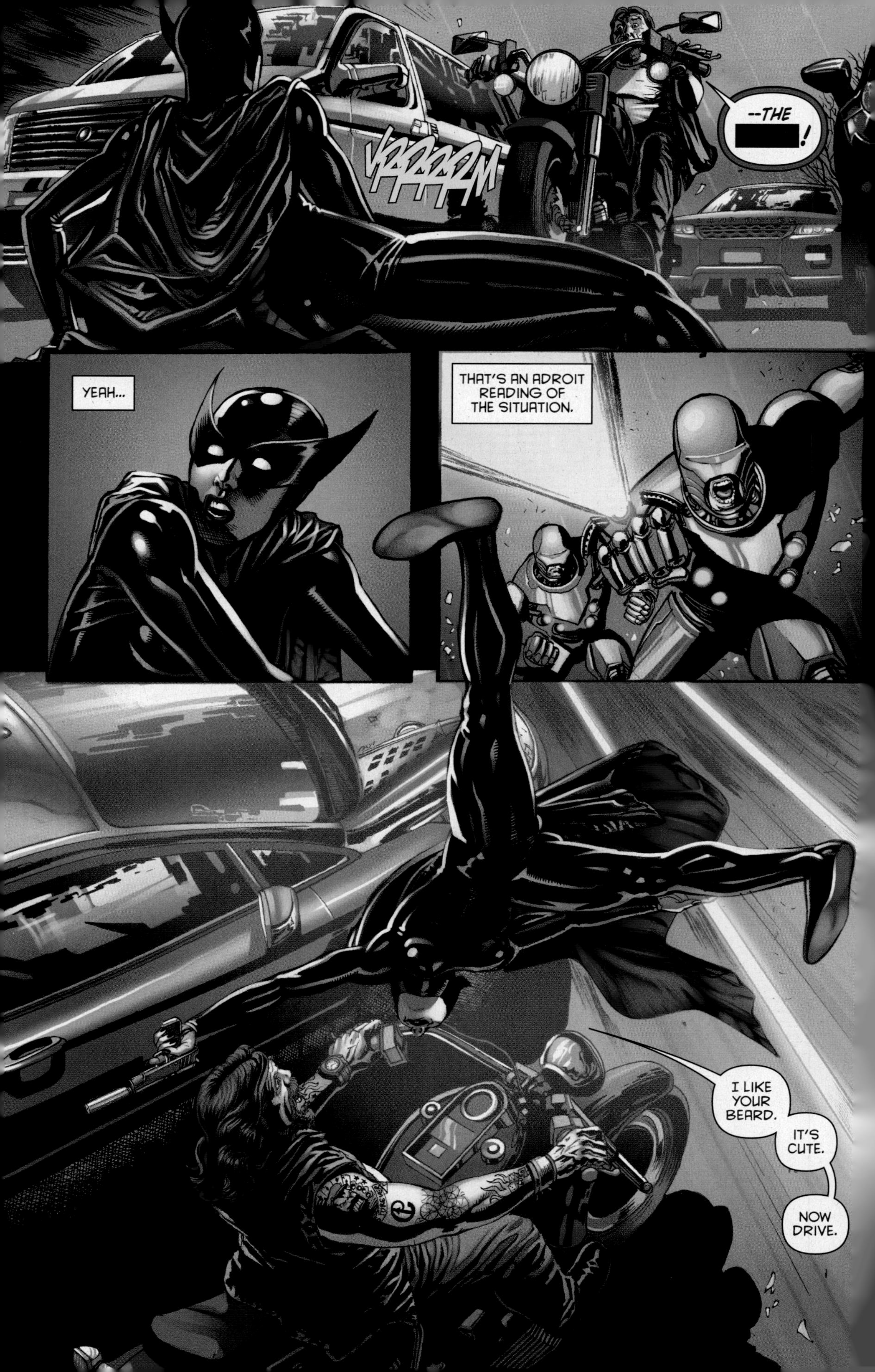
VRRRRM
--THE [redacted]!
YEAH...
THAT'S AN ADROIT READING OF THE SITUATION.
I LIKE YOUR BEARD.
IT'S CUTE.
NOW DRIVE.

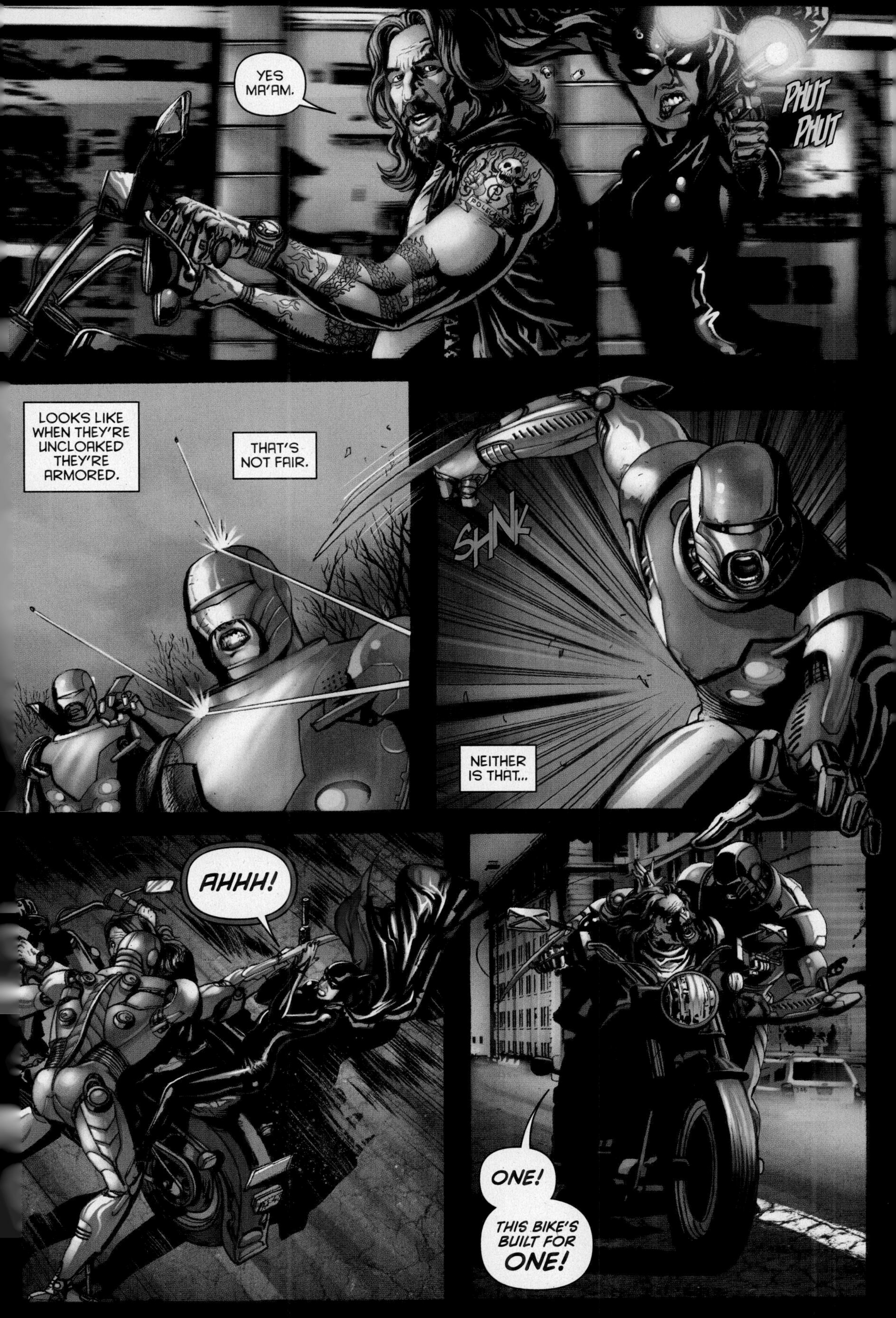
YES MA'AM.
PHUT PHUT
LOOKS LIKE WHEN THEY'RE UNCLOAKED THEY'RE ARMORED.
THAT'S NOT FAIR.
SHNK
NEITHER IS THAT...
AHHH!
ONE!
THIS BIKE'S BUILT FOR ONE!

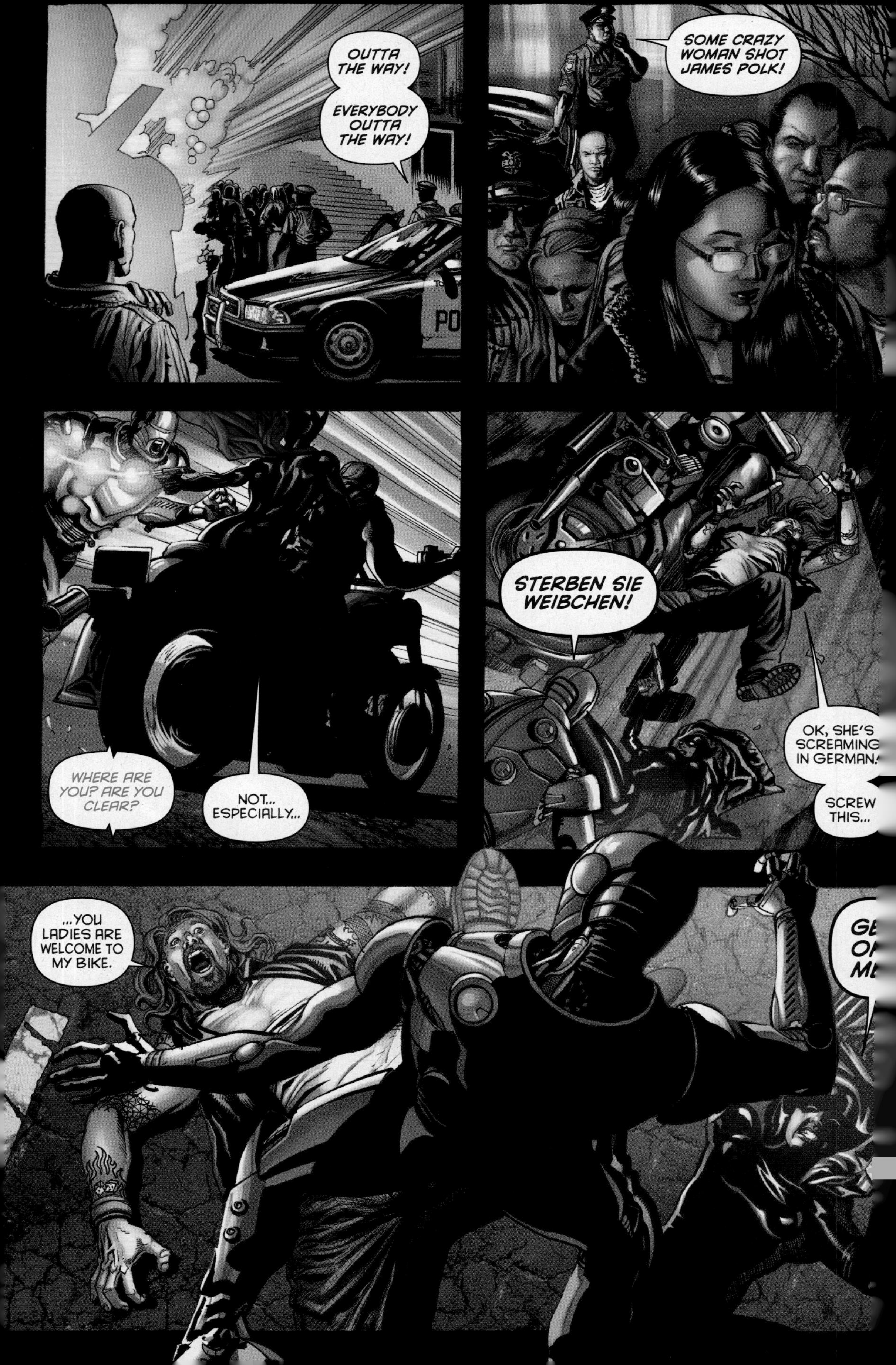
OUTTA THE WAY!
EVERYBODY OUTTA THE WAY!
SOME CRAZY WOMAN SHOT JAMES POLK!
WHERE ARE YOU? ARE YOU CLEAR?
NOT... ESPECIALLY...
STERBEN SIE WEIBCHEN!
OK, SHE'S SCREAMING IN GERMAN.
SCREW THIS...
...YOU LADIES ARE WELCOME TO MY BIKE.

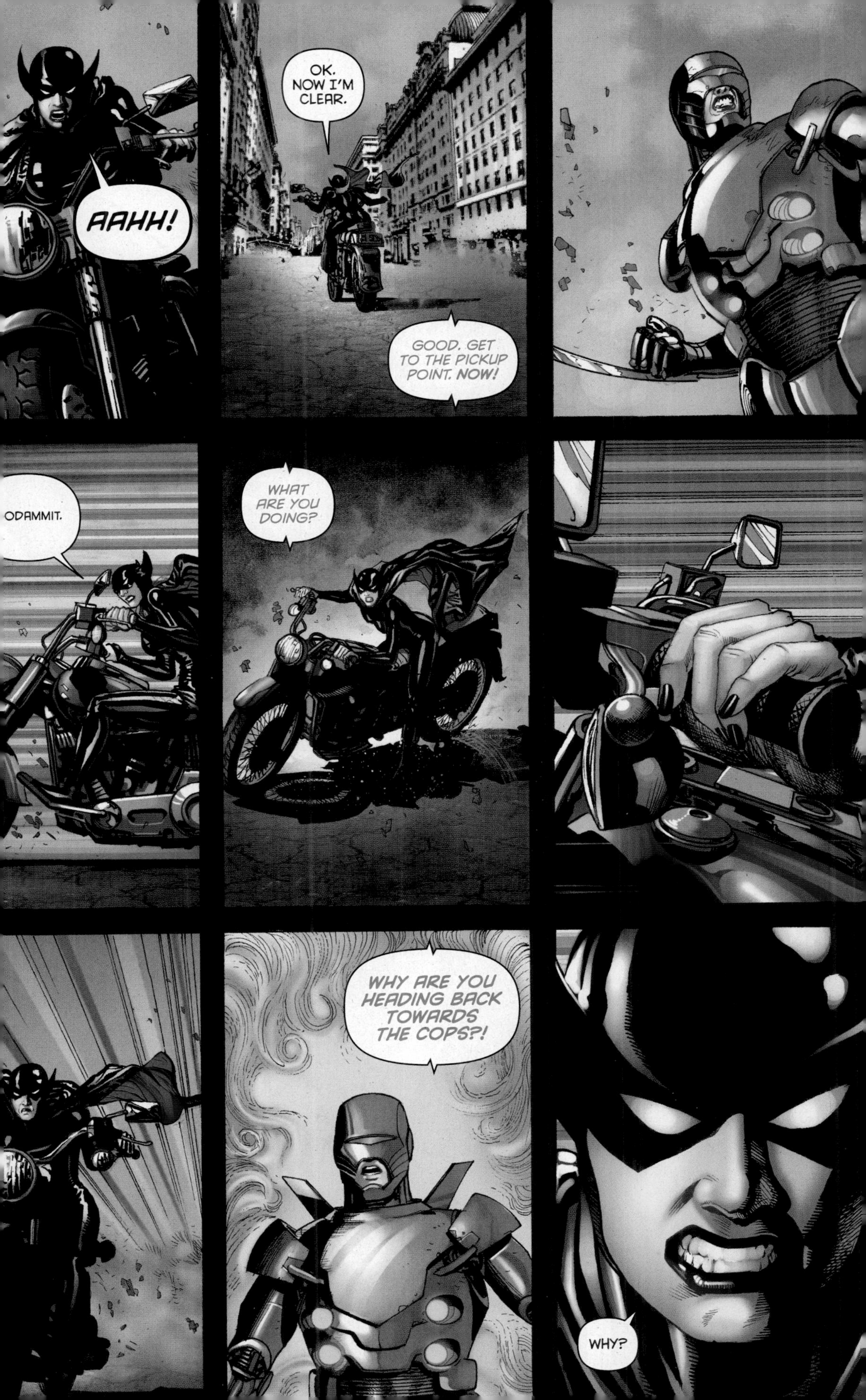
AAHH!
OK. NOW I'M CLEAR.
GOOD. GET TO THE PICKUP POINT. NOW!
ODAMMIT.
WHAT ARE YOU DOING?
WHY ARE YOU HEADING BACK TOWARDS THE COPS?!
WHY?

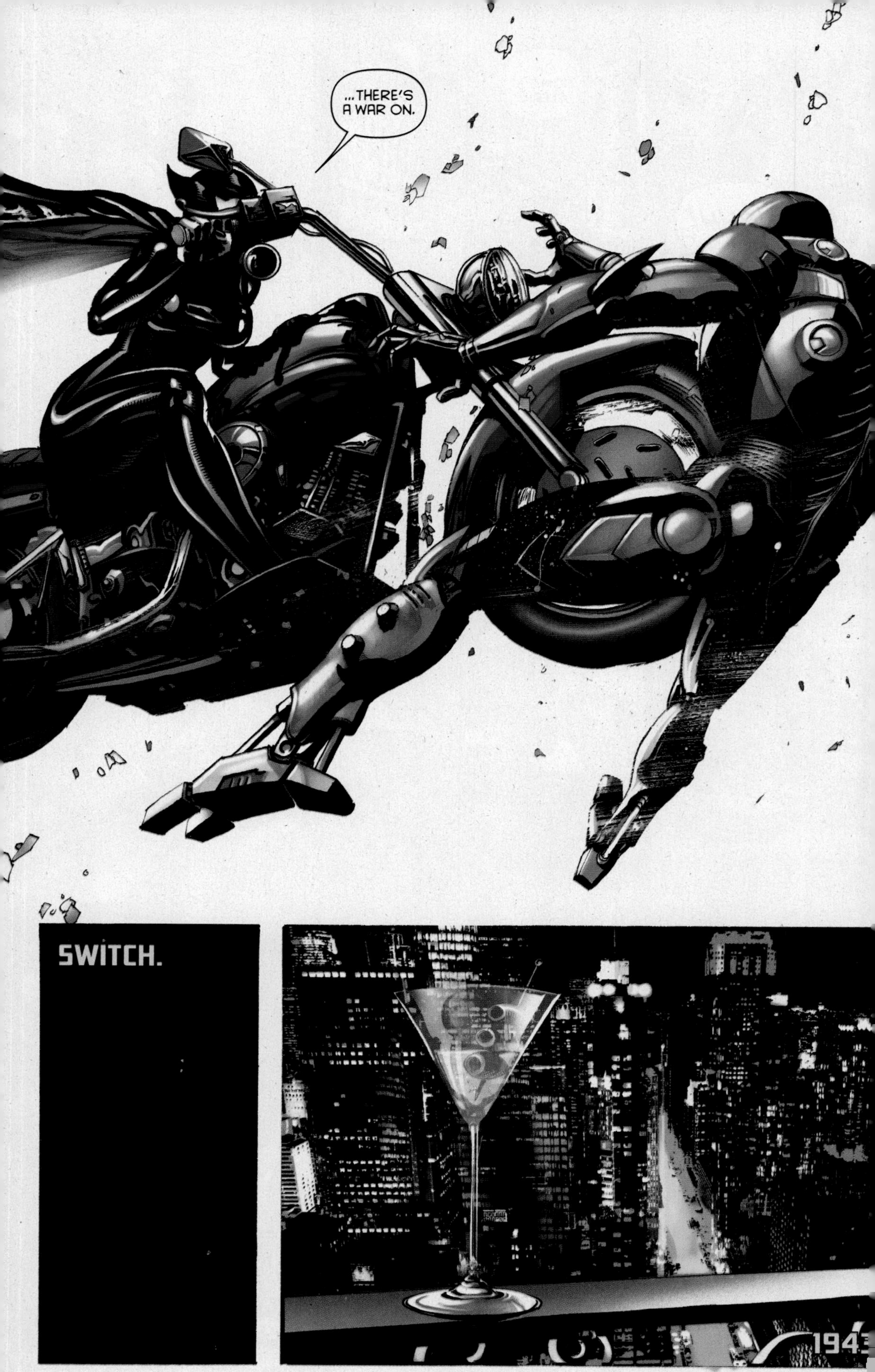
...THERE'S A WAR ON.
SWITCH.
1943

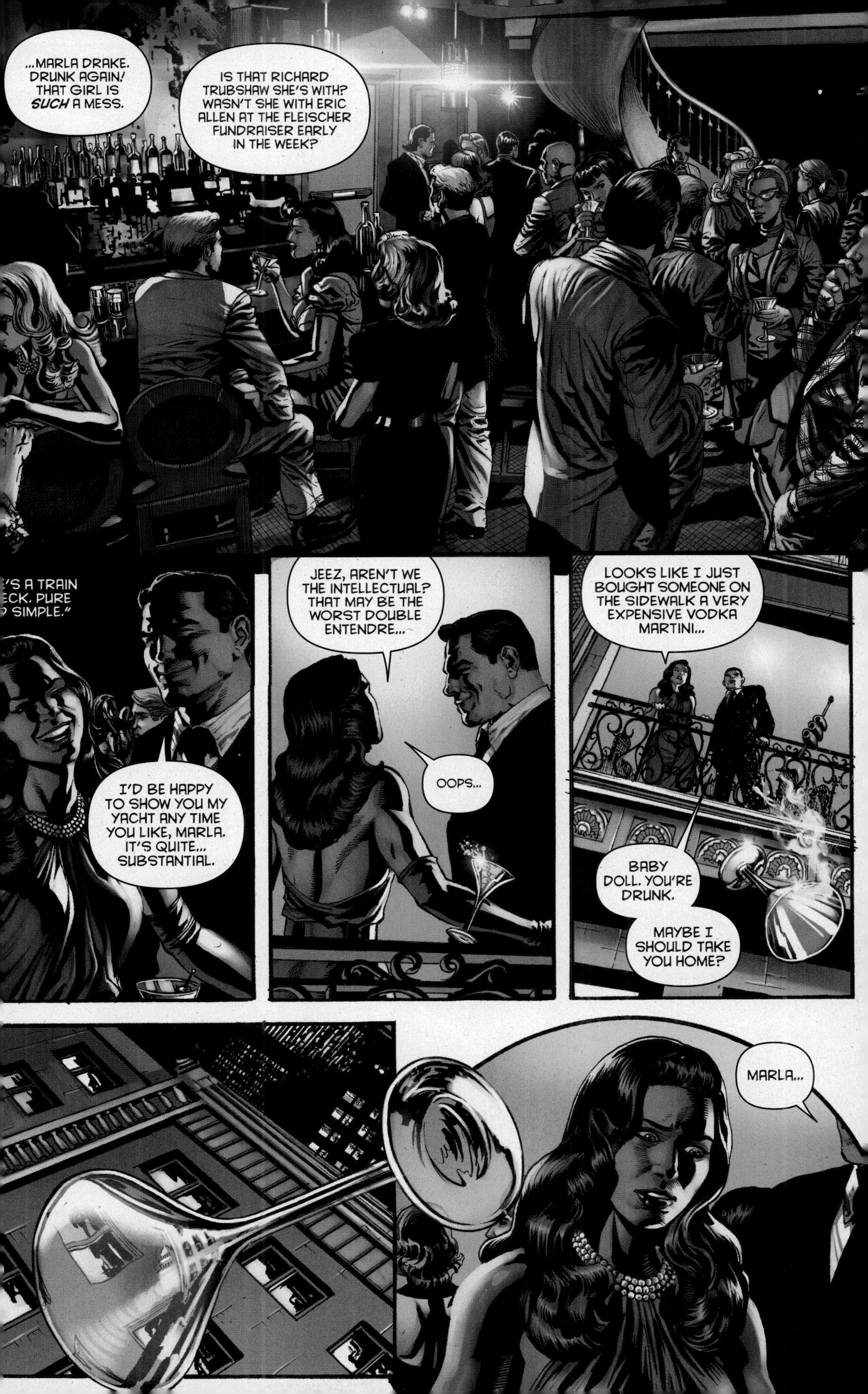
...MARLA DRAKE. DRUNK AGAIN! THAT GIRL IS SUCH A MESS.
IS THAT RICHARD TRUBSHAW SHE'S WITH? WASN'T SHE WITH ERIC ALLEN AT THE FLEISCHER FUNDRAISER EARLY IN THE WEEK?
'S A TRAIN ECK. PURE SIMPLE."
I'D BE HAPPY TO SHOW YOU MY YACHT ANY TIME YOU LIKE, MARLA. IT'S QUITE... SUBSTANTIAL.
JEEZ, AREN'T WE THE INTELLECTUAL? THAT MAY BE THE WORST DOUBLE ENTENDRE...
OOPS...
LOOKS LIKE I JUST BOUGHT SOMEONE ON THE SIDEWALK A VERY EXPENSIVE VODKA MARTINI...
BABY DOLL. YOU'RE DRUNK.
MAYBE I SHOULD TAKE YOU HOME?
MARLA...

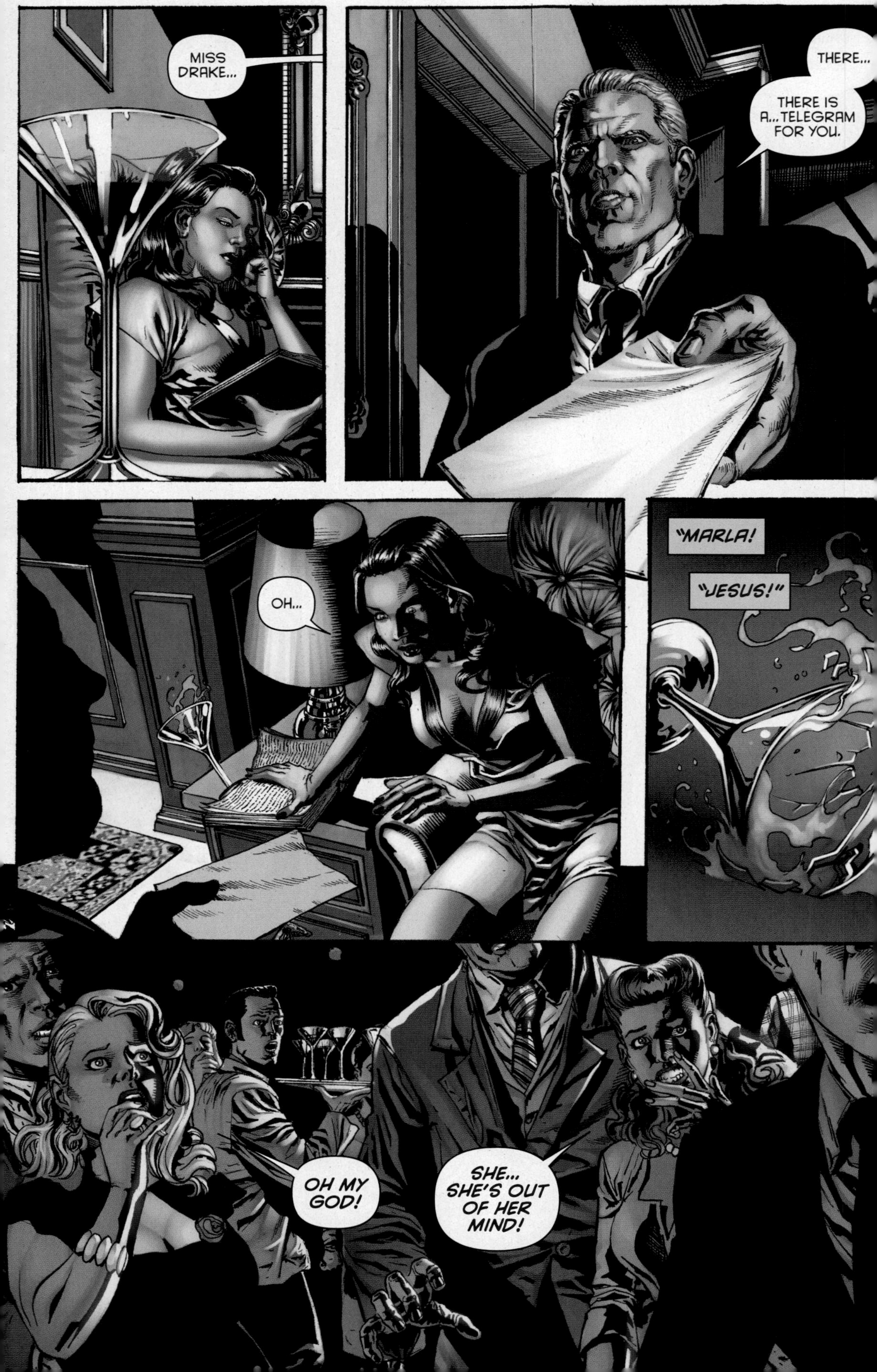
MISS DRAKE...
THERE...
THERE IS A...TELEGRAM FOR YOU.
OH...
"MARLA!
"JESUS!"
OH MY GOD!
SHE... SHE'S OUT OF HER MIND!

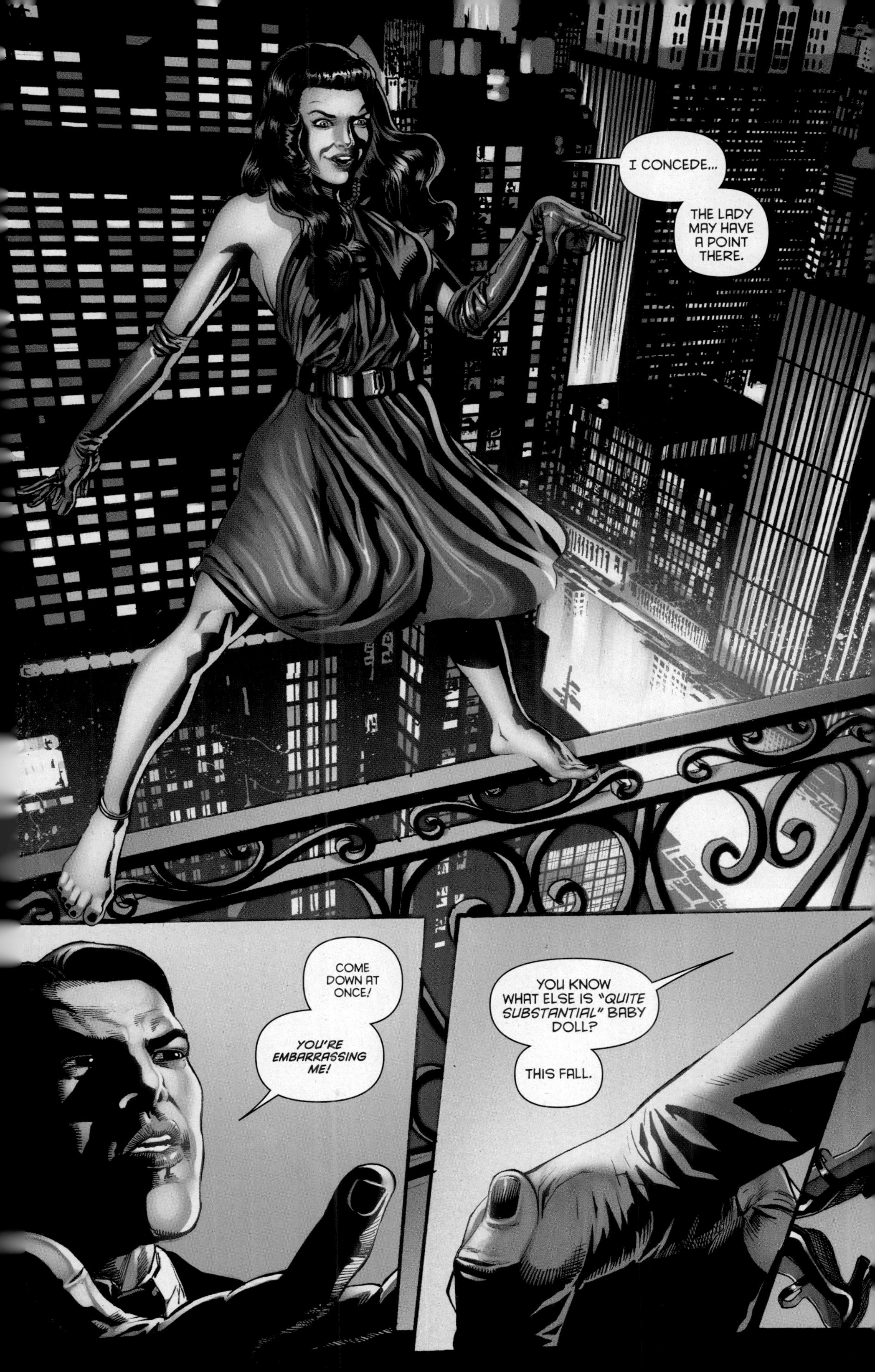
I CONCEDE...
THE LADY MAY HAVE A POINT THERE.
COME DOWN AT ONCE!
*YOU'RE* EMBARRASSING ME!
YOU KNOW WHAT ELSE IS "*QUITE SUBSTANTIAL*" BABY DOLL?
THIS FALL.

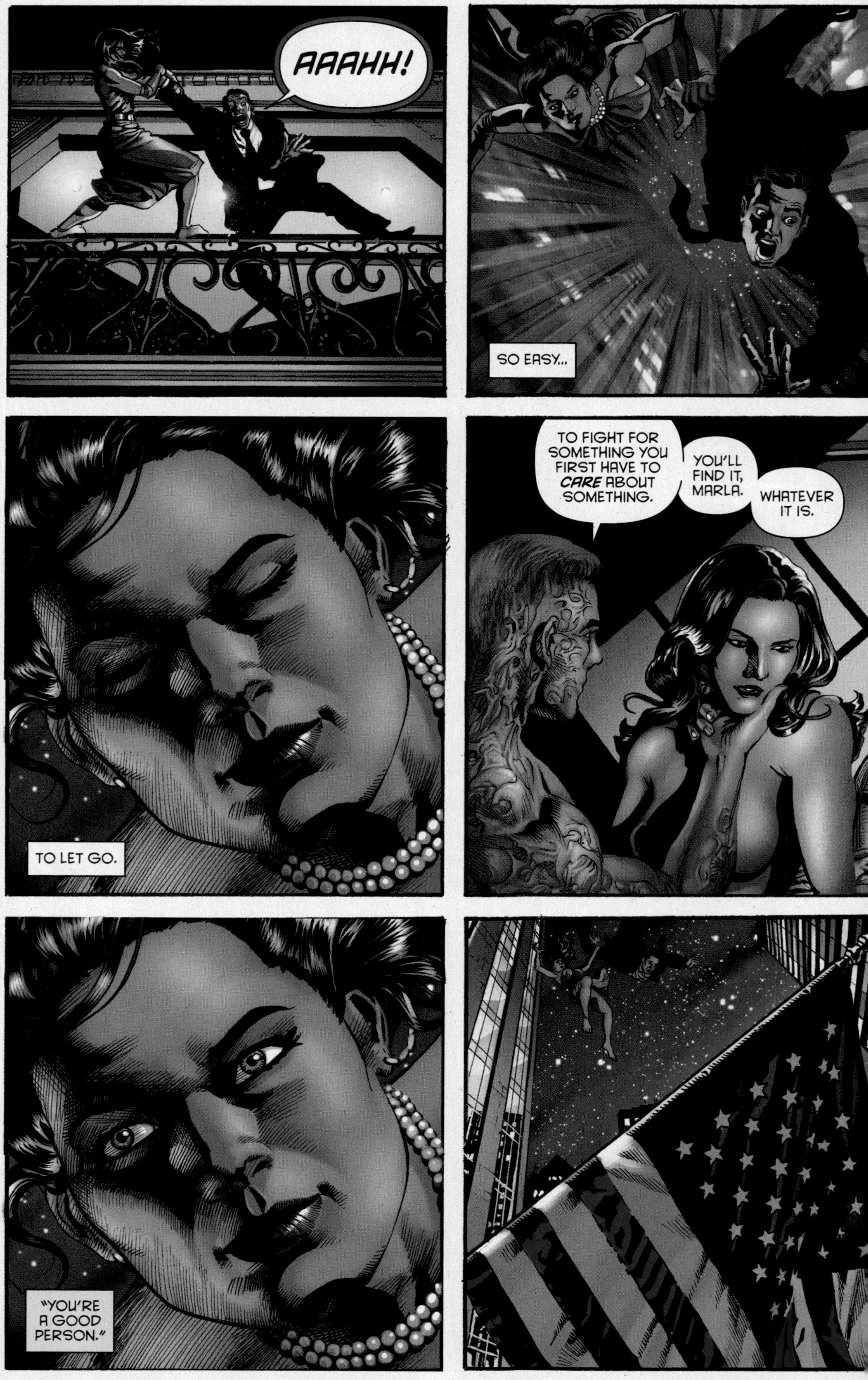
AAAHH!
SO EASY...
TO LET GO.
TO FIGHT FOR SOMETHING YOU FIRST HAVE TO *CARE* ABOUT SOMETHING.
YOU'LL FIND IT, MARLA.
WHATEVER IT IS.
"YOU'RE A GOOD PERSON."

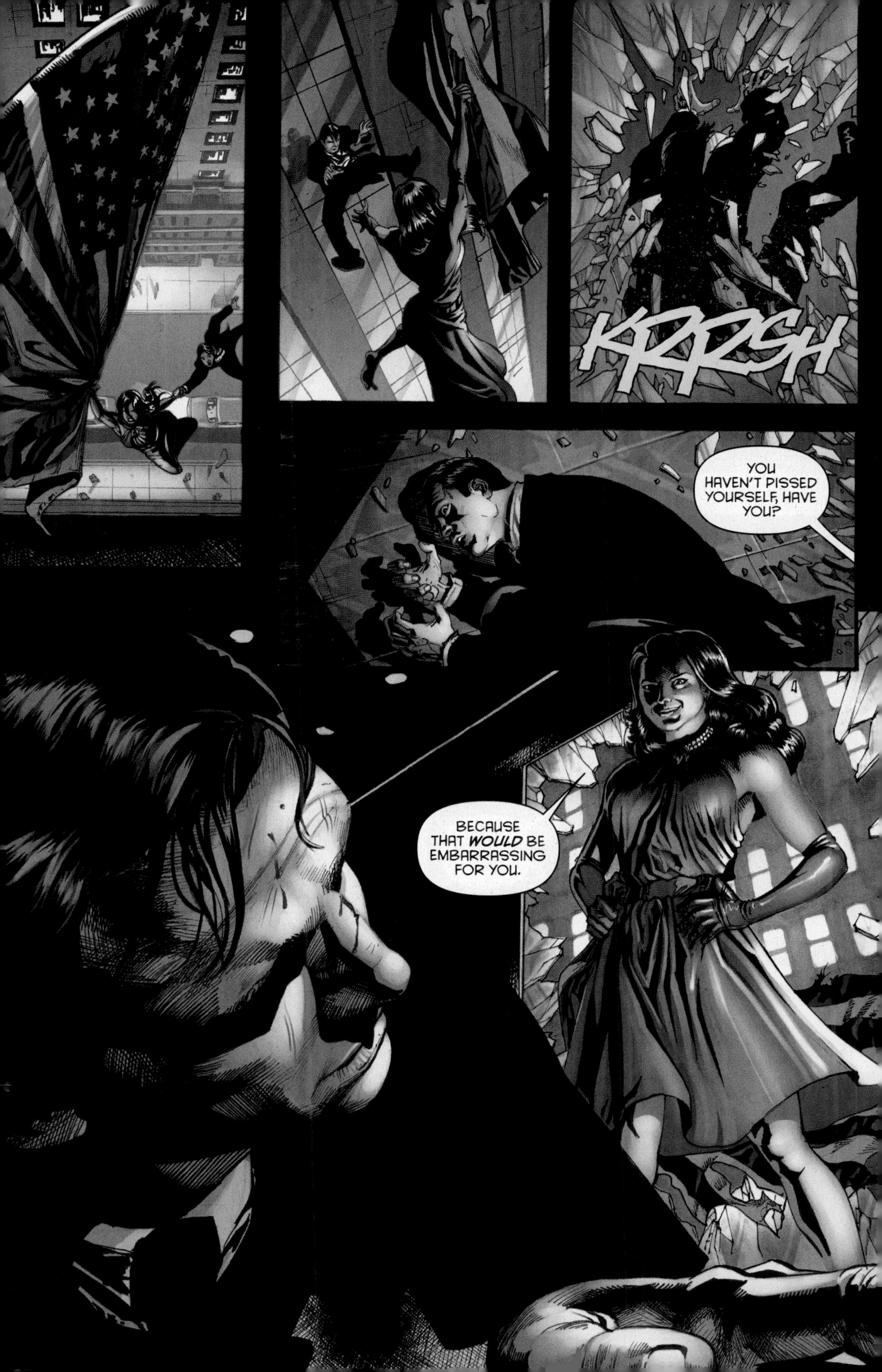
KRRSH
YOU HAVEN'T PISSED YOURSELF, HAVE YOU?
BECAUSE THAT WOULD BE EMBARRASSING FOR YOU.

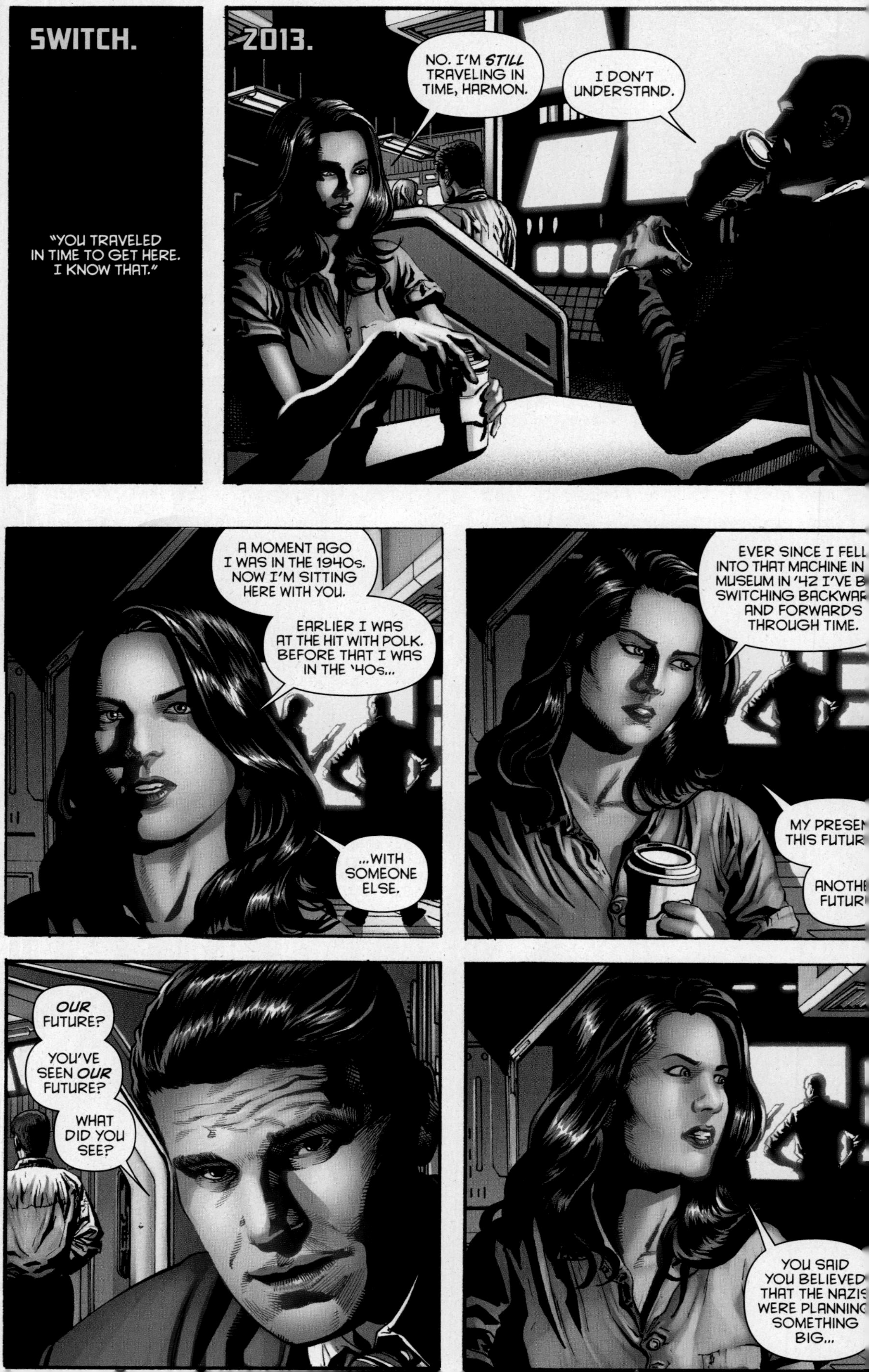
SWITCH.
"YOU TRAVELED IN TIME TO GET HERE. I KNOW THAT."
2013.
NO. I'M STILL TRAVELING IN TIME, HARMON.
I DON'T UNDERSTAND.
A MOMENT AGO I WAS IN THE 1940s. NOW I'M SITTING HERE WITH YOU.
EARLIER I WAS AT THE HIT WITH POLK. BEFORE THAT I WAS IN THE '40s...
...WITH SOMEONE ELSE.
EVER SINCE I FELL INTO THAT MACHINE IN MUSEUM IN '42 I'VE B SWITCHING BACKWAR AND FORWARDS THROUGH TIME.
MY PRESEN THIS FUTUR
ANOTH FUTUR
OUR FUTURE?
YOU'VE SEEN OUR FUTURE?
WHAT DID YOU SEE?
YOU SAID YOU BELIEVED THAT THE NAZIS WERE PLANNING SOMETHING BIG...

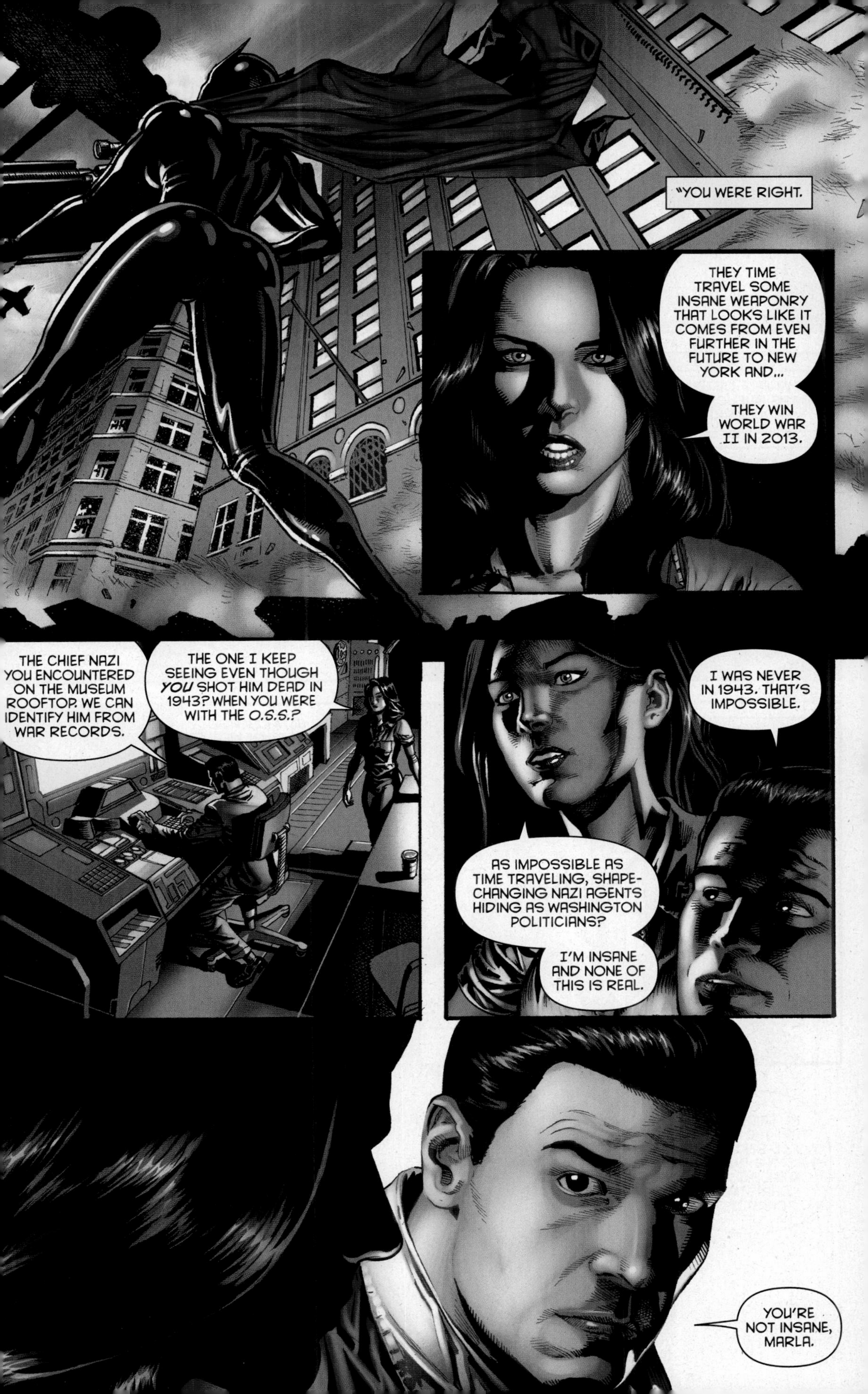
"YOU WERE RIGHT.
THEY TIME TRAVEL SOME INSANE WEAPONRY THAT LOOKS LIKE IT COMES FROM EVEN FURTHER IN THE FUTURE TO NEW YORK AND...
THEY WIN WORLD WAR II IN 2013.
THE CHIEF NAZI YOU ENCOUNTERED ON THE MUSEUM ROOFTOP. WE CAN IDENTIFY HIM FROM WAR RECORDS.
THE ONE I KEEP SEEING EVEN THOUGH *YOU* SHOT HIM DEAD IN 1943? WHEN YOU WERE WITH THE *O.S.S.*?
I WAS NEVER IN 1943. THAT'S IMPOSSIBLE.
AS IMPOSSIBLE AS TIME TRAVELING, SHAPE-CHANGING NAZI AGENTS HIDING AS WASHINGTON POLITICIANS?
I'M INSANE AND NONE OF THIS IS REAL.
YOU'RE NOT INSANE, MARLA.

HARMON'S KIND. CARING. BUT I DON'T TRUST HIM...

I CAN'T BLOCK OUT THE NAZI SCIENTIST'S WORDS ON THE MUSEUM ROOF:

WHO, EXACTLY, ARE YOU *REALLY* BEING ASKED TO KILL? AND BY WHOM?

I'M HALF-LISTENING TO HIM AS HE FLICKS THROUGH ENDLESS RECORDS.

SOMETHING ABOUT ELECTRO-MAGNETIC READINGS AND HOW THEY WERE ABLE TO DETECT THE CLOAKING DEVICES OF THE NAZI AGENTS.

CONCENTRATE ON THE MISSION. THE *WAR*.

THE CLARITY OF GOAL WILL STO ME SLIPPING INTO INSANITY

IF I MURDER THE PEOPLE HE TELLS ME TO KILL, I AM NOT MAD.

THAT'S HIM!

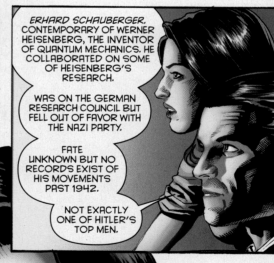

ERHARD SCHAUBERGER. CONTEMPORARY OF WERNER HEISENBERG, THE INVENTOR OF QUANTUM MECHANICS. HE COLLABORATED ON SOME OF HEISENBERG'S RESEARCH.

WAS ON THE GERMAN RESEARCH COUNCIL BUT FELL OUT OF FAVOR WITH THE NAZI PARTY.

FATE UNKNOWN BUT NO RECORDS EXIST OF HIS MOVEMENTS PAST 1942.

NOT EXACTLY ONE OF HITLER'S TOP MEN.

HE SAID TO ME THAT THE FÜHRER WOULD BEND TO HIS WILL. THEY WEREN'T ON EACH OTHERS' CHRISTMAS CARD LIST.

HE'S REAL THOUGH.

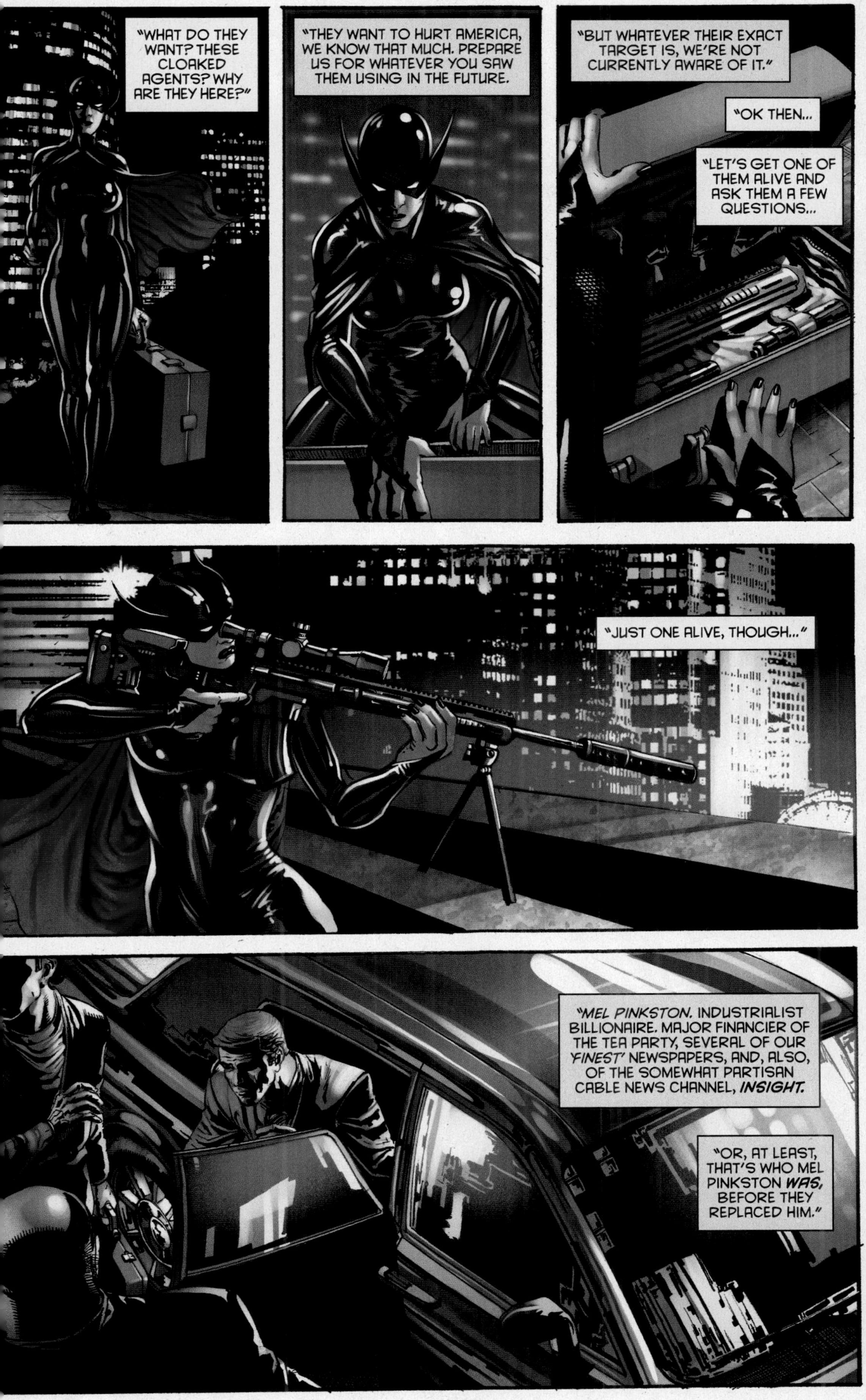
"WHAT DO THEY WANT? THESE CLOAKED AGENTS? WHY ARE THEY HERE?"
"THEY WANT TO HURT AMERICA, WE KNOW THAT MUCH. PREPARE US FOR WHATEVER YOU SAW THEM USING IN THE FUTURE.
"BUT WHATEVER THEIR EXACT TARGET IS, WE'RE NOT CURRENTLY AWARE OF IT."
"OK THEN...
"LET'S GET ONE OF THEM ALIVE AND ASK THEM A FEW QUESTIONS...
"JUST ONE ALIVE, THOUGH..."
"*MEL PINKSTON.* INDUSTRIALIST BILLIONAIRE. MAJOR FINANCIER OF THE TEA PARTY, SEVERAL OF OUR *'FINEST'* NEWSPAPERS, AND, ALSO, OF THE SOMEWHAT PARTISAN CABLE NEWS CHANNEL, ***INSIGHT.***
"OR, AT LEAST, THAT'S WHO MEL PINKSTON ***WAS,*** BEFORE THEY REPLACED HIM."

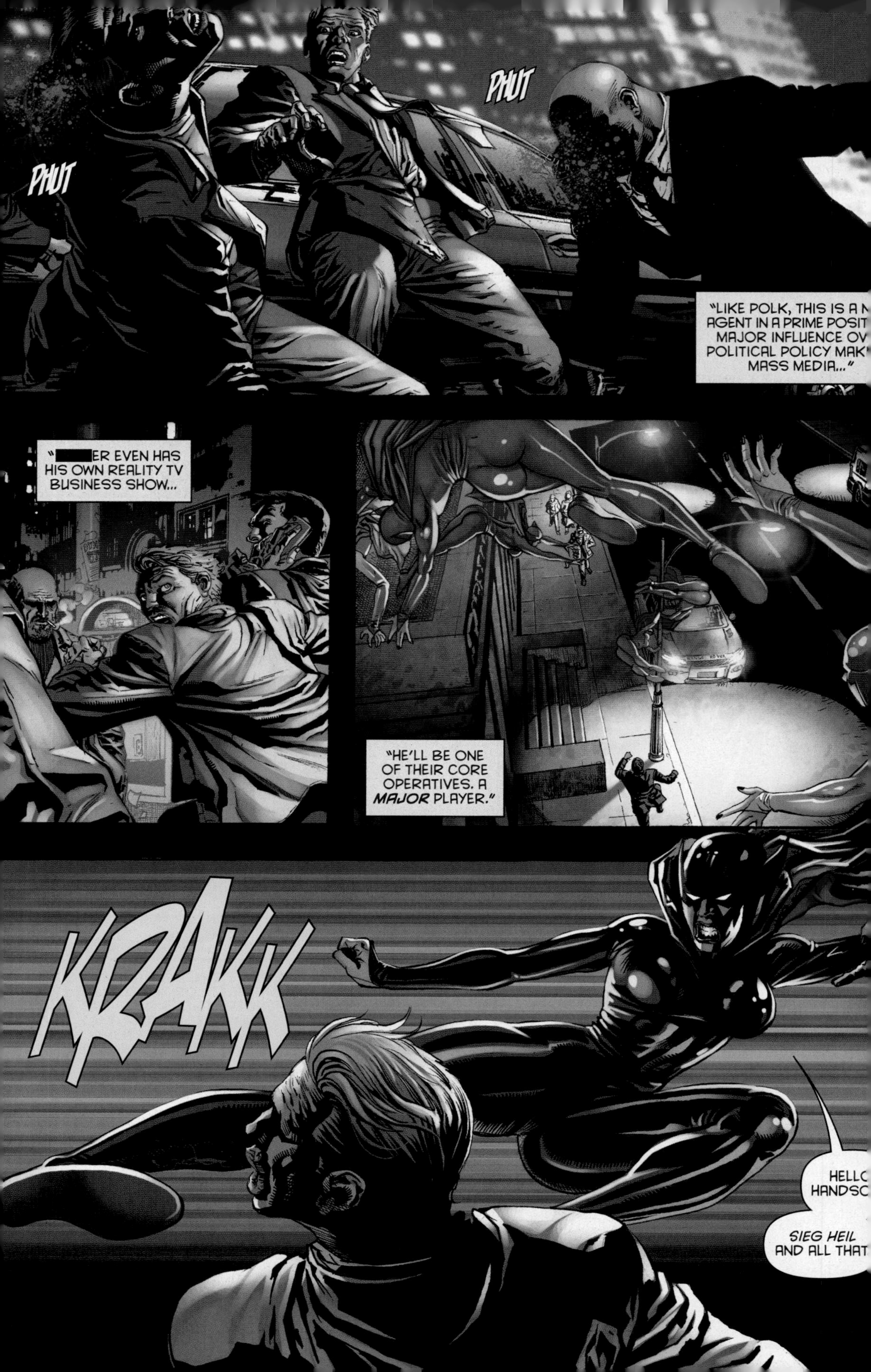
PHUT
PHUT
"LIKE POLK, THIS IS A N
AGENT IN A PRIME POSIT
MAJOR INFLUENCE OV
POLITICAL POLICY MAK
MASS MEDIA..."
"[redacted]ER EVEN HAS HIS OWN REALITY TV BUSINESS SHOW...
"HE'LL BE ONE OF THEIR CORE OPERATIVES. A *MAJOR* PLAYER."
KRAKK
HELLC HANDSC
*SIEG HEIL* AND ALL THAT

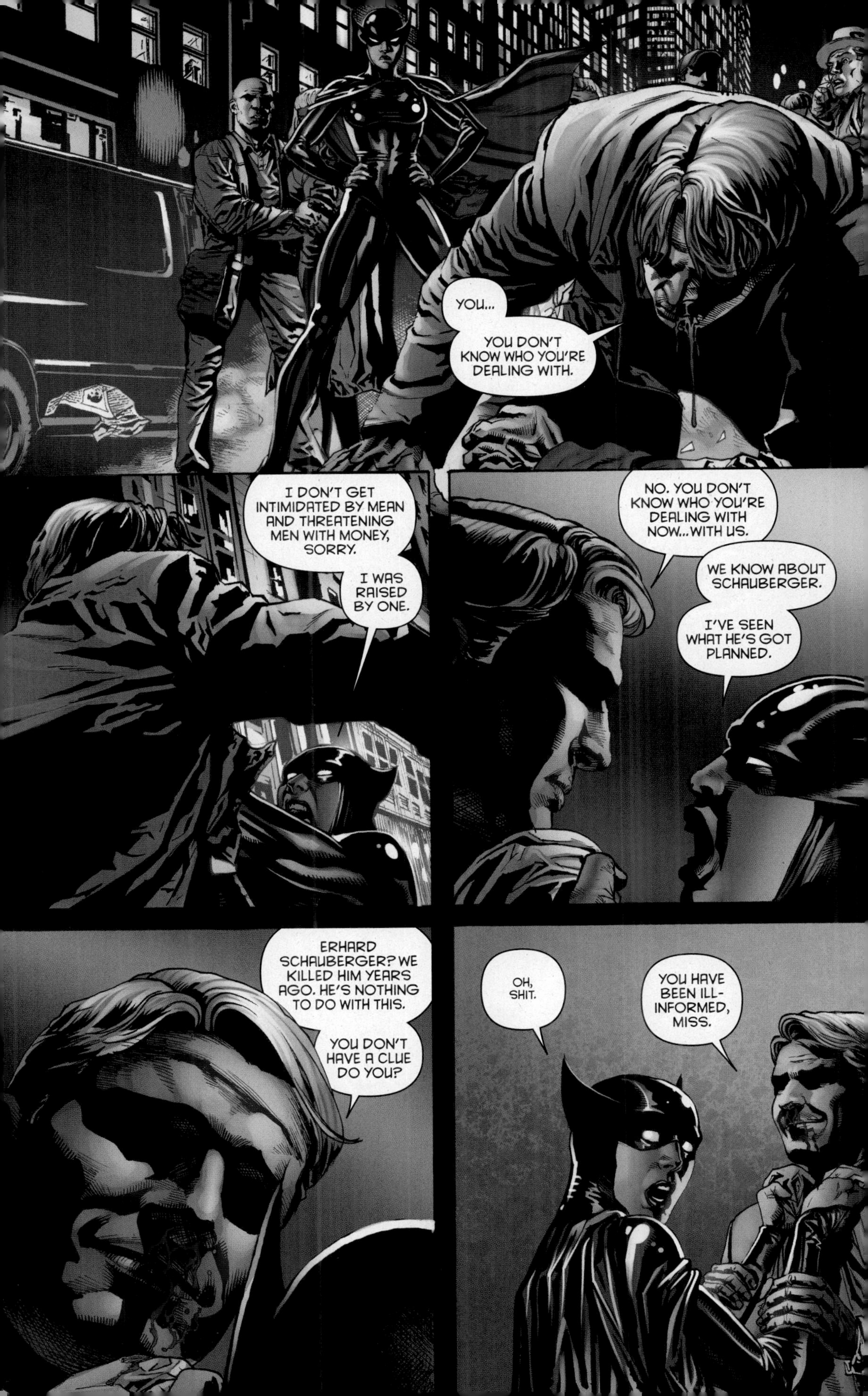
YOU...
YOU DON'T KNOW WHO YOU'RE DEALING WITH.
I DON'T GET INTIMIDATED BY MEAN AND THREATENING MEN WITH MONEY, SORRY.
I WAS RAISED BY ONE.
NO. YOU DON'T KNOW WHO YOU'RE DEALING WITH NOW...WITH US.
WE KNOW ABOUT SCHAUBERGER.
I'VE SEEN WHAT HE'S GOT PLANNED.
ERHARD SCHAUBERGER? WE KILLED HIM YEARS AGO. HE'S NOTHING TO DO WITH THIS.
YOU DON'T HAVE A CLUE DO YOU?
OH, SHIT.
YOU HAVE BEEN ILL-INFORMED, MISS.

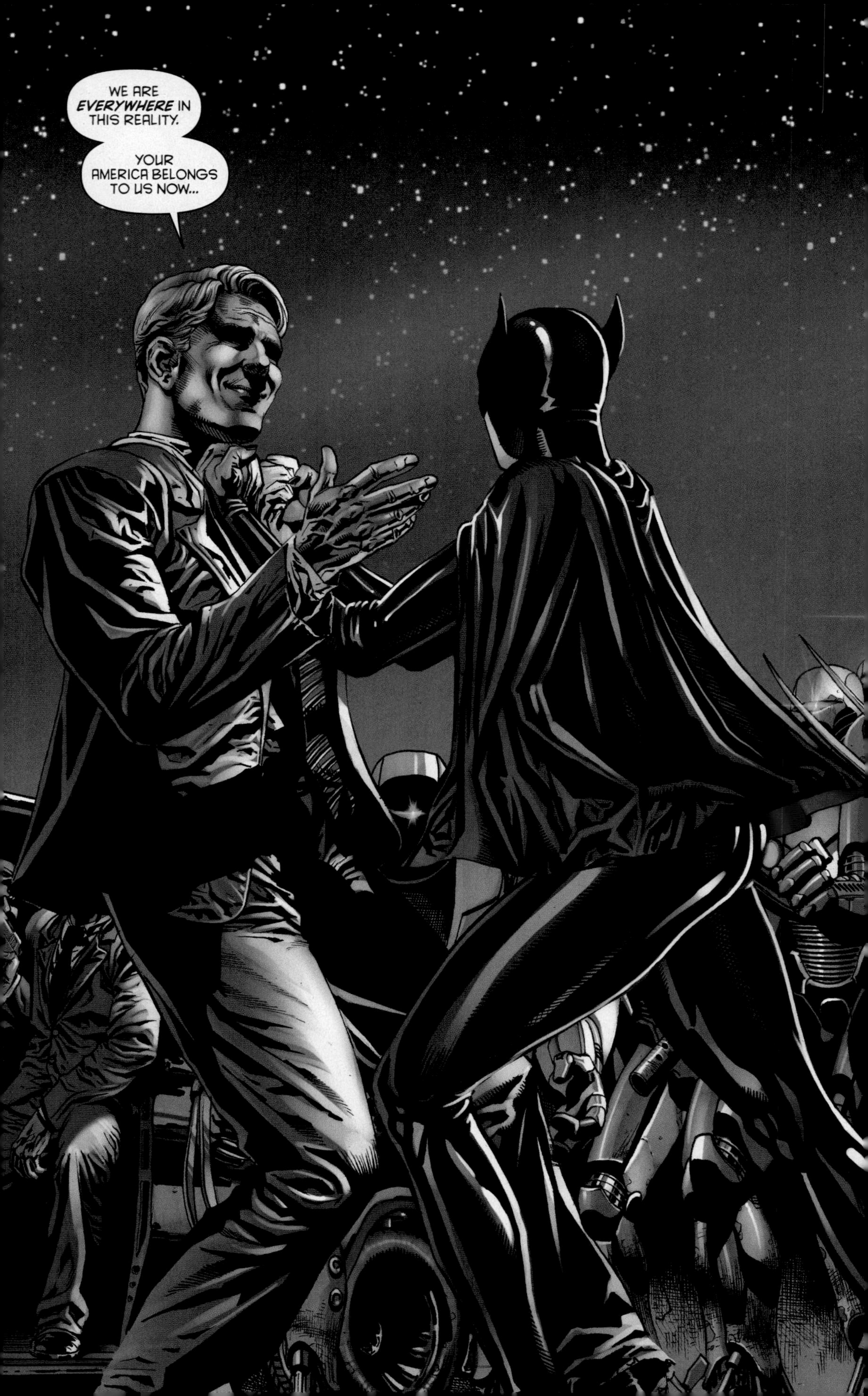
WE ARE *EVERYWHERE* IN THIS REALITY.
YOUR AMERICA BELONGS TO US NOW...

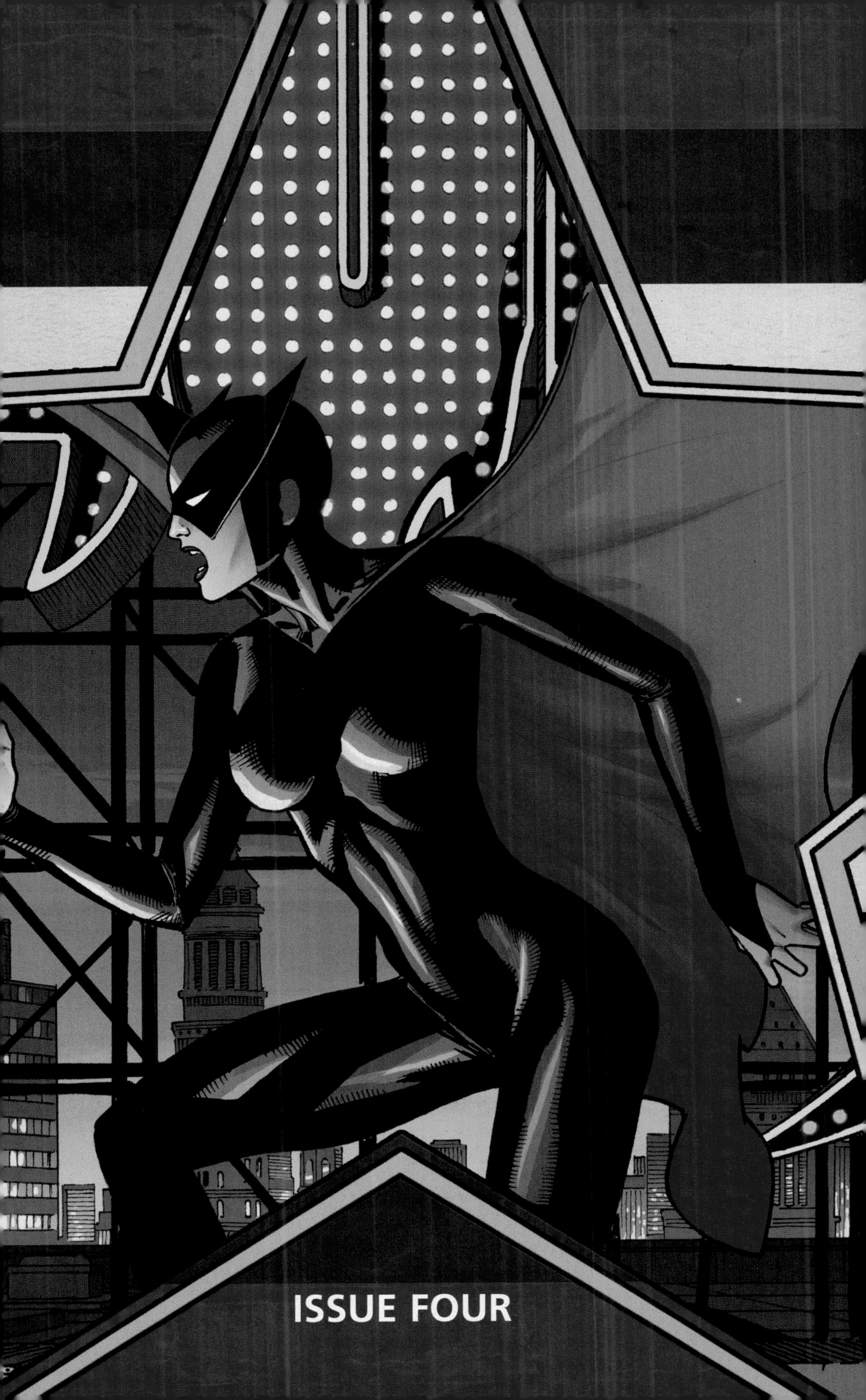
ISSUE FOUR

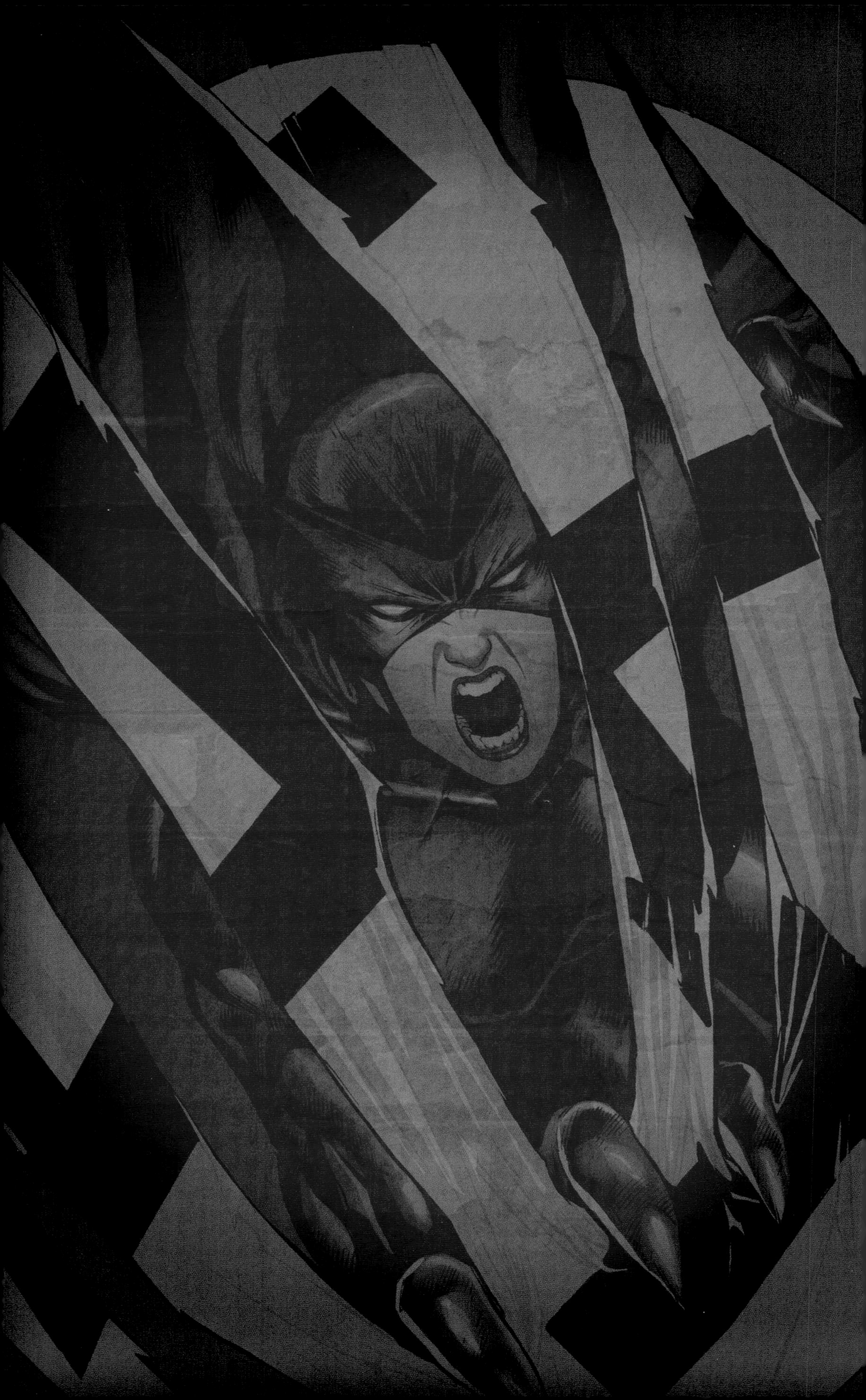

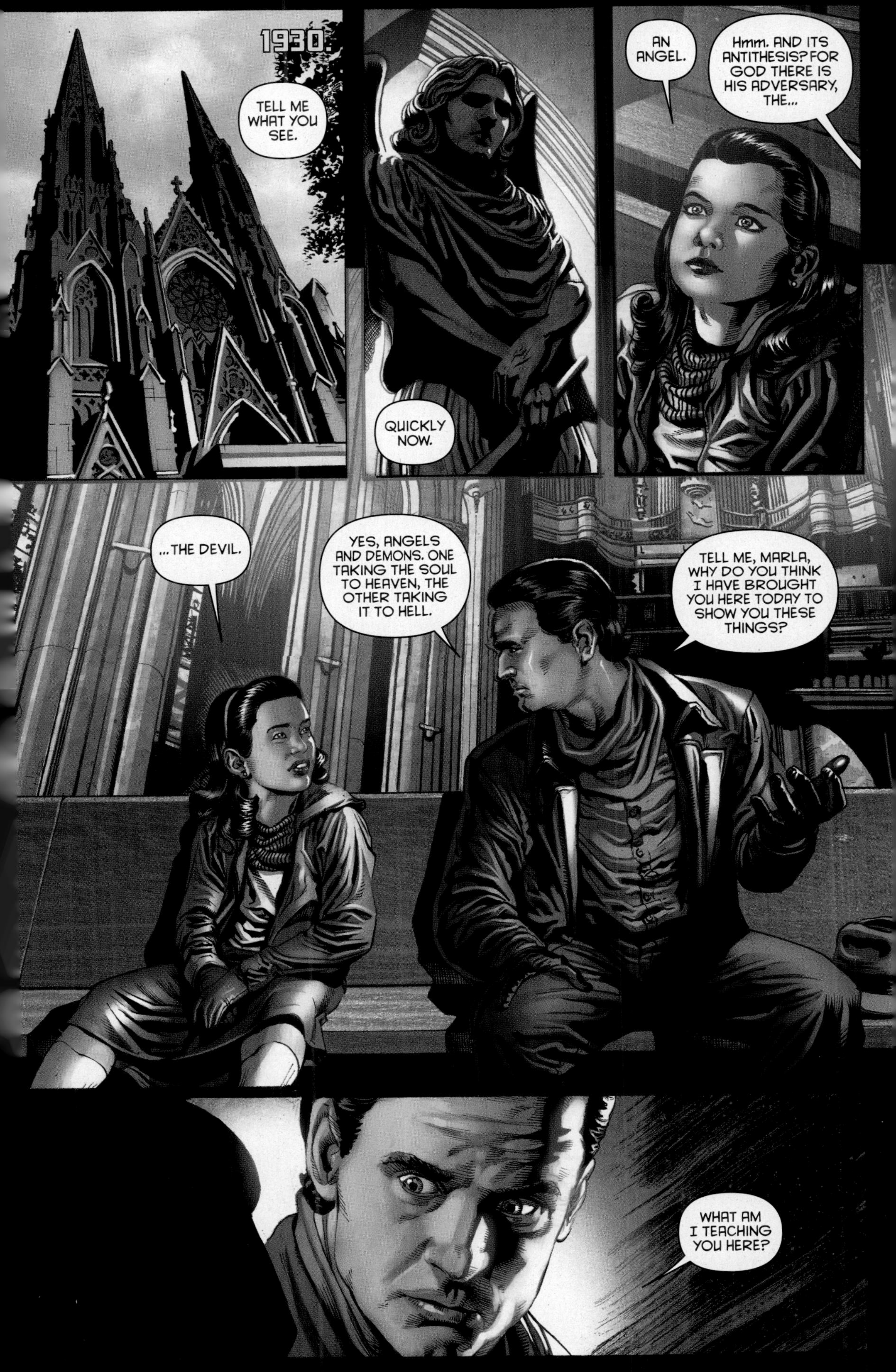
1930.
TELL ME WHAT YOU SEE.
QUICKLY NOW.
AN ANGEL.
Hmm. AND ITS ANTITHESIS? FOR GOD THERE IS HIS ADVERSARY, THE...
...THE DEVIL.
YES, ANGELS AND DEMONS. ONE TAKING THE SOUL TO HEAVEN, THE OTHER TAKING IT TO HELL.
TELL ME, MARLA, WHY DO YOU THINK I HAVE BROUGHT YOU HERE TODAY TO SHOW YOU THESE THINGS?
WHAT AM I TEACHING YOU HERE?

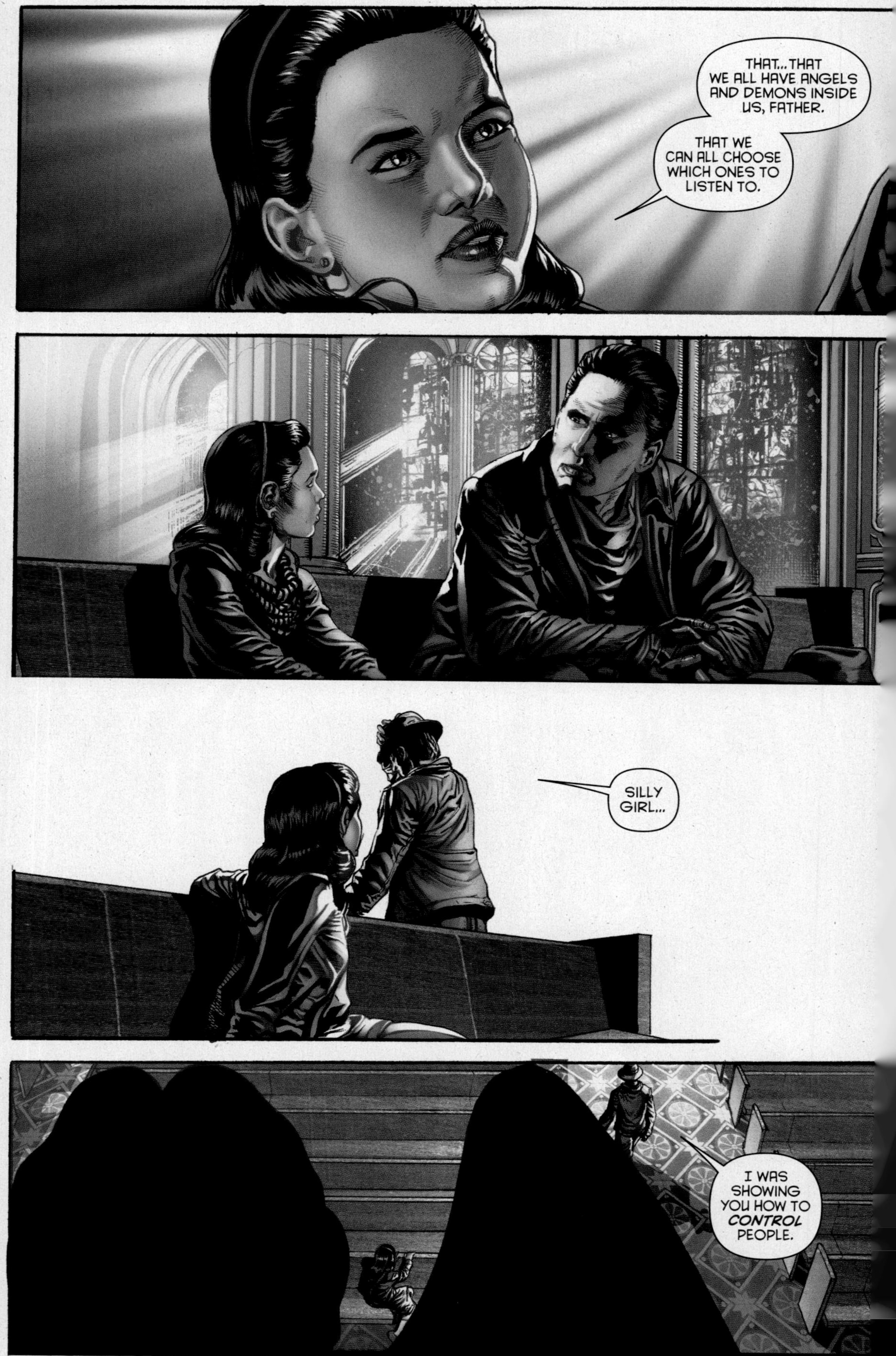
THAT... THAT WE ALL HAVE ANGELS AND DEMONS INSIDE US, FATHER.
THAT WE CAN ALL CHOOSE WHICH ONES TO LISTEN TO.
SILLY GIRL...
I WAS SHOWING YOU HOW TO CONTROL PEOPLE.

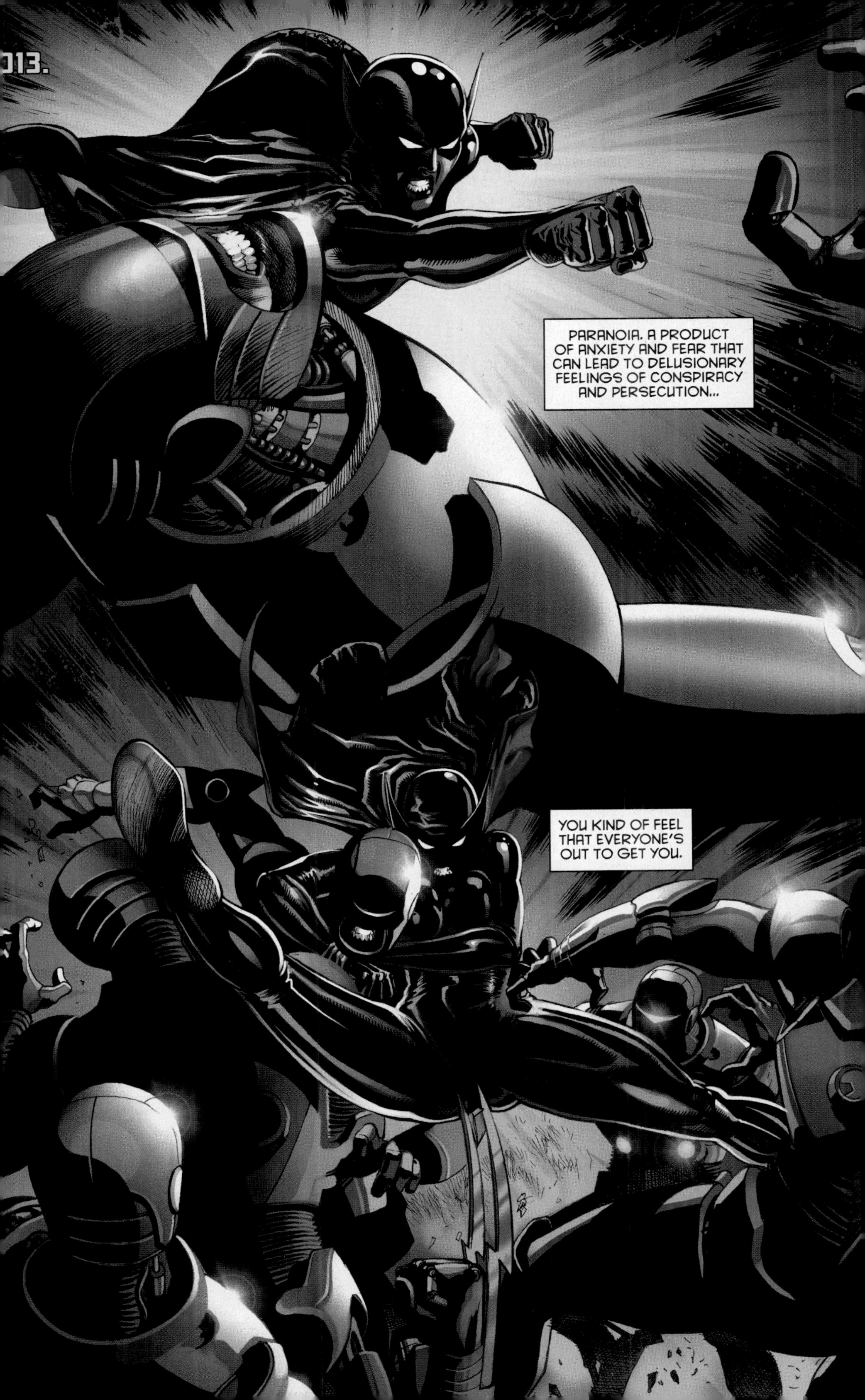
013.
PARANOIA. A PRODUCT OF ANXIETY AND FEAR THAT CAN LEAD TO DELUSIONARY FEELINGS OF CONSPIRACY AND PERSECUTION...
YOU KIND OF FEEL THAT EVERYONE'S OUT TO GET YOU.

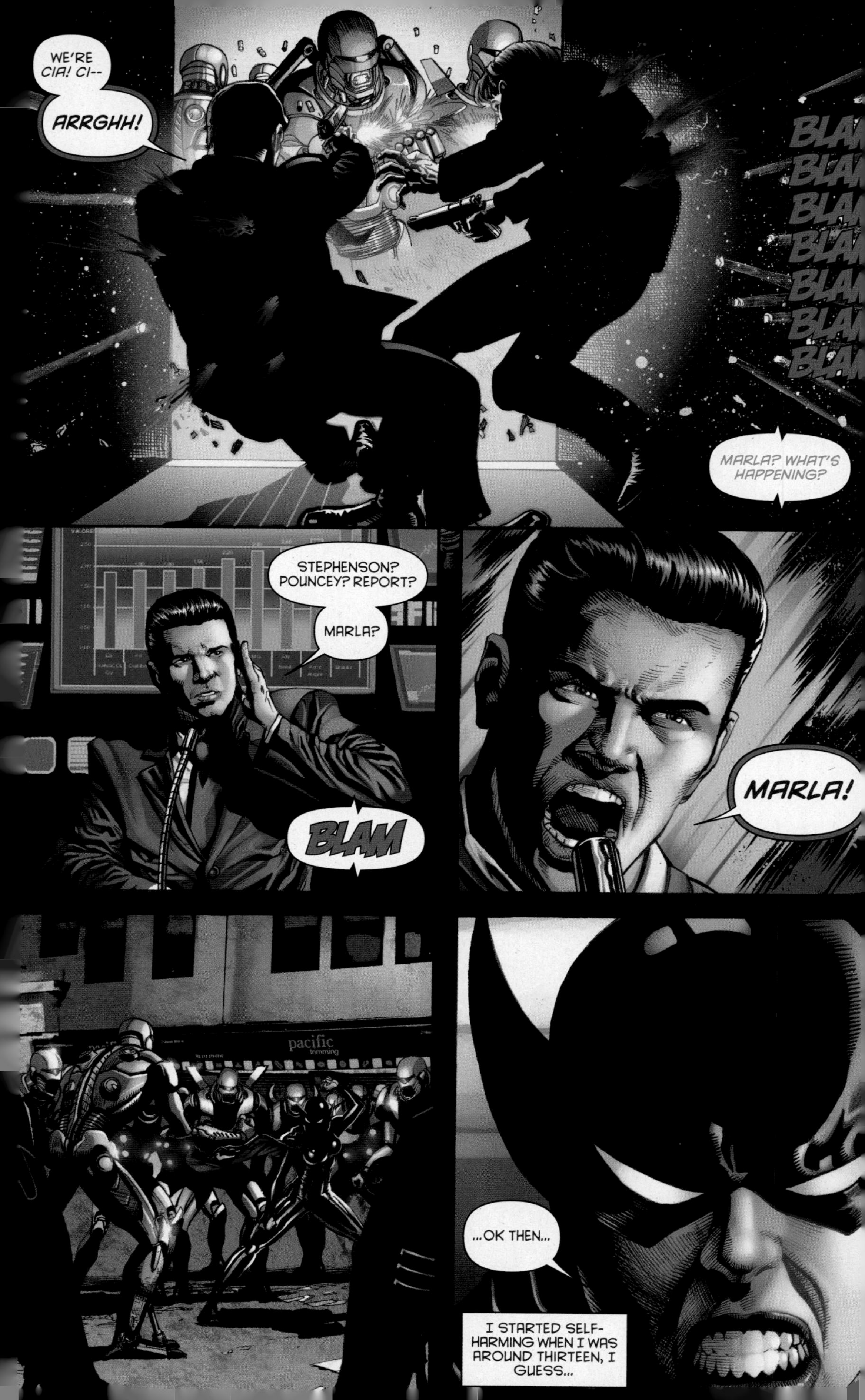
WE'RE CIA! CI--
ARRGHH!
BLAM BLAM BLAM BLAM BLAM BLAM BLAM
MARLA? WHAT'S HAPPENING?
STEPHENSON? POUNCEY? REPORT?
MARLA?
BLAM
MARLA!
pacific
...OK THEN...
I STARTED SELF-HARMING WHEN I WAS AROUND THIRTEEN, I GUESS...

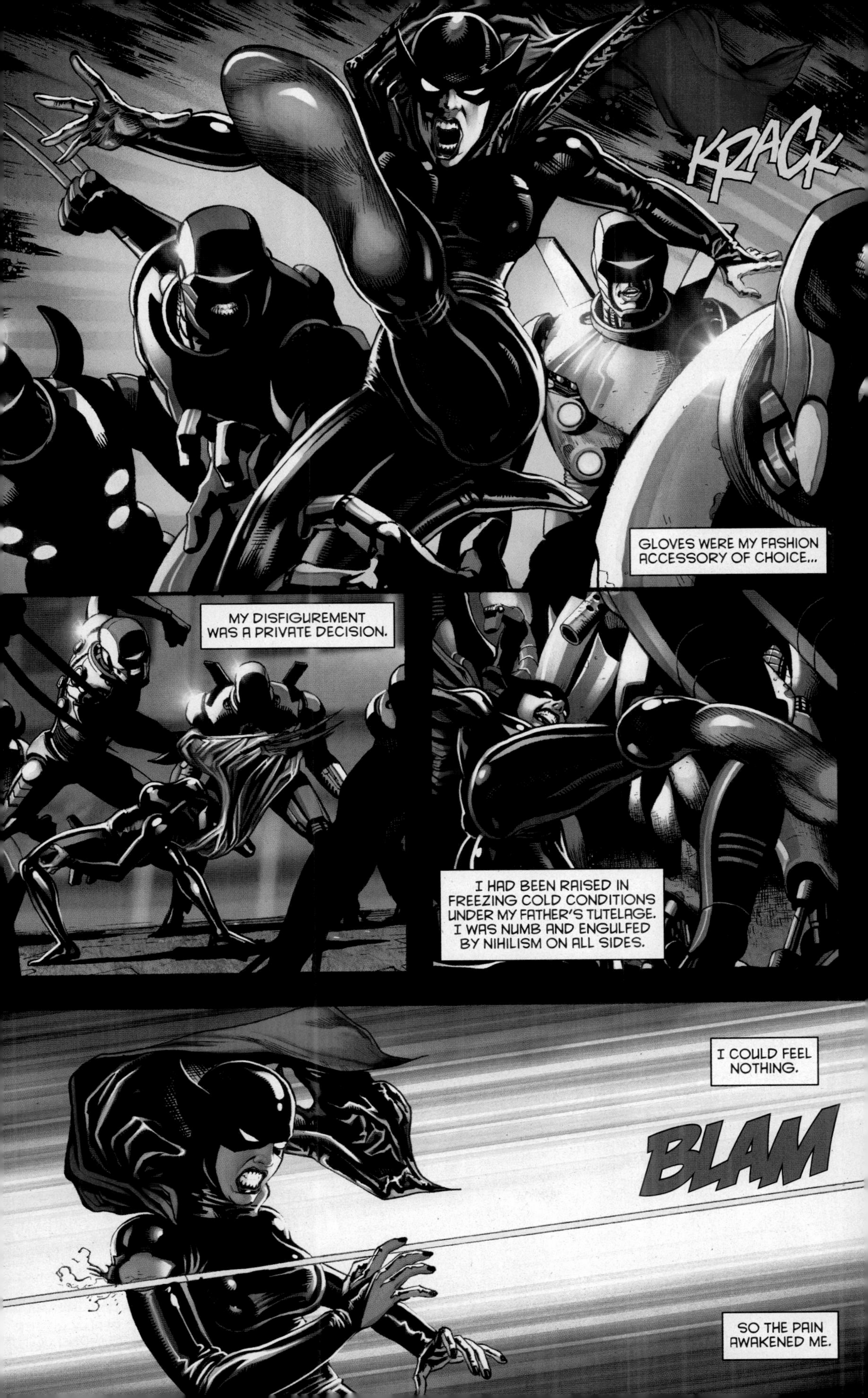
KRACK
GLOVES WERE MY FASHION ACCESSORY OF CHOICE...
MY DISFIGUREMENT WAS A PRIVATE DECISION.
I HAD BEEN RAISED IN FREEZING COLD CONDITIONS UNDER MY FATHER'S TUTELAGE. I WAS NUMB AND ENGULFED BY NIHILISM ON ALL SIDES.
I COULD FEEL NOTHING.
BLAM
SO THE PAIN AWAKENED ME.

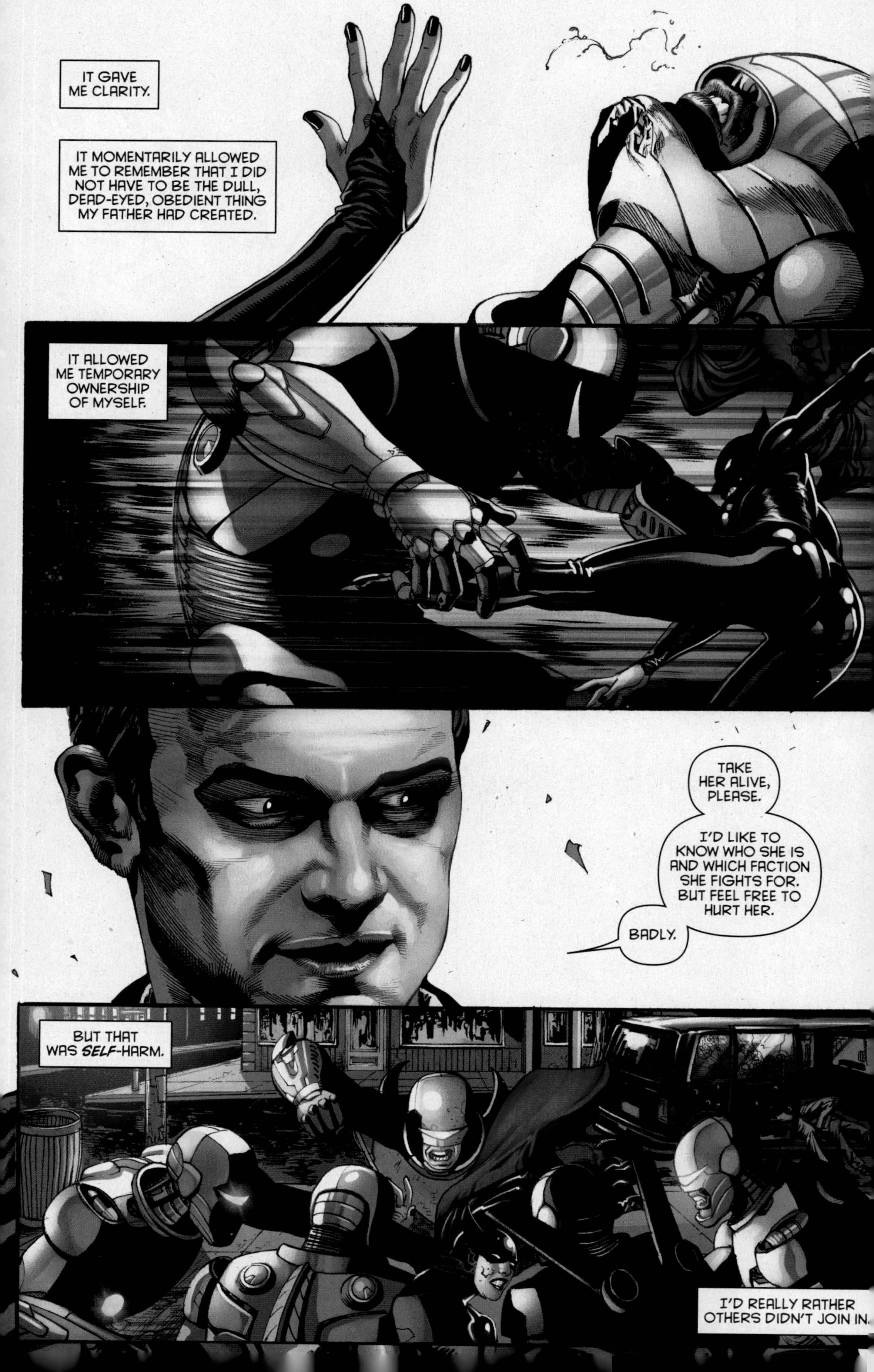
IT GAVE ME CLARITY.
IT MOMENTARILY ALLOWED ME TO REMEMBER THAT I DID NOT HAVE TO BE THE DULL, DEAD-EYED, OBEDIENT THING MY FATHER HAD CREATED.
IT ALLOWED ME TEMPORARY OWNERSHIP OF MYSELF.
TAKE HER ALIVE, PLEASE.
I'D LIKE TO KNOW WHO SHE IS AND WHICH FACTION SHE FIGHTS FOR. BUT FEEL FREE TO HURT HER.
BADLY.
BUT THAT WAS *SELF*-HARM.
I'D REALLY RATHER OTHERS DIDN'T JOIN IN.

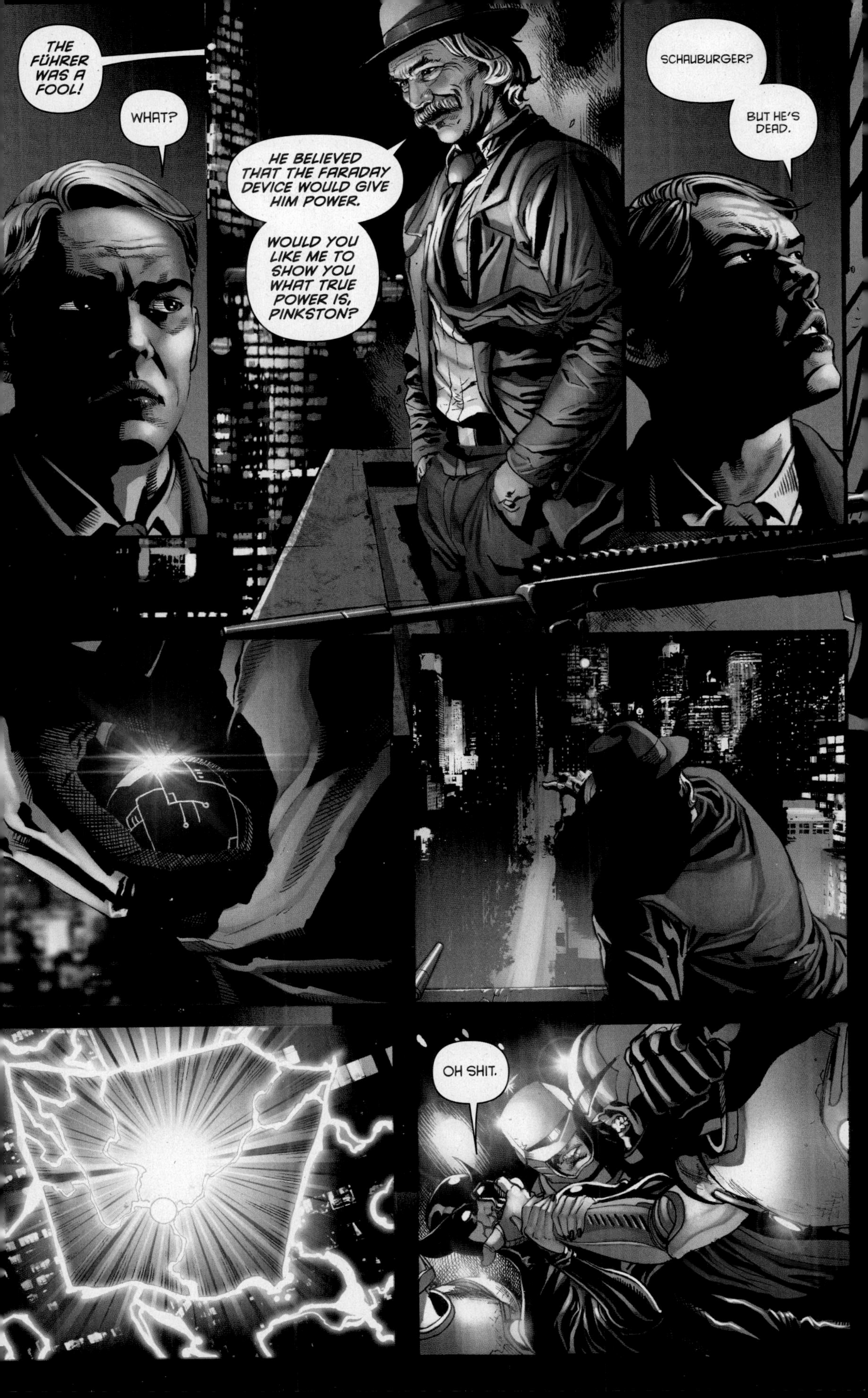
THE FÜHRER WAS A FOOL!
WHAT?
HE BELIEVED THAT THE FARADAY DEVICE WOULD GIVE HIM POWER.
WOULD YOU LIKE ME TO SHOW YOU WHAT TRUE POWER IS, PINKSTON?
SCHAUBURGER?
BUT HE'S DEAD.
OH SHIT.

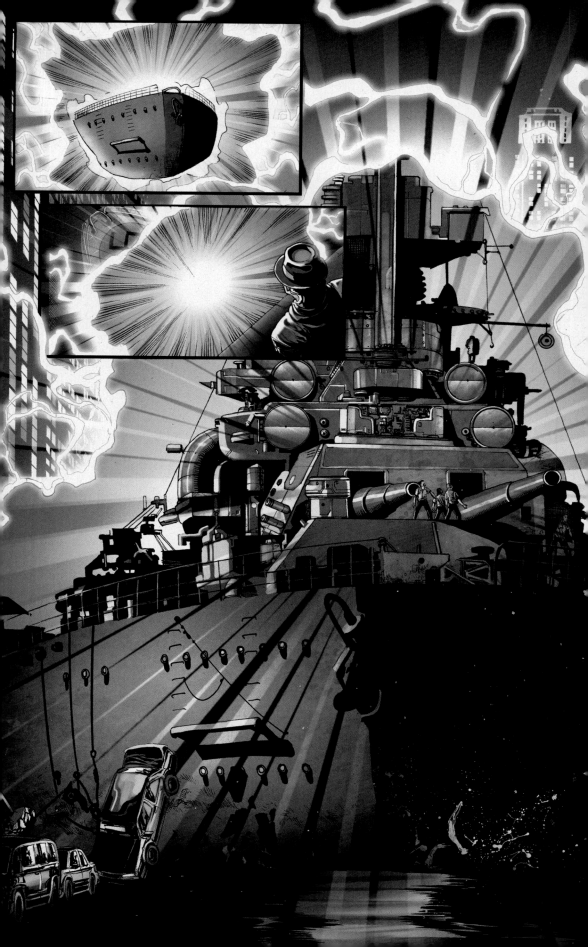

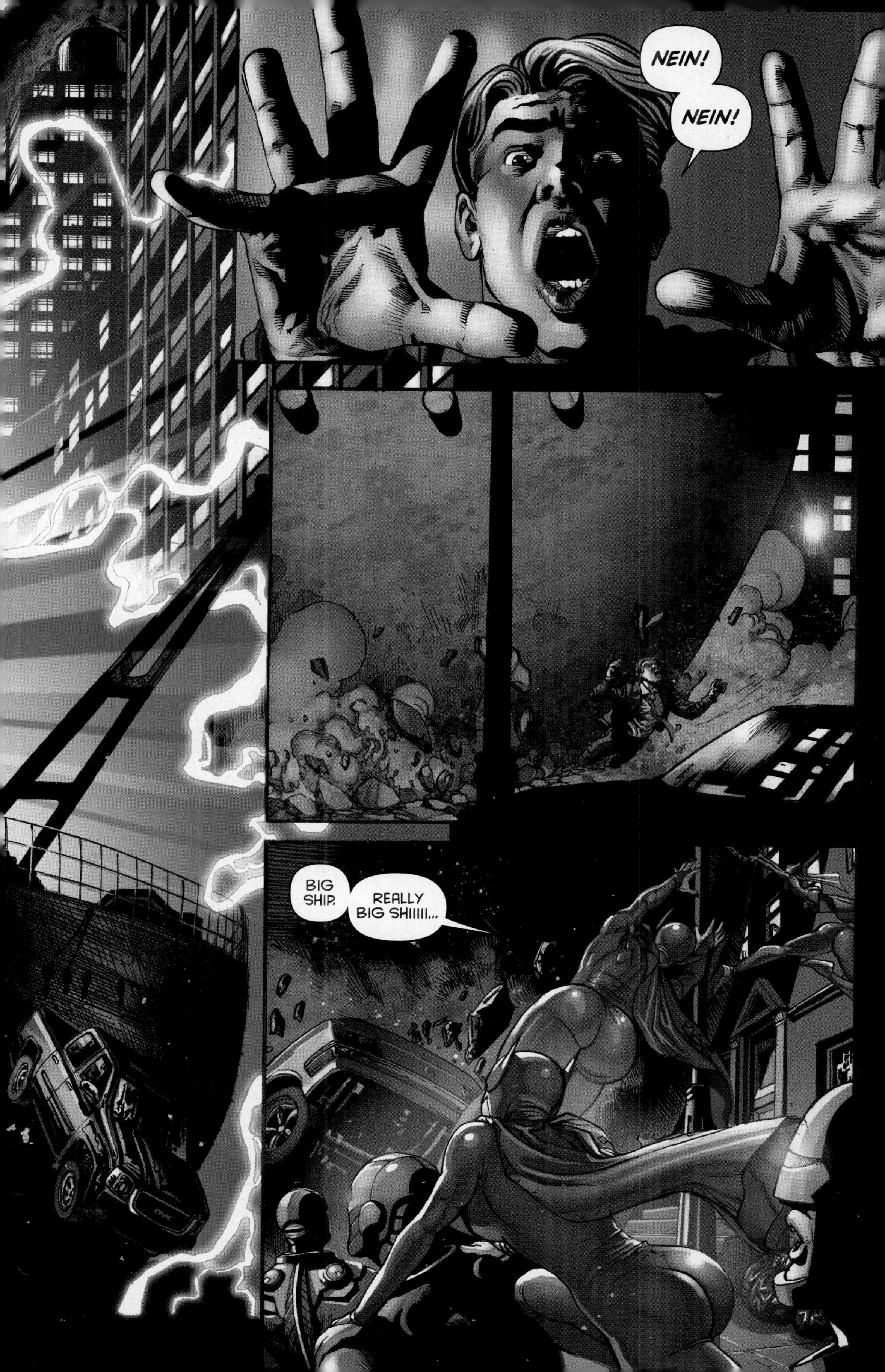
NEIN!
NEIN!
BIG SHIP.
REALLY BIG SHIIIII...

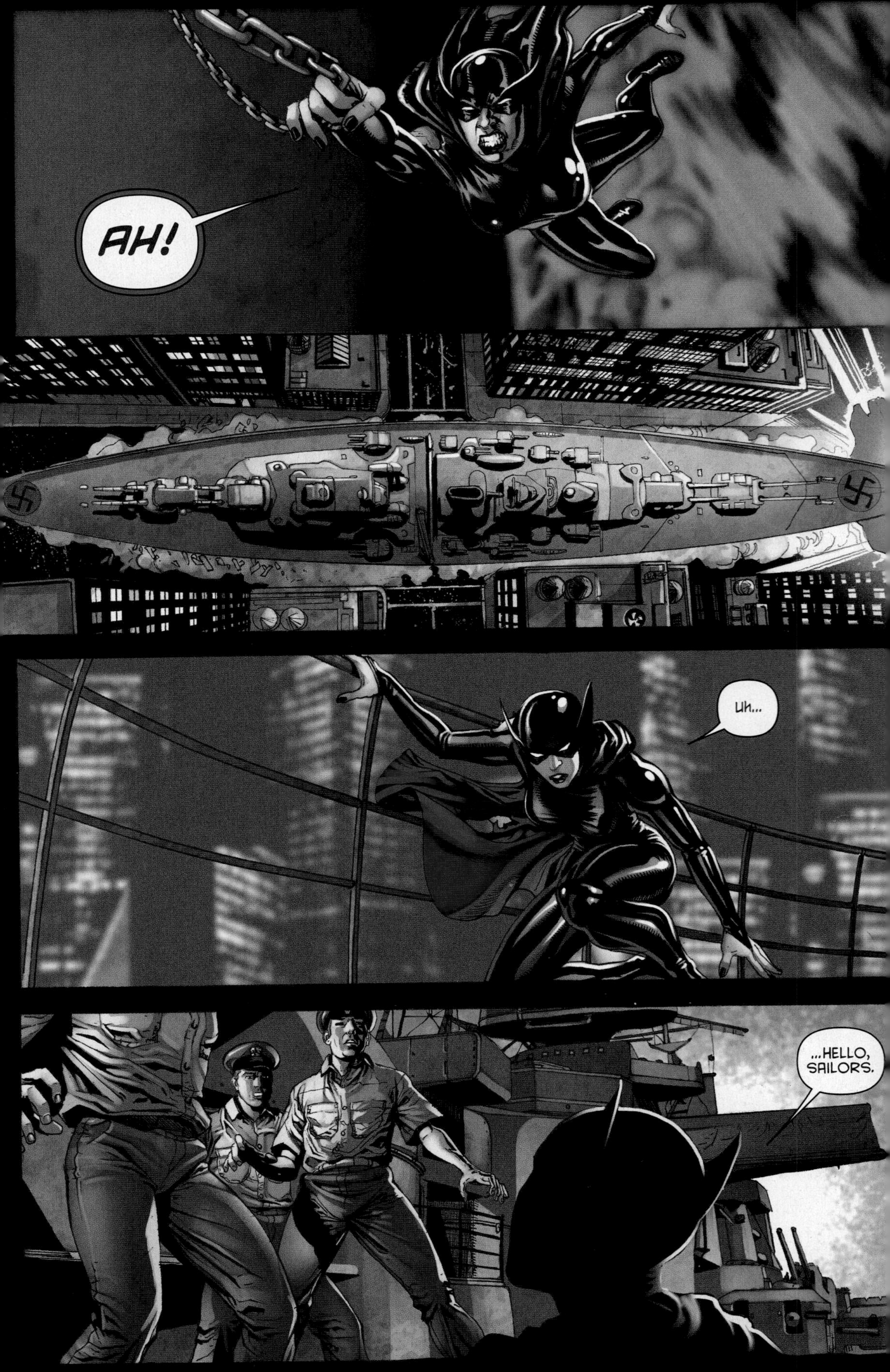
AH!
UH...
...HELLO, SAILORS.

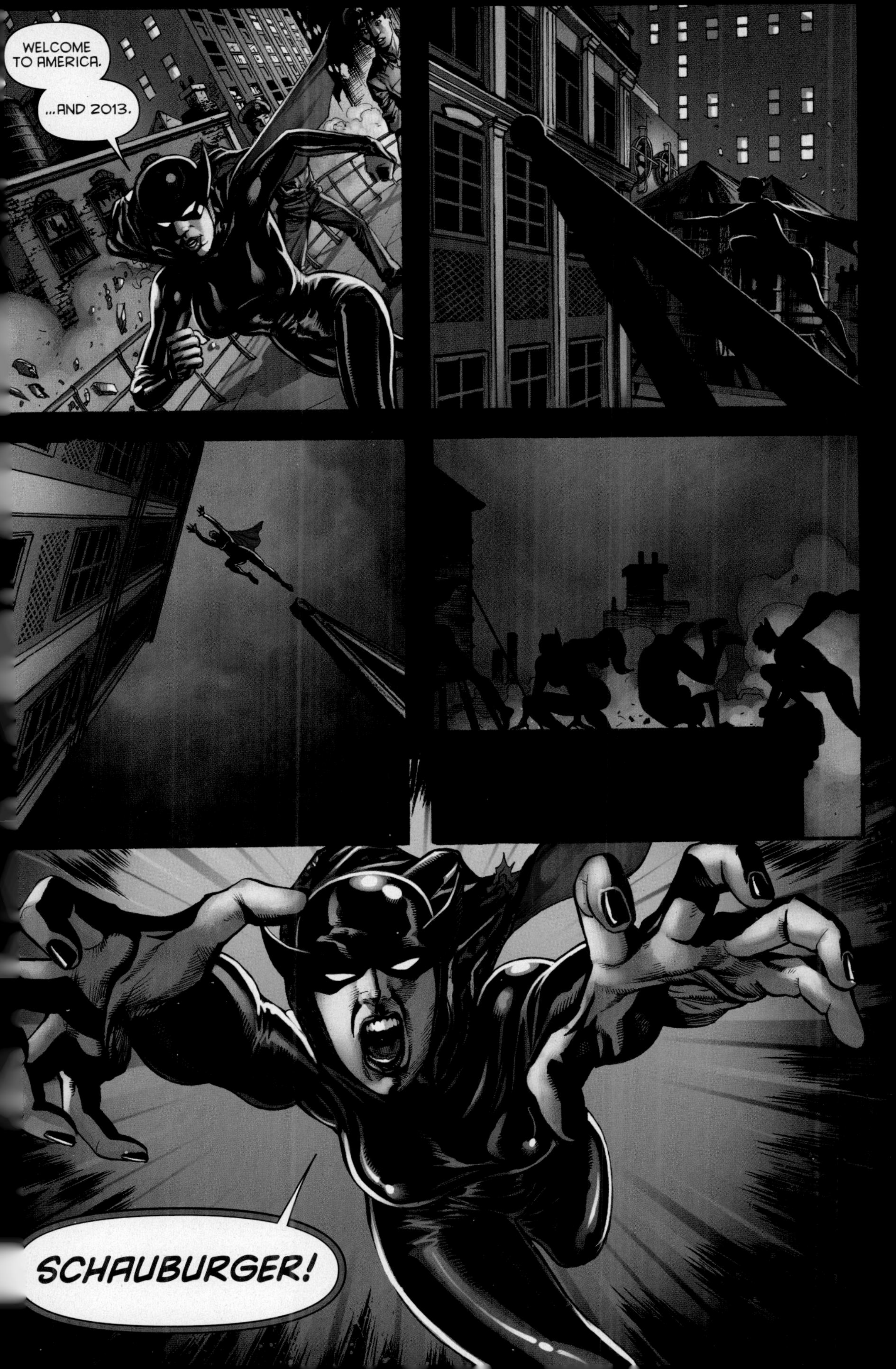
WELCOME TO AMERICA.
...AND 2013.
SCHAUBURGER!

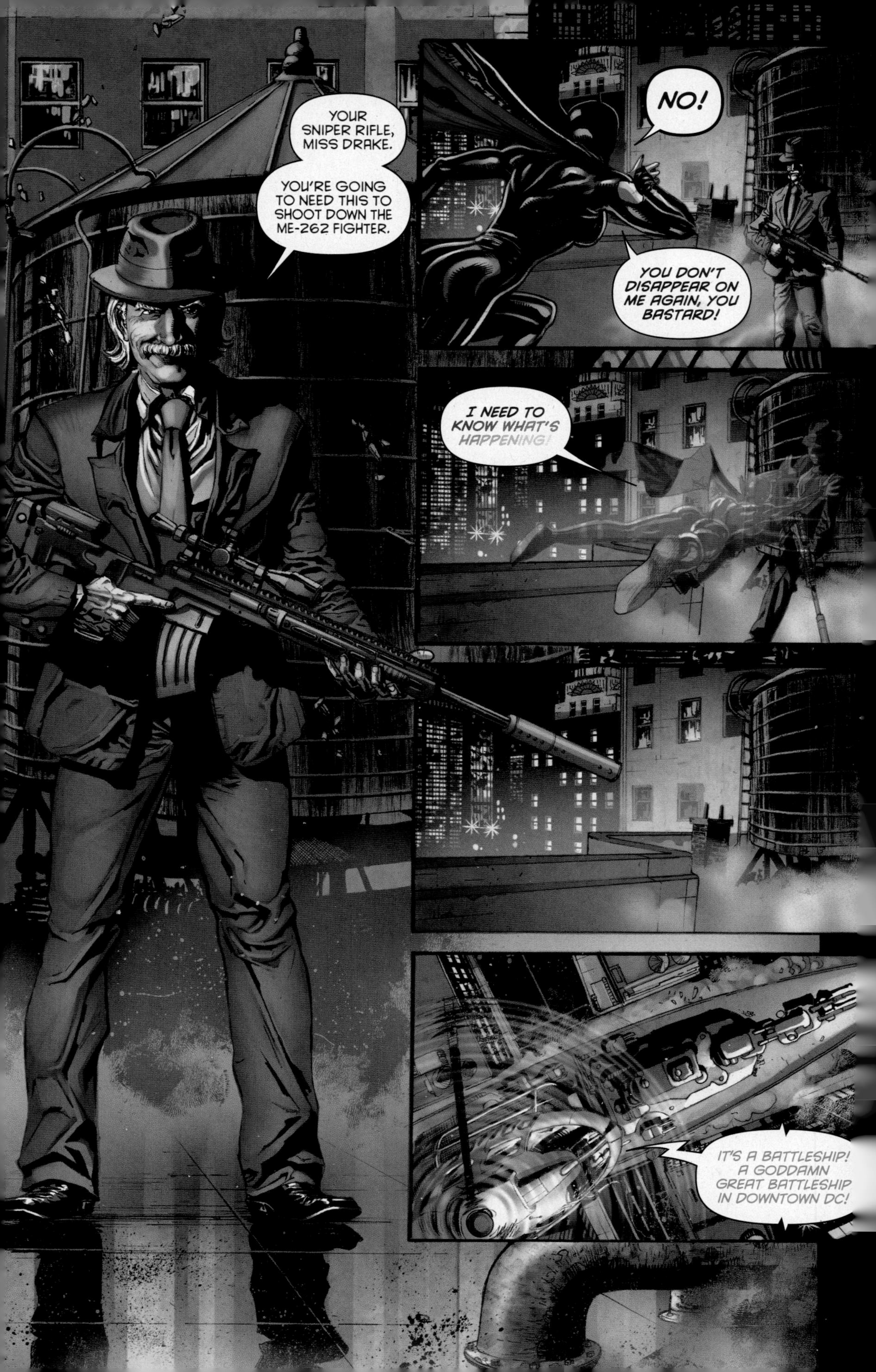
YOUR SNIPER RIFLE, MISS DRAKE.
YOU'RE GOING TO NEED THIS TO SHOOT DOWN THE ME-262 FIGHTER.
NO!
YOU DON'T DISAPPEAR ON ME AGAIN, YOU BASTARD!
I NEED TO KNOW WHAT'S HAPPENING!
IT'S A BATTLESHIP! A GODDAMN GREAT BATTLESHIP IN DOWNTOWN DC!

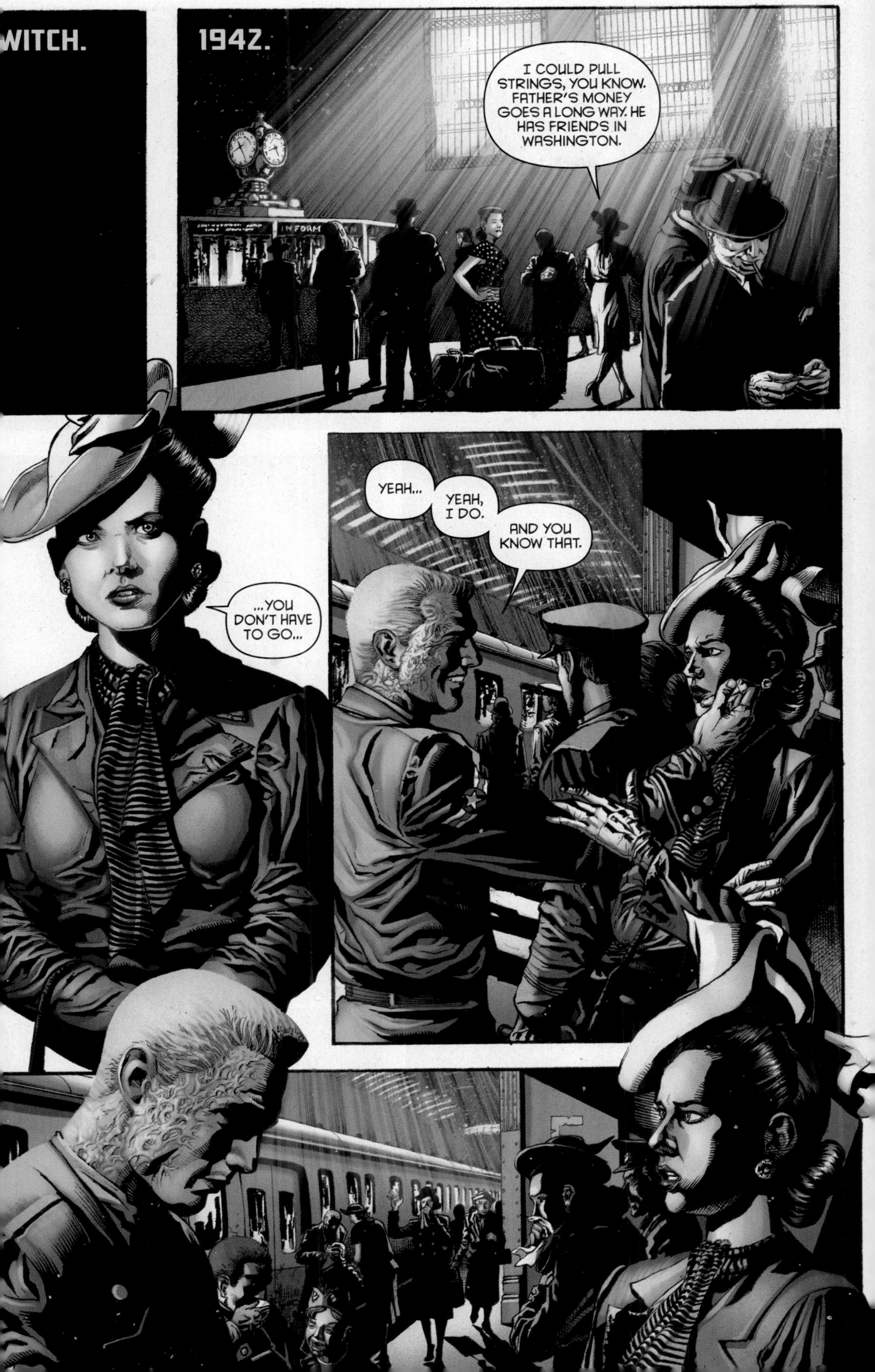
WITCH.
1942.
I COULD PULL STRINGS, YOU KNOW. FATHER'S MONEY GOES A LONG WAY. HE HAS FRIENDS IN WASHINGTON.
INFORM
...YOU DON'T HAVE TO GO...
YEAH...
YEAH, I DO.
AND YOU KNOW THAT.

I BEEN WANTING TO ASK, BUT...YOU KNOW, MARLA. WITH ALL YOUR MONEY AND YOUR HIGH SOCIETY LIFE AND YOUR UPBRINGING...

"AM I GOOD ENOUGH TO MARRY THAT PERSON," YOU ASK YOURSELF.

YOU WANNA MARRY ME?

WHEN I GET BACK FROM EUROPE?

AND YOU ARE, MARLA.

YOU'RE GOOD.

YOU JUST HAVE TO BELIEVE IT.

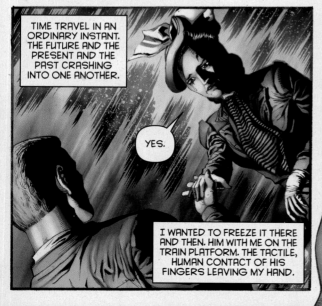

TIME TRAVEL IN AN ORDINARY INSTANT. THE FUTURE AND THE PRESENT AND THE PAST CRASHING INTO ONE ANOTHER.

YES.

I WANTED TO FREEZE IT THERE AND THEN. HIM WITH ME ON THE TRAIN PLATFORM. THE TACTILE, HUMAN CONTACT OF HIS FINGERS LEAVING MY HAND.

THE LAST MOMENT HE TOUCHED ME.

I'LL MARRY YOU.

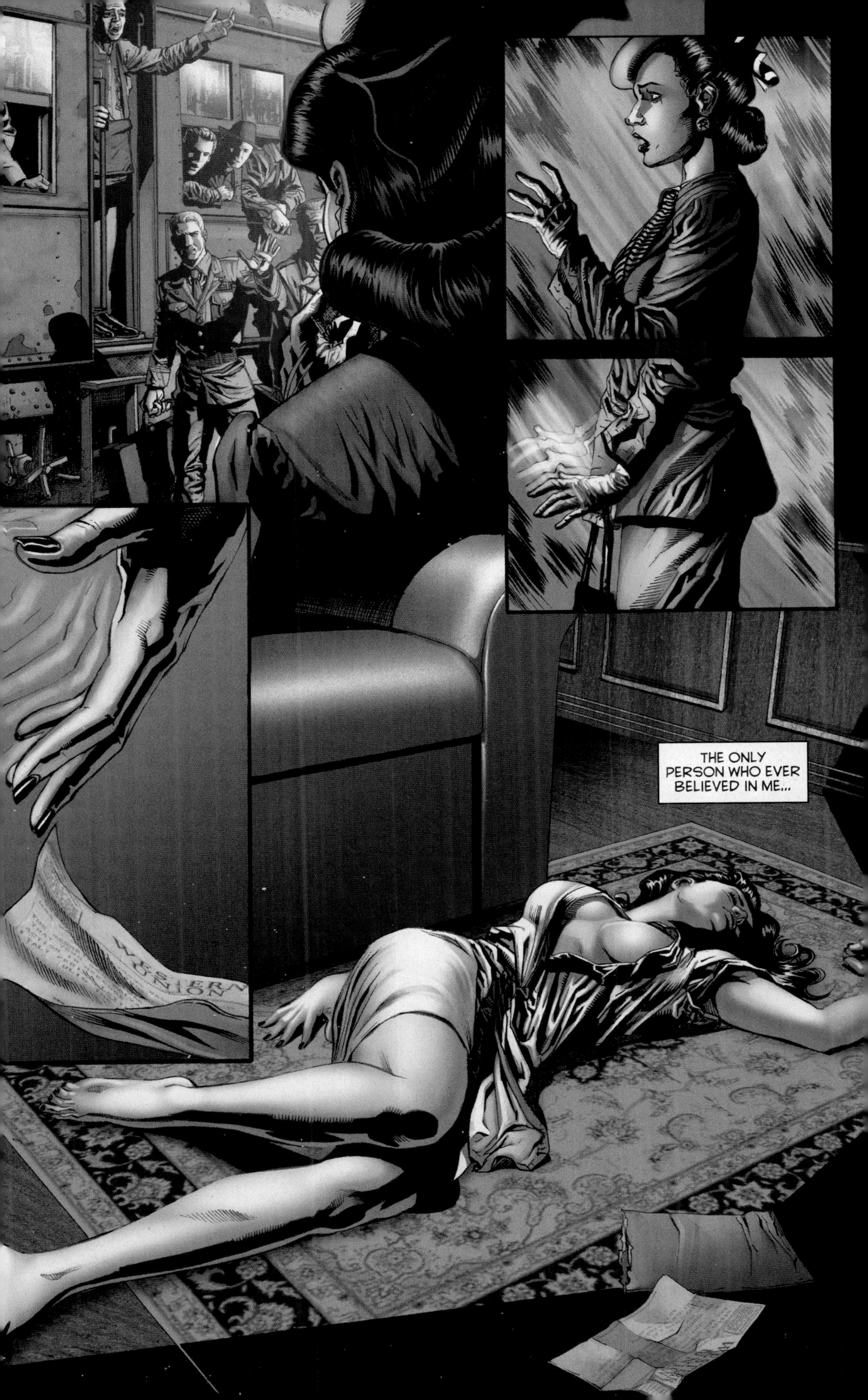
THE ONLY PERSON WHO EVER BELIEVED IN ME...
WESTERN UNION

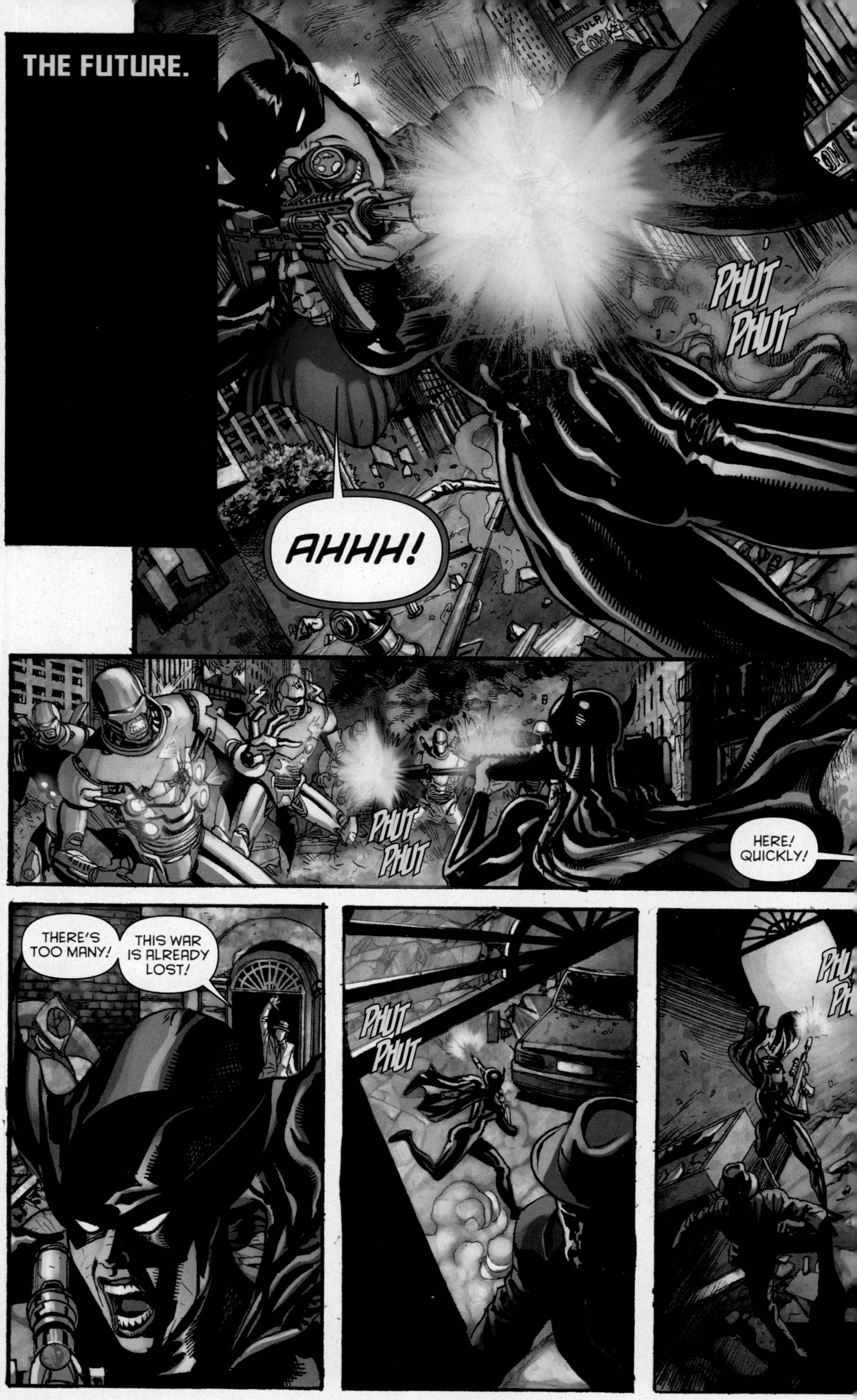
THE FUTURE.
AHHH!
PHUT PHUT
PHUT PHUT
HERE! QUICKLY!
THERE'S TOO MANY!
THIS WAR IS ALREADY LOST!
PHUT PHUT

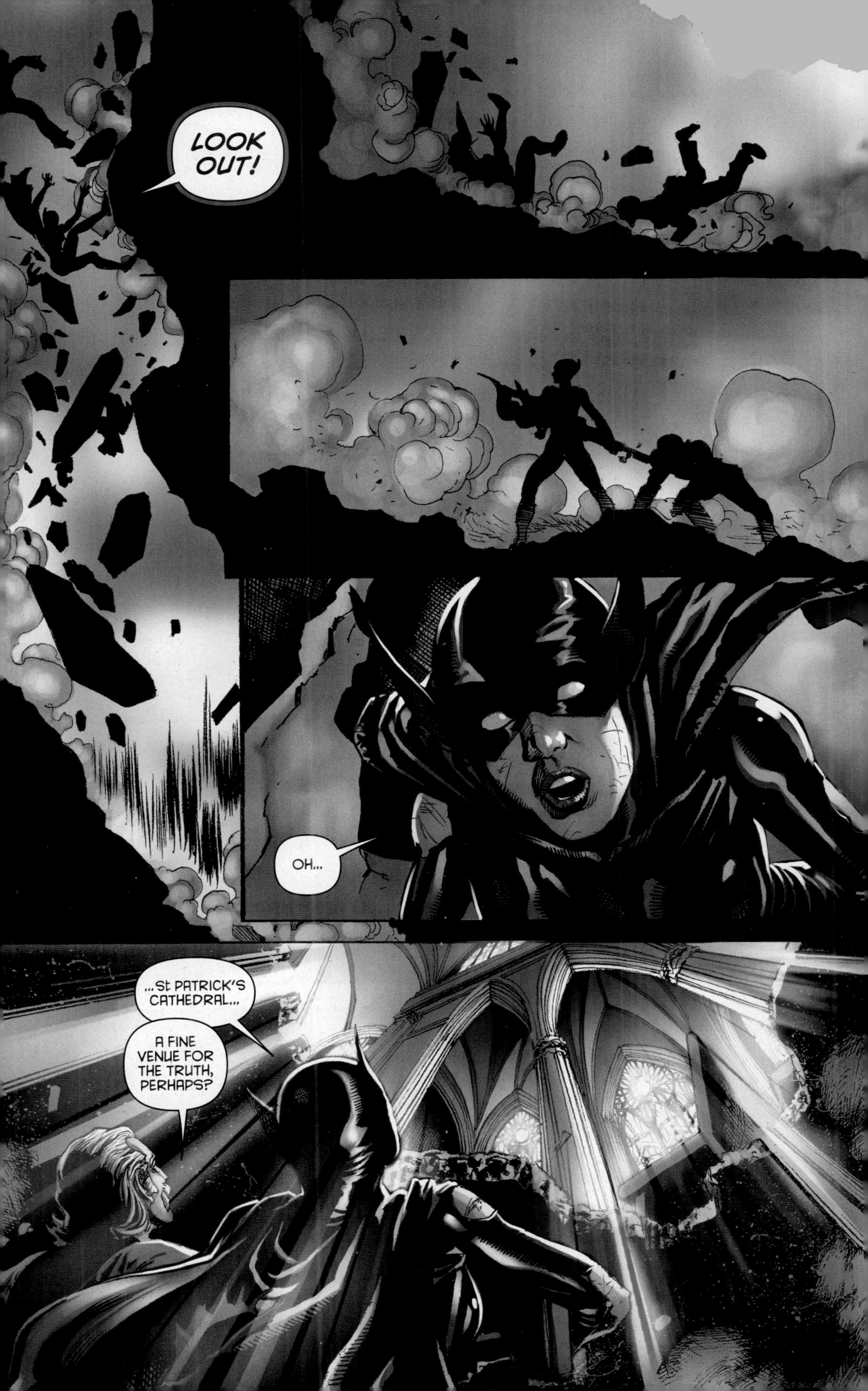
LOOK OUT!
OH...
...St PATRICK'S CATHEDRAL...
A FINE VENUE FOR THE TRUTH, PERHAPS?

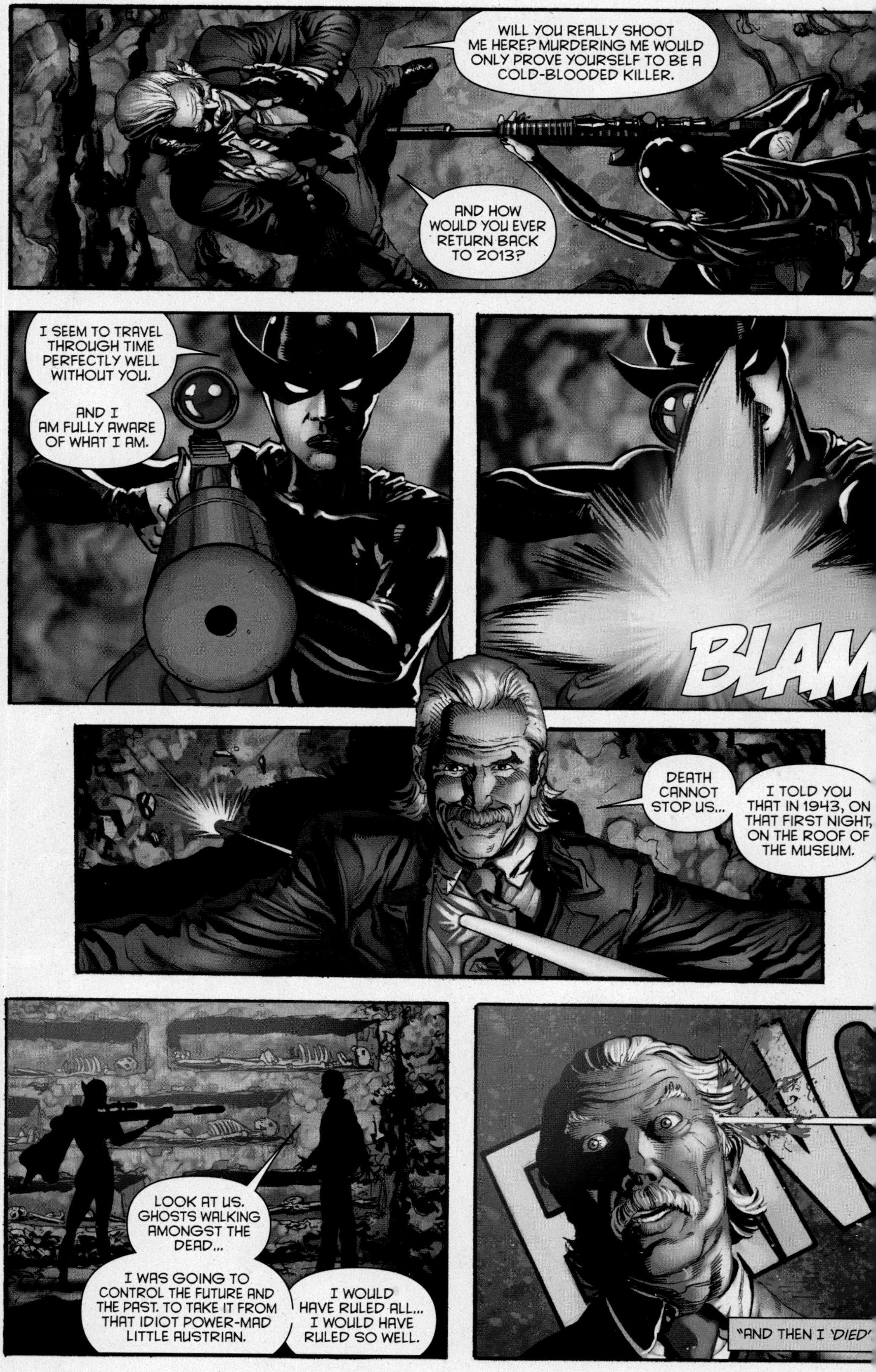
WILL YOU REALLY SHOOT ME HERE? MURDERING ME WOULD ONLY PROVE YOURSELF TO BE A COLD-BLOODED KILLER.
AND HOW WOULD YOU EVER RETURN BACK TO 2013?
I SEEM TO TRAVEL THROUGH TIME PERFECTLY WELL WITHOUT YOU.
AND I AM FULLY AWARE OF WHAT I AM.
BLAM
DEATH CANNOT STOP US...
I TOLD YOU THAT IN 1943, ON THAT FIRST NIGHT, ON THE ROOF OF THE MUSEUM.
LOOK AT US. GHOSTS WALKING AMONGST THE DEAD...
I WAS GOING TO CONTROL THE FUTURE AND THE PAST. TO TAKE IT FROM THAT IDIOT POWER-MAD LITTLE AUSTRIAN.
I WOULD HAVE RULED ALL... I WOULD HAVE RULED SO WELL.
"AND THEN I *DIED*."

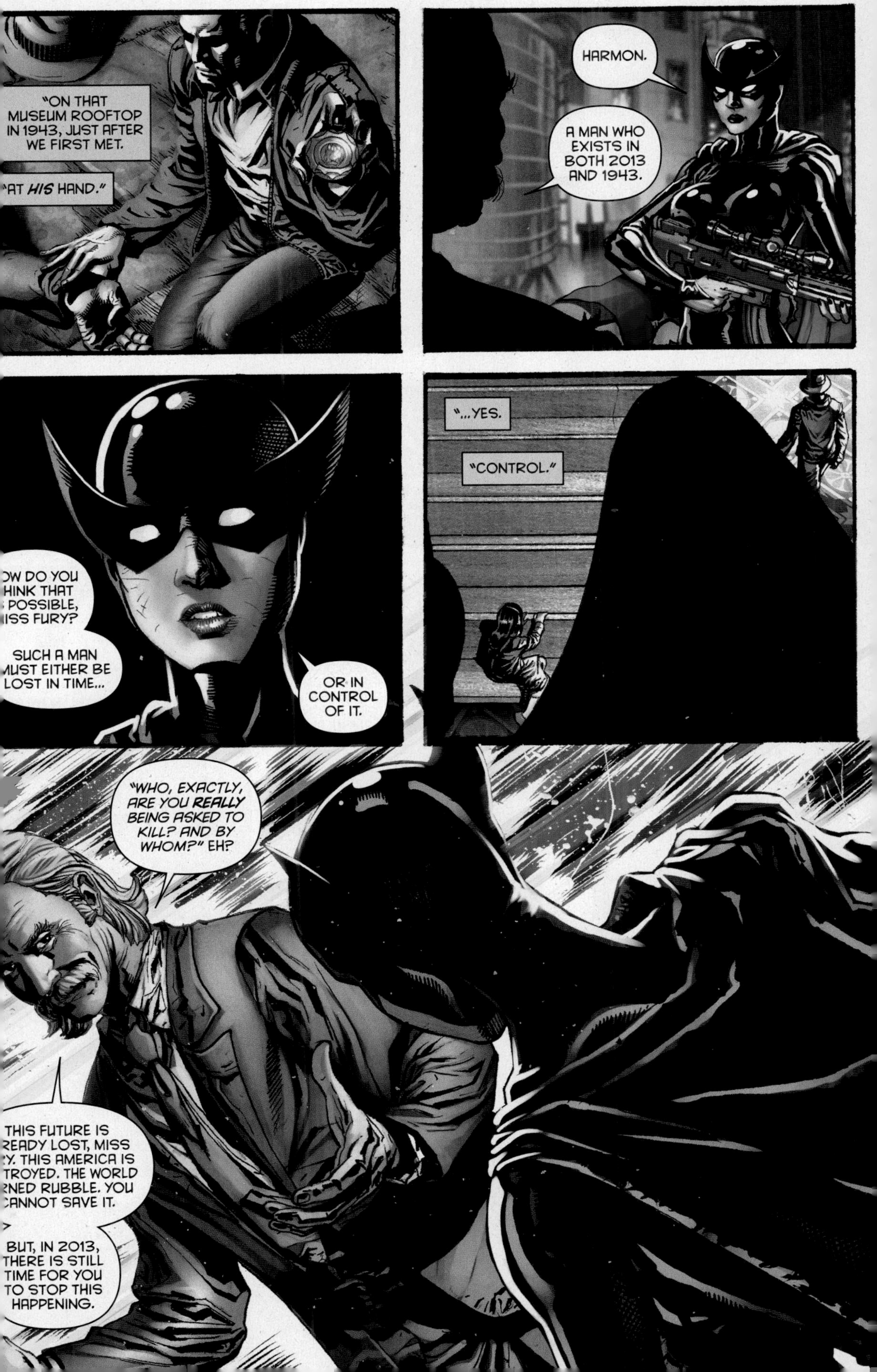

"ON THAT MUSEUM ROOFTOP IN 1943, JUST AFTER WE FIRST MET.
"AT HIS HAND."
HARMON.
A MAN WHO EXISTS IN BOTH 2013 AND 1943.
OW DO YOU HINK THAT POSSIBLE, ISS FURY?
SUCH A MAN MUST EITHER BE LOST IN TIME...
OR IN CONTROL OF IT.
"...YES.
"CONTROL."
"WHO, EXACTLY, ARE YOU REALLY BEING ASKED TO KILL? AND BY WHOM?" EH?
THIS FUTURE IS READY LOST, MISS Y. THIS AMERICA IS TROYED. THE WORLD RNED RUBBLE. YOU CANNOT SAVE IT.
BUT, IN 2013, THERE IS STILL TIME FOR YOU TO STOP THIS HAPPENING.

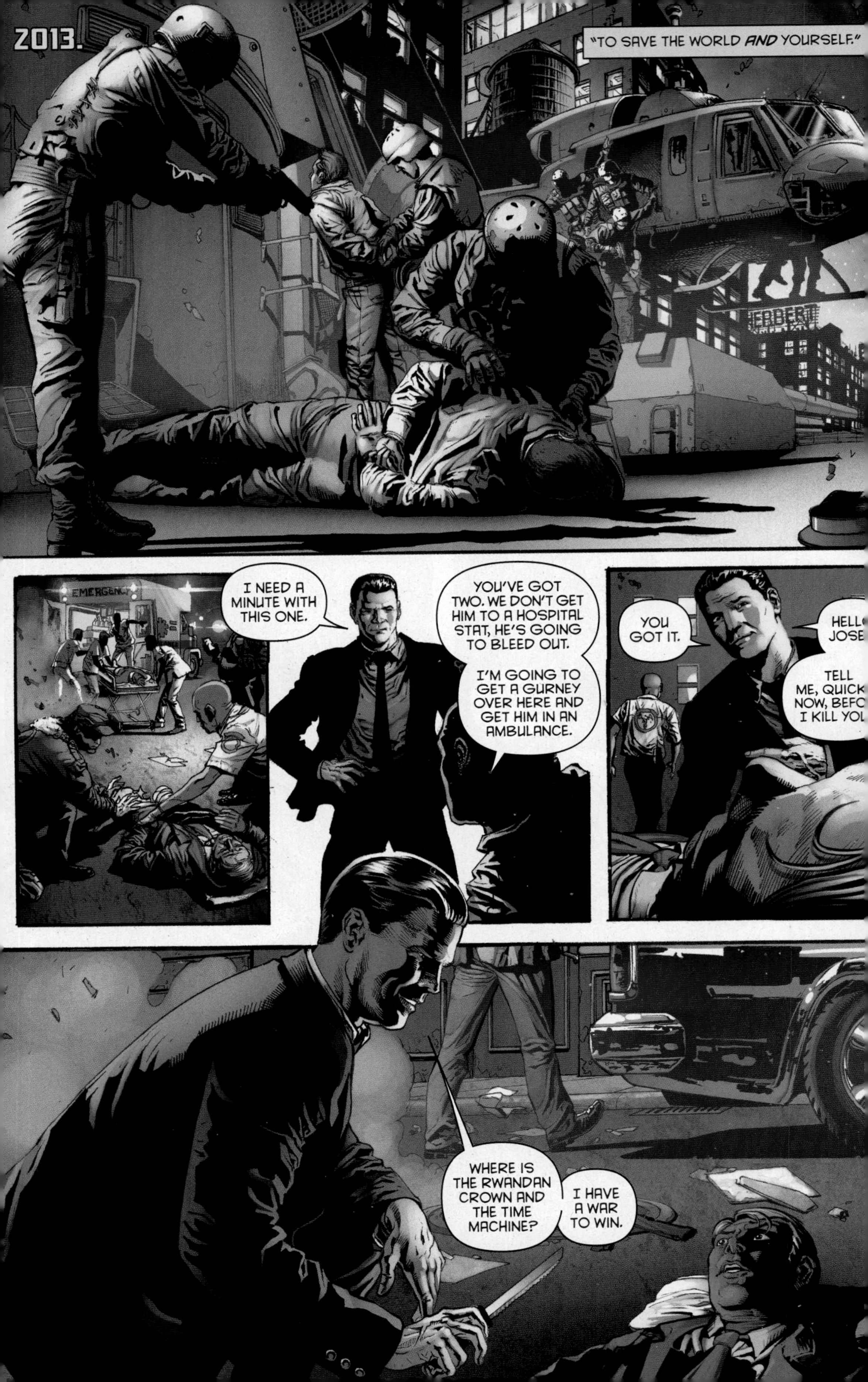
2013.
"TO SAVE THE WORLD AND YOURSELF."
EMERGENCY
I NEED A MINUTE WITH THIS ONE.
YOU'VE GOT TWO. WE DON'T GET HIM TO A HOSPITAL STAT, HE'S GOING TO BLEED OUT.
I'M GOING TO GET A GURNEY OVER HERE AND GET HIM IN AN AMBULANCE.
YOU GOT IT.
WHERE IS THE RWANDAN CROWN AND THE TIME MACHINE?
I HAVE A WAR TO WIN.

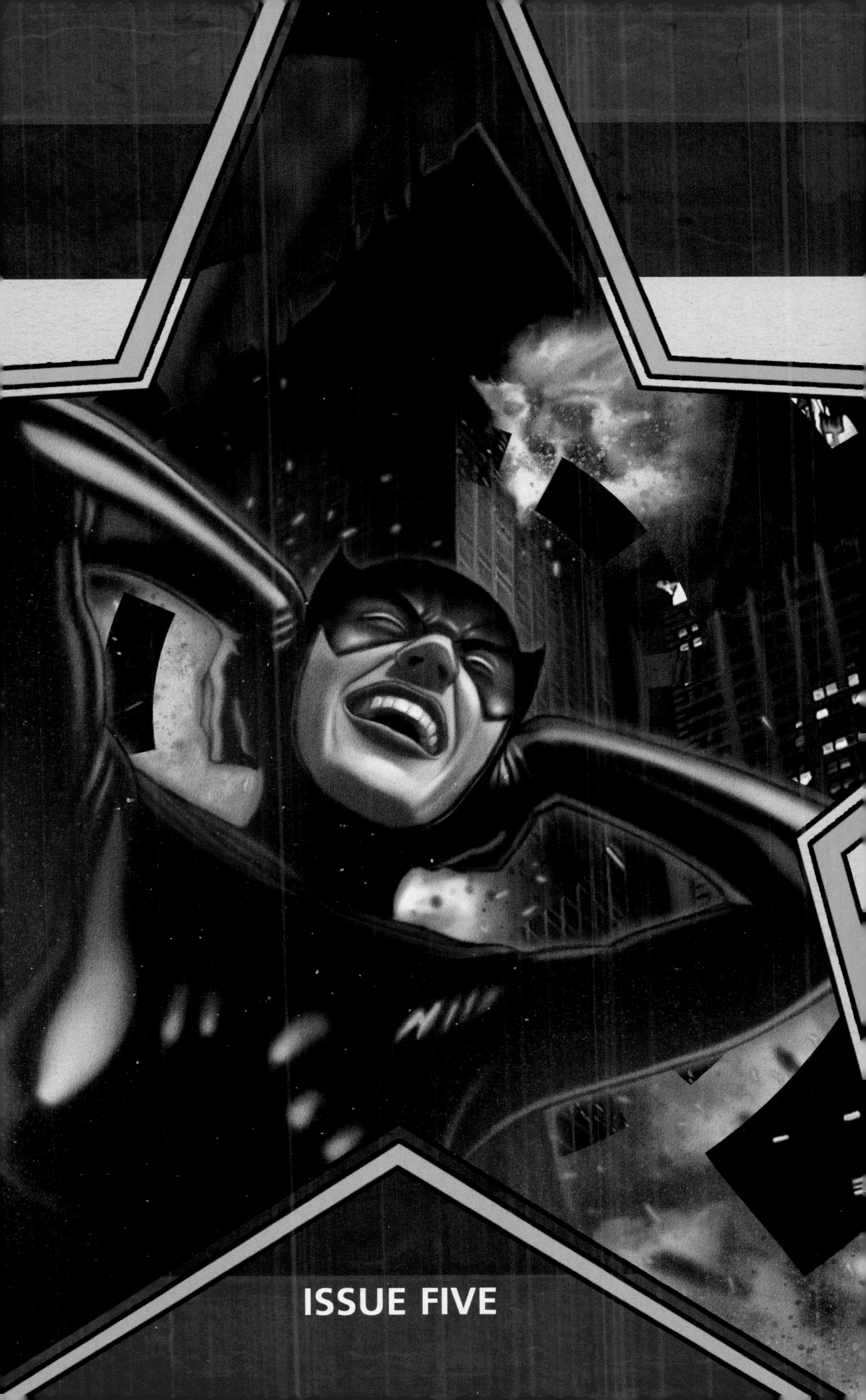
ISSUE FIVE

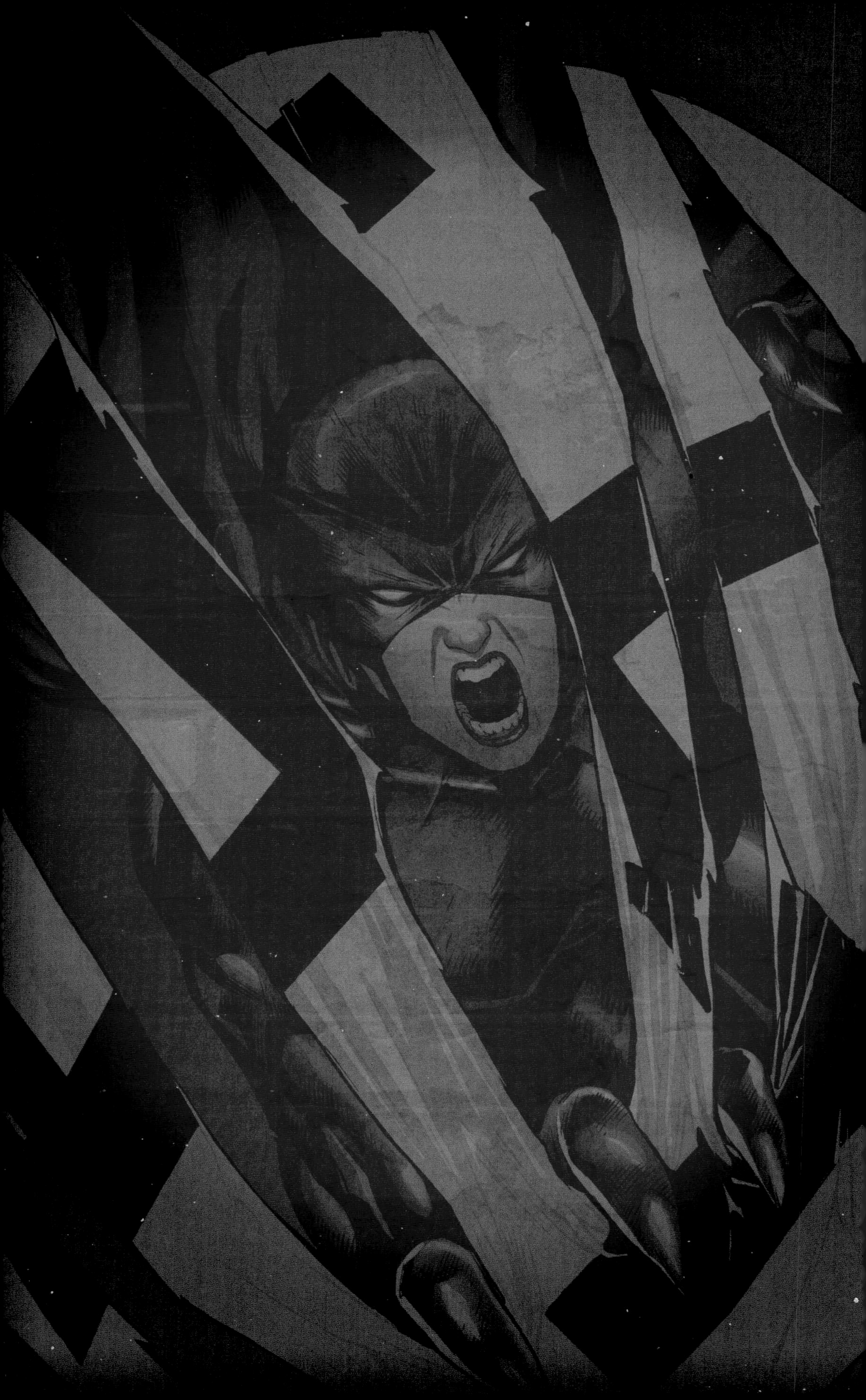

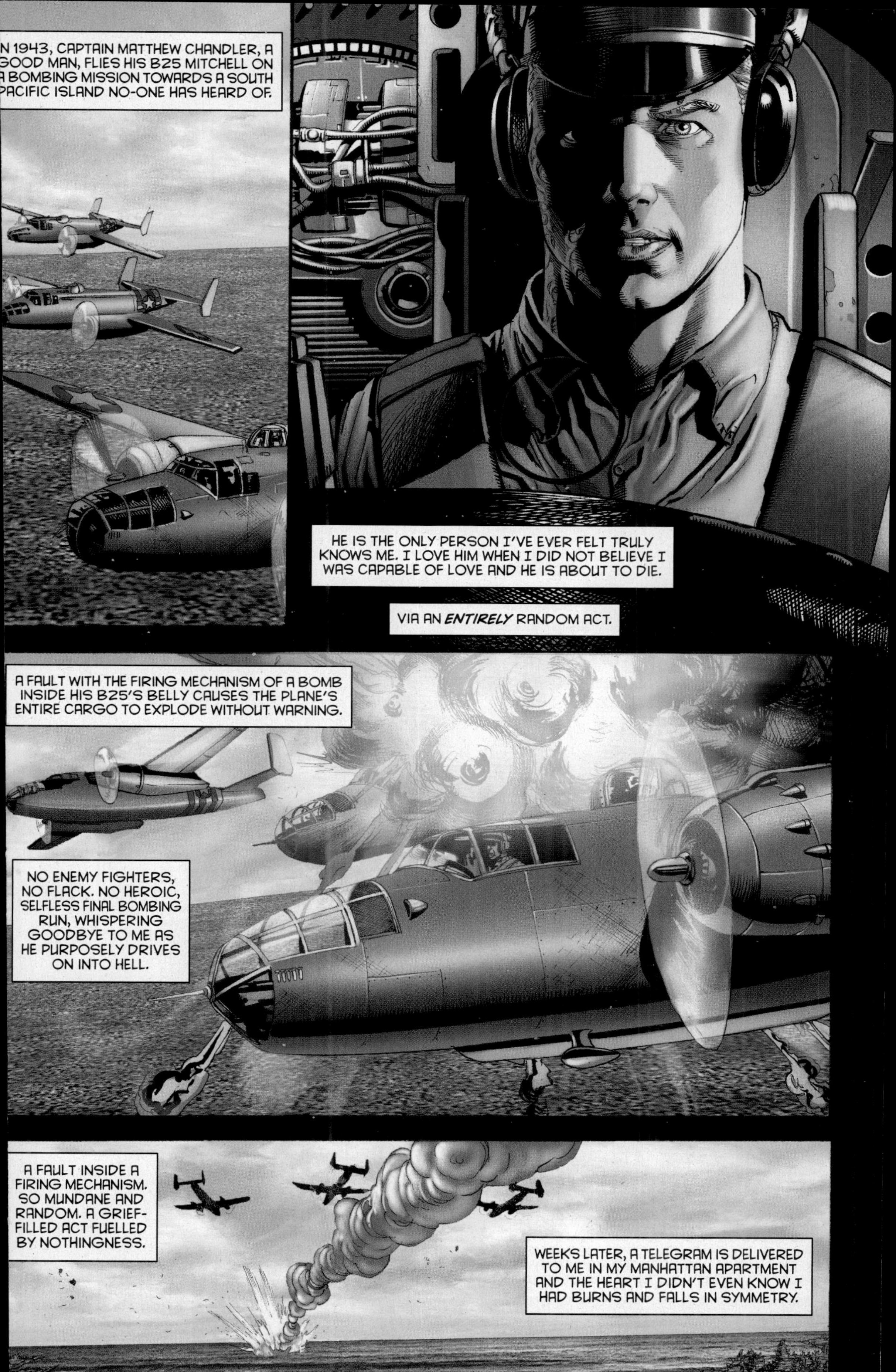
N 1943, CAPTAIN MATTHEW CHANDLER, A GOOD MAN, FLIES HIS B25 MITCHELL ON A BOMBING MISSION TOWARDS A SOUTH PACIFIC ISLAND NO-ONE HAS HEARD OF.
HE IS THE ONLY PERSON I'VE EVER FELT TRULY KNOWS ME. I LOVE HIM WHEN I DID NOT BELIEVE I WAS CAPABLE OF LOVE AND HE IS ABOUT TO DIE.
VIA AN *ENTIRELY* RANDOM ACT.
A FAULT WITH THE FIRING MECHANISM OF A BOMB INSIDE HIS B25'S BELLY CAUSES THE PLANE'S ENTIRE CARGO TO EXPLODE WITHOUT WARNING.
NO ENEMY FIGHTERS, NO FLACK. NO HEROIC, SELFLESS FINAL BOMBING RUN, WHISPERING GOODBYE TO ME AS HE PURPOSELY DRIVES ON INTO HELL.
A FAULT INSIDE A FIRING MECHANISM. SO MUNDANE AND RANDOM. A GRIEF-FILLED ACT FUELLED BY NOTHINGNESS.
WEEKS LATER, A TELEGRAM IS DELIVERED TO ME IN MY MANHATTAN APARTMENT AND THE HEART I DIDN'T EVEN KNOW I HAD BURNS AND FALLS IN SYMMETRY.

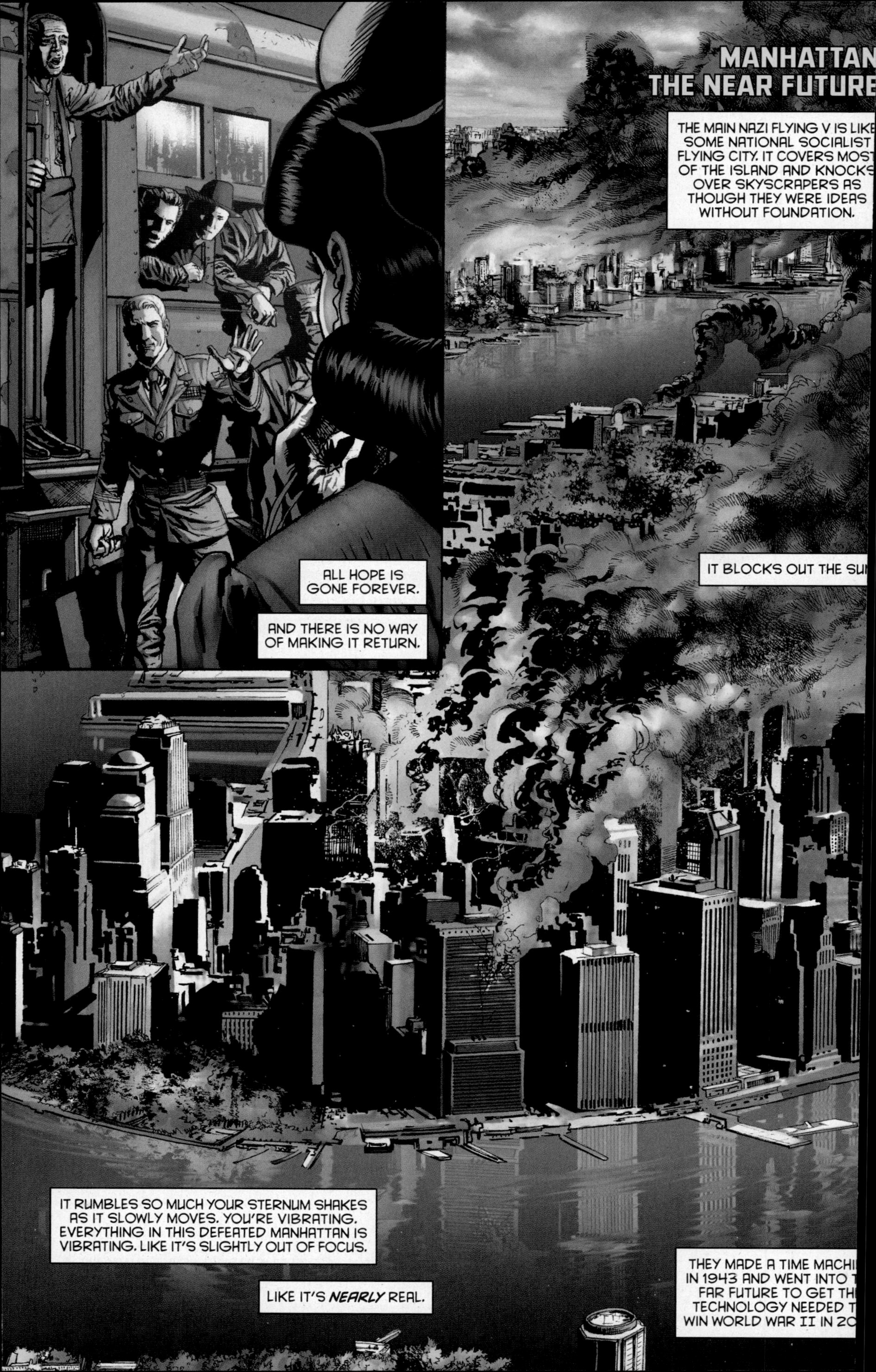

ALL HOPE IS GONE FOREVER.
AND THERE IS NO WAY OF MAKING IT RETURN.
MANHATTAN
THE NEAR FUTURE
THE MAIN NAZI FLYING V IS LIKE SOME NATIONAL SOCIALIST FLYING CITY. IT COVERS MOST OF THE ISLAND AND KNOCKS OVER SKYSCRAPERS AS THOUGH THEY WERE IDEAS WITHOUT FOUNDATION.
IT BLOCKS OUT THE SU
IT RUMBLES SO MUCH YOUR STERNUM SHAKES AS IT SLOWLY MOVES. YOU'RE VIBRATING. EVERYTHING IN THIS DEFEATED MANHATTAN IS VIBRATING. LIKE IT'S SLIGHTLY OUT OF FOCUS.
LIKE IT'S *NEARLY* REAL.
THEY MADE A TIME MACHI IN 1943 AND WENT INTO T FAR FUTURE TO GET TH TECHNOLOGY NEEDED T WIN WORLD WAR II IN 20

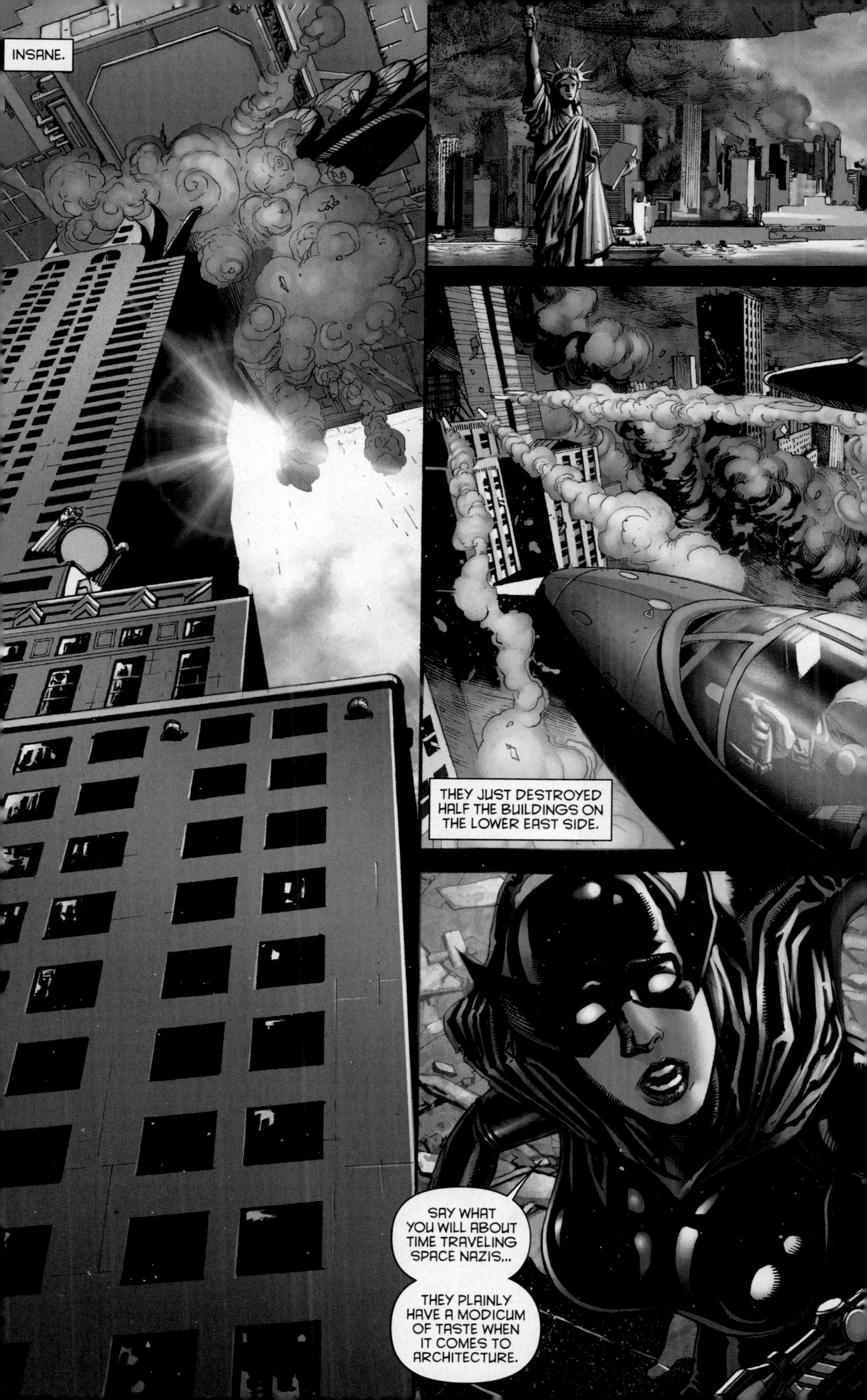
INSANE.
THEY JUST DESTROYED HALF THE BUILDINGS ON THE LOWER EAST SIDE.
SAY WHAT YOU WILL ABOUT TIME TRAVELING SPACE NAZIS...
THEY PLAINLY HAVE A MODICUM OF TASTE WHEN IT COMES TO ARCHITECTURE.

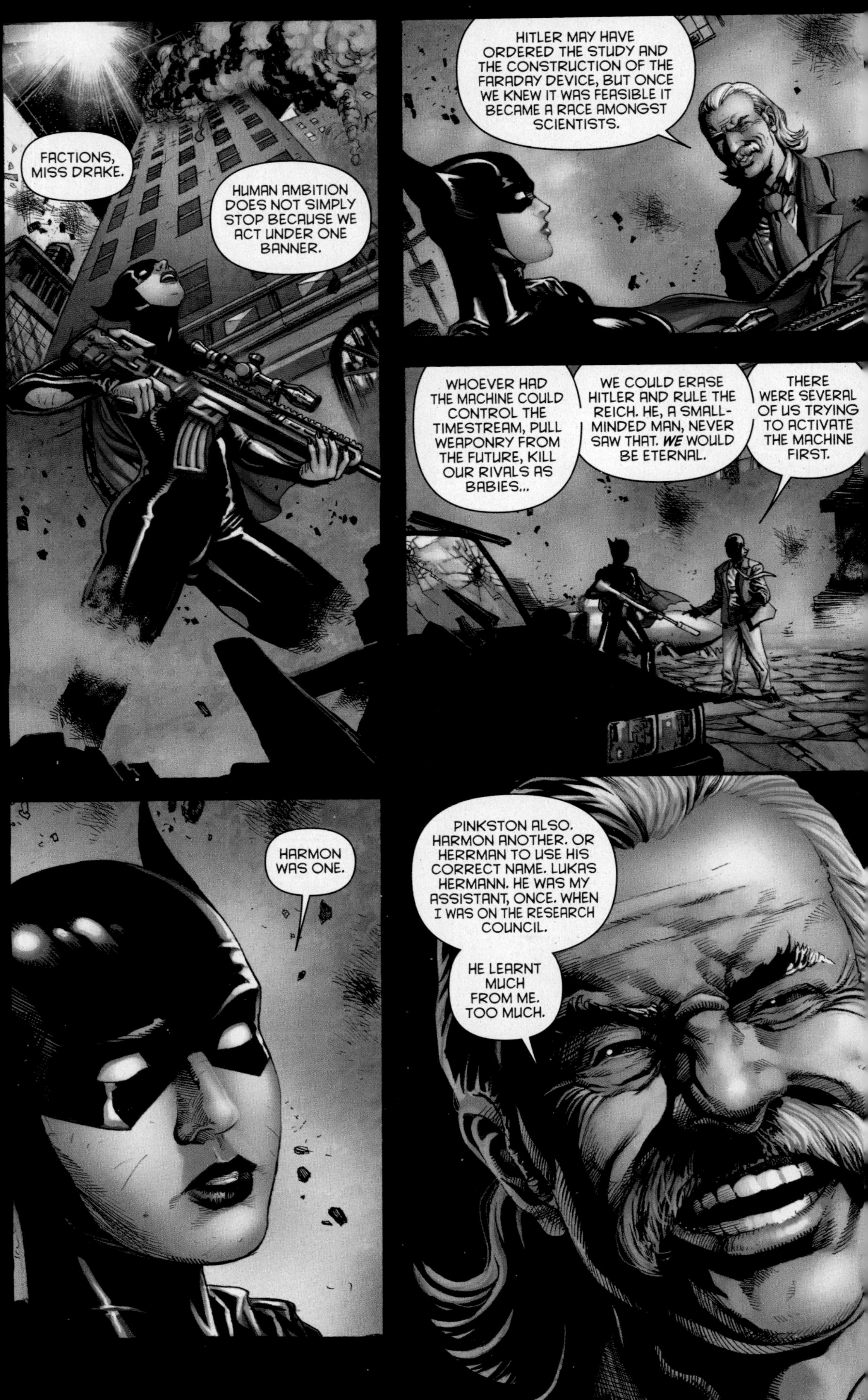
FACTIONS, MISS DRAKE.
HUMAN AMBITION DOES NOT SIMPLY STOP BECAUSE WE ACT UNDER ONE BANNER.
HITLER MAY HAVE ORDERED THE STUDY AND THE CONSTRUCTION OF THE FARADAY DEVICE, BUT ONCE WE KNEW IT WAS FEASIBLE IT BECAME A RACE AMONGST SCIENTISTS.
WHOEVER HAD THE MACHINE COULD CONTROL THE TIMESTREAM, PULL WEAPONRY FROM THE FUTURE, KILL OUR RIVALS AS BABIES...
WE COULD ERASE HITLER AND RULE THE REICH. HE, A SMALL-MINDED MAN, NEVER SAW THAT. *WE* WOULD BE ETERNAL.
THERE WERE SEVERAL OF US TRYING TO ACTIVATE THE MACHINE FIRST.
HARMON WAS ONE.
PINKSTON ALSO. HARMON ANOTHER. OR HERRMAN TO USE HIS CORRECT NAME. LUKAS HERMANN. HE WAS MY ASSISTANT, ONCE. WHEN I WAS ON THE RESEARCH COUNCIL.
HE LEARNT MUCH FROM ME. TOO MUCH.

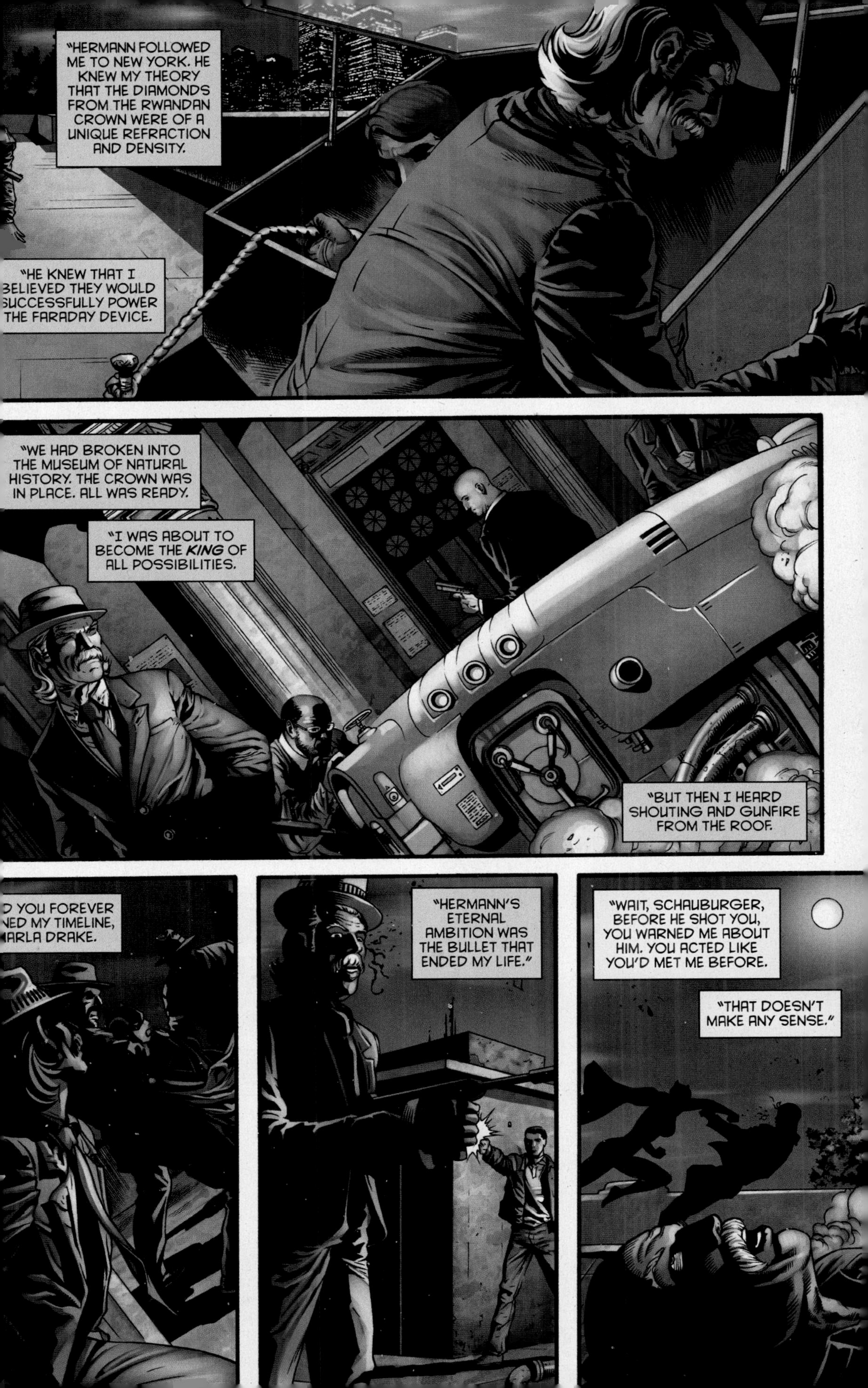
"HERMANN FOLLOWED ME TO NEW YORK. HE KNEW MY THEORY THAT THE DIAMONDS FROM THE RWANDAN CROWN WERE OF A UNIQUE REFRACTION AND DENSITY.
"HE KNEW THAT I BELIEVED THEY WOULD SUCCESSFULLY POWER THE FARADAY DEVICE.
"WE HAD BROKEN INTO THE MUSEUM OF NATURAL HISTORY. THE CROWN WAS IN PLACE. ALL WAS READY.
"I WAS ABOUT TO BECOME THE *KING* OF ALL POSSIBILITIES.
"BUT THEN I HEARD SHOUTING AND GUNFIRE FROM THE ROOF.
D YOU FOREVER NED MY TIMELINE, MARLA DRAKE.
"HERMANN'S ETERNAL AMBITION WAS THE BULLET THAT ENDED MY LIFE."
"WAIT, SCHAUBURGER, BEFORE HE SHOT YOU, YOU WARNED ME ABOUT HIM. YOU ACTED LIKE YOU'D MET ME BEFORE.
"THAT DOESN'T MAKE ANY SENSE."

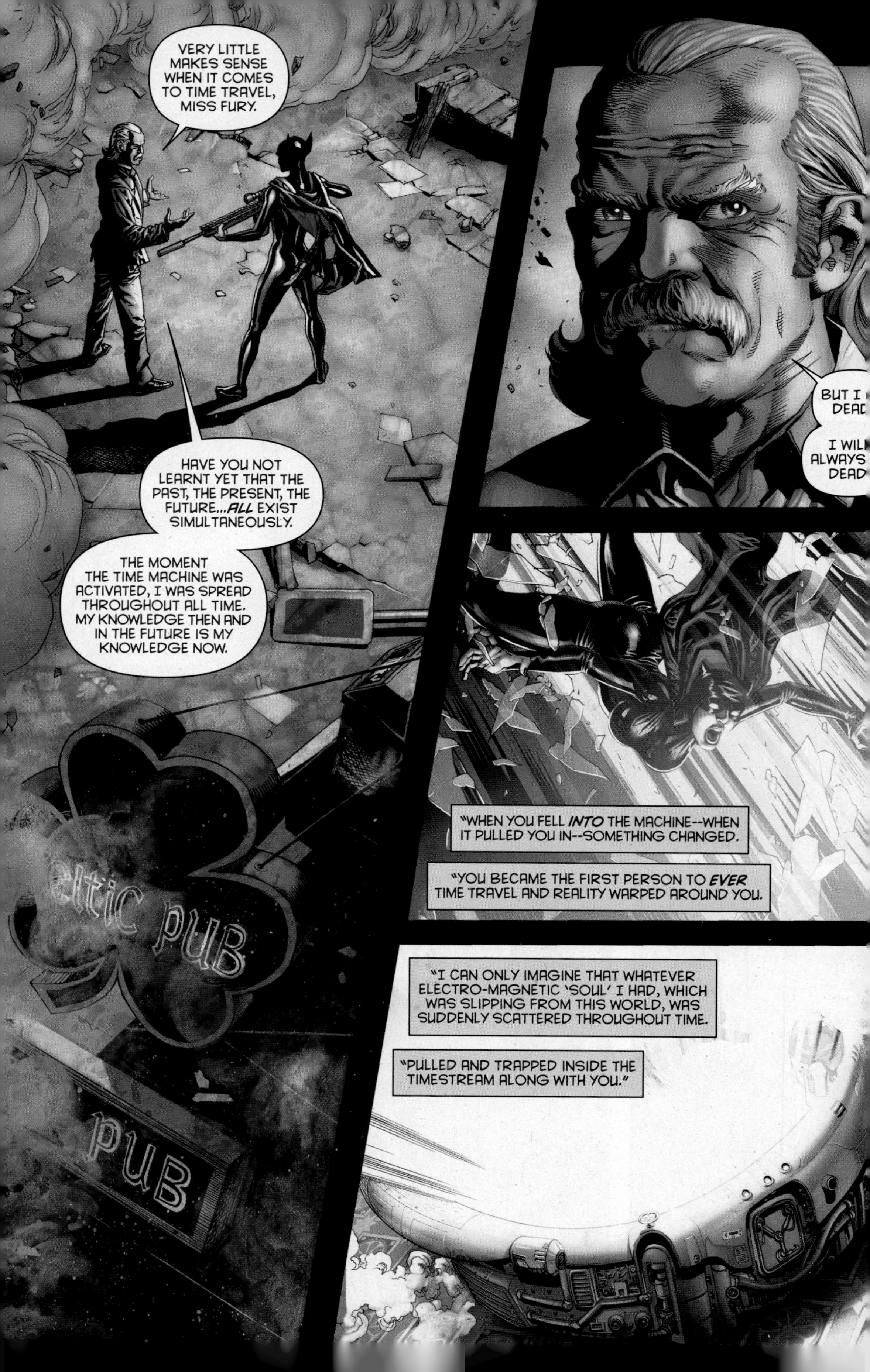
VERY LITTLE MAKES SENSE WHEN IT COMES TO TIME TRAVEL, MISS FURY.
HAVE YOU NOT LEARNT YET THAT THE PAST, THE PRESENT, THE FUTURE...ALL EXIST SIMULTANEOUSLY.
THE MOMENT THE TIME MACHINE WAS ACTIVATED, I WAS SPREAD THROUGHOUT ALL TIME. MY KNOWLEDGE THEN AND IN THE FUTURE IS MY KNOWLEDGE NOW.
eltic PUB
PUB
"WHEN YOU FELL INTO THE MACHINE--WHEN IT PULLED YOU IN--SOMETHING CHANGED.
"YOU BECAME THE FIRST PERSON TO EVER TIME TRAVEL AND REALITY WARPED AROUND YOU.
"I CAN ONLY IMAGINE THAT WHATEVER ELECTRO-MAGNETIC 'SOUL' I HAD, WHICH WAS SLIPPING FROM THIS WORLD, WAS SUDDENLY SCATTERED THROUGHOUT TIME.
"PULLED AND TRAPPED INSIDE THE TIMESTREAM ALONG WITH YOU."

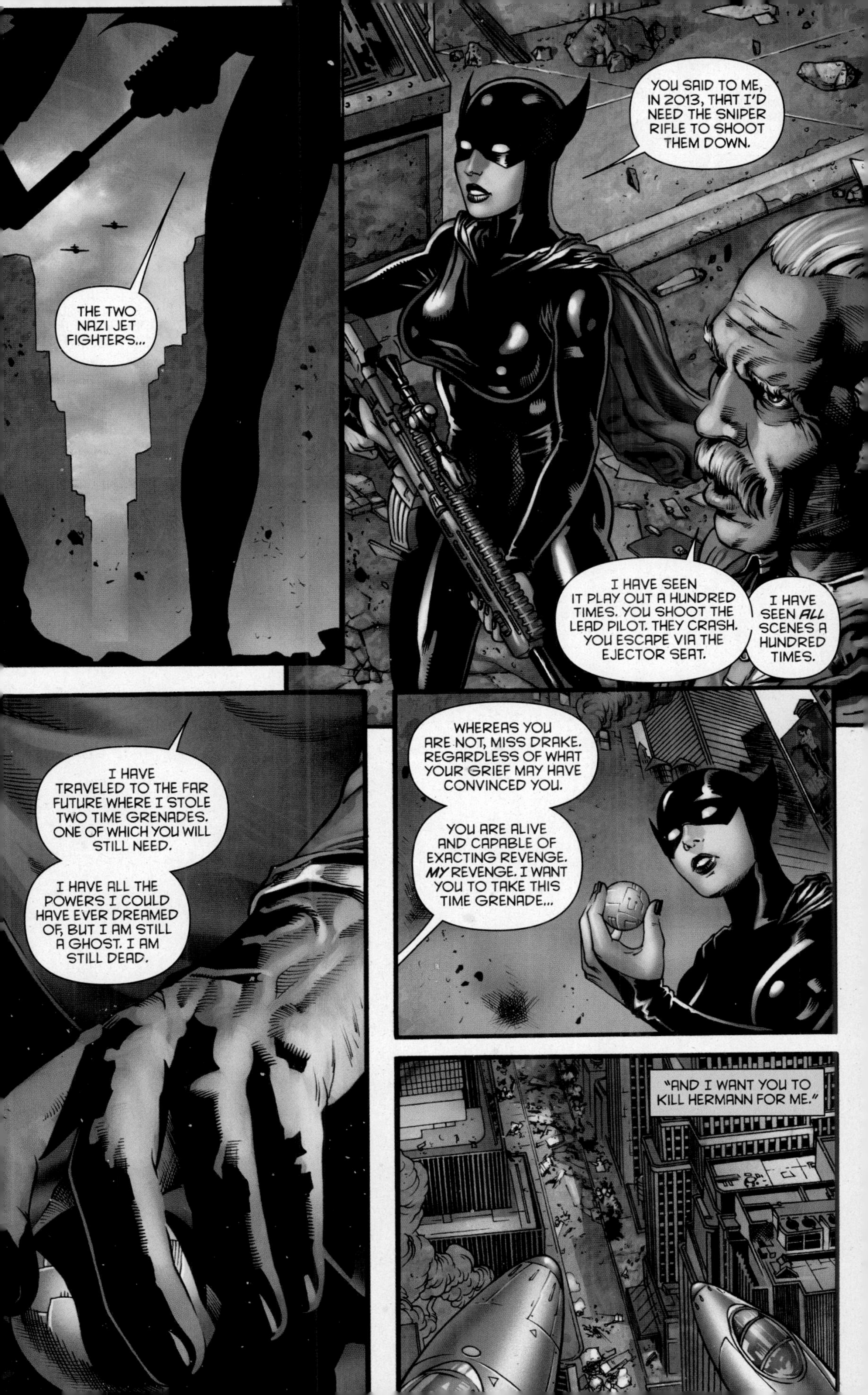
THE TWO NAZI JET FIGHTERS...
YOU SAID TO ME, IN 2013, THAT I'D NEED THE SNIPER RIFLE TO SHOOT THEM DOWN.
I HAVE SEEN IT PLAY OUT A HUNDRED TIMES. YOU SHOOT THE LEAD PILOT. THEY CRASH. YOU ESCAPE VIA THE EJECTOR SEAT.
I HAVE SEEN *ALL* SCENES A HUNDRED TIMES.
I HAVE TRAVELED TO THE FAR FUTURE WHERE I STOLE TWO TIME GRENADES. ONE OF WHICH YOU WILL STILL NEED.
I HAVE ALL THE POWERS I COULD HAVE EVER DREAMED OF, BUT I AM STILL A GHOST. I AM STILL DEAD.
WHEREAS YOU ARE NOT, MISS DRAKE. REGARDLESS OF WHAT YOUR GRIEF MAY HAVE CONVINCED YOU.
YOU ARE ALIVE AND CAPABLE OF EXACTING REVENGE. *MY* REVENGE. I WANT YOU TO TAKE THIS TIME GRENADE...
"AND I WANT YOU TO KILL HERMANN FOR ME."

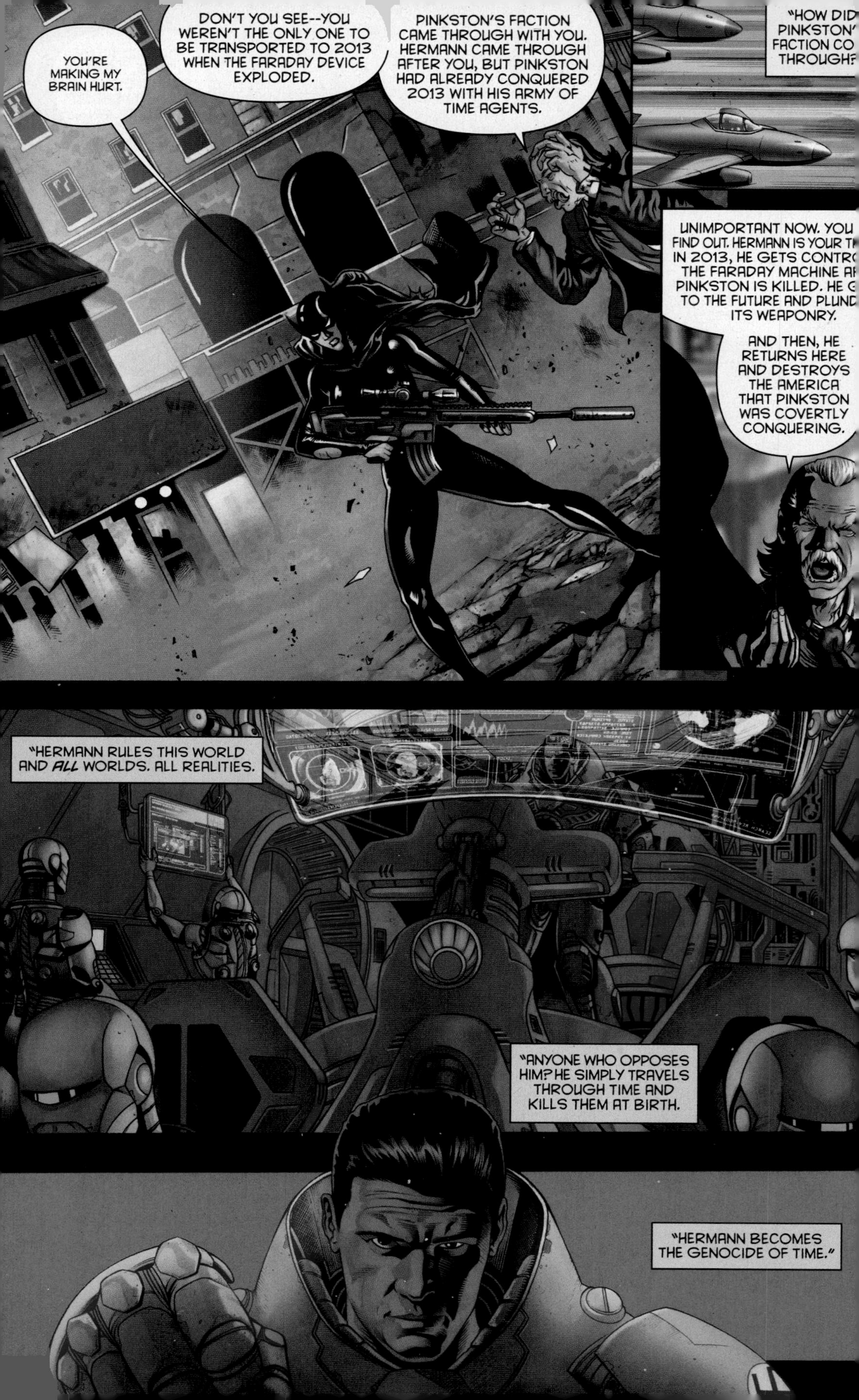
YOU'RE MAKING MY BRAIN HURT.
DON'T YOU SEE--YOU WEREN'T THE ONLY ONE TO BE TRANSPORTED TO 2013 WHEN THE FARADAY DEVICE EXPLODED.
PINKSTON'S FACTION CAME THROUGH WITH YOU. HERMANN CAME THROUGH AFTER YOU, BUT PINKSTON HAD ALREADY CONQUERED 2013 WITH HIS ARMY OF TIME AGENTS.
"HOW DID PINKSTON' FACTION CO THROUGH?
UNIMPORTANT NOW. YOU FIND OUT. HERMANN IS YOUR T IN 2013, HE GETS CONTR THE FARADAY MACHINE A PINKSTON IS KILLED. HE G TO THE FUTURE AND PLUND ITS WEAPONRY.
AND THEN, HE RETURNS HERE AND DESTROYS THE AMERICA THAT PINKSTON WAS COVERTLY CONQUERING.
"HERMANN RULES THIS WORLD AND *ALL* WORLDS. ALL REALITIES.
"ANYONE WHO OPPOSES HIM? HE SIMPLY TRAVELS THROUGH TIME AND KILLS THEM AT BIRTH.
"HERMANN BECOMES THE GENOCIDE OF TIME."

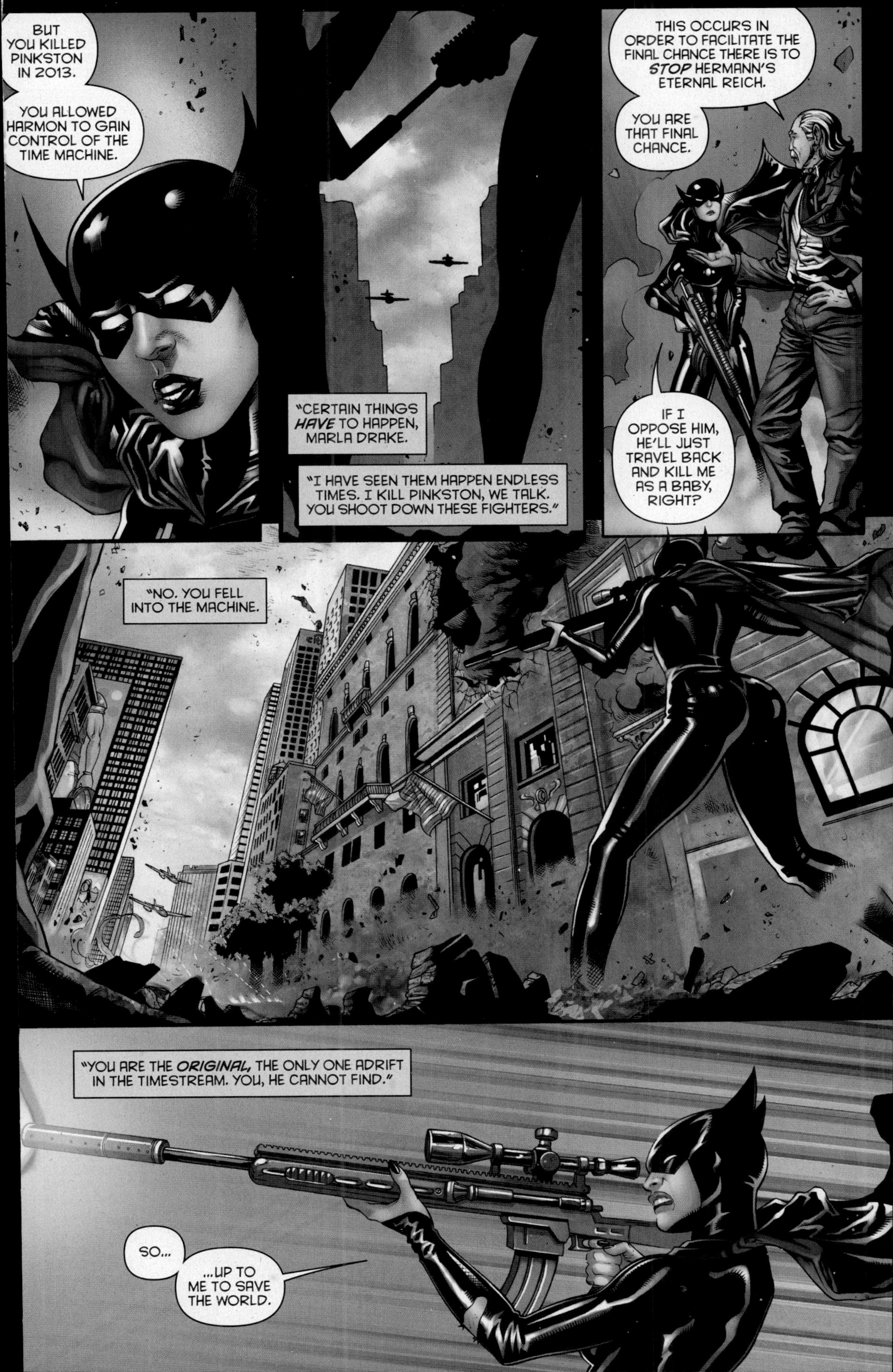
BUT YOU KILLED PINKSTON IN 2013.
YOU ALLOWED HARMON TO GAIN CONTROL OF THE TIME MACHINE.
"CERTAIN THINGS *HAVE* TO HAPPEN, MARLA DRAKE.
"I HAVE SEEN THEM HAPPEN ENDLESS TIMES. I KILL PINKSTON, WE TALK. YOU SHOOT DOWN THESE FIGHTERS."
THIS OCCURS IN ORDER TO FACILITATE THE FINAL CHANCE THERE IS TO *STOP* HERMANN'S ETERNAL REICH.
YOU ARE THAT FINAL CHANCE.
IF I OPPOSE HIM, HE'LL JUST TRAVEL BACK AND KILL ME AS A BABY, RIGHT?
"NO. YOU FELL INTO THE MACHINE.
"YOU ARE THE *ORIGINAL*, THE ONLY ONE ADRIFT IN THE TIMESTREAM. YOU, HE CANNOT FIND."
SO...
...UP TO ME TO SAVE THE WORLD.

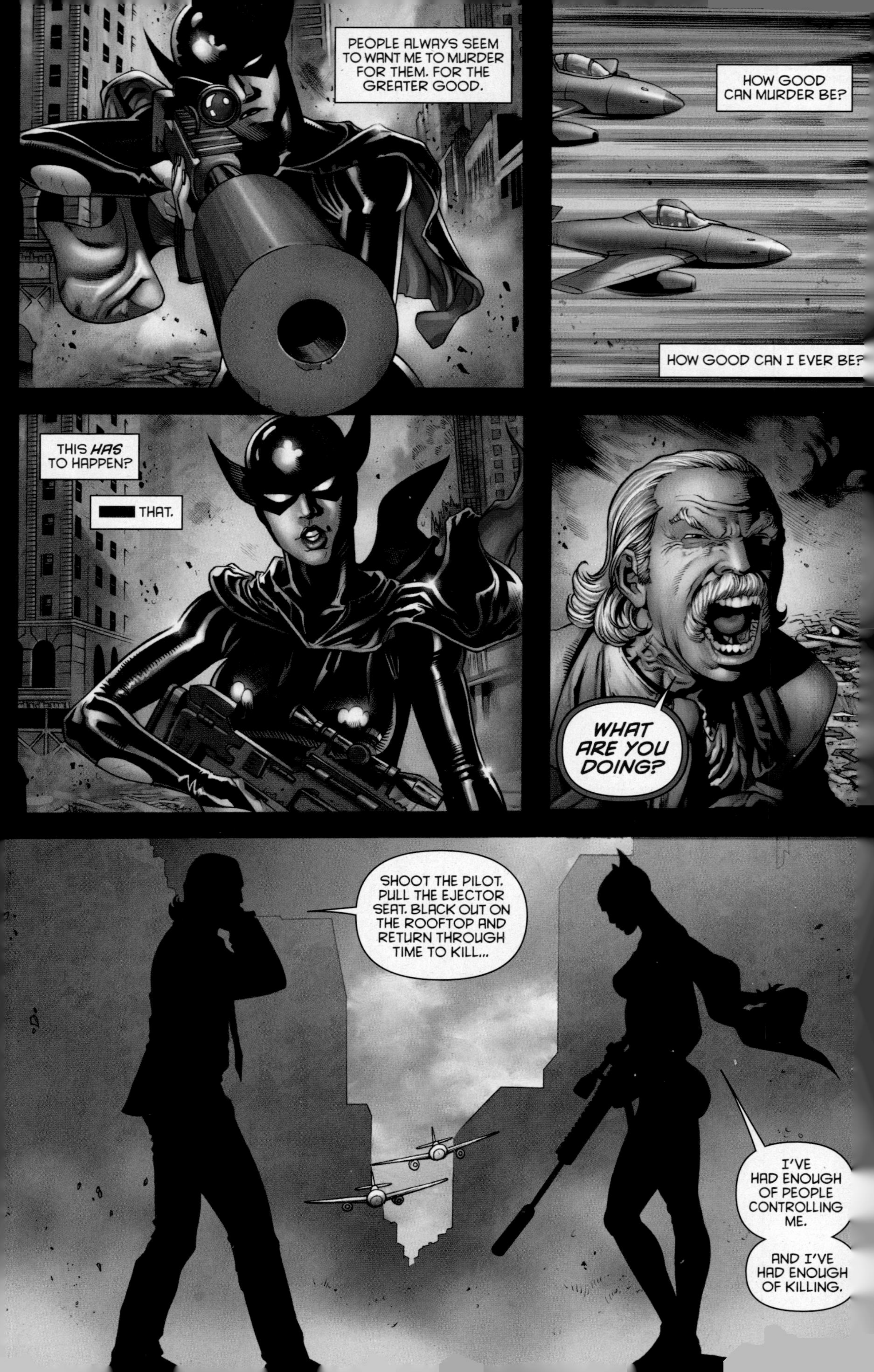
PEOPLE ALWAYS SEEM TO WANT ME TO MURDER FOR THEM. FOR THE GREATER GOOD.
HOW GOOD CAN MURDER BE?
HOW GOOD CAN I EVER BE?
THIS *HAS* TO HAPPEN?
[redacted] THAT.
WHAT ARE YOU DOING?
SHOOT THE PILOT. PULL THE EJECTOR SEAT. BLACK OUT ON THE ROOFTOP AND RETURN THROUGH TIME TO KILL...
I'VE HAD ENOUGH OF PEOPLE CONTROLLING ME.
AND I'VE HAD ENOUGH OF KILLING.

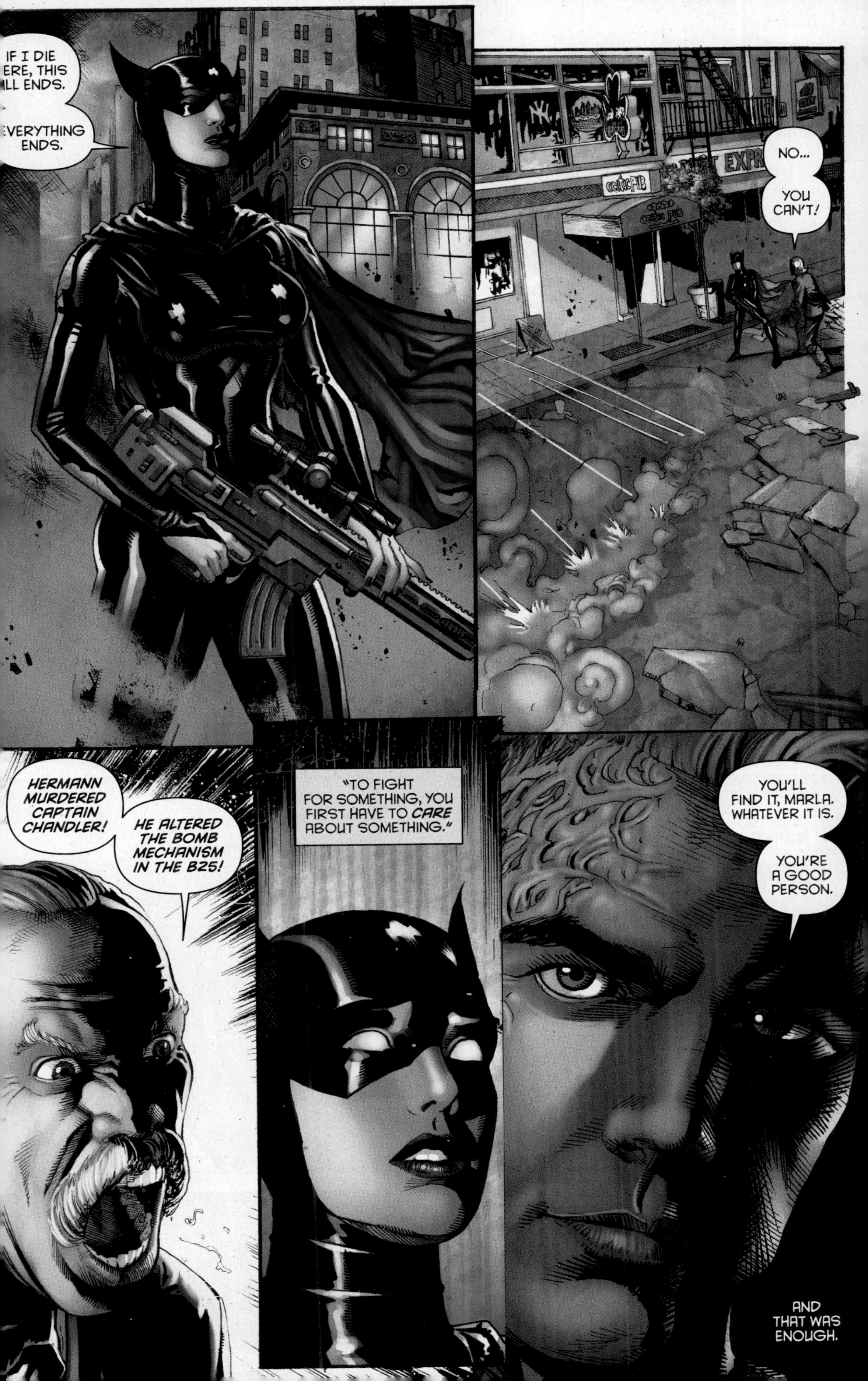
IF I DIE
ERE, THIS
LL ENDS.
EVERYTHING
ENDS.
NO...
YOU
CAN'T!
HERMANN MURDERED CAPTAIN CHANDLER!
HE ALTERED THE BOMB MECHANISM IN THE B25!
"TO FIGHT FOR SOMETHING, YOU FIRST HAVE TO CARE ABOUT SOMETHING."
YOU'LL FIND IT, MARLA. WHATEVER IT IS.
YOU'RE A GOOD PERSON.
AND THAT WAS ENOUGH.

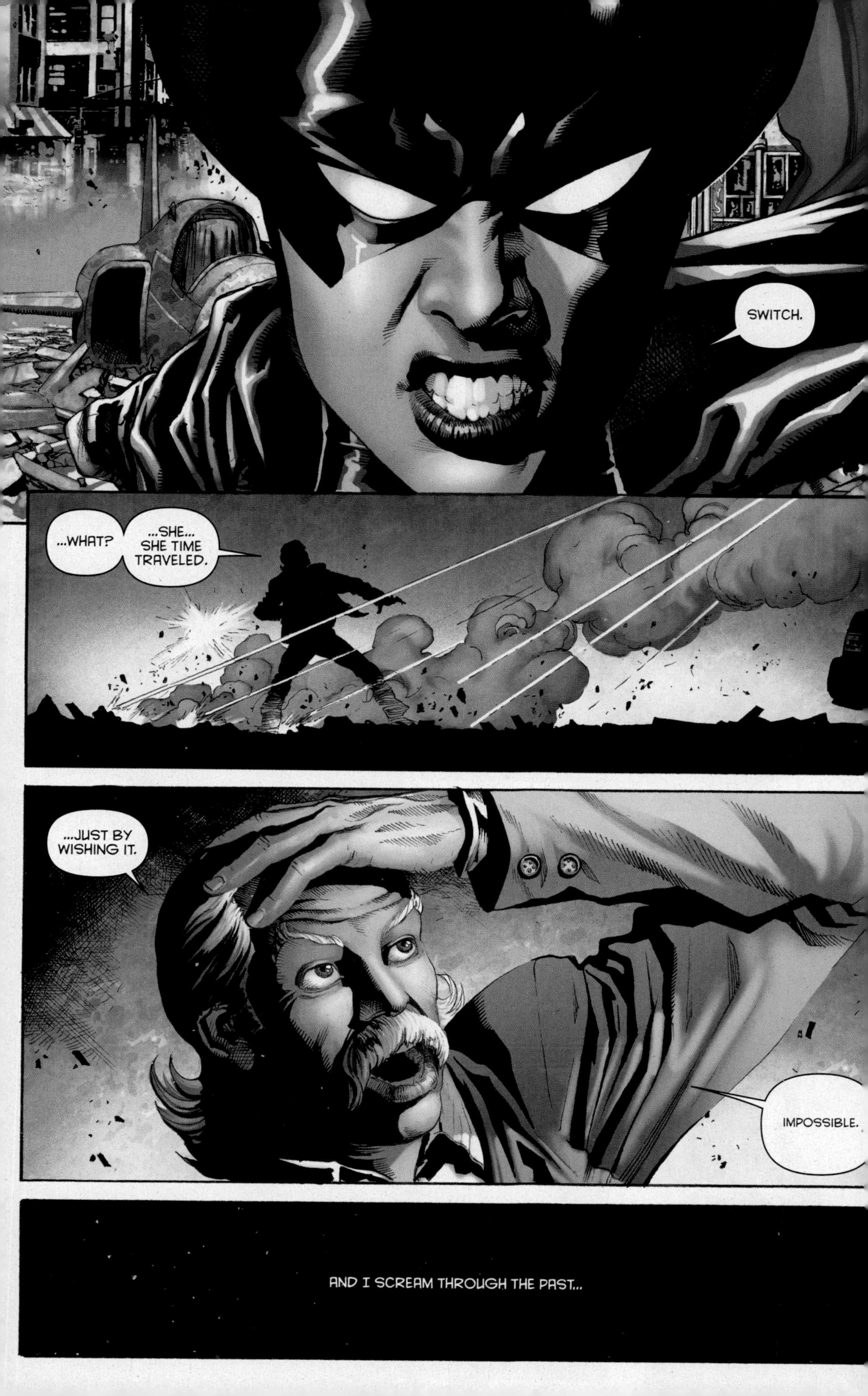
SWITCH.
...WHAT?
...SHE... SHE TIME TRAVELED.
...JUST BY WISHING IT.
IMPOSSIBLE.
AND I SCREAM THROUGH THE PAST...

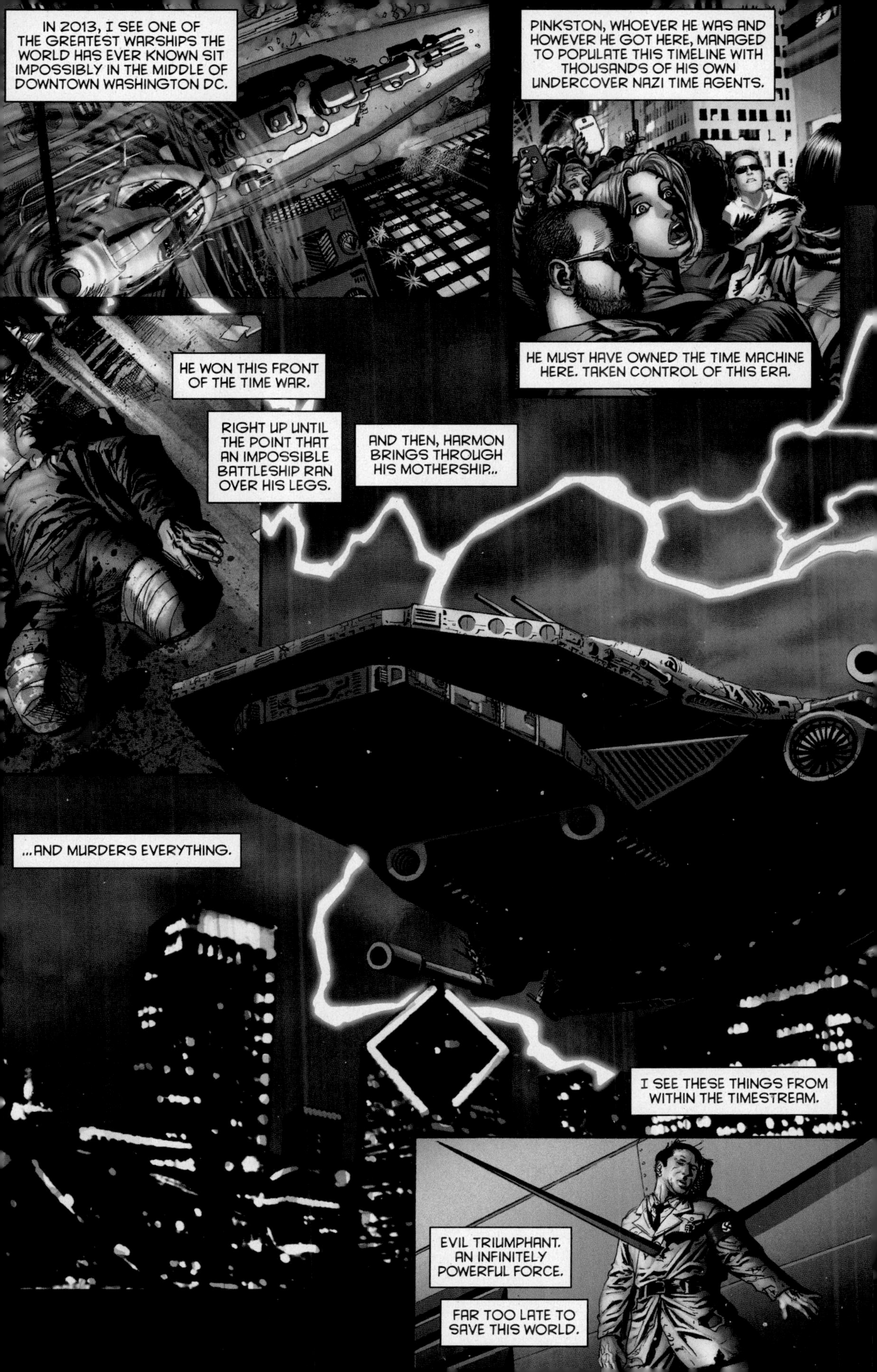
IN 2013, I SEE ONE OF THE GREATEST WARSHIPS THE WORLD HAS EVER KNOWN SIT IMPOSSIBLY IN THE MIDDLE OF DOWNTOWN WASHINGTON DC.
PINKSTON, WHOEVER HE WAS AND HOWEVER HE GOT HERE, MANAGED TO POPULATE THIS TIMELINE WITH THOUSANDS OF HIS OWN UNDERCOVER NAZI TIME AGENTS.
HE MUST HAVE OWNED THE TIME MACHINE HERE. TAKEN CONTROL OF THIS ERA.
HE WON THIS FRONT OF THE TIME WAR.
RIGHT UP UNTIL THE POINT THAT AN IMPOSSIBLE BATTLESHIP RAN OVER HIS LEGS.
AND THEN, HARMON BRINGS THROUGH HIS MOTHERSHIP...
...AND MURDERS EVERYTHING.
I SEE THESE THINGS FROM WITHIN THE TIMESTREAM.
EVIL TRIUMPHANT. AN INFINITELY POWERFUL FORCE.
FAR TOO LATE TO SAVE THIS WORLD.

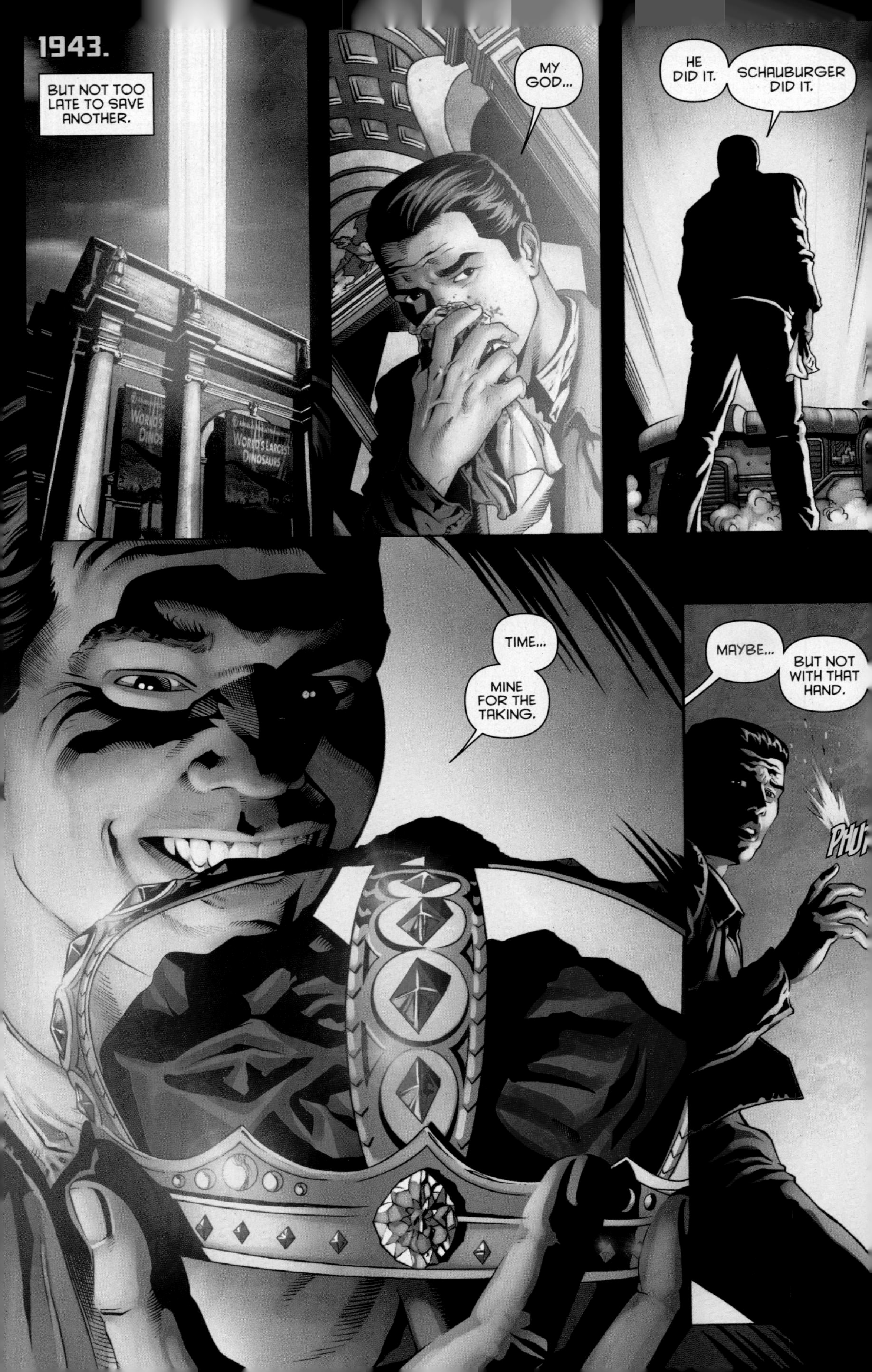
1943.
BUT NOT TOO LATE TO SAVE ANOTHER.
WORLD'S LARGEST DINOSAURS
MY GOD...
HE DID IT.
SCHAUBURGER DID IT.
TIME...
MINE FOR THE TAKING.
MAYBE...
BUT NOT WITH THAT HAND.
PHU

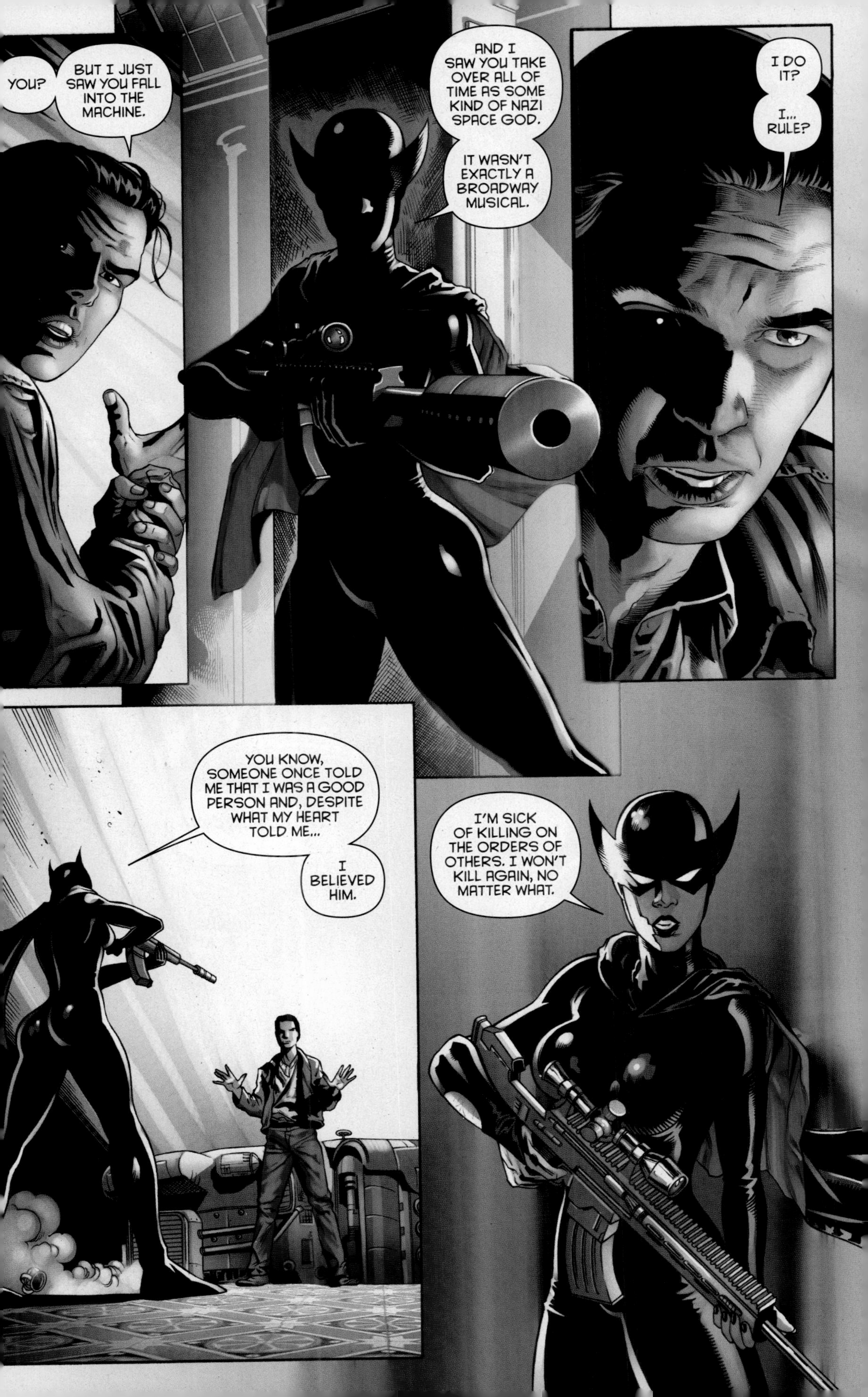
YOU?
BUT I JUST SAW YOU FALL INTO THE MACHINE.
AND I SAW YOU TAKE OVER ALL OF TIME AS SOME KIND OF NAZI SPACE GOD.
IT WASN'T EXACTLY A BROADWAY MUSICAL.
I DO IT?
I... RULE?
YOU KNOW, SOMEONE ONCE TOLD ME THAT I WAS A GOOD PERSON AND, DESPITE WHAT MY HEART TOLD ME...
I BELIEVED HIM.
I'M SICK OF KILLING ON THE ORDERS OF OTHERS. I WON'T KILL AGAIN, NO MATTER WHAT.

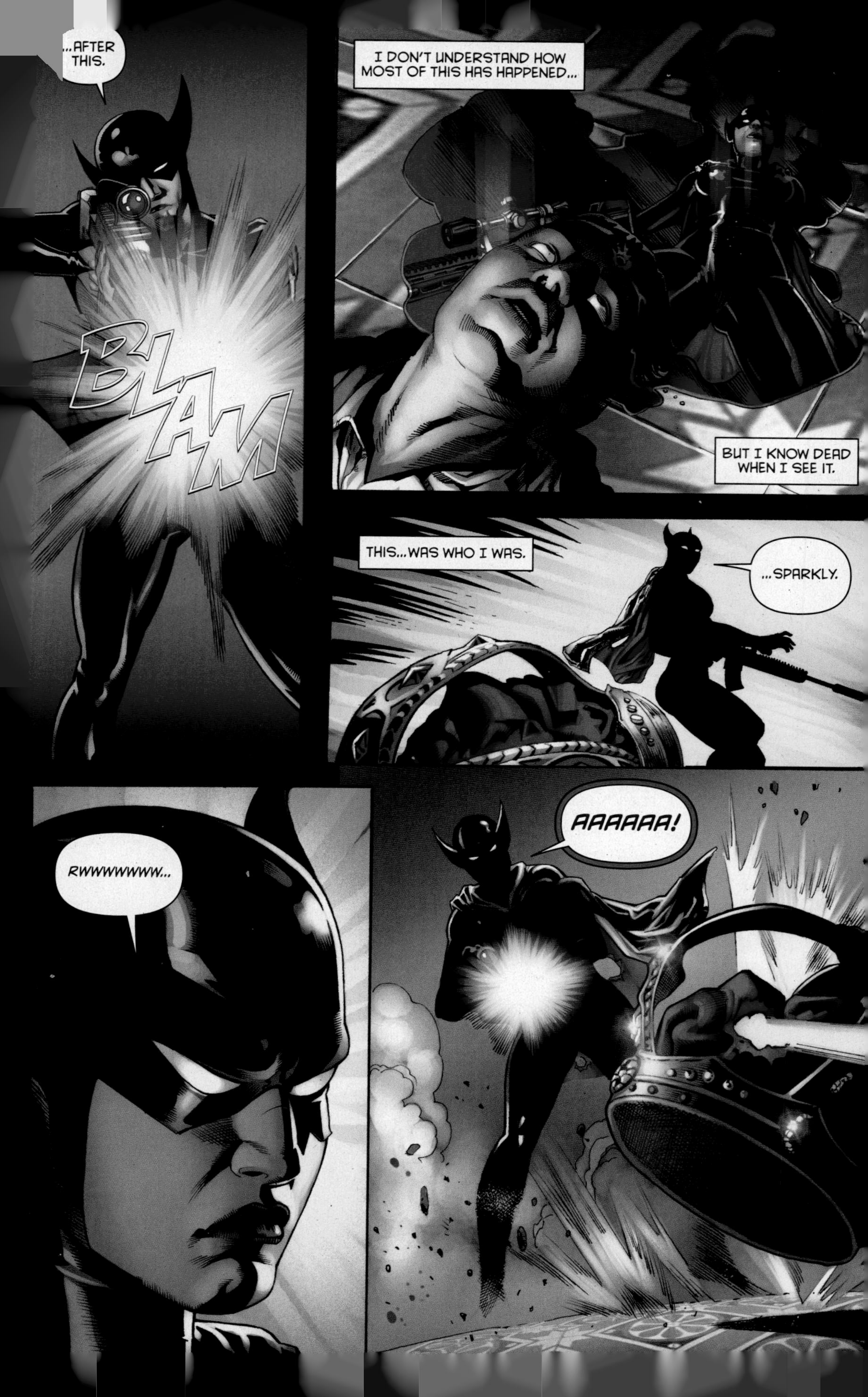
...AFTER THIS.
BLAM
I DON'T UNDERSTAND HOW MOST OF THIS HAS HAPPENED...
BUT I KNOW DEAD WHEN I SEE IT.
THIS...WAS WHO I WAS.
...SPARKLY.
RWWWWWWW...
AAAAAA!

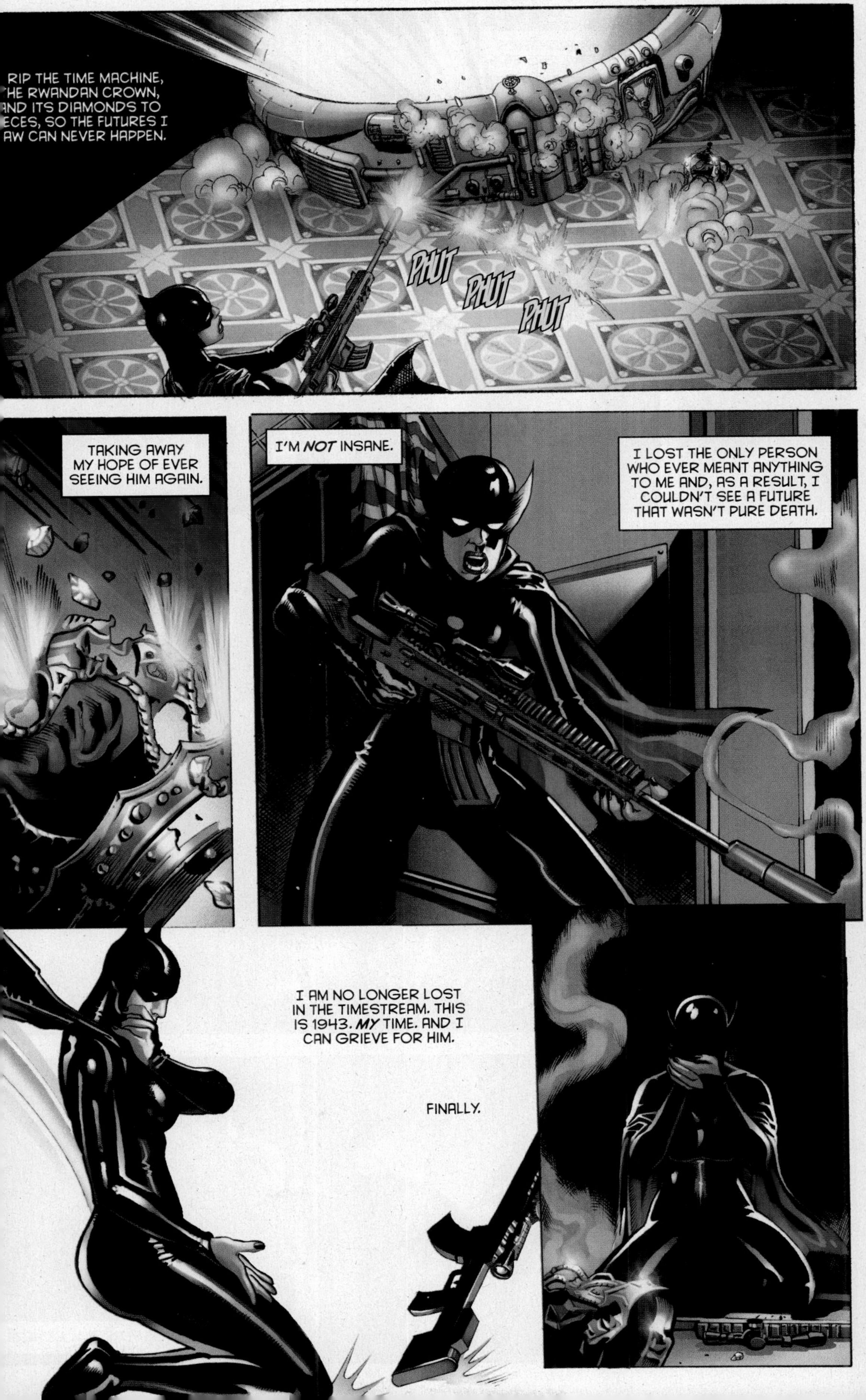

RIP THE TIME MACHINE, HE RWANDAN CROWN, AND ITS DIAMONDS TO ECES, SO THE FUTURES I AW CAN NEVER HAPPEN.
PHUT
PHUT
PHUT
TAKING AWAY MY HOPE OF EVER SEEING HIM AGAIN.
I'M *NOT* INSANE.
I LOST THE ONLY PERSON WHO EVER MEANT ANYTHING TO ME AND, AS A RESULT, I COULDN'T SEE A FUTURE THAT WASN'T PURE DEATH.
I AM NO LONGER LOST IN THE TIMESTREAM. THIS IS 1943. *MY* TIME. AND I CAN GRIEVE FOR HIM.
FINALLY.

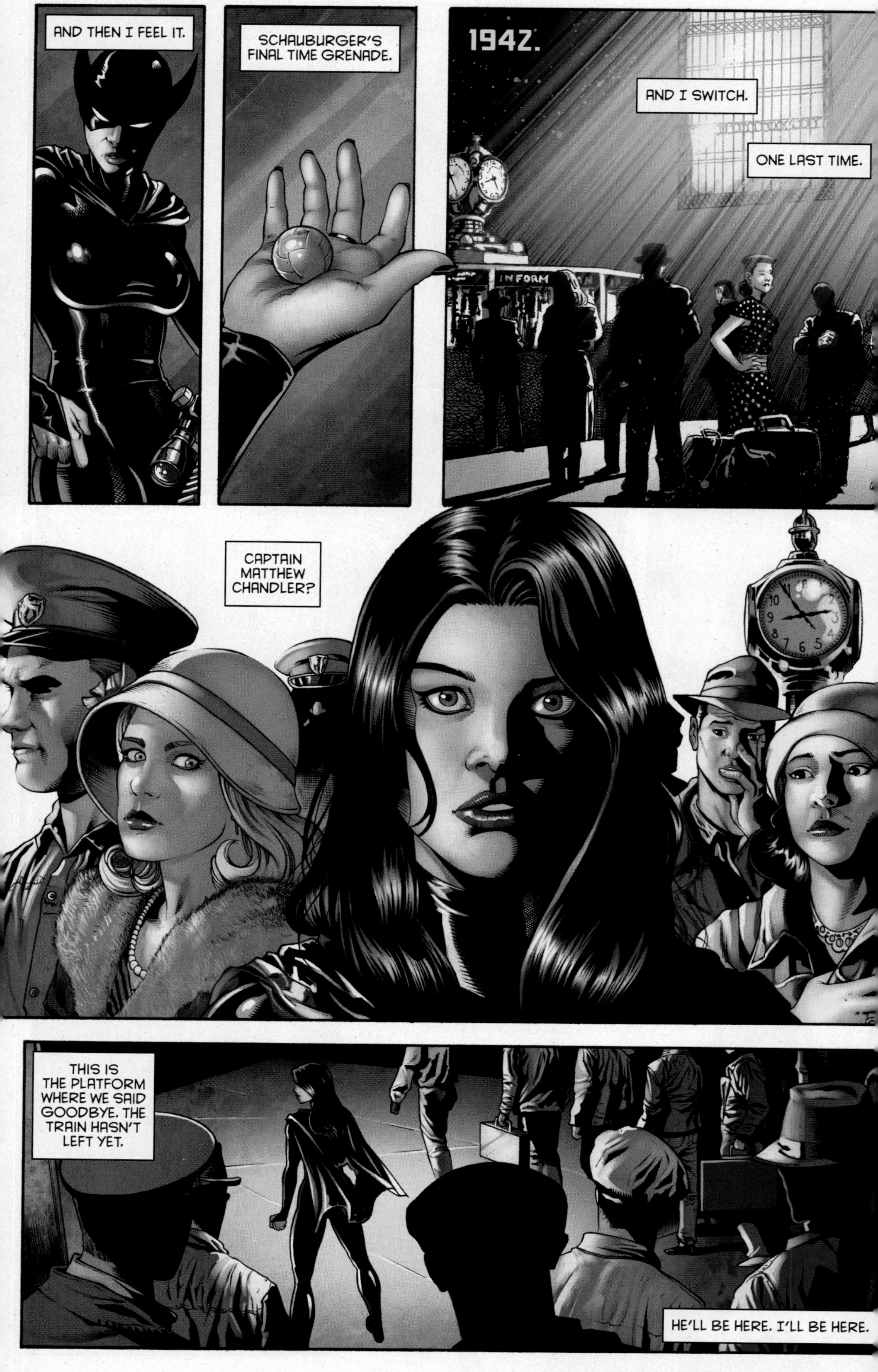
AND THEN I FEEL IT.
SCHAUBURGER'S FINAL TIME GRENADE.
1942.
AND I SWITCH.
ONE LAST TIME.
INFORM
CAPTAIN MATTHEW CHANDLER?
THIS IS THE PLATFORM WHERE WE SAID GOODBYE. THE TRAIN HASN'T LEFT YET.
HE'LL BE HERE. I'LL BE HERE.

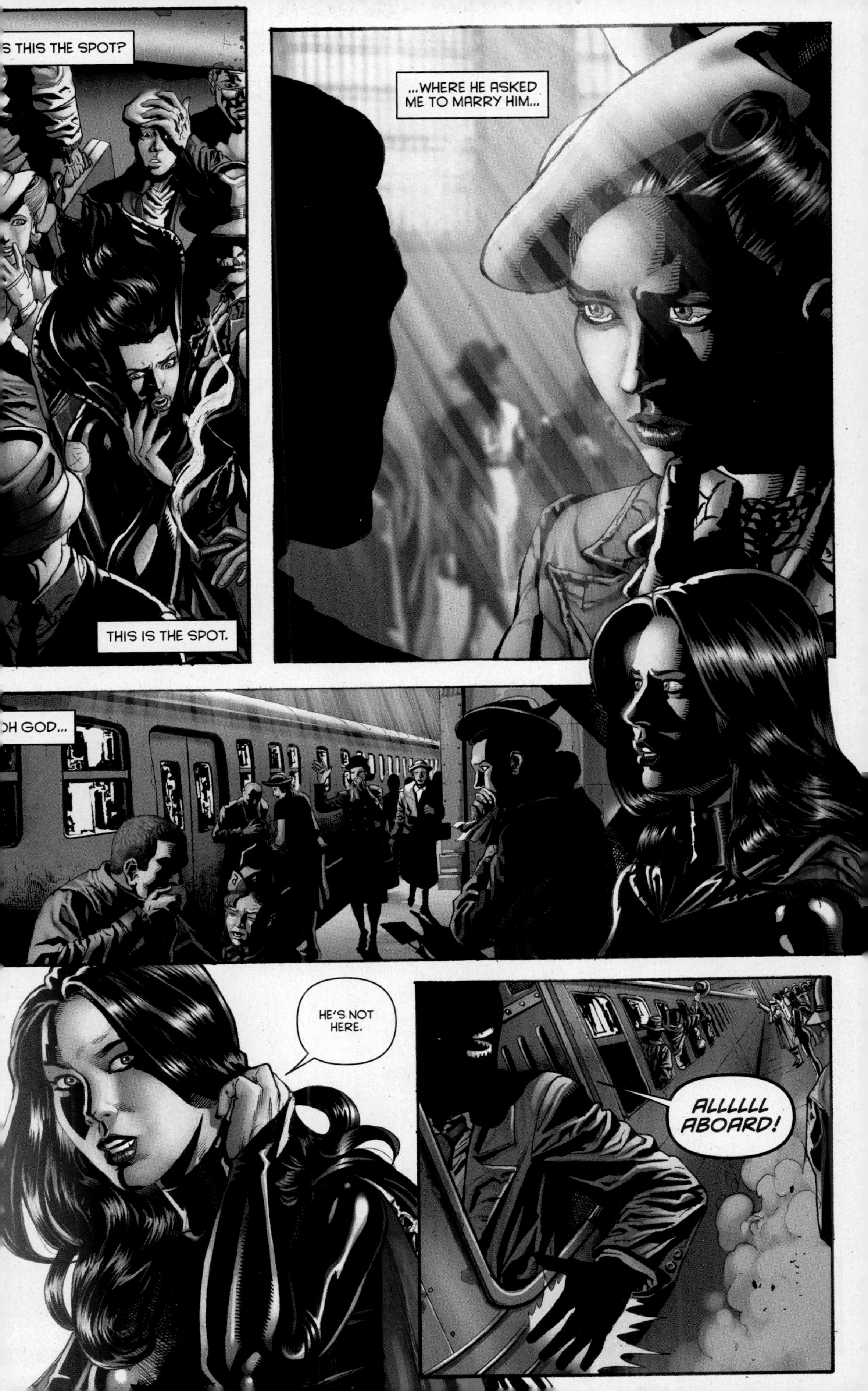
S THIS THE SPOT?
THIS IS THE SPOT.
...WHERE HE ASKED ME TO MARRY HIM...
OH GOD...
HE'S NOT HERE.
ALLLLLL ABOARD!

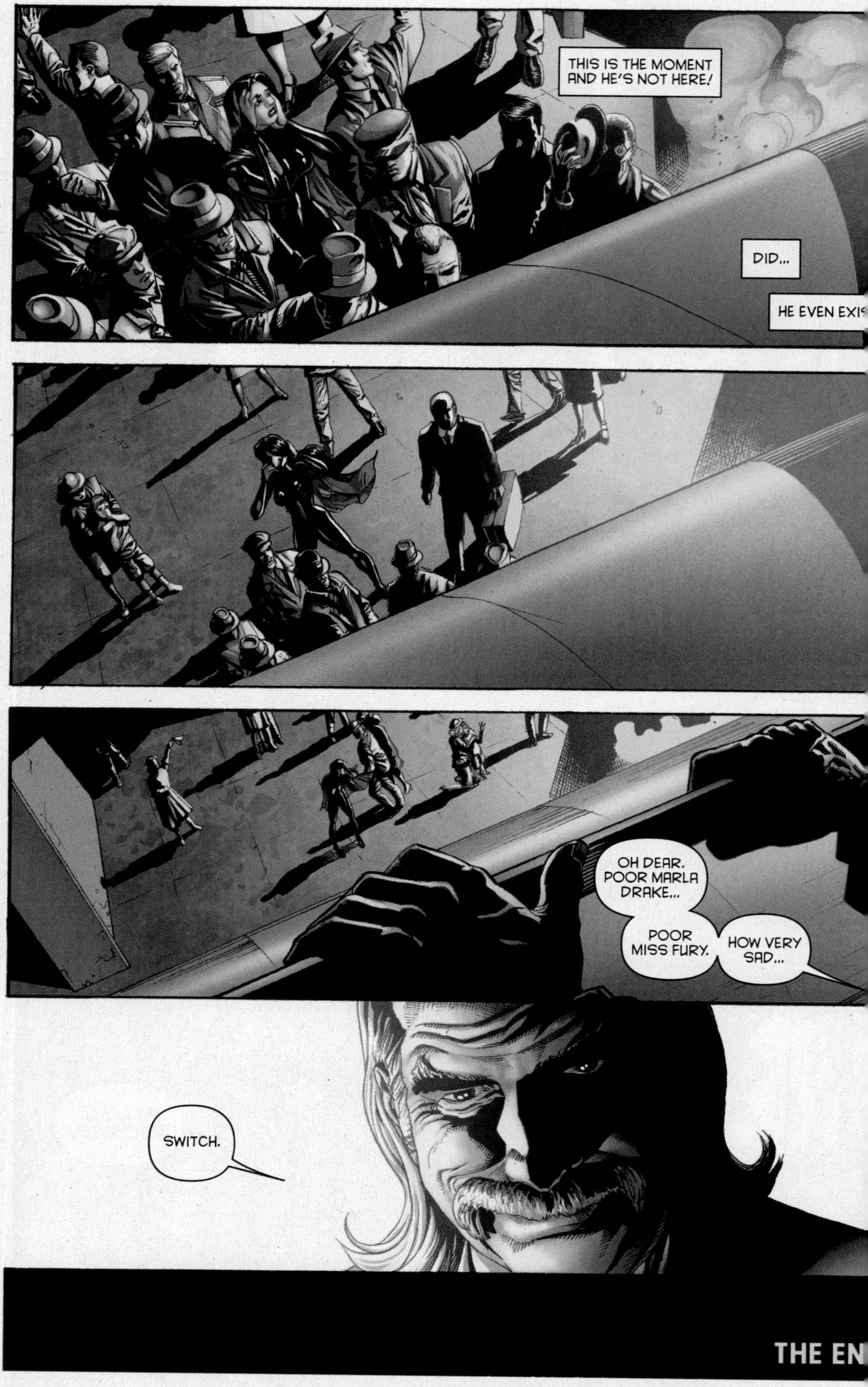
THIS IS THE MOMENT AND HE'S NOT HERE!
DID...
OH DEAR. POOR MARLA DRAKE...
POOR MISS FURY.
HOW VERY SAD...
SWITCH.

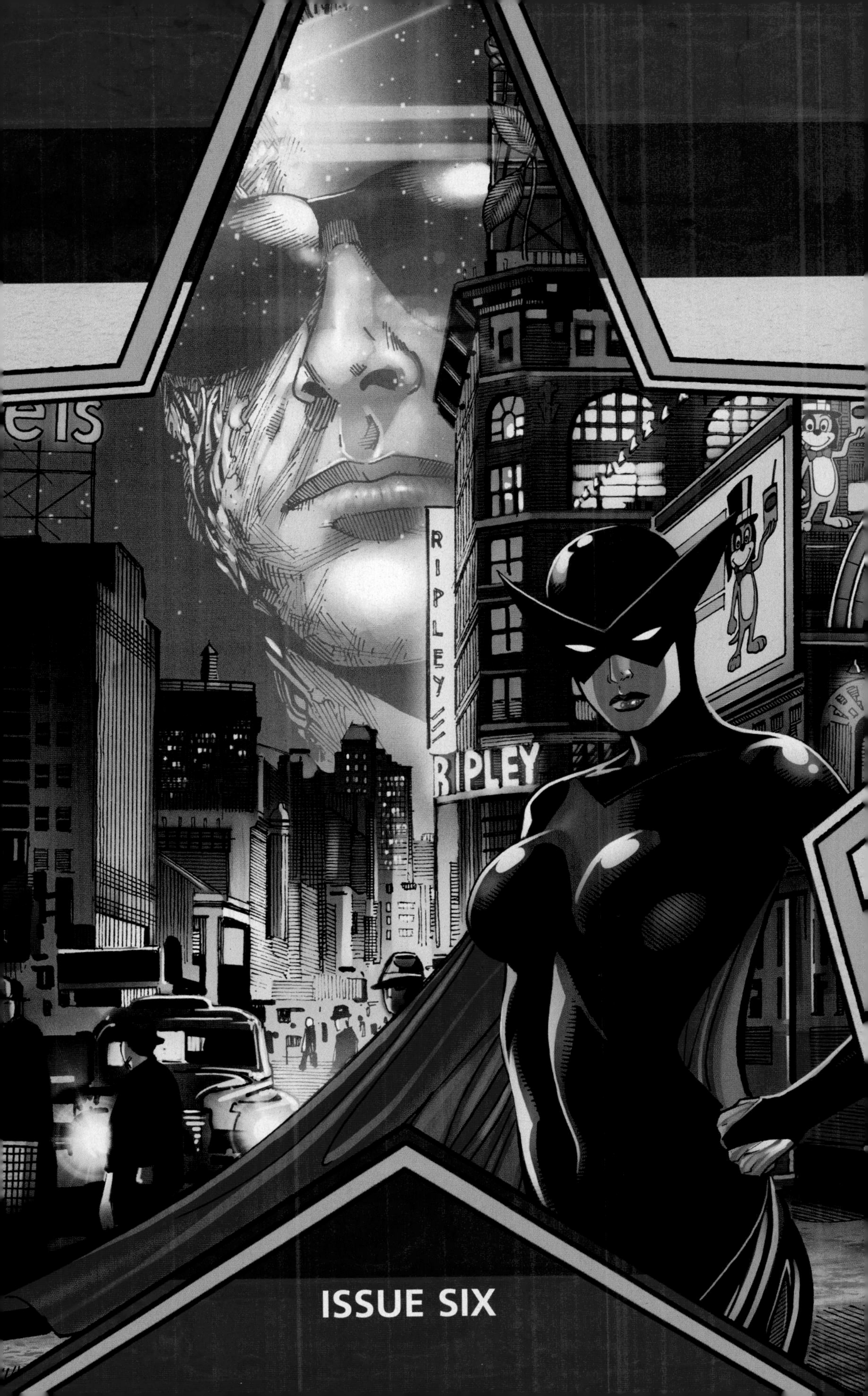
RIPLEY
RIPLEY
ISSUE SIX

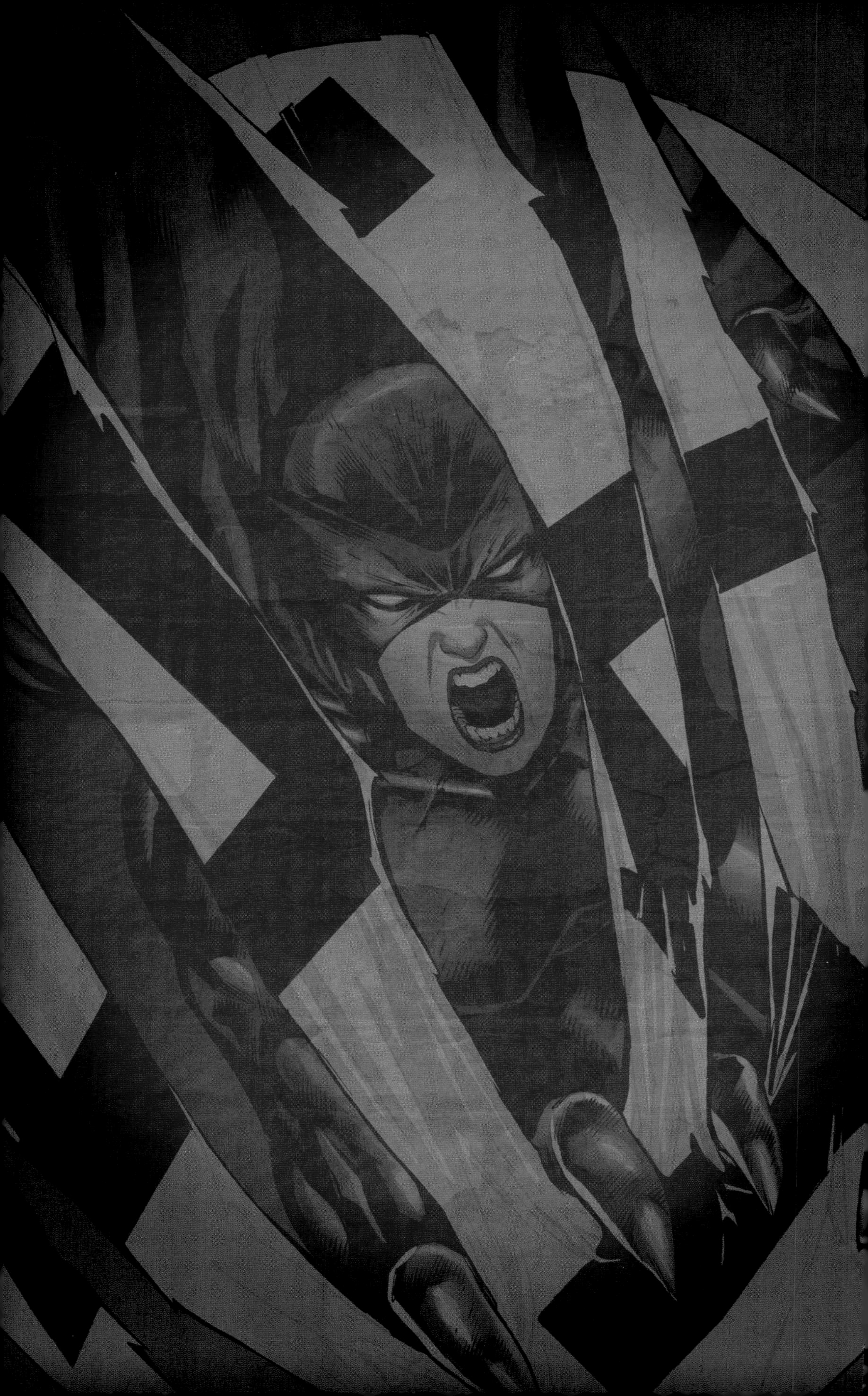

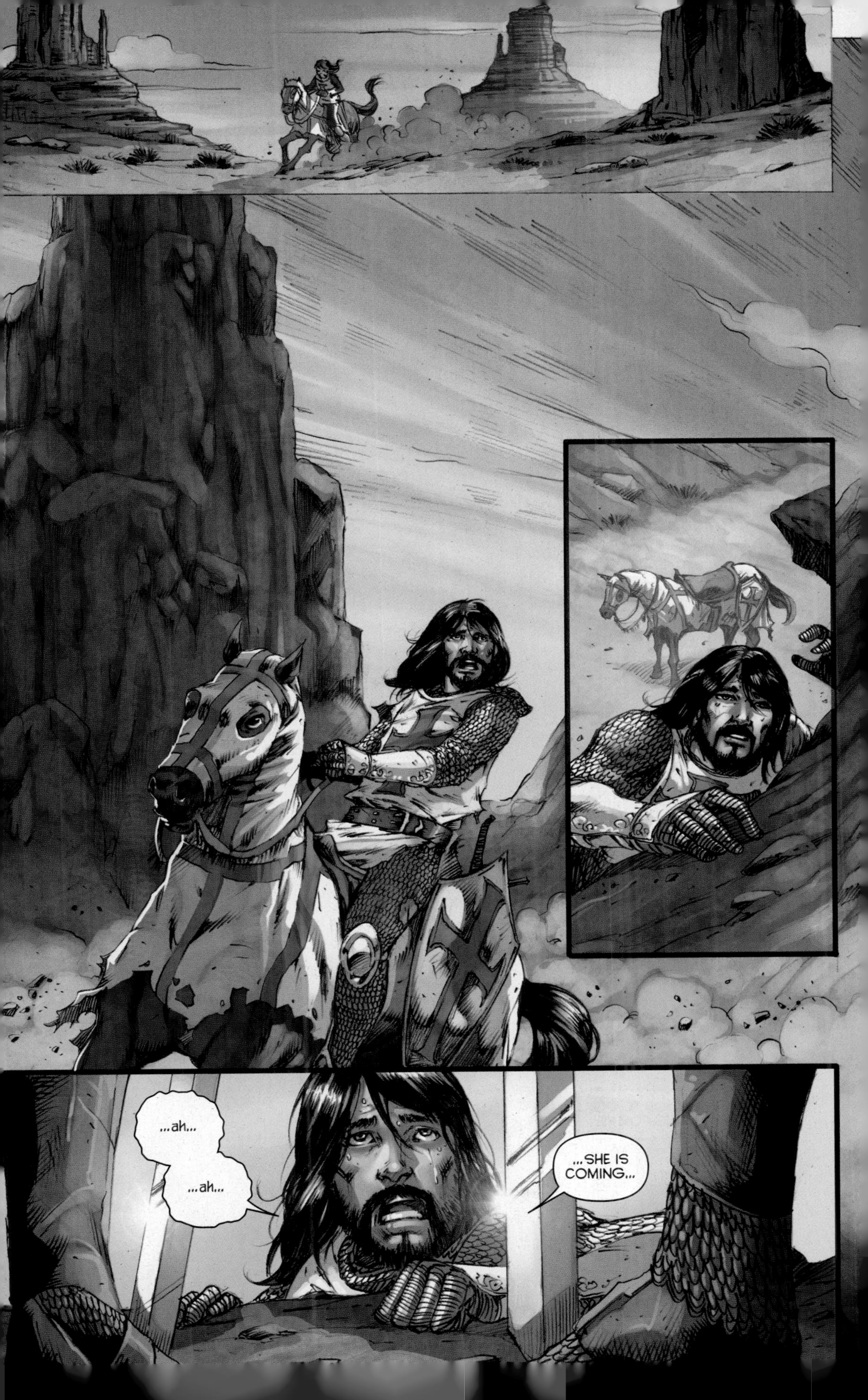
...ah...
...ah...
...SHE IS COMING...

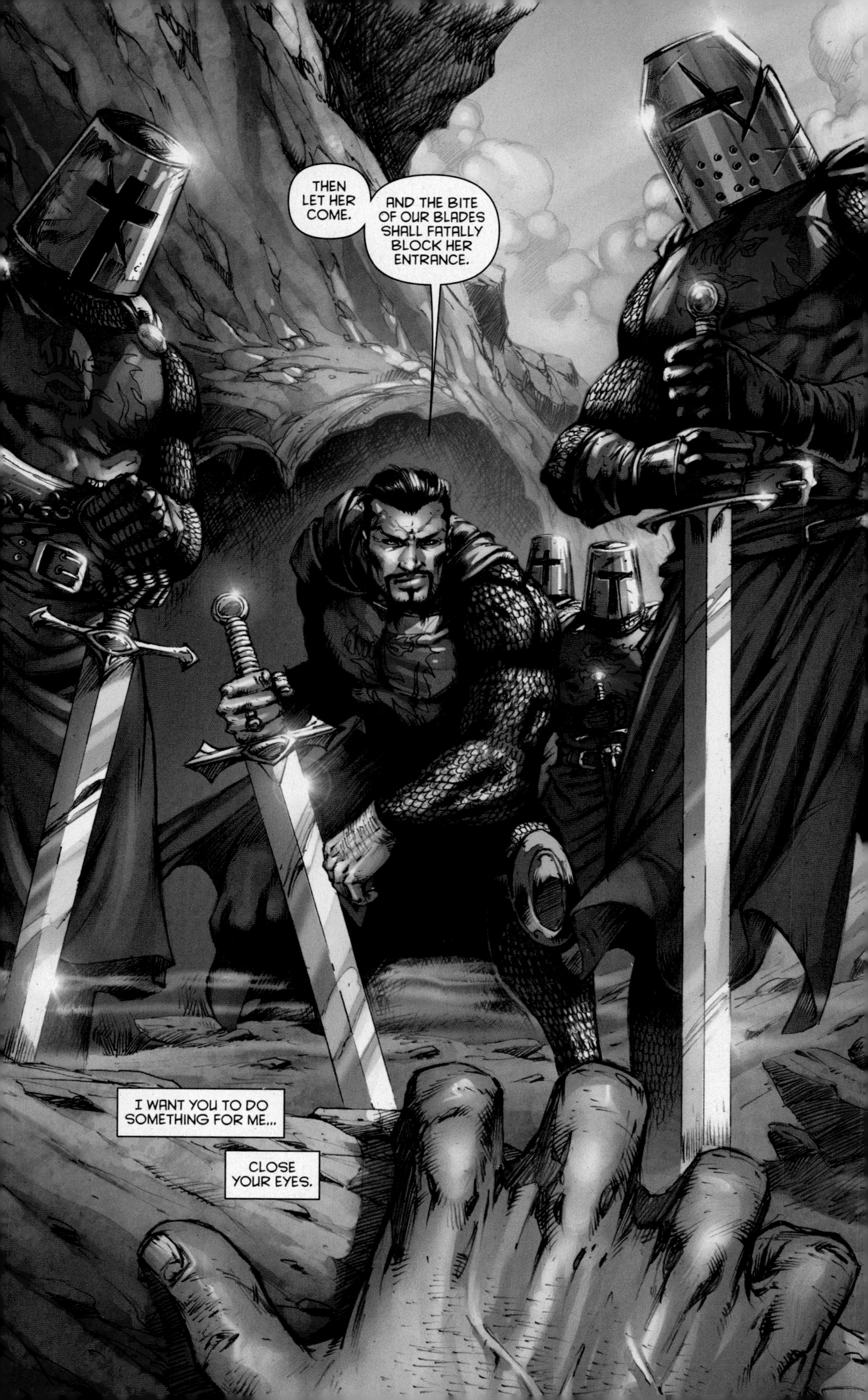
THEN LET HER COME.
AND THE BITE OF OUR BLADES SHALL FATALLY BLOCK HER ENTRANCE.
I WANT YOU TO DO SOMETHING FOR ME...
CLOSE YOUR EYES.

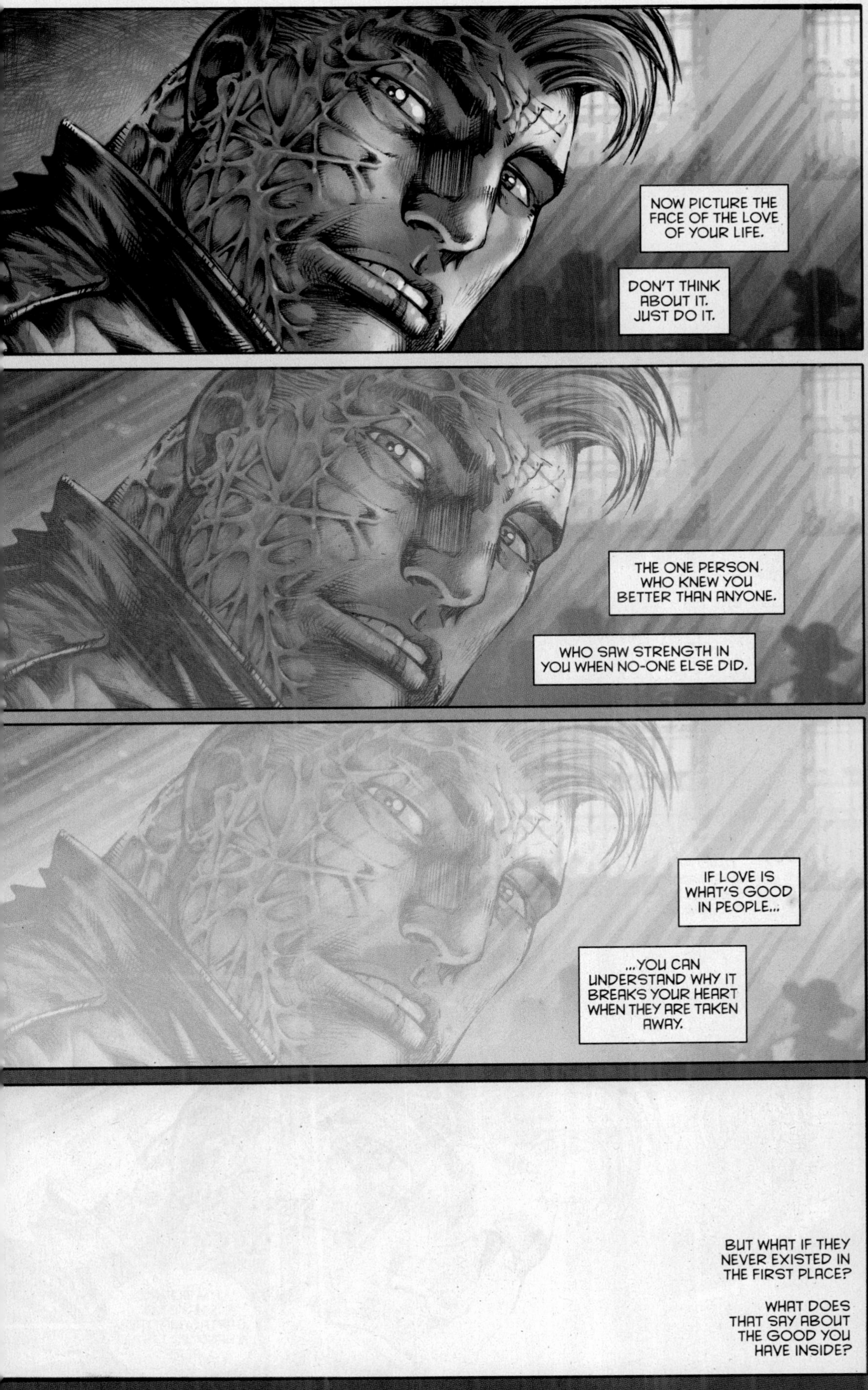
NOW PICTURE THE FACE OF THE LOVE OF YOUR LIFE.
DON'T THINK ABOUT IT. JUST DO IT.
THE ONE PERSON WHO KNEW YOU BETTER THAN ANYONE.
WHO SAW STRENGTH IN YOU WHEN NO-ONE ELSE DID.
IF LOVE IS WHAT'S GOOD IN PEOPLE...
...YOU CAN UNDERSTAND WHY IT BREAKS YOUR HEART WHEN THEY ARE TAKEN AWAY.
BUT WHAT IF THEY NEVER EXISTED IN THE FIRST PLACE?
WHAT DOES THAT SAY ABOUT THE GOOD YOU HAVE INSIDE?

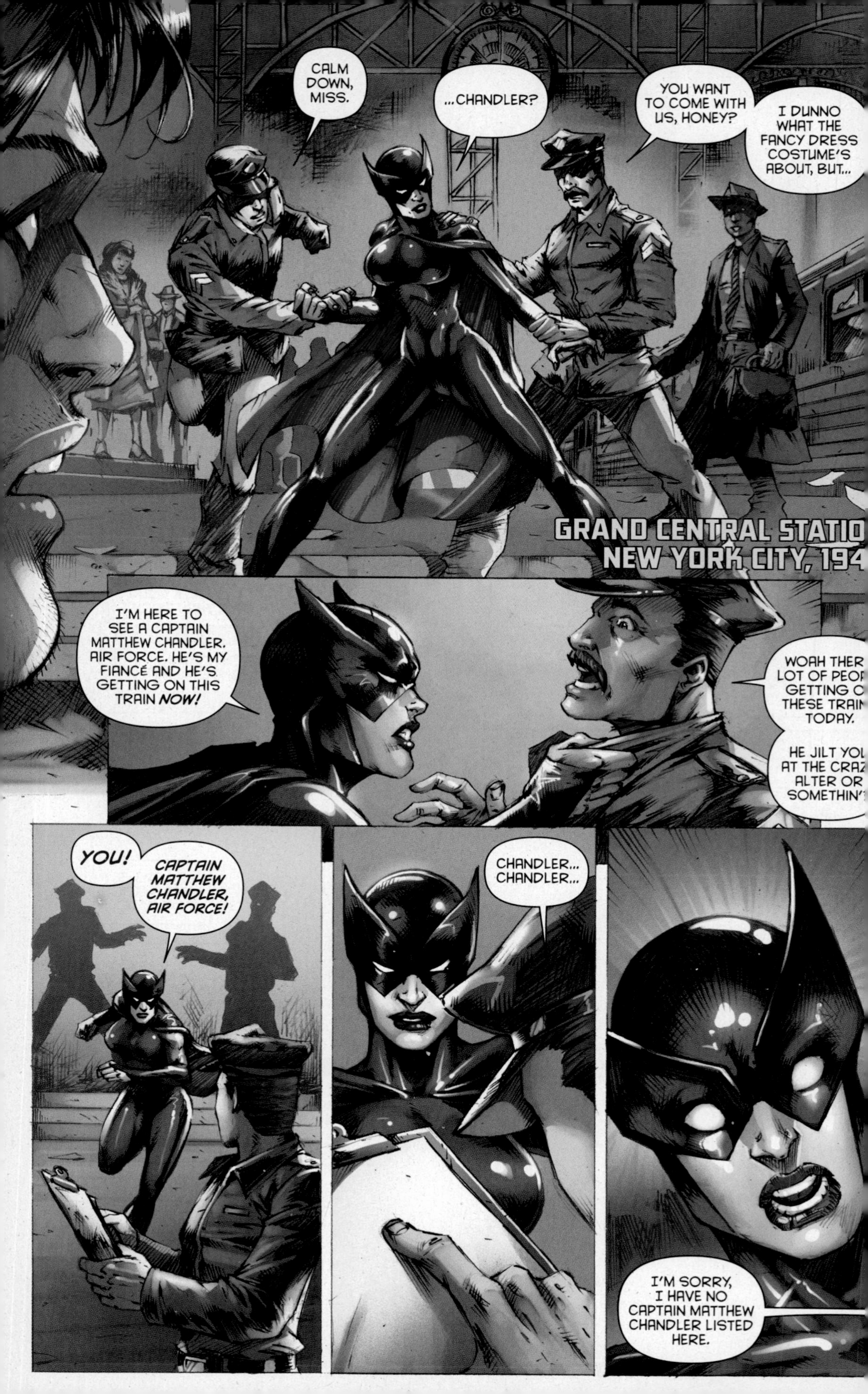
CALM DOWN, MISS.
...CHANDLER?
YOU WANT TO COME WITH US, HONEY?
I DUNNO WHAT THE FANCY DRESS COSTUME'S ABOUT, BUT...
GRAND CENTRAL STATIO
NEW YORK CITY, 194
I'M HERE TO SEE A CAPTAIN MATTHEW CHANDLER. AIR FORCE. HE'S MY FIANCÉ AND HE'S GETTING ON THIS TRAIN NOW!
WOAH THER LOT OF PEOP GETTING O THESE TRAIN TODAY.
HE JILT YO AT THE CRAZ ALTER OR SOMETHIN'
YOU!
CAPTAIN MATTHEW CHANDLER, AIR FORCE!
CHANDLER... CHANDLER...
I'M SORRY, I HAVE NO CAPTAIN MATTHEW CHANDLER LISTED HERE.

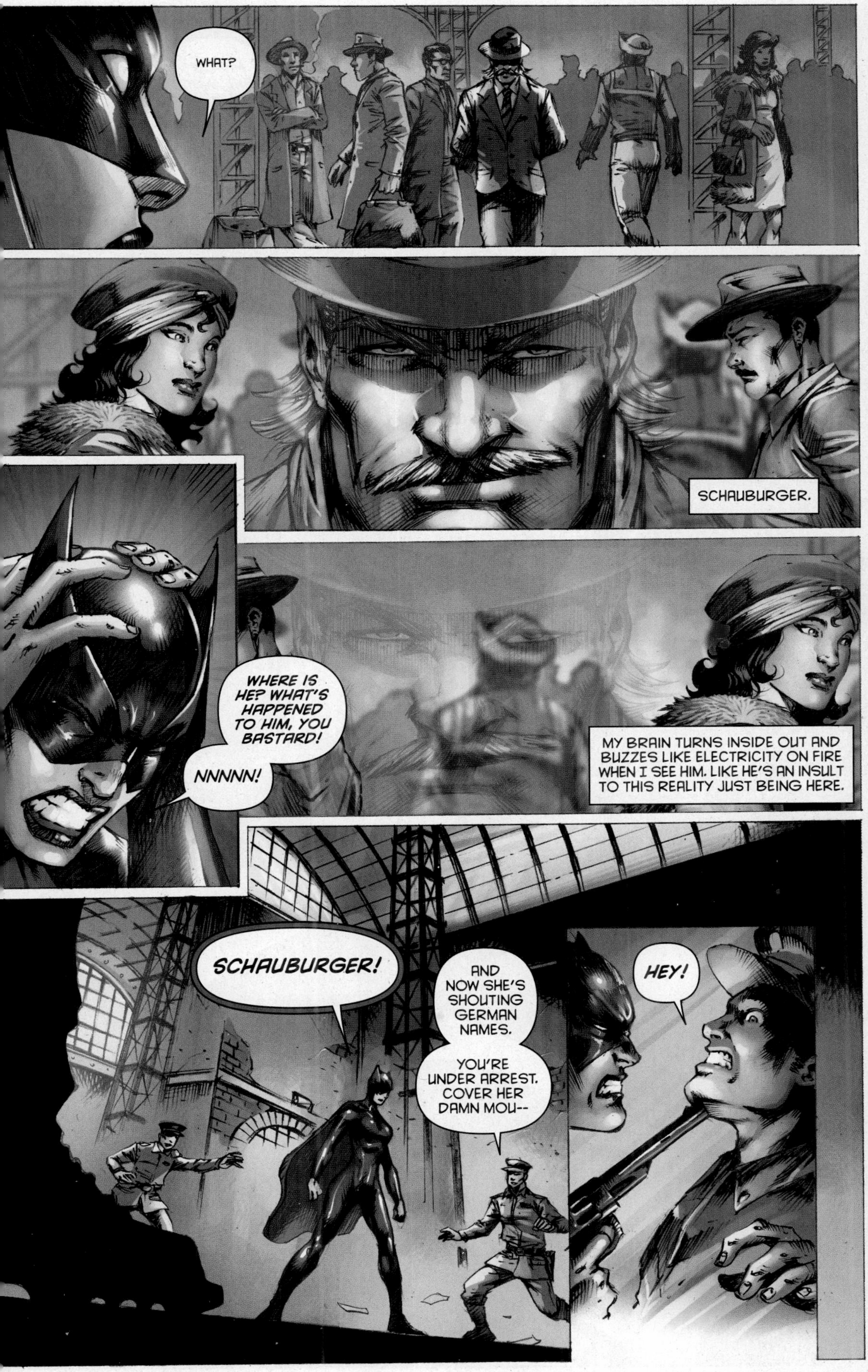
WHAT?
SCHAUBURGER.
WHERE IS HE? WHAT'S HAPPENED TO HIM, YOU BASTARD!
NNNNN!
MY BRAIN TURNS INSIDE OUT AND BUZZES LIKE ELECTRICITY ON FIRE WHEN I SEE HIM. LIKE HE'S AN INSULT TO THIS REALITY JUST BEING HERE.
SCHAUBURGER!
AND NOW SHE'S SHOUTING GERMAN NAMES.
YOU'RE UNDER ARREST. COVER HER DAMN MOU--
HEY!

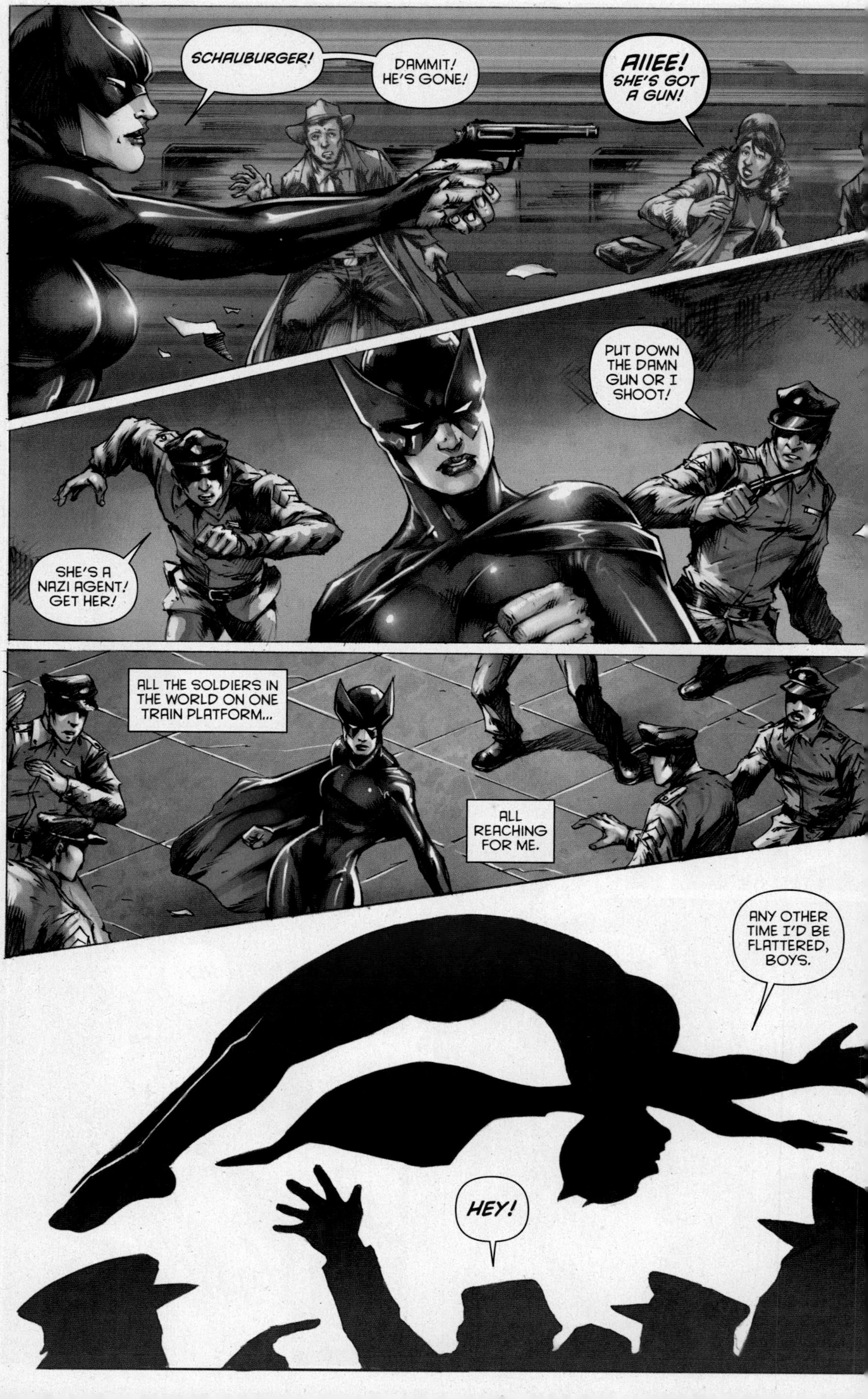
SCHAUBURGER!
DAMMIT! HE'S GONE!
AIIEE! SHE'S GOT A GUN!
PUT DOWN THE DAMN GUN OR I SHOOT!
SHE'S A NAZI AGENT! GET HER!
ALL THE SOLDIERS IN THE WORLD ON ONE TRAIN PLATFORM...
ALL REACHING FOR ME.
ANY OTHER TIME I'D BE FLATTERED, BOYS.
HEY!

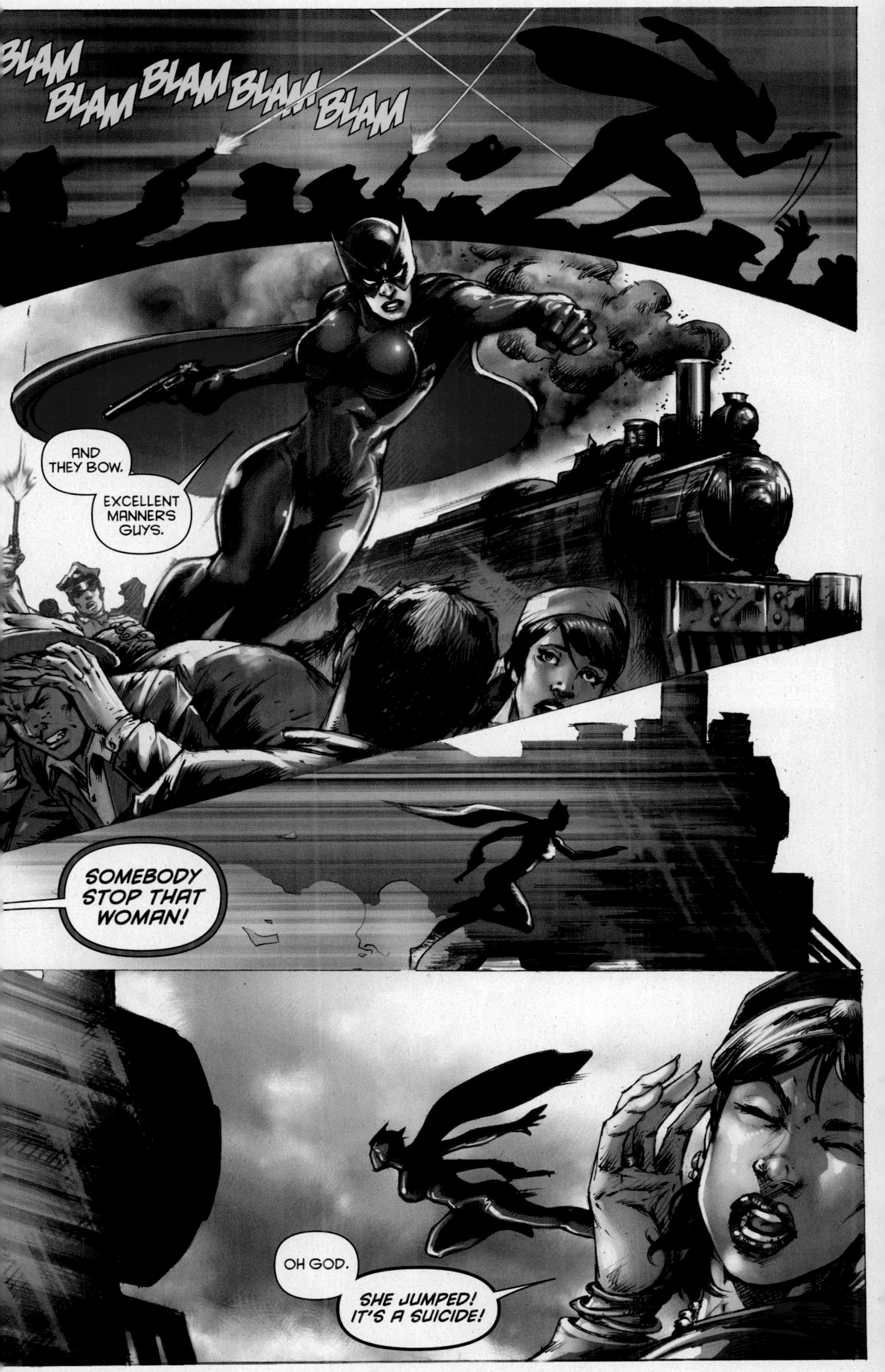
BLAM BLAM BLAM BLAM BLAM
AND THEY BOW.
EXCELLENT MANNERS GUYS.
SOMEBODY STOP THAT WOMAN!
OH GOD.
SHE JUMPED! IT'S A SUICIDE!

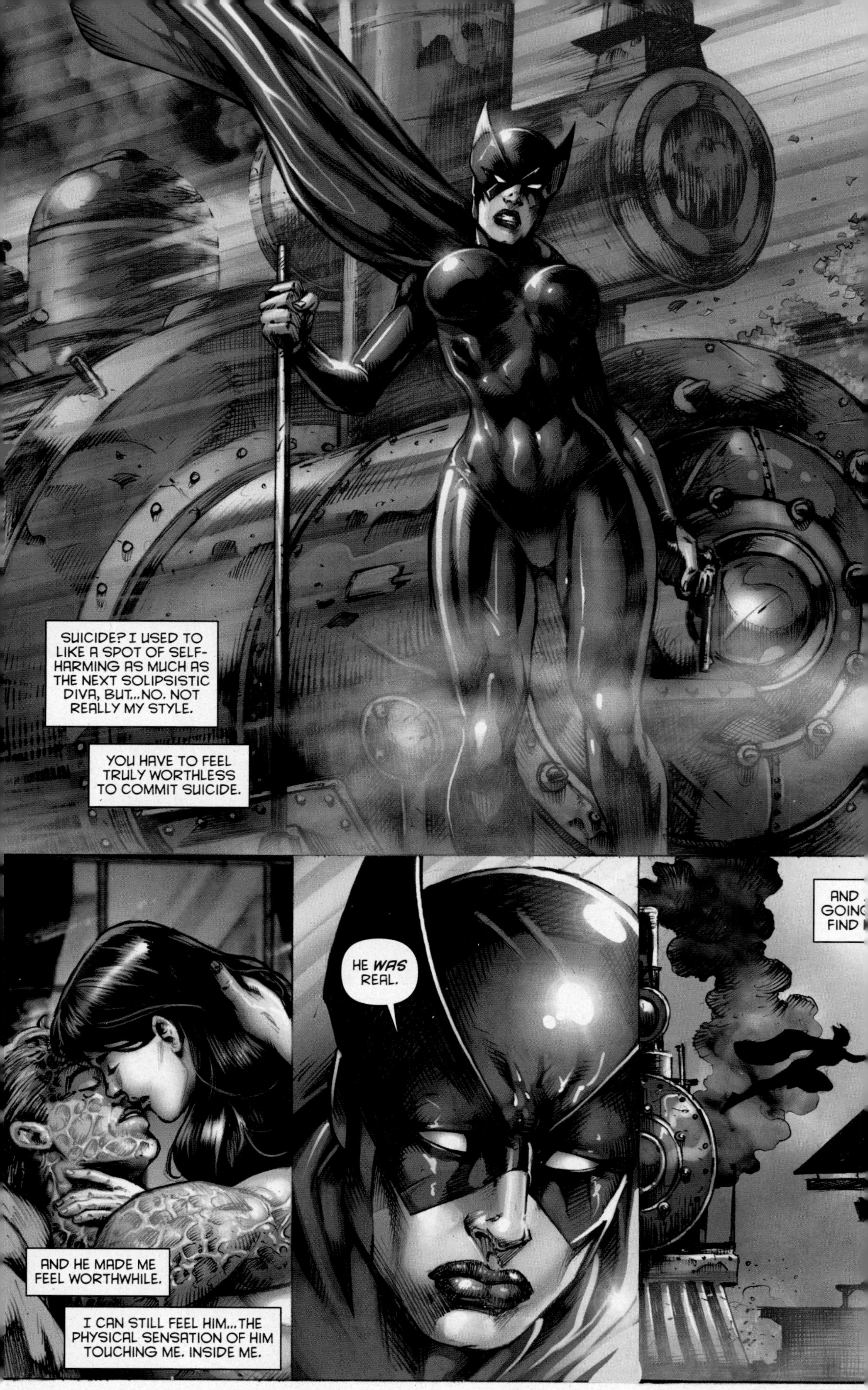
SUICIDE? I USED TO LIKE A SPOT OF SELF-HARMING AS MUCH AS THE NEXT SOLIPSISTIC DIVA, BUT...NO. NOT REALLY MY STYLE.
YOU HAVE TO FEEL TRULY WORTHLESS TO COMMIT SUICIDE.
AND HE MADE ME FEEL WORTHWHILE.
I CAN STILL FEEL HIM...THE PHYSICAL SENSATION OF HIM TOUCHING ME. INSIDE ME.
HE *WAS* REAL.

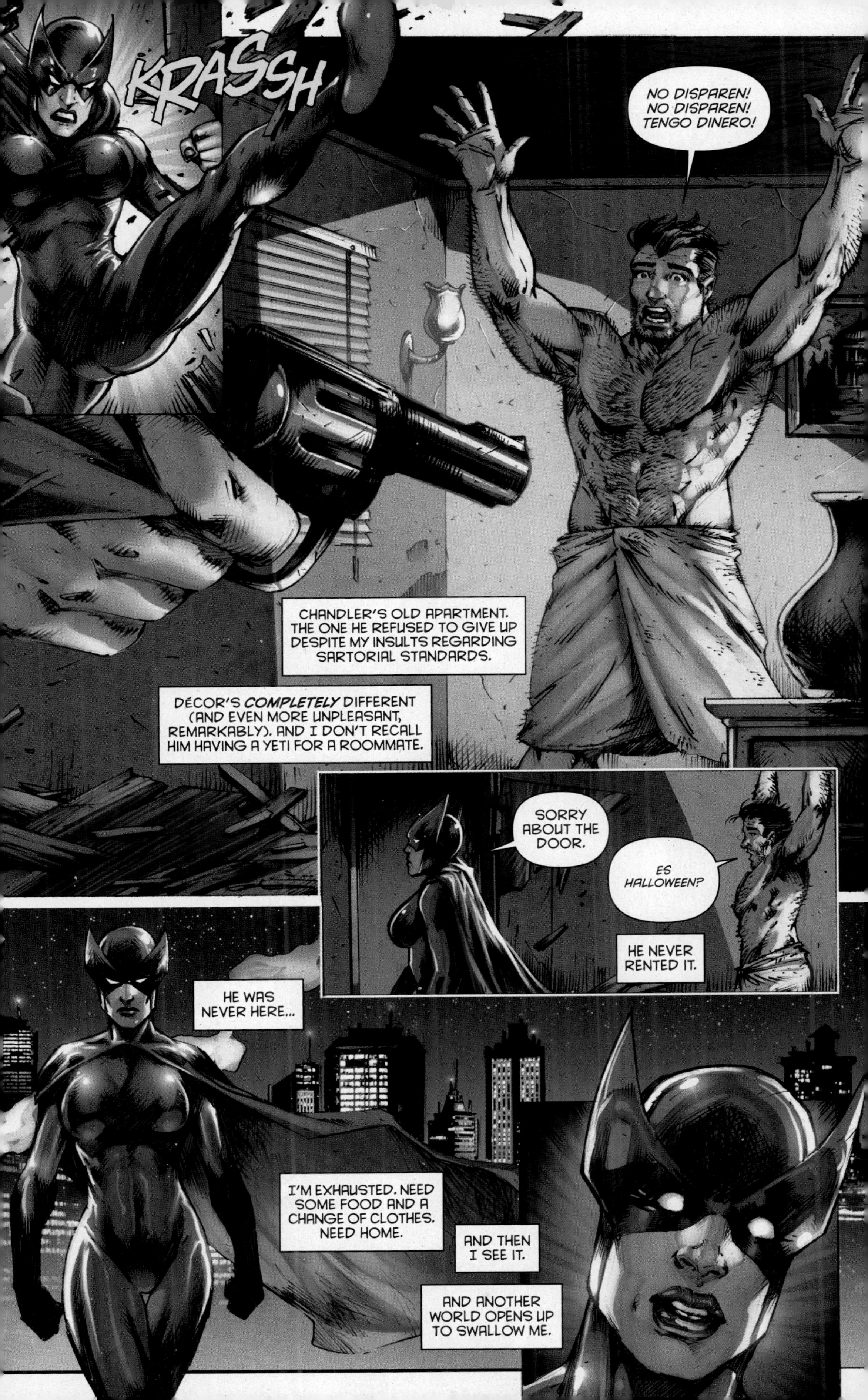
KRASSH
NO DISPAREN! NO DISPAREN! TENGO DINERO!
CHANDLER'S OLD APARTMENT. THE ONE HE REFUSED TO GIVE UP DESPITE MY INSULTS REGARDING SARTORIAL STANDARDS.
DÉCOR'S COMPLETELY DIFFERENT (AND EVEN MORE UNPLEASANT, REMARKABLY). AND I DON'T RECALL HIM HAVING A YETI FOR A ROOMMATE.
SORRY ABOUT THE DOOR.
ES HALLOWEEN?
HE NEVER RENTED IT.
HE WAS NEVER HERE...
I'M EXHAUSTED. NEED SOME FOOD AND A CHANGE OF CLOTHES. NEED HOME.
AND THEN I SEE IT.
AND ANOTHER WORLD OPENS UP TO SWALLOW ME.

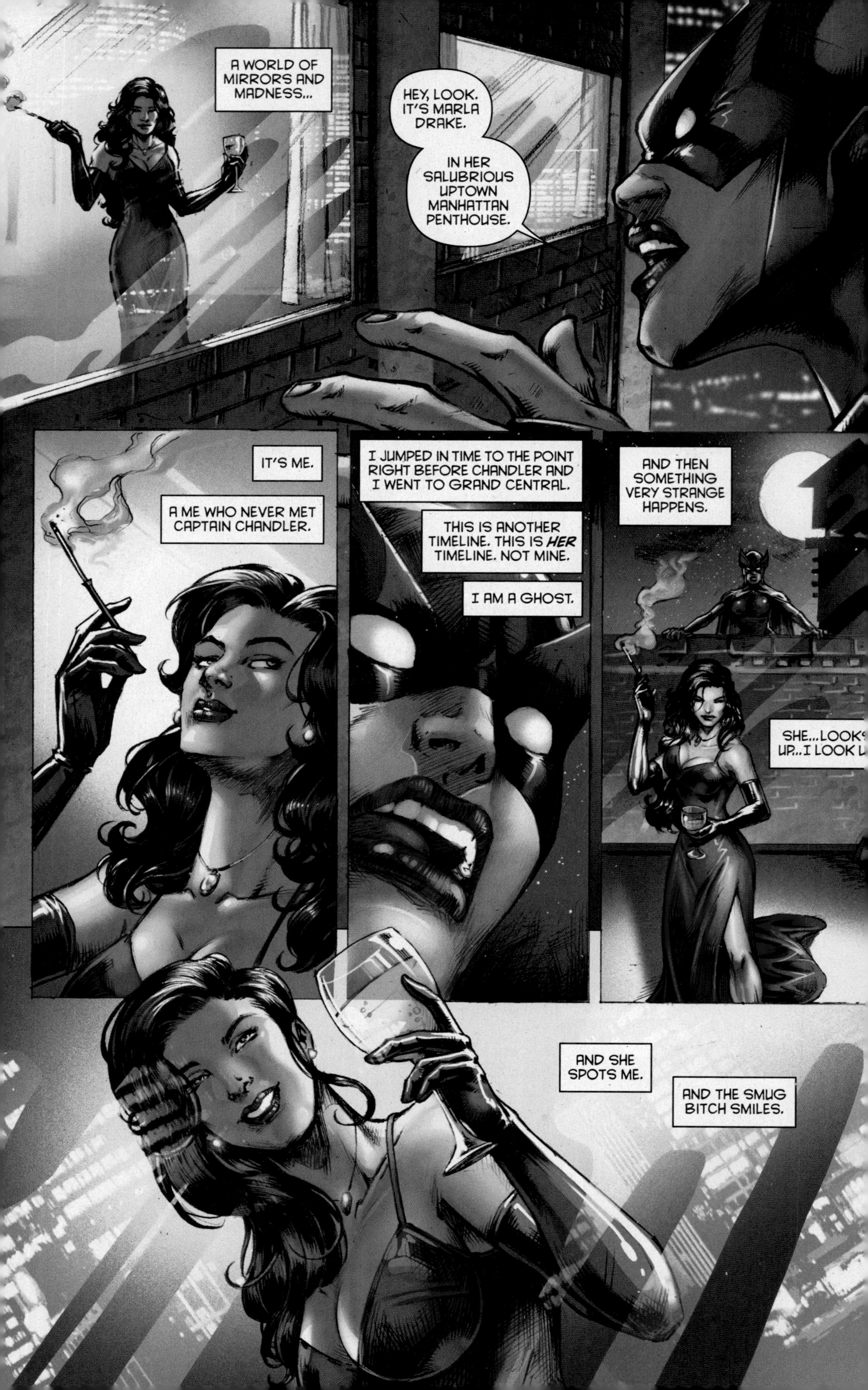
A WORLD OF MIRRORS AND MADNESS...
HEY, LOOK. IT'S MARLA DRAKE.
IN HER SALUBRIOUS UPTOWN MANHATTAN PENTHOUSE.
IT'S ME.
A ME WHO NEVER MET CAPTAIN CHANDLER.
I JUMPED IN TIME TO THE POINT RIGHT BEFORE CHANDLER AND I WENT TO GRAND CENTRAL.
THIS IS ANOTHER TIMELINE. THIS IS *HER* TIMELINE. NOT MINE.
I AM A GHOST.
AND THEN SOMETHING VERY STRANGE HAPPENS.
AND SHE SPOTS ME.
AND THE SMUG BITCH SMILES.

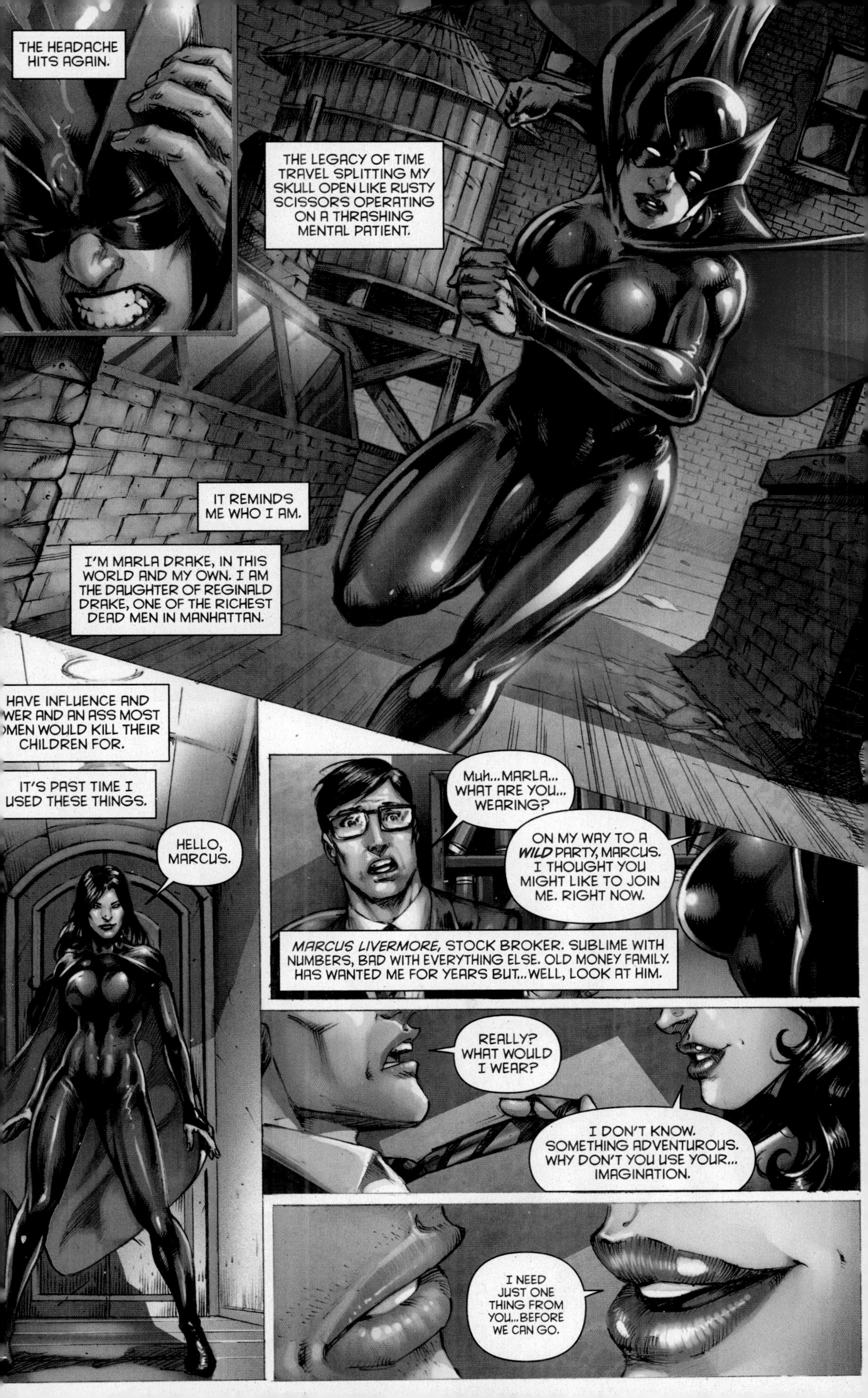
THE HEADACHE HITS AGAIN.
THE LEGACY OF TIME TRAVEL SPLITTING MY SKULL OPEN LIKE RUSTY SCISSORS OPERATING ON A THRASHING MENTAL PATIENT.
IT REMINDS ME WHO I AM.
I'M MARLA DRAKE, IN THIS WORLD AND MY OWN. I AM THE DAUGHTER OF REGINALD DRAKE, ONE OF THE RICHEST DEAD MEN IN MANHATTAN.
HAVE INFLUENCE AND WER AND AN ASS MOST OMEN WOULD KILL THEIR CHILDREN FOR.
IT'S PAST TIME I USED THESE THINGS.
HELLO, MARCUS.
Muh... MARLA... WHAT ARE YOU... WEARING?
ON MY WAY TO A *WILD* PARTY, MARCUS. I THOUGHT YOU MIGHT LIKE TO JOIN ME. RIGHT NOW.
*MARCUS LIVERMORE,* STOCK BROKER. SUBLIME WITH NUMBERS, BAD WITH EVERYTHING ELSE. OLD MONEY FAMILY. HAS WANTED ME FOR YEARS BUT... WELL, LOOK AT HIM.
REALLY? WHAT WOULD I WEAR?
I DON'T KNOW. SOMETHING ADVENTUROUS. WHY DON'T YOU USE YOUR... IMAGINATION.
I NEED JUST ONE THING FROM YOU... BEFORE WE CAN GO.

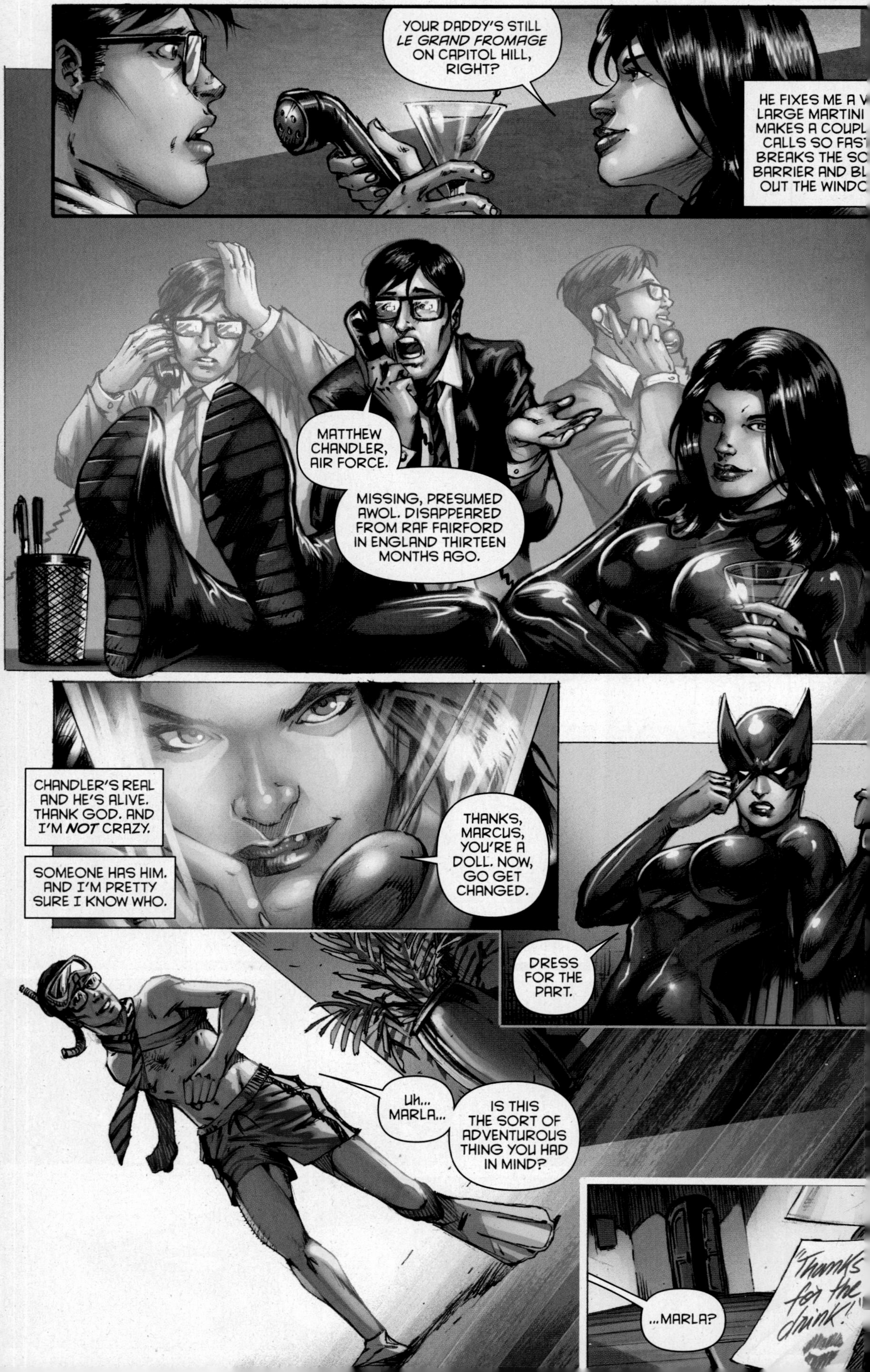

YOUR DADDY'S STILL *LE GRAND FROMAGE* ON CAPITOL HILL, RIGHT?
MATTHEW CHANDLER, AIR FORCE.
MISSING, PRESUMED AWOL. DISAPPEARED FROM RAF FAIRFORD IN ENGLAND THIRTEEN MONTHS AGO.
CHANDLER'S REAL AND HE'S ALIVE. THANK GOD. AND I'M ***NOT*** CRAZY.
SOMEONE HAS HIM. AND I'M PRETTY SURE I KNOW WHO.
THANKS, MARCUS, YOU'RE A DOLL. NOW, GO GET CHANGED.
DRESS FOR THE PART.
UH... MARLA...
IS THIS THE SORT OF ADVENTUROUS THING YOU HAD IN MIND?
...MARLA?
"Thanks for the drink!"

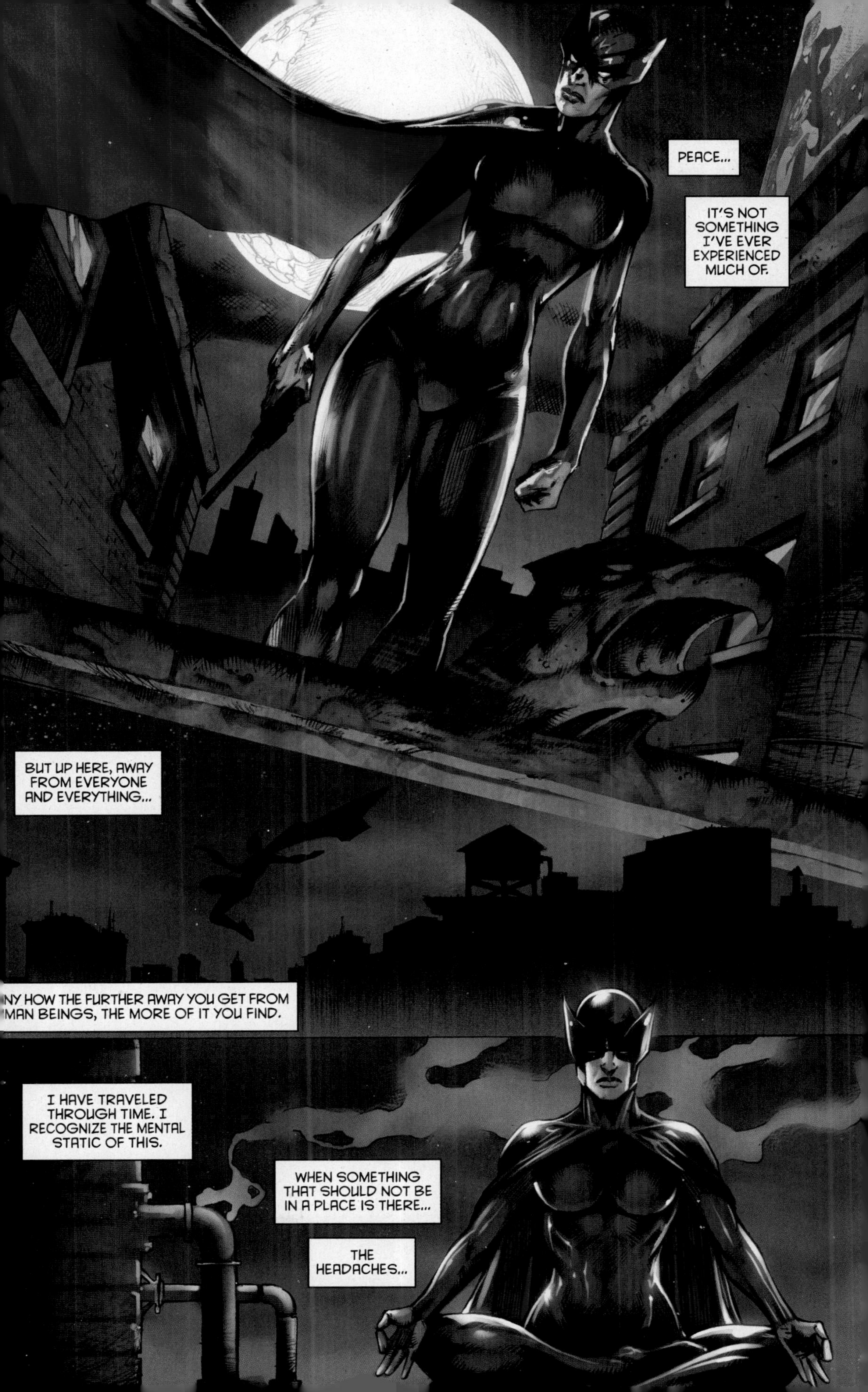
PEACE...
IT'S NOT SOMETHING I'VE EVER EXPERIENCED MUCH OF.
BUT UP HERE, AWAY FROM EVERYONE AND EVERYTHING...
NY HOW THE FURTHER AWAY YOU GET FROM
MAN BEINGS, THE MORE OF IT YOU FIND.
I HAVE TRAVELED THROUGH TIME. I RECOGNIZE THE MENTAL STATIC OF THIS.
WHEN SOMETHING THAT SHOULD NOT BE IN A PLACE IS THERE...
THE HEADACHES...

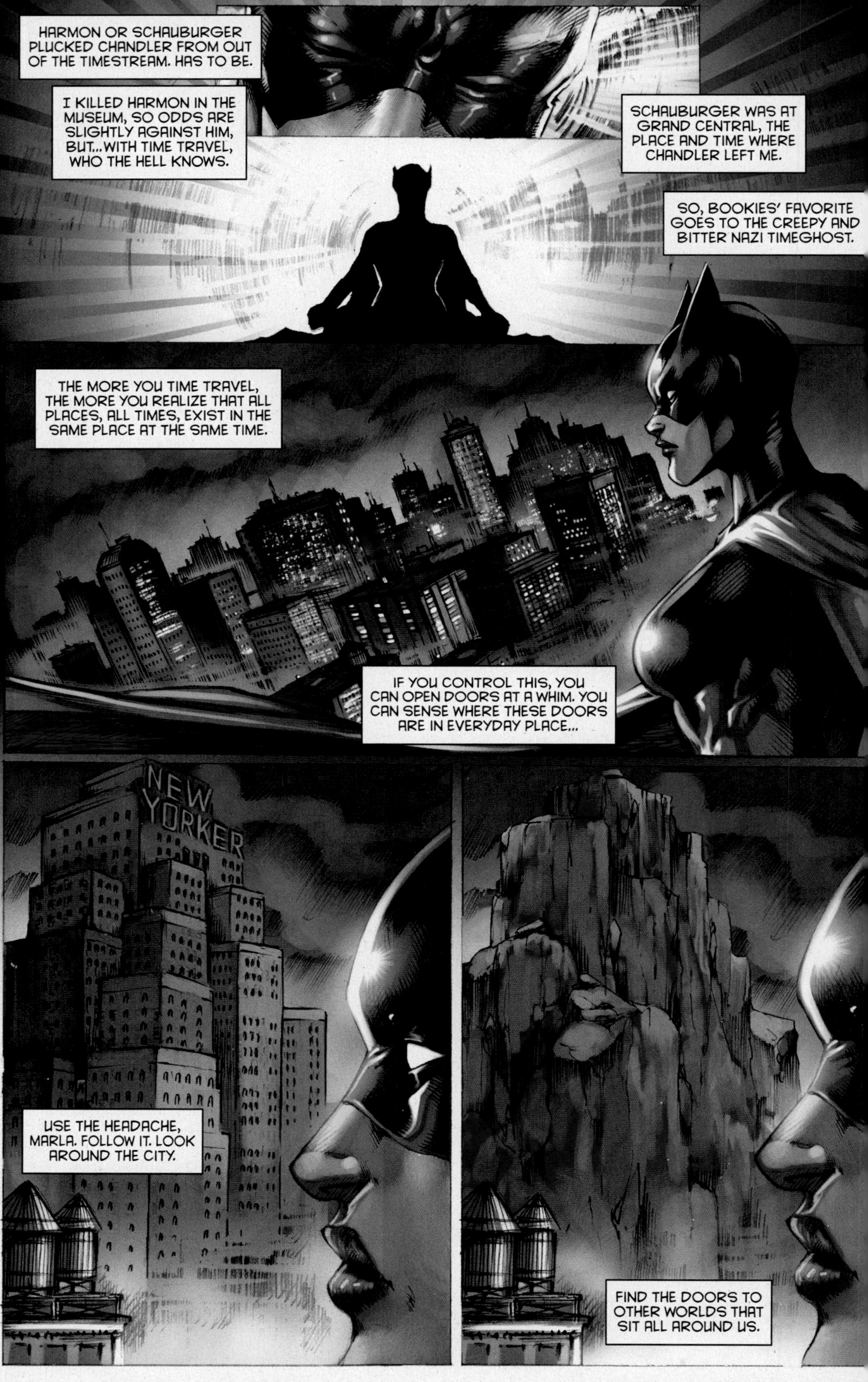
HARMON OR SCHAUBURGER PLUCKED CHANDLER FROM OUT OF THE TIMESTREAM. HAS TO BE.
I KILLED HARMON IN THE MUSEUM, SO ODDS ARE SLIGHTLY AGAINST HIM, BUT...WITH TIME TRAVEL, WHO THE HELL KNOWS.
SCHAUBURGER WAS AT GRAND CENTRAL, THE PLACE AND TIME WHERE CHANDLER LEFT ME.
SO, BOOKIES' FAVORITE GOES TO THE CREEPY AND BITTER NAZI TIMEGHOST.
THE MORE YOU TIME TRAVEL, THE MORE YOU REALIZE THAT ALL PLACES, ALL TIMES, EXIST IN THE SAME PLACE AT THE SAME TIME.
IF YOU CONTROL THIS, YOU CAN OPEN DOORS AT A WHIM. YOU CAN SENSE WHERE THESE DOORS ARE IN EVERYDAY PLACE...
NEW YORKER
USE THE HEADACHE, MARLA. FOLLOW IT. LOOK AROUND THE CITY.
FIND THE DOORS TO OTHER WORLDS THAT SIT ALL AROUND US.

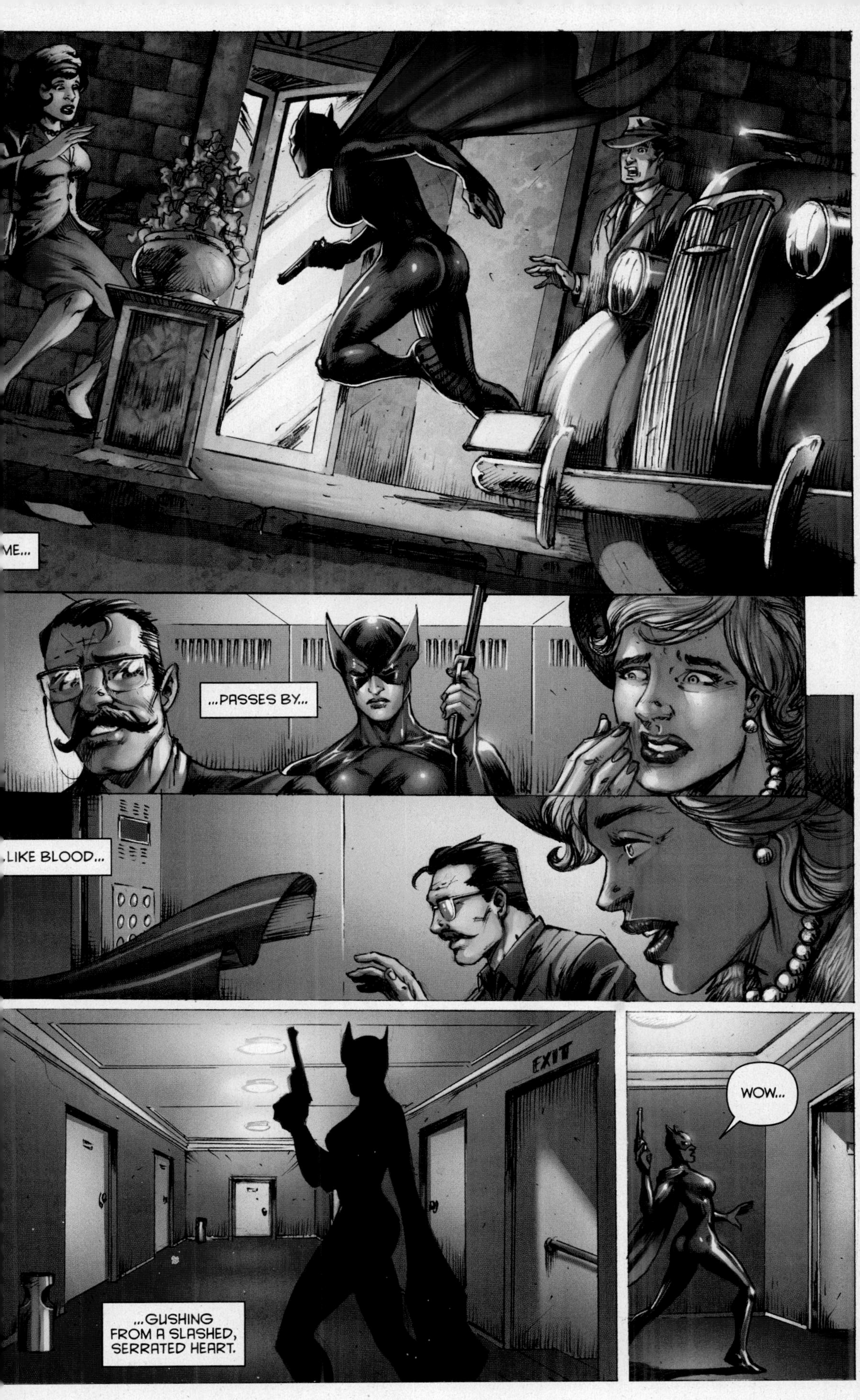
ME...
...PASSES BY...
.LIKE BLOOD...
...GUSHING FROM A SLASHED, SERRATED HEART.
EXIT
WOW...

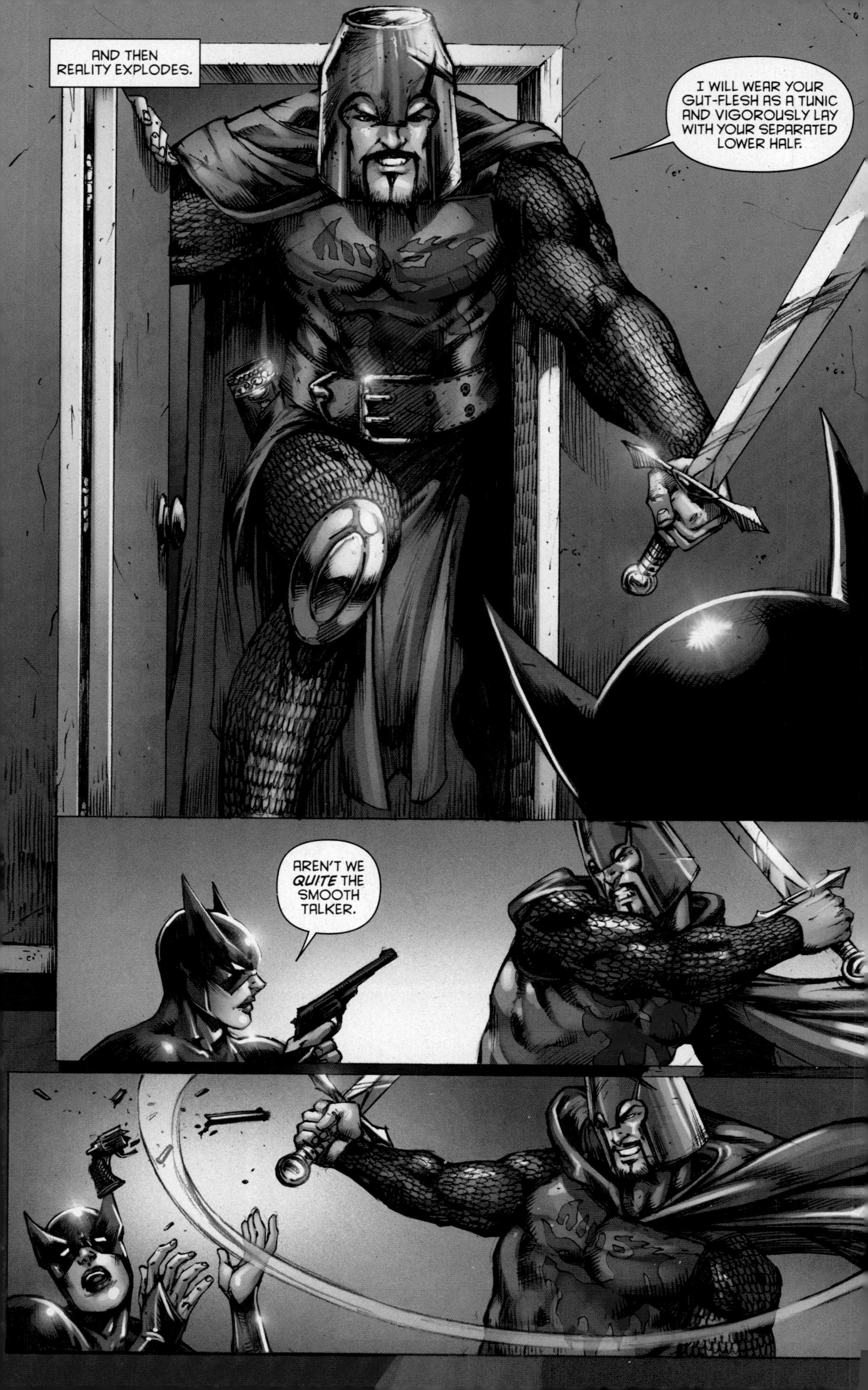
AND THEN REALITY EXPLODES.
I WILL WEAR YOUR GUT-FLESH AS A TUNIC AND VIGOROUSLY LAY WITH YOUR SEPARATED LOWER HALF.
AREN'T WE *QUITE* THE SMOOTH TALKER.

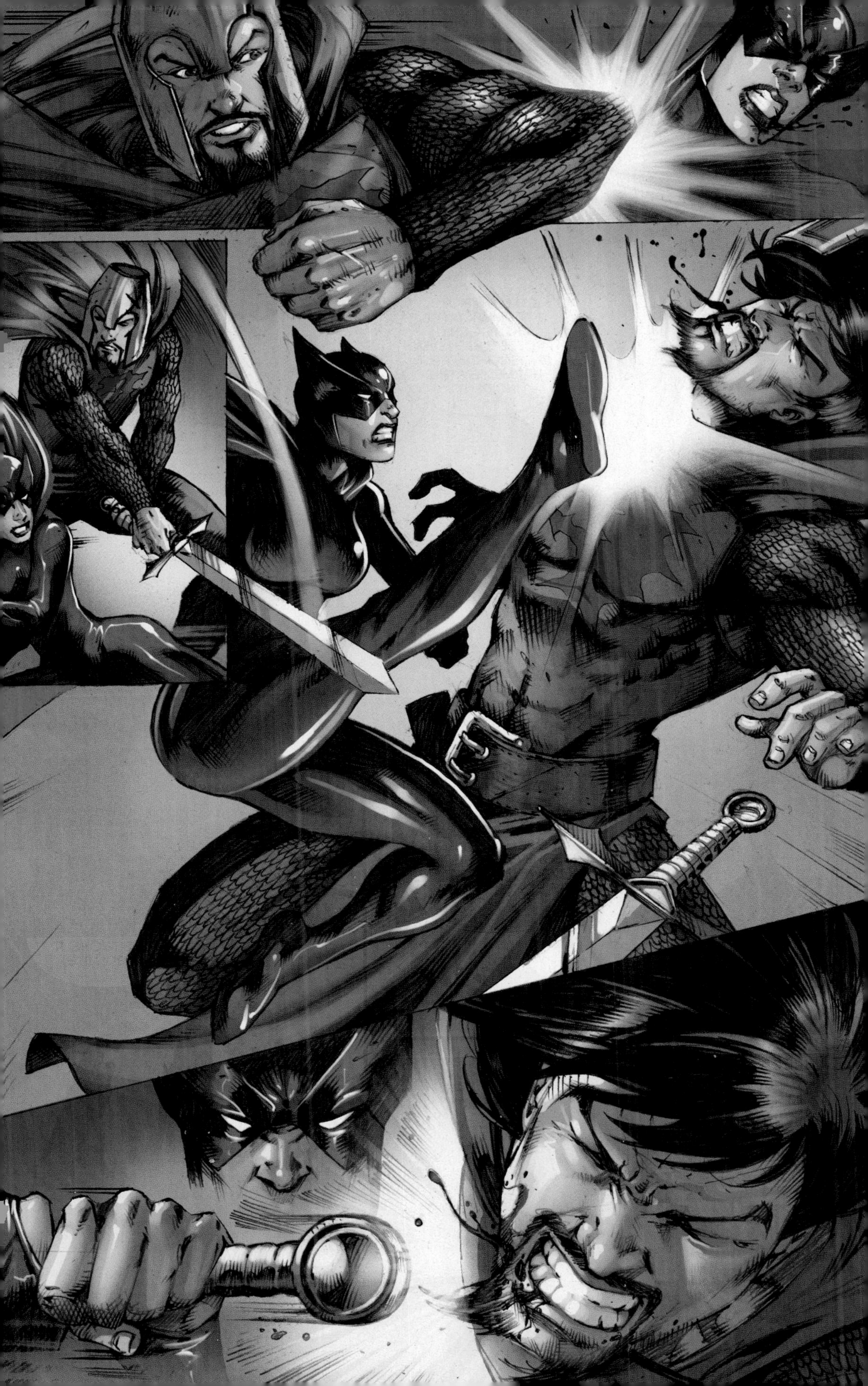

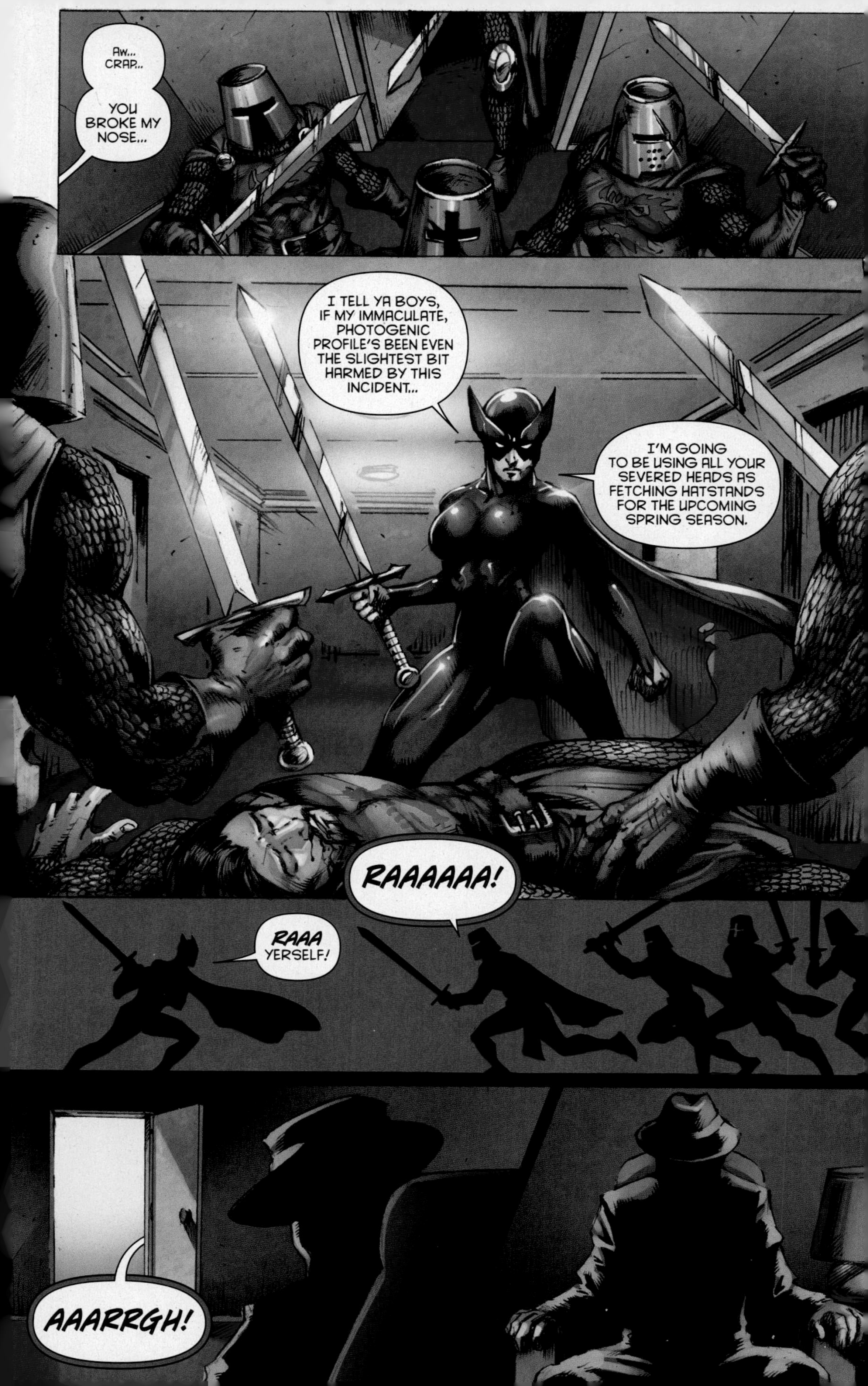
AW... CRAP...
YOU BROKE MY NOSE...
I TELL YA BOYS, IF MY IMMACULATE, PHOTOGENIC PROFILE'S BEEN EVEN THE SLIGHTEST BIT HARMED BY THIS INCIDENT...
I'M GOING TO BE USING ALL YOUR SEVERED HEADS AS FETCHING HATSTANDS FOR THE UPCOMING SPRING SEASON.
RAAAAAA!
RAAA YERSELF!
AAARRGH!

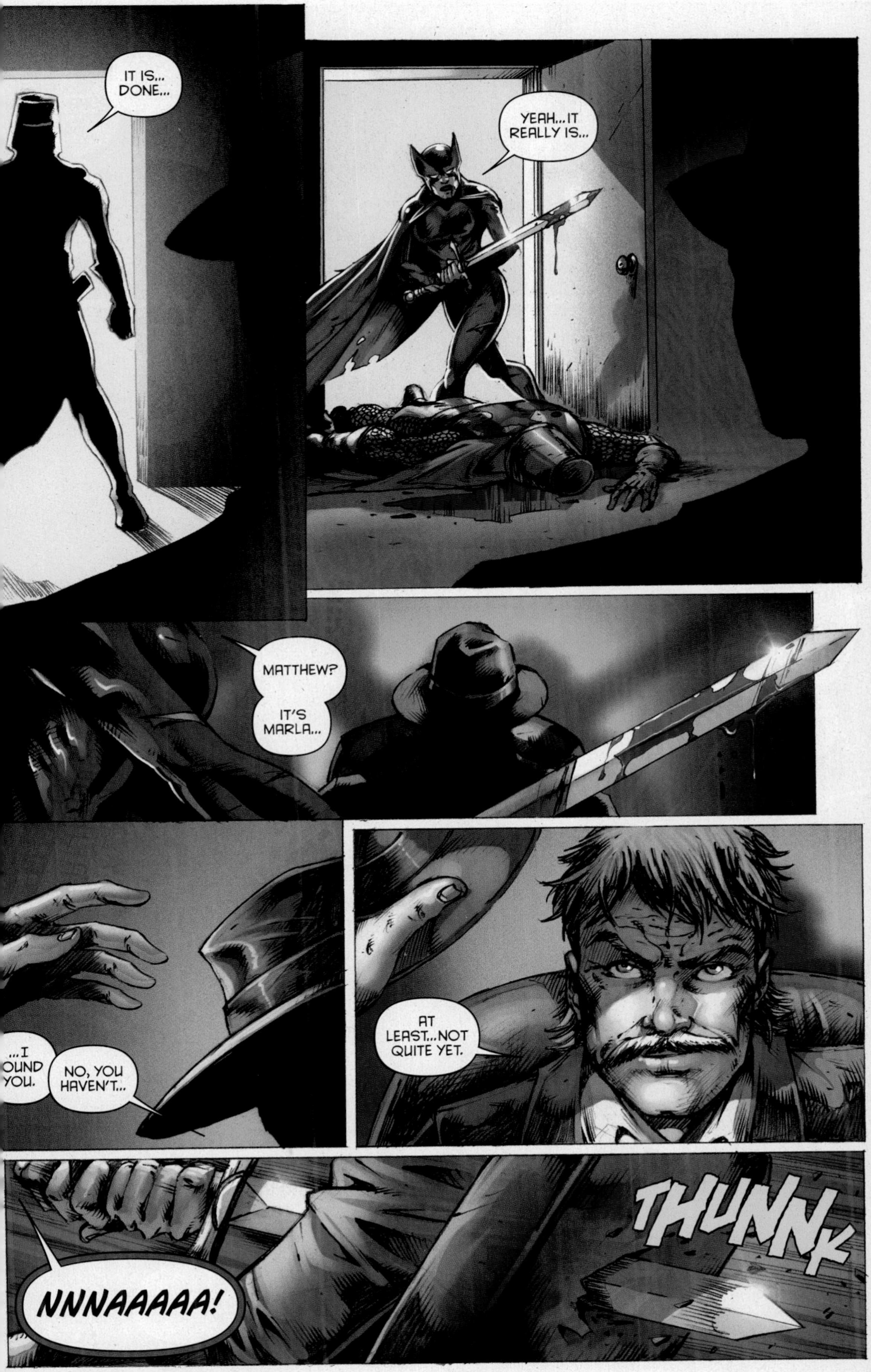
IT IS... DONE...
YEAH...IT REALLY IS...
MATTHEW?
IT'S MARLA...
...I OUND YOU.
NO, YOU HAVEN'T...
AT LEAST...NOT QUITE YET.
THUNNK
NNNAAAAA!

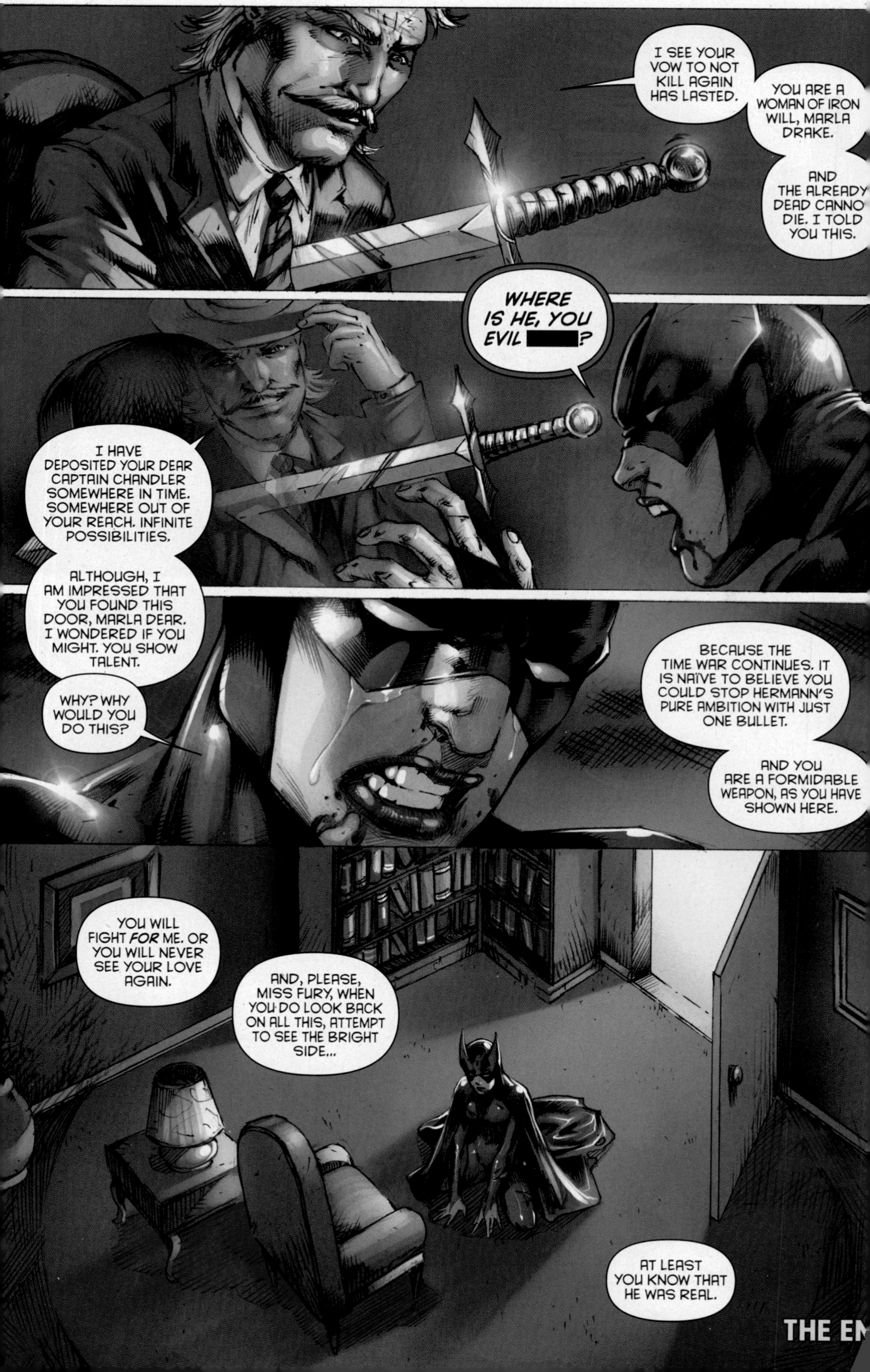
I SEE YOUR VOW TO NOT KILL AGAIN HAS LASTED.
YOU ARE A WOMAN OF IRON WILL, MARLA DRAKE.
AND THE ALREADY DEAD CANNO DIE. I TOLD YOU THIS.
*WHERE IS HE, YOU EVIL* [redacted]*?*
I HAVE DEPOSITED YOUR DEAR CAPTAIN CHANDLER SOMEWHERE IN TIME. SOMEWHERE OUT OF YOUR REACH. INFINITE POSSIBILITIES.
ALTHOUGH, I AM IMPRESSED THAT YOU FOUND THIS DOOR, MARLA DEAR. I WONDERED IF YOU MIGHT. YOU SHOW TALENT.
WHY? WHY WOULD YOU DO THIS?
BECAUSE THE TIME WAR CONTINUES. IT IS NAÏVE TO BELIEVE YOU COULD STOP HERMANN'S PURE AMBITION WITH JUST ONE BULLET.
AND YOU ARE A FORMIDABLE WEAPON, AS YOU HAVE SHOWN HERE.
YOU WILL FIGHT *FOR* ME. OR YOU WILL NEVER SEE YOUR LOVE AGAIN.
AND, PLEASE, MISS FURY, WHEN YOU DO LOOK BACK ON ALL THIS, ATTEMPT TO SEE THE BRIGHT SIDE...
AT LEAST YOU KNOW THAT HE WAS REAL.
THE EN

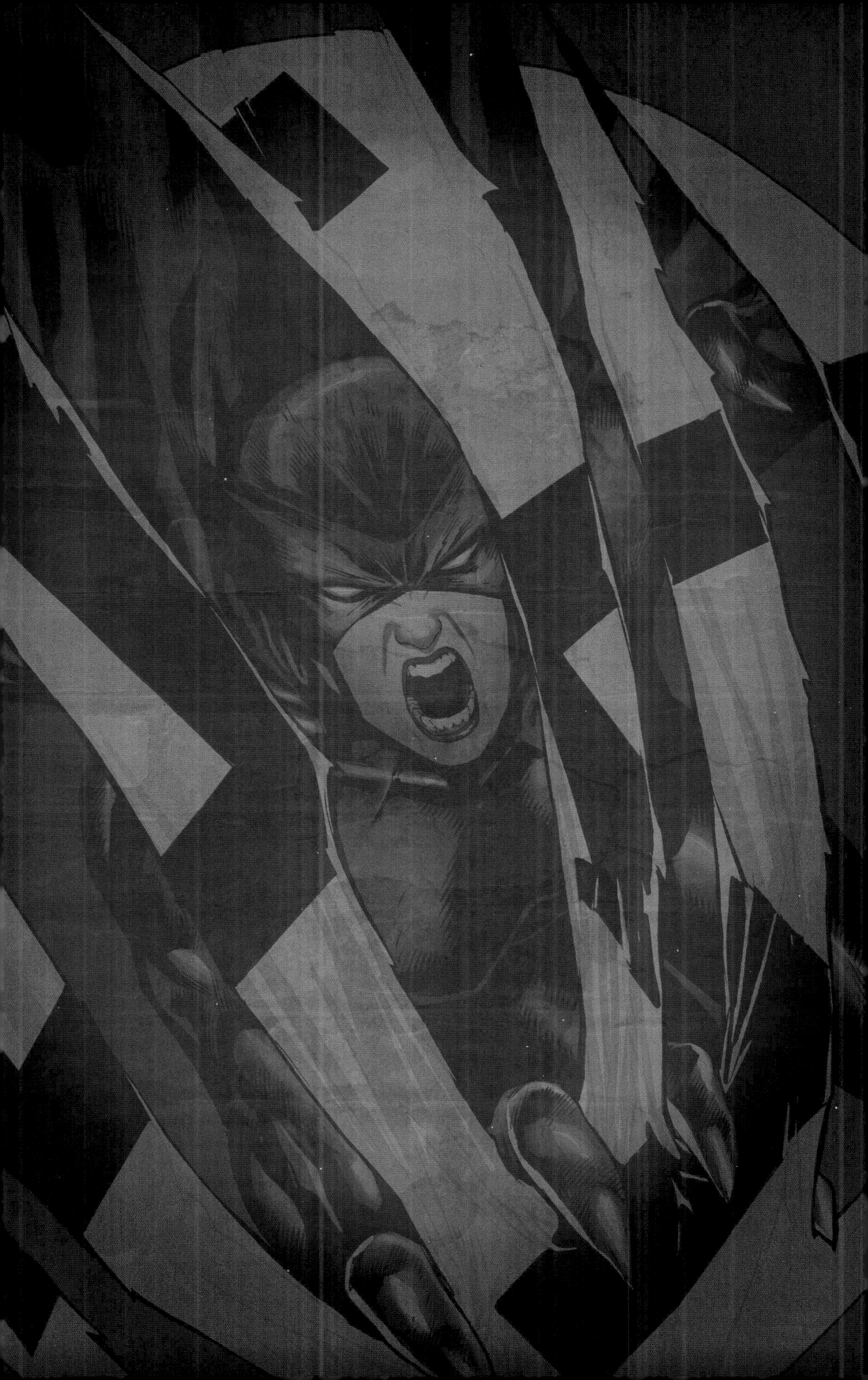

# MISS FURY #1
## WRITTEN BY ROB WILLIAMS

**Page One (Five Page-wide Panels)**

Panel One
A three-panel incremental sequence to open. Massively tight close up on Miss Fury's face – she's in full costume here – but the mask is slightly ripped and she's plainly in the middle of a huge battle. Her teeth are gritted and she's lost in rage and, yes, fury. Slashing her claws across the face and neck of one goon. Blood splatter flies through the air from the damage she's doing to someone. She's fighting four goons here – '40s G-Men types in suits and fedoras with knives and handguns. Don't worry about establishing them or the room. This is all about a close-up on Miss Fury and her incredible fucking RAGE. She's called Miss Fury for a reason and we're going to get to the heart of that in this story. BTW – if this were a movie Miss Fury is played by Olivia Munn from The Newsroom. Plenty of reference here: http://www.imdb.com/media/rm1247652352/nm1601397 In terms of setting, this is all taking place on a Manhattan rooftop at night, but we'll establish that on page two. For now, just go in tight on her and get tighter. Miss Fury is in her main outfit – it's a skin-tight black catsuit with a small red cape. Plenty of reference here: http://tinyurl.com/cmhnnsc **Let's largely stick to the original but with a couple of amends – let's lose the cat ears. She's already way too close to Catwoman. Similar for the cat's tail. Let's lose that. I think the small red cape helps distance the look from Catwoman too, so keep that.**

CAPTION:        "Everyone is doing themselves a weak and cowardly disservice if they don't ask them selves this question…"

Panel Two
Same sequence but even closer in here on Miss Fury's face. If she looked angry last panel she's even angrier here. She's not trying to win a fight, she's lost in red mist. She wants to fucking HURT these people. She wants to hurt everything and everyone. The blood splatter hits her face here. Hitting across her cheek and the edge of her mouth. She lets fly another hit – blood on her claws - as on one of the G-Men grabs her round the shoulders from behind.

NO DIALOGUE

Panel Three
Cut to different scene. Close up on female hands holding a 1940s telegram from Western Union – 'we regret to inform you…' the type of telegram sent to people who've lost loved ones in the war, Reference here http://tinyurl.com/cf4sj65

NO DIALOGUE

Panel Four
Back to the angry sequence but even closer in on her face here. Her rage even HIGHER. The blood's on the edge of her lips, like she's a vampire. She's lost in the rage. Reaching behind her to claw at the eyes of the guy who's grabbed her. Three things should be apparent here – 1) she's incredible badass and a fearsome fighter. 2) She's got serious anger management issues. 3) This is no quippy do-gooder. This is an extremely troubled individual.

CAPTION:        "What are YOU angry about?"

Panel Five
The guy she's been attacking – deep slash marks across his face – much blood - looks up at 'us'/her – fear in his eyes. Pleading! MERCY!

GOON:           Please…
GOON:           … don't.

**Page Two (Six Panels)**

Panel One
Pullback now so we get some context. The 1940s Midtown Manhattan rooftop (this is the museum of natural hoistory, so a beautiful stonework rooftop) at night. Beautiful moonlight shining down, lighting this scene. Empire State Building shining in the background etc. Miss Fury slashes her claws right across the throat of the pleading goon. Ripping his throat out. The other goon – big guy – has his arm around her throat, she's already reaching up to deal with him next. Three other goons are nearby – one is coming in with a knife, one has a luger pistol fitted with a silencer. They're all wearing suits and fedoras. NB – there's a skylight on the roof behind this fight, we'll go crashing through that soon enough. These goons are Nazi agents, as we'll soon see.

LOCATOR: 1943.

FX: SLASSSH!

THROAT RIP GOON: Ack.

Panel Two
Miss Fury reaches up and stabs her claws into the eyes of the goon who had her round the neck. Nasty.

FX: PHLOKK!

GOON: AAAAAHHHHHH!!!!

Panel Three
The goon with the Luger/silencer fires it twice at 'us'/Miss Fury. She's reached over with both hands and grabbed the collars of the now-blind goon.

FX: THONK!!
FX: THONK!!

Panel Four
Miss Fury, with incredible strength and dexterity pulls the now-blind guy right over her head so he comes crashing over her and the bullets pound into him instead.

FX: THONK!!
FX: THONK!!

Panel Five
Miss Fury throws the now dead goon right at the guy with the Luger – amazing strength!

NO DIALOGUE

Panel Six
The remaining goon throws that big old knife with amazing skill right at Miss Fury – its blade whizzing right through the air towards 'us'. It looks utterly sharp and deadly.

FX: WHOOOOSH!!!

**Page Three (Six Panels)**

Panel One
Miss Fury acrobatically grabs the knife from mid-air with phenomenal dexterity, seemingly just barely touching it with her fingertips – she's already turning – going to use the momentum of the knife and send it back.

NO DIALOGUE

Panel Two
She sends it back and it thunks right into the forehead of the goon with the Luger and the silencer.
Deadly.

FX:        THUNK!!!

Panel Three
The goon who did have the knife now looks on, terrified, running his options in a mental panic – no
weapons left. He's edging backwards to the edge of the roof. In the foreground of the shot, very calmly,
Miss Fury coolly kneels down to pick up the luger from the dead goon.

GOON:           Ah…
GOON:           Ah…

MISS FURY:      You know, a really good distraction in the maelstrom of Midtown Midtown is SO dif
                ficult to come by these days.

Panel Four
Miss Fury, looking sensational and cool in the moonlight, points the luger with the silencer, right at 'us'.
And fires it.

MISS FURY:      Jump.
MISS FURY:      Please.

FX:        THONK!

Panel Five
The goon, bug eyed, sweating and terrified, right on the edge of the building, stares at us in shock as his
right knee explodes as the bullet hits it.

MISS FURY (o/s):        And here's your incentive.

FX:        THONK!

Panel Six
We're below the building as the goon falls/jumps off the edge, into mid-air. A lethal fall, this. The build-
ing is the American Museum Of Natural History. Plenty of reference here http://tinyurl.com/c7jw7hr
Man frozen in mid-air, plainly falling to his death.

NO DIALOGUE

**Page Four (Six Panels)**

Panel One
Miss Fury stands on the edge of the building, looking down, that luger in her hand, admiring her handi-
work.

SCHAUBERGER (from behind her):        Death cannot stop us. We are more powerful than that…

Panel Two
Miss Fury whirls around but a brief blast of machine gun fire hits the luger out of her hand. For the first
time she's out of her comfort zone.

FX:        BRAAAPPPP!!

MISS FURY:      AH!

**Panel Three**
Standing on the roof in front of her is a strange old man in suit and fedora. Far older, thinner and STRANGER than the goons thus far. Pure white hair. He's early 70s but somehow looks older, face lined like he's smoked 200 cigarettes a day his entire adult life. He holds a machine gun, pointing at her. And there's intelligence and madness in his eyes. This is a key player in our story. A nazi scientist named Schauberger.

SCHAUBERGER:       Death, by definition, is finite. We are not finite.
SCHAUBERGER:       Time is a lie. We are told that it overpowers us but WE are its masters. We
                   will conquer this land in both times.

**Panel Four**
Same panel/angle but Schauberger flickers weirdly, like he's here but not. Pixelates round the edges slightly. What the hell is this? Is he a ghost, a hologram? No, he's still physically here, but part of him suddenly… isn't. Like he's trapped in time.

SCHAUBERGER:       We HAVE conquered it in both times.

**Panel Five**
Miss Fury, looking confused/worried here. He's got her dead-to-rights.

SCHAUBERGER (o/s):  It has bent to the Fuhrer's will.
SCHAUBERGER (o/s):  And he will bend to mine.

**Panel Six**
Close up on Schauberger here, and the creepy old fuck smiles a knowing smile.

SCHAUBERGER:       The machine is ready. Goodbye, Miss Drake. Enjoy your journey and ask
                   yourself this…
SCHAUBERGER:       Who, exactly, are you REALLY being asked to kill? And by whom?

**Page Five (Five Panels)**

**Panel One**
Schauberger is suddenly shot through the head from someone off panel. He pixelates again ever so lightly as this occurs. But there's no doubting the physical presence he has to be shot through the brain this way.

FX:     BANG!!

**Panel Two**
Miss Fury, shocked, looks up and sees a CIA/OSS agent holding a smoking revolver. He's a mid-thirties, manly, square-jawed type. Good looking, confident. Think Don Draper/Jon Hamm from Mad Men. Wearing a fedora and suit. This is HARMON. He smiles at her.

HARMON:       Nazi agents in New York City.
HARMON:       Right in the heart of America.
HARMON:       Makes you kind of sick, don't it?

**Panel Three**
Harmon kneels and checks Schauberger's pulse on the floor, holding out his OSS badge to show Miss Fury in the process, Miss Fury in the background. Schauberger is quite dead, eyes open. Miss Fury approaches, behind. She's unreadable.

HARMON: Name's Harmon. OSS. I've been tracking this group but they gave me the slip.
HARMON: Glad to see that there's ordinary citizens able to protect America too.
HARMON: Well, I say ordinary…

Panel Four
He looks up at Miss Fury, smiling at her (they're on the same side!).

HARMON: You're one of those new costume adventurers, right?
HARMON: Wadda they call you? Superheroes?

Panel Five
Miss Fury slashes/smashes Harmon across the face with a HUGE hit that'll draw blood, knock him out and seriously mark him. And the look on her face here is just plain mean.

MISS FURY: I'm NOT a superhero.

FX: THWAKKKKKK!!!!

**Page Six (Five Panels)**

Panel One
Pull back for a wide shot. Miss Fury has the roof to herself. Everyone dead or unconscious and bleeding. She looks over to the side to the skylight we established earlier, and it's aglow. Loads of light streaming out of the room below, a huge amount of light. Unnatural amount. This gets her attention.

NO DIALOGUE

Panel Two
We're below the skylight now, looking up out of it. Miss Fury looks down at 'us', leaning on the skylight for a better look. The incredible light shining up.

NO DIALOGUE

Panel Three
Close-up on Miss Fury's face. Shock, amazement, wonder. Light engulfing her, flooding up from below. We're still below the skylight though, and the glass is starting to shatter. Lots of little cracks on the glass. This looks like Miss Fury's face/her mind is cracking.

NO DIALOGUE

Panel Four
Repeat of the telegram panel from page one, panel three.

MISS FURY CAPTION: "Time…"

Panel Five
The glass on the skylight shatters and Miss Fury comes crashing through it, falling down into the source of the light below.

NO DIALOGUE

**Page Seven (Four Panels)**

Panel One
Cut to, in the middle of an astonishing burning flame – the source of this light – an African crown with six huge diamonds in it. The light is burning through and out of those diamonds. We'll pull back in a second for context.

MISS FURY CAPTION:            "... such a PRECIOUS thing."

Panel Two
Miss Fury falling down into the light here, shattered glass around her, and, in her panic, she reaches out towards and for that African crown – the thing she came here to steal, as we'll see. The character's drive appears to be riches, but actually it's time, as we'll see. A wish for times past and lost.

NO DIALOGUE

Panel Three
Pull back now for a wide shot of the room, Miss Fury falling down from the ceiling – and she's falling down into the incredible light that is emanating from a very strange looking piece of machinery. Disappearing into the light. This is a '40s style mad Nazi tech Faraday Machine. A TIME MACHINE, effectively. Go crazy with the mad period tech here. At its heart is the crown and the diamonds, which are powering it. The light its creating is, in fact, a portal. NB – the machine sits at the heart of a large museum room, which we'll return to later. Plenty of ancient artefacts in displays around the room. Time is a theme in this room.

CAPTION:            "Time..."

Panel Four
Thin, page-wide black panel.

CAPTION:            "...switch."

**Page Eight (Five Panels)**

Panel One
Cut to daylight. Close-up on Miss Fury in costume, unharmed, on top of a skyscraper in Manhattan. But this is 2013 Manhattan as we'll see. She's lying down in sniper pose (we'll pull back to show her rifle in a second). She looks like she's woken with a jolt here. Shock on her face. Like she's been startled out of a dream.

MISS FURY:       Huh?

Panel Two
Pull back now and we see that, on a tripod in front of her, is the MOTHER of hi-tech 21st century sniper rifles. Incredible size on this thing, crazy barrel. Think Sienkiewicz Elektra-ish. Don't be afraid to make this thing OTT and oversized. It looks like it could take out an elephant from a mile away. Miss Fury looks at the gun in confusion and shock. In her costume and with this gun she looks like an amazing sleek assassin.

NO DIALOGUE

Panel Three
She gets to her feet, slowly, stunned, looking around. Confusion.

MISS FURY:       What the...

Panel Four
Large panel. Pull back for a widescreen shot now, we're behind Miss Fury as she looks out at the skyline of 21st century, modern-day Manhattan. She's in the future here, as far as she's concerned, and has no clue how she got here.

MISS FURY:       ... hell?

Panel Five
Small, thin black panel again.

LOCATOR:      SWITCH.

**Page Nine (Splash Page)**

Cut to a new scene. 1943. Side on shot Miss Fury, naked in a salubrious bubble bath – and it's a huge art deco bath that only the very rich could afford. The bubbles cover her to an extent, although one leg's stretched out of the bath, the other's playing with the ornate taps. NB – she's wearing long silk gloves that go up to her elbows,, which makes no sense in the bath but we'll reveal why. She's reading a newspaper (and it's a 1943 newspaper). She's beautiful, aloof and aristocratic-looking. Long black hair tied up. Again, go to Olivia Munn for reference. The bath sits in the middle of huge room in a millionaire's apartment in Manhattan, steam rising from it. Oak wood floorboards that shine, they're so well kept. Moneyed paintings on the wall, a candelabra hangs from the centre of the ceiling. Everything in this room says money and luxury. Everything plays as the polar opposite of the dialogue. If people are out there dying and suffering due to World War 2, it's not apparent here. And, what's more, she doesn't give a fuck. She is utterly cocky and confident. If page one said anger, this image says complete nonchalance.

LOCATOR:      1943.

MISS FURY CAPTION:        "There's a war on you know."
MISS FURY CAPTION:        "It's a terrible business."

**Page Ten (Six Panels)**

Panel One
Close-up on Miss Fury's eyes. Her face sweaty from the bath heat. Reading.

NO DIALOGUE

Panel Two
Now we see the front cover of the paper she's reading: THE NEW YORK POST (it's the NY Times but we're changing the title for legal reasons). Reference: http://tinyurl.com/cjxwfhq Same headline too - ROOSEVELT, CHURCHILL MAP 1943 WAR STRATEGY etc.

NO DIALOGUE

Panel Three
Back to Miss Fury's eyes, and she rolls them. Bored.

MISS FURY:      Booooring.

Panel Four
Back to the newspaper but a small story, halfway down and to the left. The headline reads: RWANDAN DIAMOND CROWN COMES TO AMERICAN MUSEUM OF NATURAL HISTORY.

NO DIALOGUE

Panel Five
Close-up on the eyes. She likes this.

MISS FURY:      Not boring.
MISS FURY:      Sparkly.

Panel Six

A few moments later, with her back to us and soap suds dripping down her (she looks sensational), she walks away from the bath, leaving wet foot marks behind her. An effete-haughty-looking plainly furiously gay butler in his early sixties, averting his eyes (he's well trained) holds out a towel for her to take.

MISS FURY:     Prepare my prettiest outfit, please.
MISS FURY:     BOTH my prettiest outfits.

## Page Eleven (Five panels)

Panel One

Out on the sidewalk. Miss Fury in a SENSATIONAL high society dress with gloves going up to her elbows (that cover her lower arms) diamond necklace (why does she need to steal a diamond crown? That's the question here) walks to enter the back of her pure white limousine – the door held open by the same butler. It's a Rolls Royce, obviously. Ref: http://tinyurl.com/cyp5td4 People on the sidewalk look and stare – she looks sensational, she reeks of money in tough times.

CAPTION:       "My name is Marla Drake…"
CAPTION:       "I am one of the wealthiest women in Manhattan and I have the occasional penchant for high-end robbery."

Panel Two

Aerial shot now as we look down on that limo as it drives through the streets of Midtown Manhattan. It stands out, being white and amazing. The streets are as busy as ever – the city full of life and lights. Plenty of amazing reference pics here: http://tinyurl.com/cqrhuy8 The Roller is getting snarled up in traffic here, some drunken revellers spilling into the roads from the sidewalk.

CAPTION:       "A Midtown girl will have her peccadilloes."

Panel Three

Miss Fury in the back of the limo, gazing out at the lights of Times Square as they pass. She looks bored.

CAPTION:       "A life of privilege and riches inherited is a flickering, sensual and glamorous thing."
CAPTION:       "But, where are the challenges?"

Panel Four

Close-up on her now, and she's troubled. But this is more than boredom. There's depression here.

CAPTION:       "Where is the…"

Panel Five

We're in the back of the car now, looking up at her as she gazes up out of the window. One of those sleeves has rolled down and we can see self-inflicted cuts and claw marks on her lower arms. She's a self-harmer. And they're deep too. No cry for help, these.

CAPTION:       "…substance?"

## Page Twelve (Six panels)

Panel One

Out on the busy street as she drives along. Lots of people on the sidewalks. In the middle of them. And the middle of our panel - Schauberger stands there, smiling at 'us' in his evil, creepy, way. Like he knows what's coming.

CAPTION: "In a world of dull comfort the only truly sane thing to do is dress in an African black leopardskin costume and make your own fun…"

Panel Two
Same panel but Schauberger has disappeared. Like he was never there.

CAPTION: "Hmmm…"
CAPTION: "… strange."

Panel Three
Miss Fury in the back of the limo now, lost in thought.

CAPTION: "It was on my trip to Kenya, my present from daddy on my 21st birthday, that my 'alter ego' first presented itself."
CAPTION: "Another identity…"

Panel Four
Cut to a campfire at night in the Masai Mara. A hunky, manly late-thirties western white hunter type – Tyron Woodrell - shielding a seemingly terrified Miss Fury (in impeccable safari garb etc) as a huge bull elephant approaches them and angrily stomps its feet at them. He has a large hunting shotgun in his hands. She's playing the part of the terrified heroine. He the gallant hero. Very clichéd and stereotypical, this image. Think a young Oliver Reed for Woodrell.

CAPTION: "Daddy had hired the legendary and oh-so-gallant English aristocratic adventurer Tyron Woodrell to be my guide across the Savannah."
CAPTION: "Such adventures we had!"

Panel Five
Cut to Woodrell being a right shit to some Masai men who are carrying their gear, hitting one small Masai tribesman his shotgun belt right across the jaw, knocking out teeth. The man's plainly an enormous bully. Miss Fury looks on.

CAPTION: "Unfortunately the only thing Woodrell liked more than the endless sound of his tiresome tales of personal glory was bullying and brutalising our Masai Safari helpers."
CAPTION: "He beat one boy to-death for accidentally dropping and losing one of the myriad elephant tusks he had taken as his prize."

Panel Six
Woodrell, oppressively coming onto Miss Fury here against a tree – his strong arm barring her way from leaving. Smug smile on his face. Very drunk. She plainly finds him rather disgusting.

CAPTION: "The Masai helpers rather tired of his company from that point on."
CAPTION: "As did I of his increasingly numerous whiskey-soaked advances…"

**Page Thirteen (Five panels)**

Panel One
Cut to Woodrell tied to a wooden stake, panic written on his face as a pack of hungering, slavering hyenas approach him. He's been left as dinner.

CAPTION: "After that a mutual agreement was made that I would press on with the Masai and Woodrell would be free to enjoy the African plains at his leisure."
CAPTION: "I helped agree an appropriate severance package and thanked him for his service."
CAPTION: "There were no hard feelings."

Panel Two

As the Masai group and Miss Fury walk through the bush, she exchanges a glance with a tall, hunky, muscled Masai tribesman. Sexual chemistry here.

CAPTION:        "After that, the trip was FAR more relaxed."
CAPTION:        "The landscape quite breathtaking..."

Panel Three
Around a campfire at night, with colourful markings on both their faces, the Masai tribesman hands Miss Fury a wooden cup with a potion in it. This is the start of a magic ritual. The other Masai people sat around the fire. Similar markings.

CAPTION:        "One of the Masai, a striking figure called Kapalei, befriended me and offered me a local potion one night."
CAPTION:        "Combined with a magic ritual and the implicit local hallucinogenic he claimed it would provide me with GREAT superhuman powers."

Panel Four
Large panel. 'Crane' shot now as we're above the camp as rains pour down at biblical levels. All the Masai and Miss Fury are dancing, raising their arms to the heavens and as naked as the day is born. This looks like a magical ceremony. Off to the side is jungle.

CAPTION:        "Although, to be fair, he may have just been trying it on."

Panel Five
Ground level shot now of the same scene and lightning fills the skies as they dance. This sure seems like a magical scene where great power is being embued. The rain crashes down.

NO DIALOGUE

**Page Fourteen (Three panels)**

Panel One
Miss Fury and Kapalei turn towards 'us' as something large emerges from the jungle shrubbery and they see it – not fear in their eyes but fascination. Both they and the other Masai tribespeople are tripping their arses off here. Miss Fury reaches down to the ground to pick up a large Masai knife. Rain still hammering down.

CAPTION:        "Certainly, something changed in me that night."

Panel Two
Large panel as a HUGE black panther – this is enhanced by the hallucinogenic to look like the king of all panthers. Emerges from the jungle darkness towards them, to attack.

CAPTION:        "The cripplingly dull futility of high society conventions fell away and instead I was empowered by something other..."

Panel Three
Large panel. The huge panther leaps through the air towards Miss Fury, to attack as a lightning bolt flashes across the sky, she goes for the animal's heart with her knife, meeting the attack with equal ferocity.

CAPTION:        "I was alive for the first time."

Panel Four
Miss Fury, covered in blood – the panther's - in bed with the Masai guy in one of their tents. But she's on top. She's in command. Let's not make this too explicit, eh? But it's pretty obvious what's occurring.

CAPTION:        "Yes...."
CAPTION:        "I did enjoy the Dark Continent."

## Page Fifteen (Five Panels)

Panel One
Cut to an plush late 1930s ocean liner travelling across the sea. Heading home.

CAPTION:        "After that the gowns and courting politics of Manhattan aristocracy seemed trivial to the point of agony."

Panel Two
Miss Fury, politely dressed, on the deck of the ship. She looks sad.

CAPTION:        "Father passed away from a heart attack during my journey home. Word reached me that I was now alone in the world."

CAPTION:        "Little changed. He had been an awkward, distant man with strict, strange rules for his only child."

CAPTION:        "But he was my only remaining blood and now he was gone."

Panel Three
We're behind the liner now as it comes into dock in 1930s Manhattan. Spires gleaming.

CAPTION:        "I had money."
CAPTION:        "But I had always had money..."

Panel Four
Miss Fury leaving the ship, coming down the gangway, she looks sad. Lots of people around. Big crowd getting off the ship.

CAPTION:        "I had experienced the wonder of a fleeting moment of otherness that could not be repeated. Its glory only existed in the fact that it was unique."

CAPTION:        "I was wise enough to be thankful for this but also to realise that to attempt to repeat it would only cause incremental, diving levels of desperation."

Panel Five
Close-up on Miss Fury's amazed face as, through the crowd, she sees someone. And it's a subtle little jaw dropping moment. This is the moment she sees the love of her life for the first time.

CAPTION:        "And then, just as all seemed decay..."
CAPTION:        "The universe showed me something entirely unexpected..."

## Page Sixteen (Four Panels)

Panel One
Large panel. Strong introductory shot of Captain Matthew Chandler. He's a good-looking US Air Force Captain in uniform. He smiles at 'us' as the crowd parts here and it's not a smug smile, despite his good looks. It's a kind smile. There's a good heart in this guy, we can see it. The complication is that half his face is recovering from horrible burns that he suffered in an aeroplane crash. Some of the crowd are parting and staring in horror at him. But he's unaffected. Plenty of WW2 USAF air force uniform reference here. http://tinyurl.com/cw555m8 This is a bombshell moment for Miss Fury. The love of her life emerging unexpectedly from the crowd.

MISS FURY CAPTION:              "Hope."

Panel Two

Miss Fury and Captain Chandler smiling at each other as the crowd moves around them, a frozen moment.

CAPTION:          "His name was Chandler…"
CAPTION:          "He had only come to the dockside that day to pick up his the father of a friend as a favour."

Panel Three
Cut to a repeat of that telegram panel from page one, panel three.

NO DIALOGUE

Panel Four
Entirely black panel again.

LOCATOR:          SWITCH.

## Page Seventeen (Six Panels)

Panel One
Cut to a wide establishing shot of a high society party at the Museum. This is the large room where we saw the time machine earlier. Lots of champagne glasses and entrees on trays. Miss Fury is centre of this panel in her stunning dress (don't forget the long arm length gloves). There's several exhibits dotted around in glass cases. One of them that she's staring at, is the crown with the diamonds in it.

LOCATOR:          1943.

Panel Two
Close-up of the African crown in the case. Those diamonds showing.

NO DIALOGUE

Panel Three
Miss Fury, champagne glass in hand, staring at 'us'/the crown. One of the museum's administrators – a man in his 60s in a tuxedo – leans across and smiles at Miss Fury.

ADMINSTRATOR:          It's wonderful, isn't it?

MISS FURY:          Hmmm…
MISS FURY:          It is, yes.

Panel Four
The administrator leans into Miss Fury. She doesn't even notice him. Just staring at the crowd.

ADMINSTRATOR:          You're Reginald Drake's daughter. I understand.
ADMINSTRATOR:          Great man, Reginald. Great, great man. Very sadly missed. We were happy to enjoy his patronage here at the museum.

MISS FURY:          He was a fucking asshole whose heart finally gave out 50 years after it had ACTUALLY died..

Panel Five
The adminstrator's eyes near pop out of his head and he goes very red. Miss Fury, coolly, hardly looks at him. Still staring at the crown.

ADMINSTRATOR (small):          Ummm… well, yes… ummm… every… every family has its…

MISS FURY:      You came over here either because you're hoping I'll give money to the museum like
                daddy did or because you're a lecherous old man and you'd like to screw me, right?
MISS FURY:      So, which one is it?

ADMINSTRATOR:        (small) The money…

Panel Six
Miss Fury turns and smiles at 'us'/him here. Cocky.

MISS FURY:      I didn't come here to give you money.
MISS FURY:      I came here to work out how I'm going to steal this crown.
MISS FURY:      Tonight.

**Page Eighteen (Six Panels)**

Panel One
The Administrator looks shocked & slightly annoyed.

ADMINISTRATOR:       My god…
ADMINSTRATOR:        The way you speak and act…
ADMINSTRATOR:        Reginald was one of the richest men in America. YOU are one of the richest
                     women in America…
Panel Two
Miss Fury, nonchalant, downs her champagne.

ADMINISTRATOR (o/s):         Why on earth would you want to steal this crown?
ADIMINISTRATOR (o/s):        Don't you have any morals whatsoever?

Panel Three
Full length shot of Miss Fury as she strides away towards us, throwing the empty champagne glass over
her shoulder and not looking, or caring, where it lands. The Administrator, in panic, tries to catch it.

MISS FURY:      Hmm…
MISS FURY:      Aren't those interesting questions.

Panel Four
In the crowd of shocked people in the museum, looking on, we can see SCHAUBERGER, smiling at all
this. Like he knows how it will play out. Miss Fury walking towards him, but she hasn't noticed him
here.

MISS FURY:      I'm rather interested to find out the answers myself.

Panel Five
Schauberger grabs Miss Fury's arm as she passes and smiles at her – she looks him in the eyes, sur-
prised. She doesn't recognise him. Lots of people looking on.

SCHAUBERGER:        I look forward to seeing you on the roof. Tonight.
SCHAUBERGER:        Where our journey begins… and ends.

Panel Six
Miss Fury, slightly unnerved and losing her cool (for once) pushes his hand away.

MISS FURY:      Crazy…

**Page Nineteen (Five Panels)**

Panel One
Page-wide, entirely black panel.

MISS FURY CAPTION:                "You..."

LOCATOR:        SWITCH.

Panel Two
Miss Fury, in costume, breathing hard, distraught, exhausted. Costume ripped from battle. She's just been through an incredible battle. She's holding that huge oversized sniper rifle we saw from earlier and it's smoking where she's been firing it. Behind her are dead bodies and carnage. This is a Midtown Manhattan street that's been turned into a war zone. Craters, tanks, dead soldiers, ruined buildings. Midtown turned into a scene from Call Of Duty Modern Warfare.

NO DIALOGUE

Panel Three
Close-up on Miss Fury, tears in her eyes, as she looks up at the sky. Something big coming in over the top. Ground shaking with the low rumble of huge engines.

NO DIALOGUE

Panel Four
We're at her feet now, looking up at battle-scarred skyscrapers as a massive shape blocks out the sky. This is a monster-sized Nazi Flying wing jet bomber (we'll establish this next page, for here it looks like a massive mothership). A third of the size of Manhattan. There's small shapes whizzing beneath it. These are Messerschmitt 262 jet fighters (reference http://tinyurl.com/cdckea8). Little squadrons of them whizzing by.

NO DIALOGUE

Panel Five
Miss Fury looks down the street. Tears in her eyes now. DESPERATE. Is she going out of her mind?

CAPTION:        "You're crazy."

## Page Twenty (Splash Page)

Aerial wide shot of the island of Manhattan here, and it's a war zone. And hovering above it are four of those HUGE Nazi Flying wing jet bombers (make sure we get the HUGE swastikas on the wings here). The air is filled with squadrons of the Me 262 fighters. And the battle is plainly over and New York has been taken over and largely destroyed. The Nazis triumphant.

LOCATOR:        2013.

CAPTION:        "So..."
CAPTION:        "What have YOU got to be angry about?"


TO BE CONTINUED...

# WRITER'S COMMENTARY

## BEHIND MISS FURY #1 WITH ROB WILLIAMS

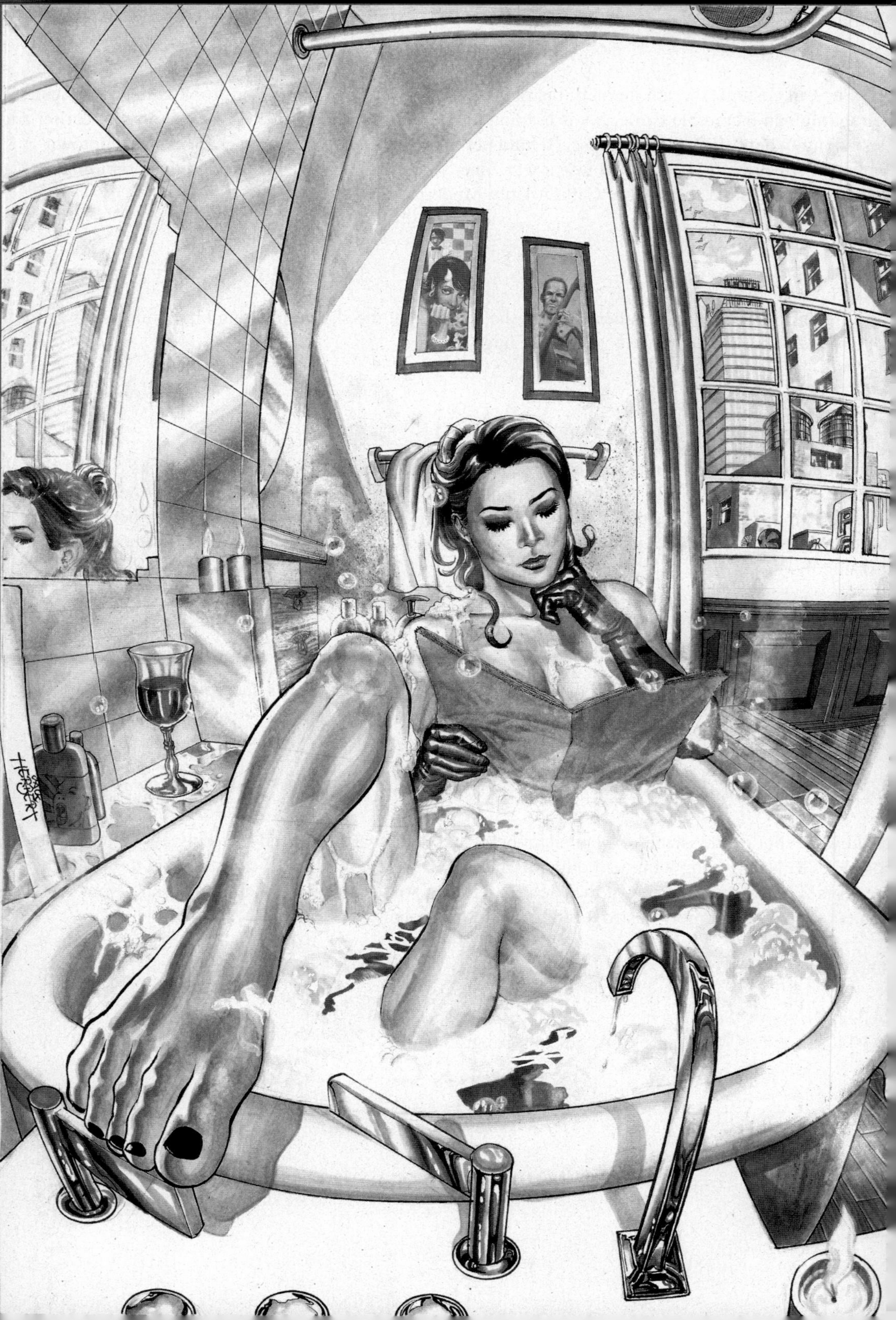

Everyone is doing themselves a weak and cowardly disservice if they don't ask them-selves this question… What are YOU angry about?" Start a storyline with the control-ing idea front and centre. It's on the nose, yes, but it's effective. And this was the key question for Miss Fury when I approached the book. She's called 'fury' yet she's a super rich Manhattan socialite who's incredibly good looking. What's she got to be angry about? Over the course of the first arc – that's the core question. And we open in 1943. The world's at war. America's at war. Millions dying and suffering. Yet Marla Drake's life is all roses. She hasn't found herself yet.

Anger is an energy," was something I wrote in the pitch, stealing from John Lydon.

And that telegram in panel 3 is a flashback, by the way. To a key moment in her jour-ey towards her own anger. We'll find out more as we go.

PG 2

My first draft of the script I started things further on with some character-setting dia-ogue, but then I decided this was an issue one, we probably needed some action straight out of the blocks.

More punching. And kicking. This is a superhero book.

We're establishing here that a) Miss Fury is a fearsome, superhumanly quick fighter she twists an assailant around in time to get his body to take the bullets meant for her - that's quick). And b) she's not a squeaky clean, morally black and white figure. She's lashing and drawing blood here.

Also: Jack Herbert, our seriously impressive artist, is establishing that he can draw an ction sequence really, REALLY well.

PG 3

She catches a knife in mid-air and returns it at the thrower, getting him right between he eyes!

You know, for kids!

When I saw these pages in B&W I was delighted. I hadn't worked with Jack before but here's a real fluidity to the action here, and Miss Fury looks terrific in panel 4. Lots of swagger there. The colours are wonderful too. Ivan Nunes did a killer job on the book. Really talented colourist.

Love the 'Thunk!' sound effect there too. Nice job by Simon Bowland, our letterer, hroughout.

PG 6

The idea here was, on a kind of suggestive level, that Miss Fury doesn't just fall hrough the skylight into the Nazi's time machine, but the time machine rather pulls her through. It wants her. None of this is established in text, and to have her saying "It almost feels like it… wants me," would've been plain bad writing. A bit of ambiguity here and there isn't necessarily a bad thing, I think. Let readers fill in the blanks as ong as the narrative us clear. Even if no one gets what the intention was, she still falls nto the time machine so the plot is serviced.

The whole idea of Miss Fury's time travel in the arc is so personal to her. It's meant to be ambiguous to an extent. Is she really travelling through time or is she still in 1943 and insane?

## PG 9
Jack drew this to be a real highlight of the issue. And it's completely different from the script and what I imagined. But who cares when it looks this amazing.

The script called for a side-on shot of an art deco bath, which sits in the middle of a huge room in Miss Fury's Manhattan apartment. The idea being that this room is enormous but she's kind of so emotionally empty that there's nothing in it, just a luxury bath. Jack changed the angle, the sense of this huge room with just a small bath in it. But she's still wearing the gloves in the bath (that's not for 'cool and sexy' aesthetic reasons, we'll reveal why later). She's reading the '43 newspaper, and the contradiction of the salubrious image and the dialogue "there's a war on, you know. It's a terrible business" is still there. I don't mind an artist changing what I've asked for as long as the narrative point is served. It is here.

And it looks fantastic. So shut up Mr. Writer.

## PG 13
Miss Fury's new origin. Her voice is more than a little tongue-in-cheek here. "The implicit local hallucinogenic…" "he may have just been trying it on." The humour hopefully lifts this scene beyond being the typical superhero origin. And I liked the fact that she isn't 100% sure if she has superpowers. It's, again, a little ambiguous.

## PG 14
Sex Panther! It stings the nostrils.

Is the panther real? She doesn't know.

Although, she is covered in blood during sex in the final panel, so there's a hint. She's a dark one, eh? I wanted to show her as being in control here. She drives the action

Titillating? Yes. But true to her character. These are all little snapshots of Marla Drake. The entire initial arc is something of a jigsaw puzzle for her and, hopefully, by the end of the first storyline, you have something of a three-dimensional woman.

And who among us can say that we haven't had sex with a Masai tribesman while under the influence of a powerful hallucinogen and covered in the blood of a MASSIVE jungle cat that we've just killed in hand-to-paw combat? I know I have.

### PG 18
Who's this bloke then? Badly burnt face? He's a super-villain, surely.

This is Captain Chandler. Who'll make a big difference in Marla Drake's life. A key figure in her journey.

Great faces in the crowd scene behind Captain Chandler. Jack does great faces..

And there's that telegram again in panel three. If it repeats like this, it's a key moment.

### PG 21
And suddenly we're in a scene from Modern Warfare. Tanks, guns, jet fighters, a street scene where Manhattan's been turned into Chechnya. Romance is very much over and Miss Fury's suddenly thrust into war. Her war.

And something big overhead is blocking out the sun. That can't be good.

The script, by the way, asked for her to be carrying a 'Sienkiewicz rifle', as in Bill. I used the same phrase in an issue of Daken: Dark Wolverine and it's become shorthand for an impossibly large and deadly weapon. The language of comics… I'm going to keep using it.

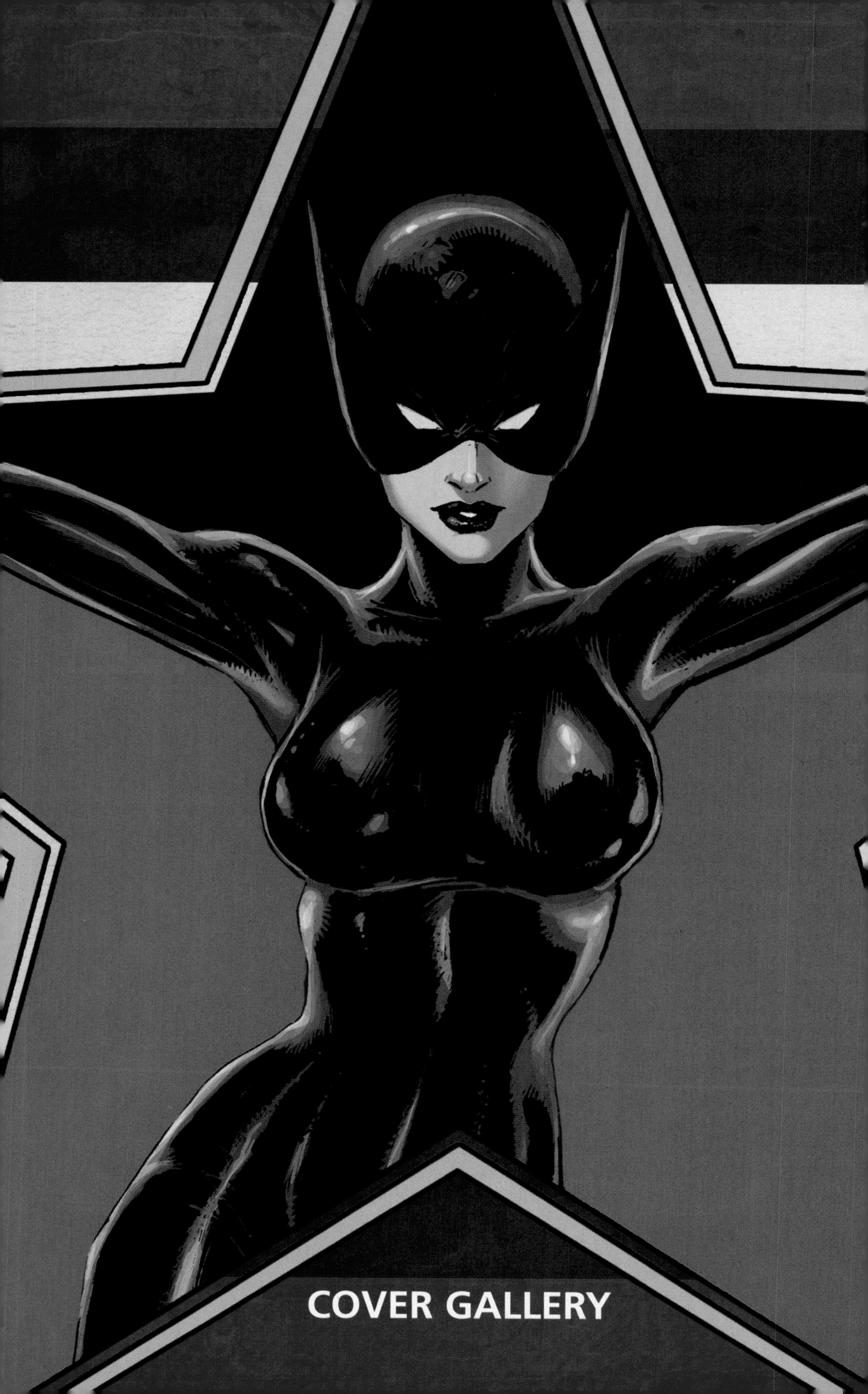

# COVER GALLERY

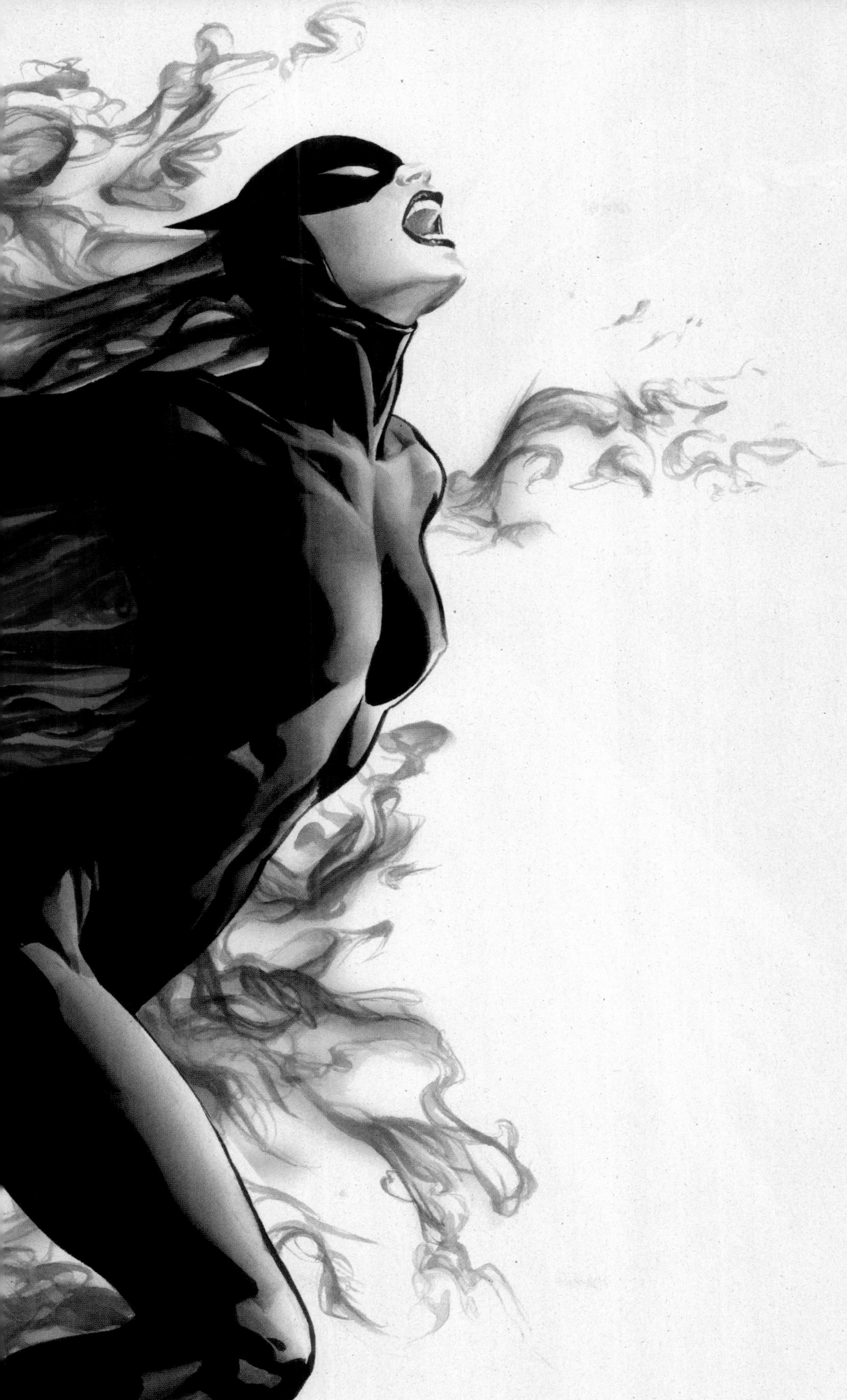

issue #1 cover by ALEX ROSS

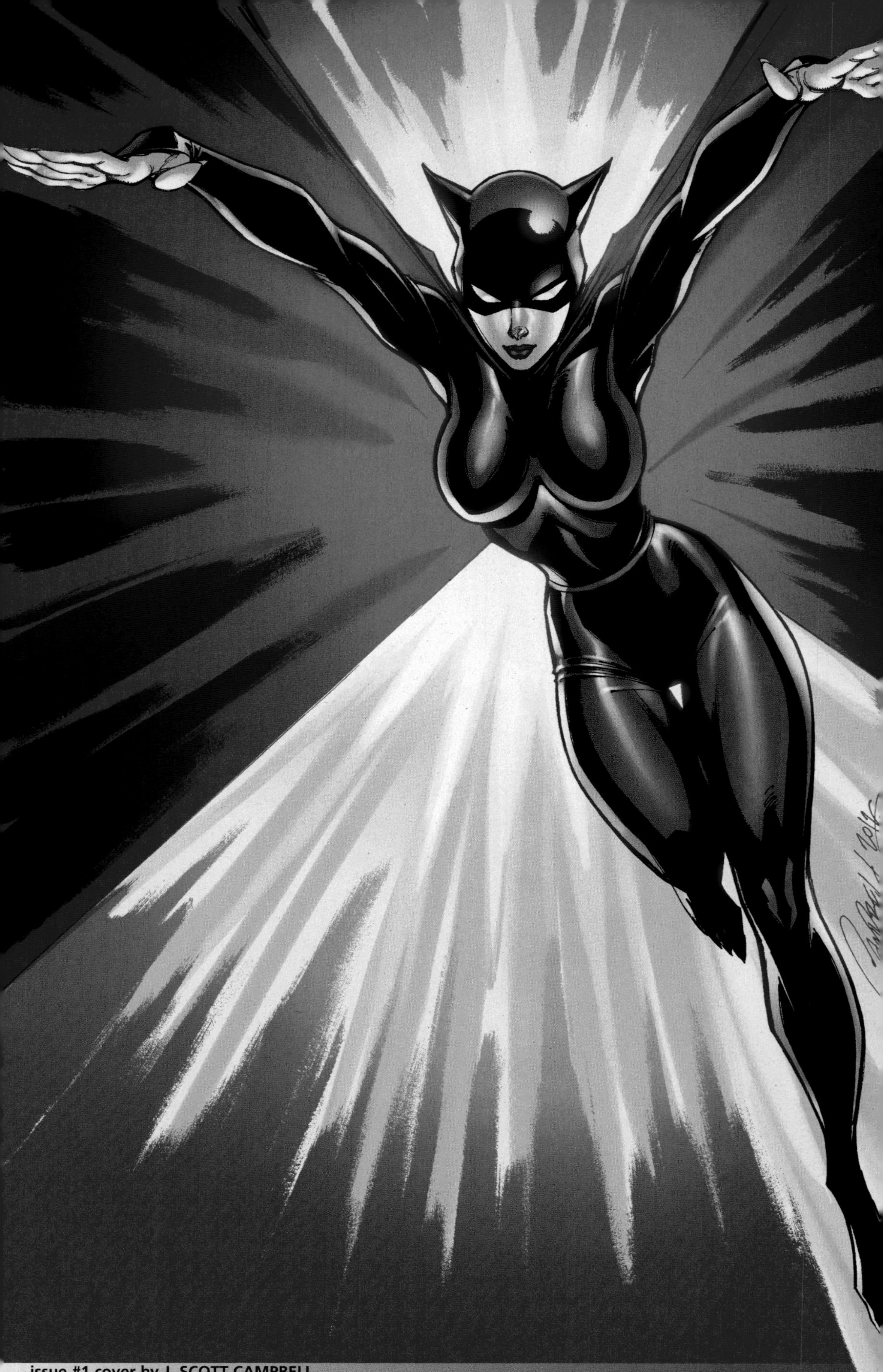

issue #1 cover by J. SCOTT CAMPBELL

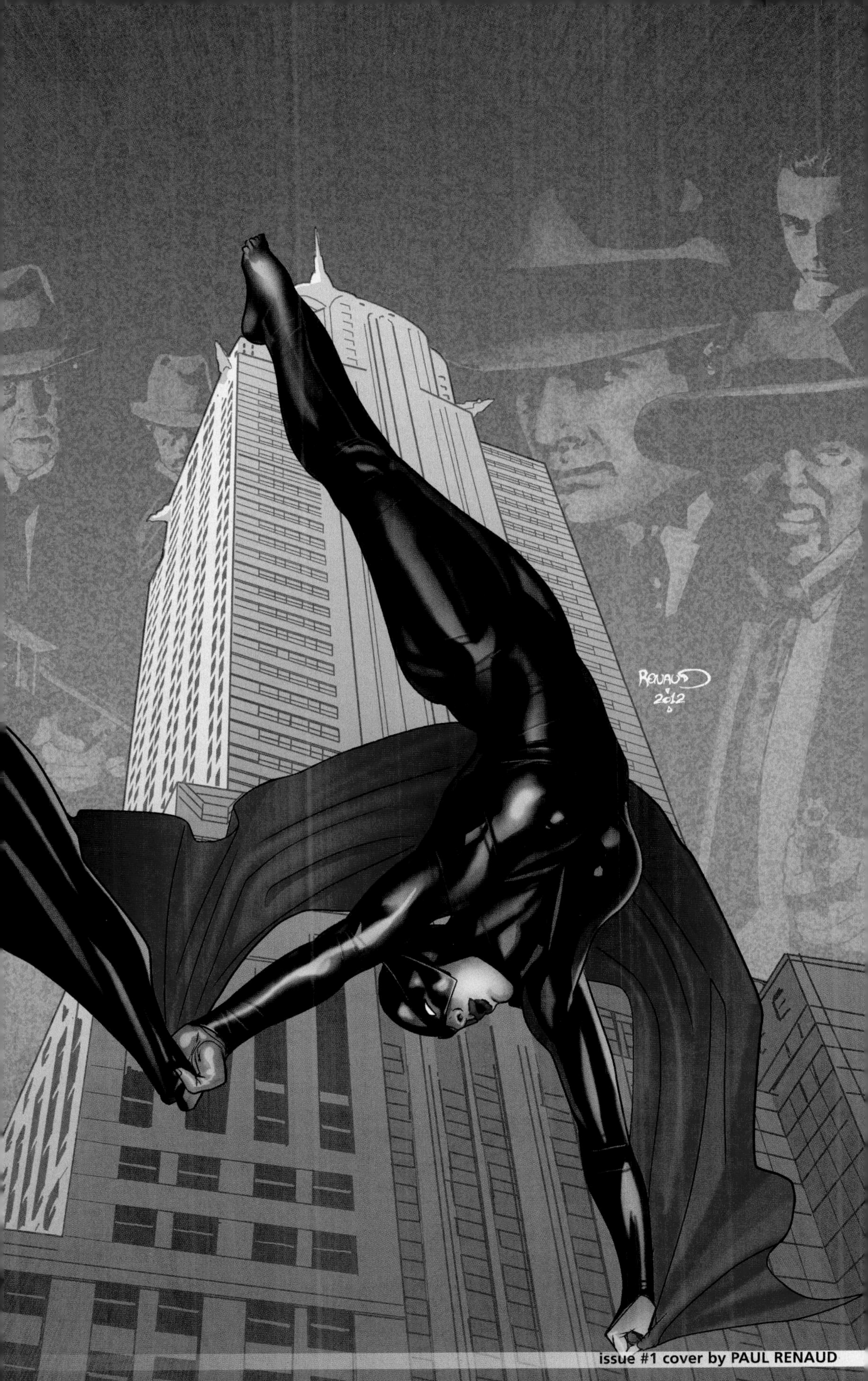
RENAUD
2012
issue #1 cover by PAUL RENAUD

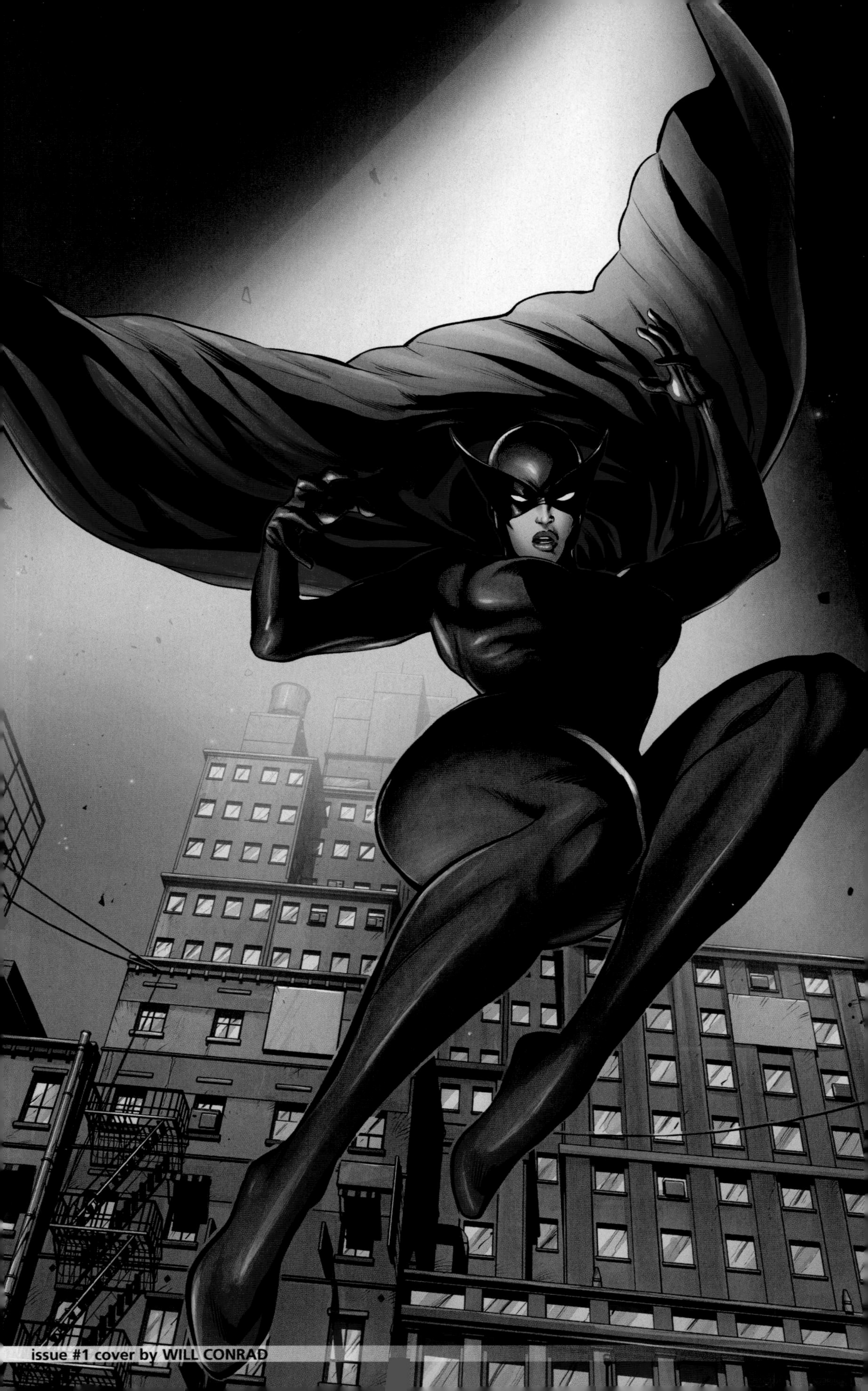

issue #1 cover by WILL CONRAD

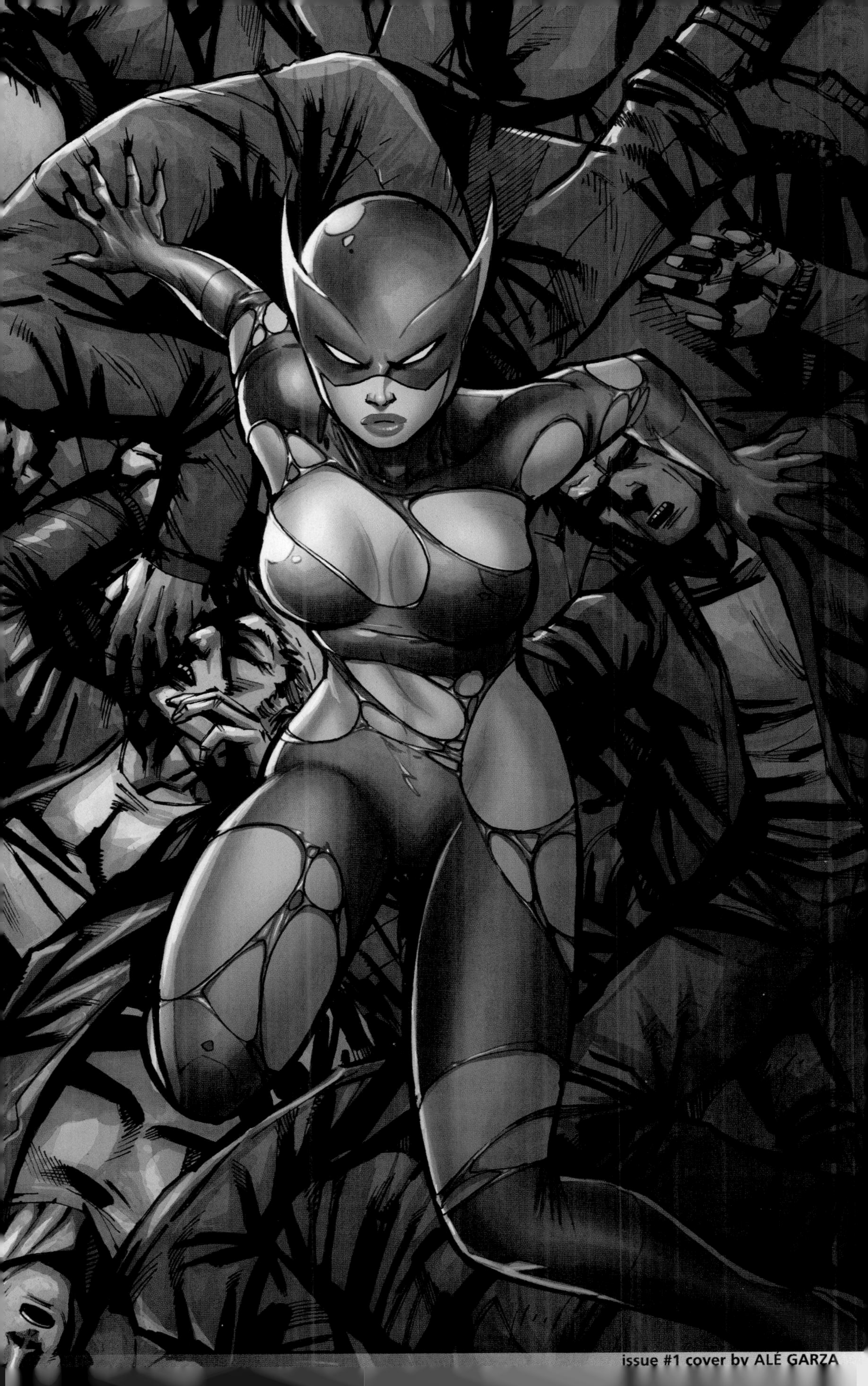

issue #1 cover by ALÉ GARZA

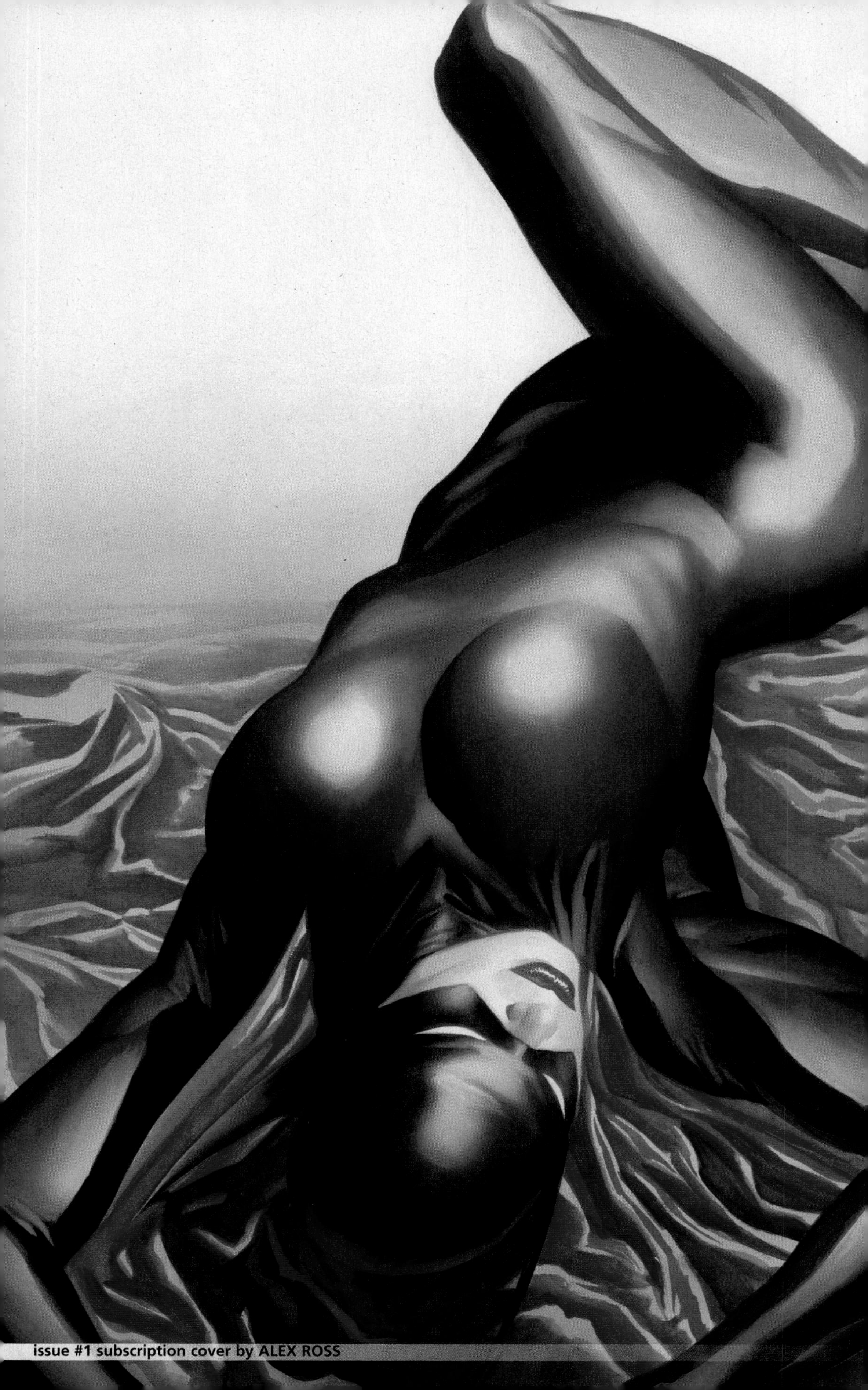

issue #1 subscription cover by ALEX ROSS

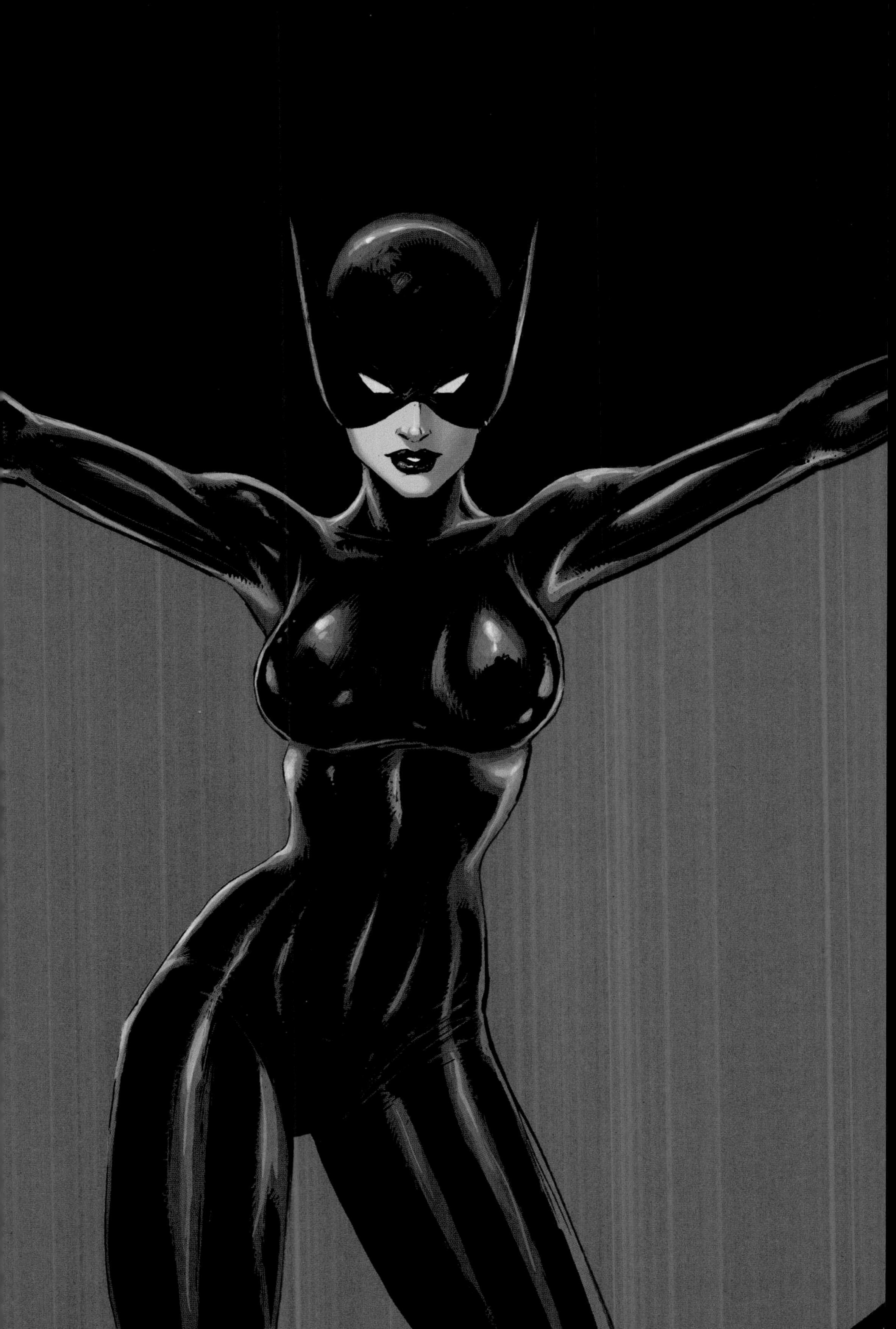

issue #2 cover by JOE BENITEZ

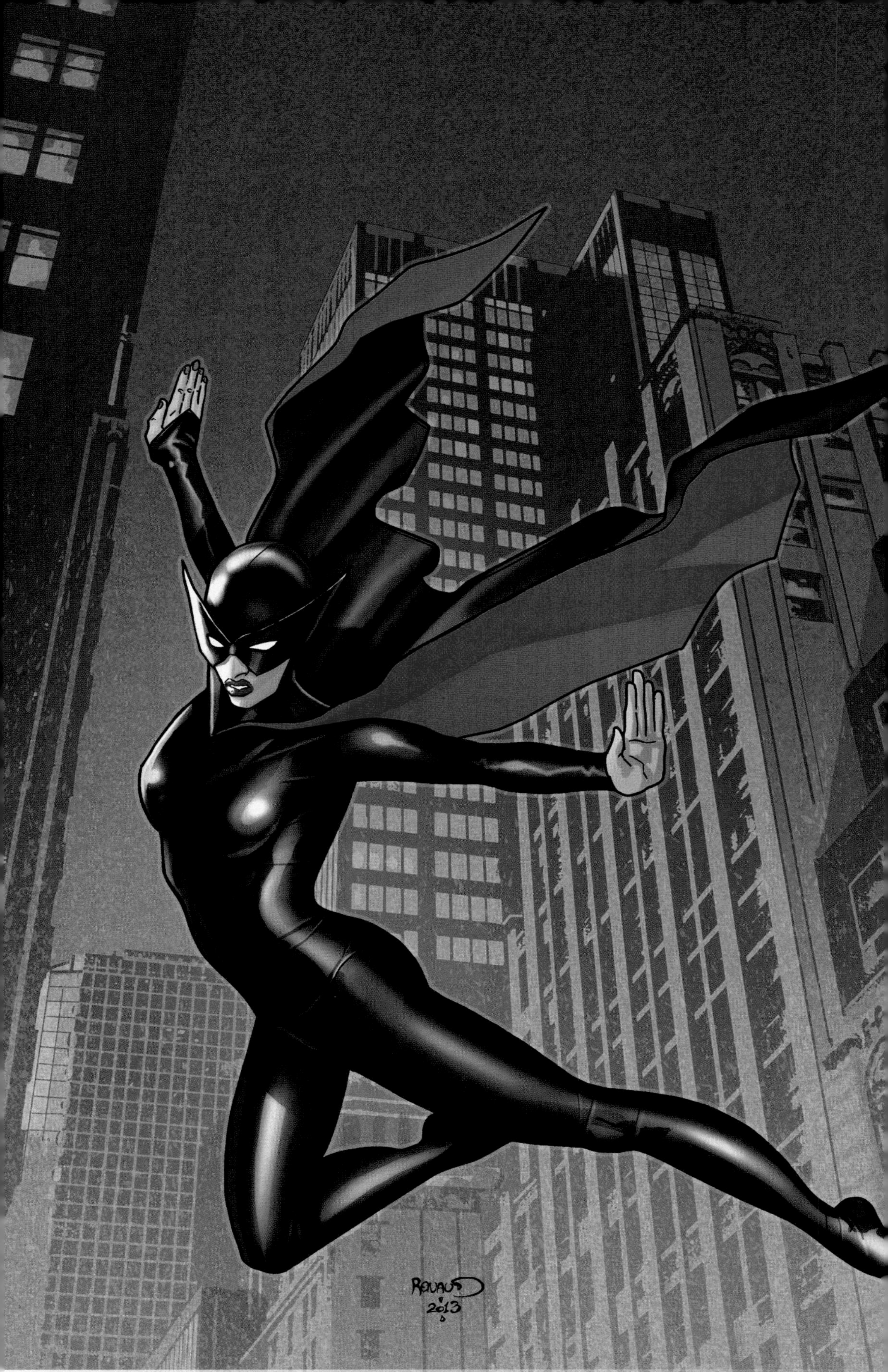
RENAUD
2013
issue #2 cover by PAUL RENAUD

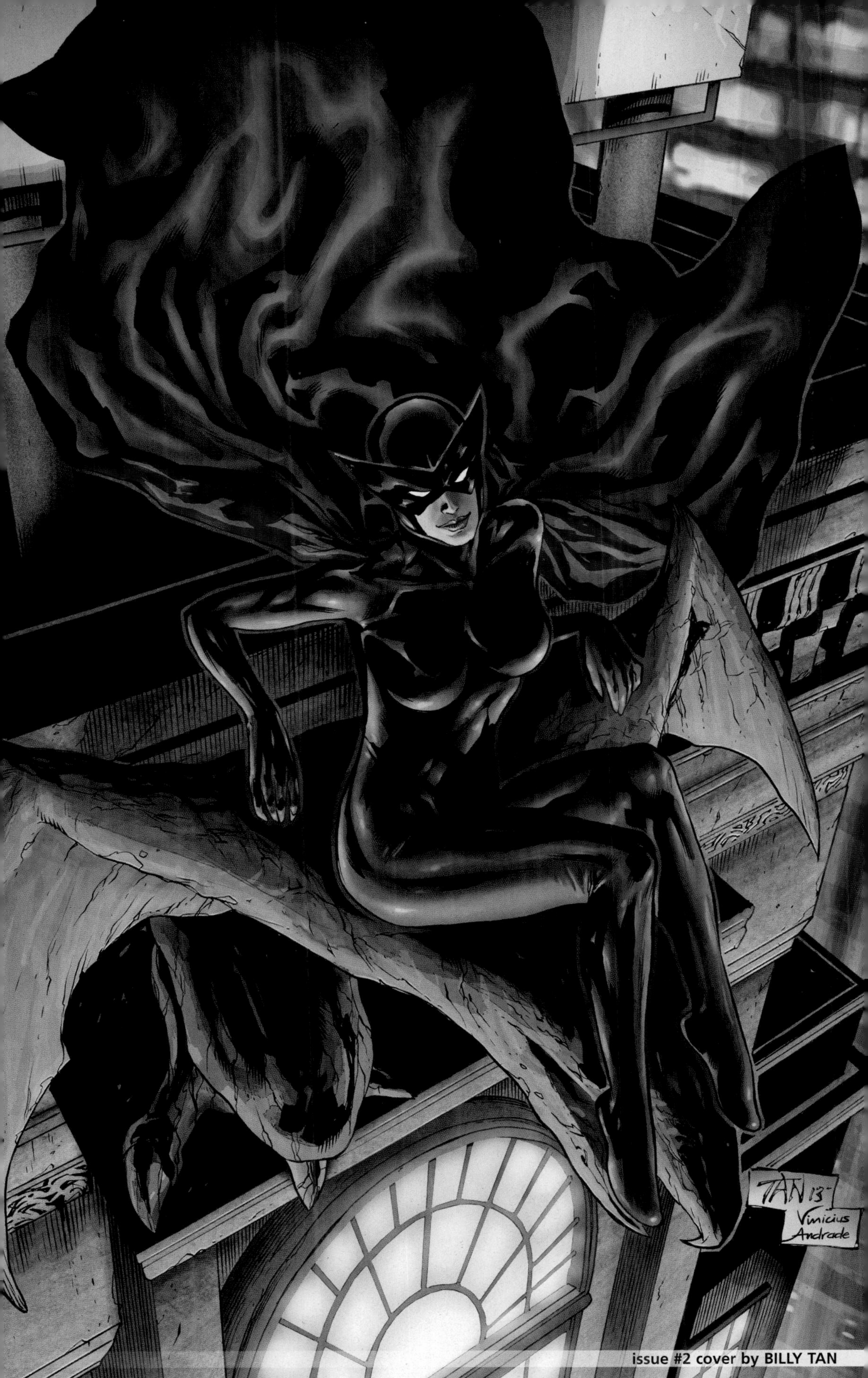
TAN 13
Vinicius
Andrade

issue #2 cover by BILLY TAN

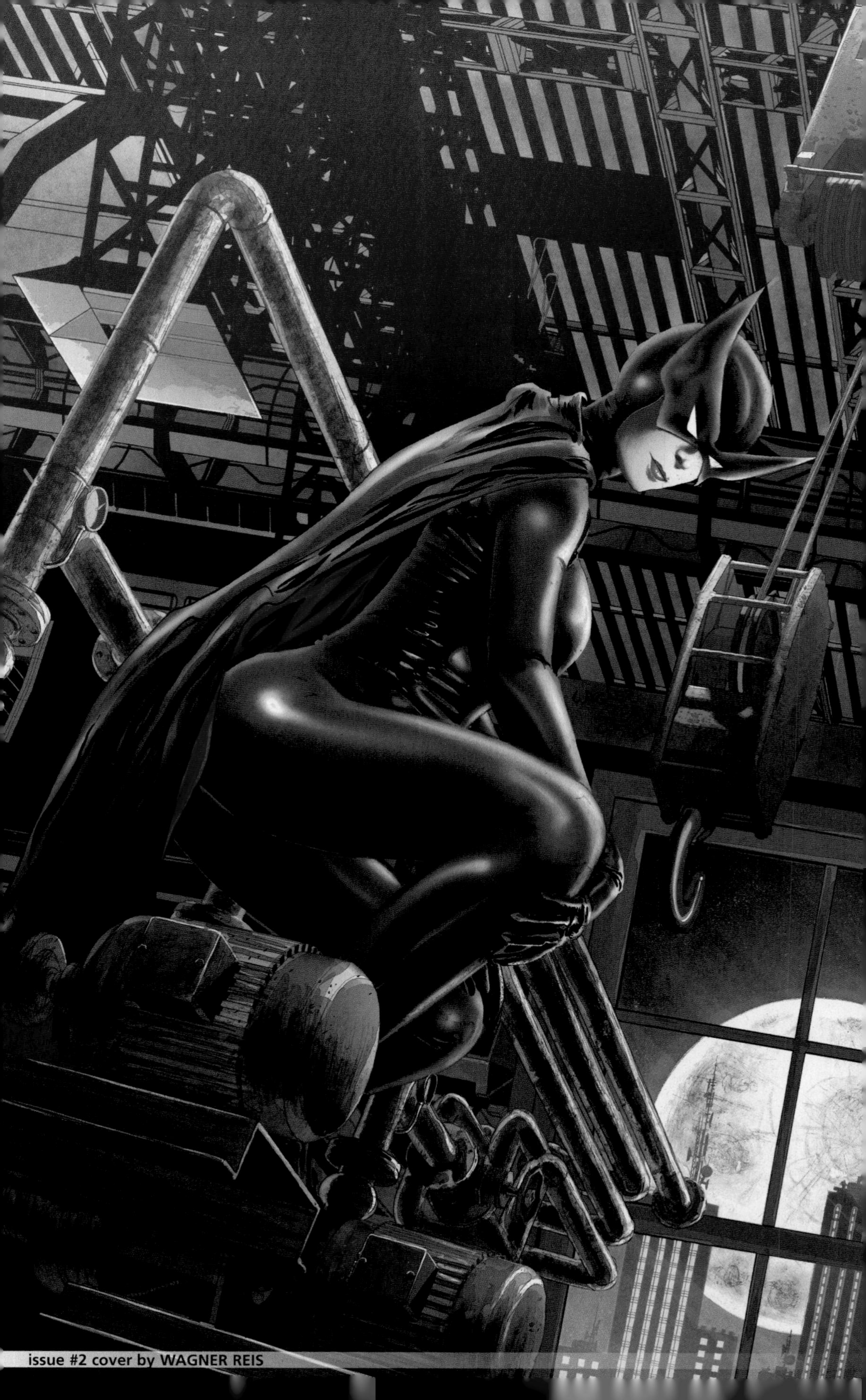

issue #2 cover by WAGNER REIS

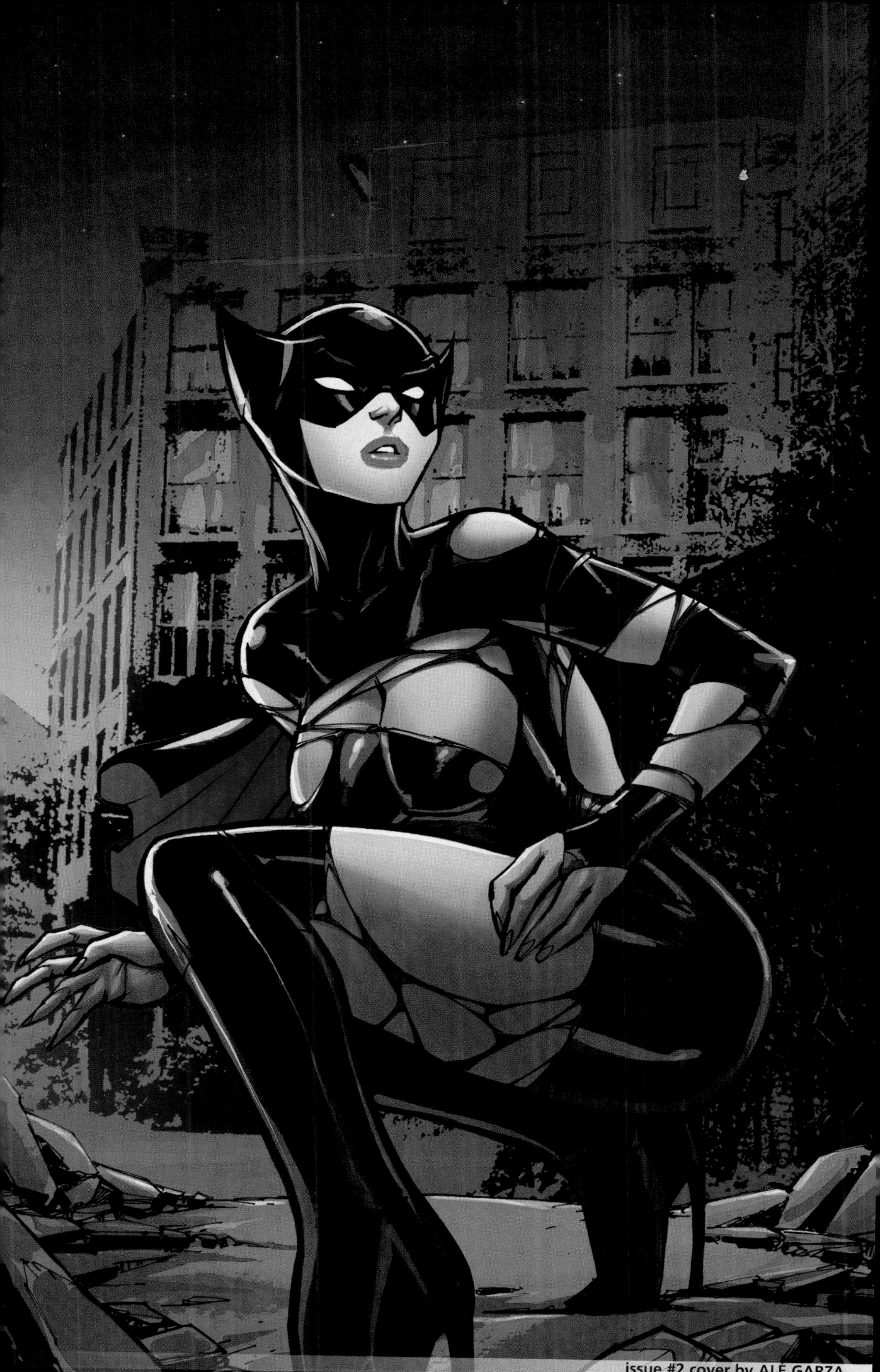

issue #2 cover by ALÉ GARZA

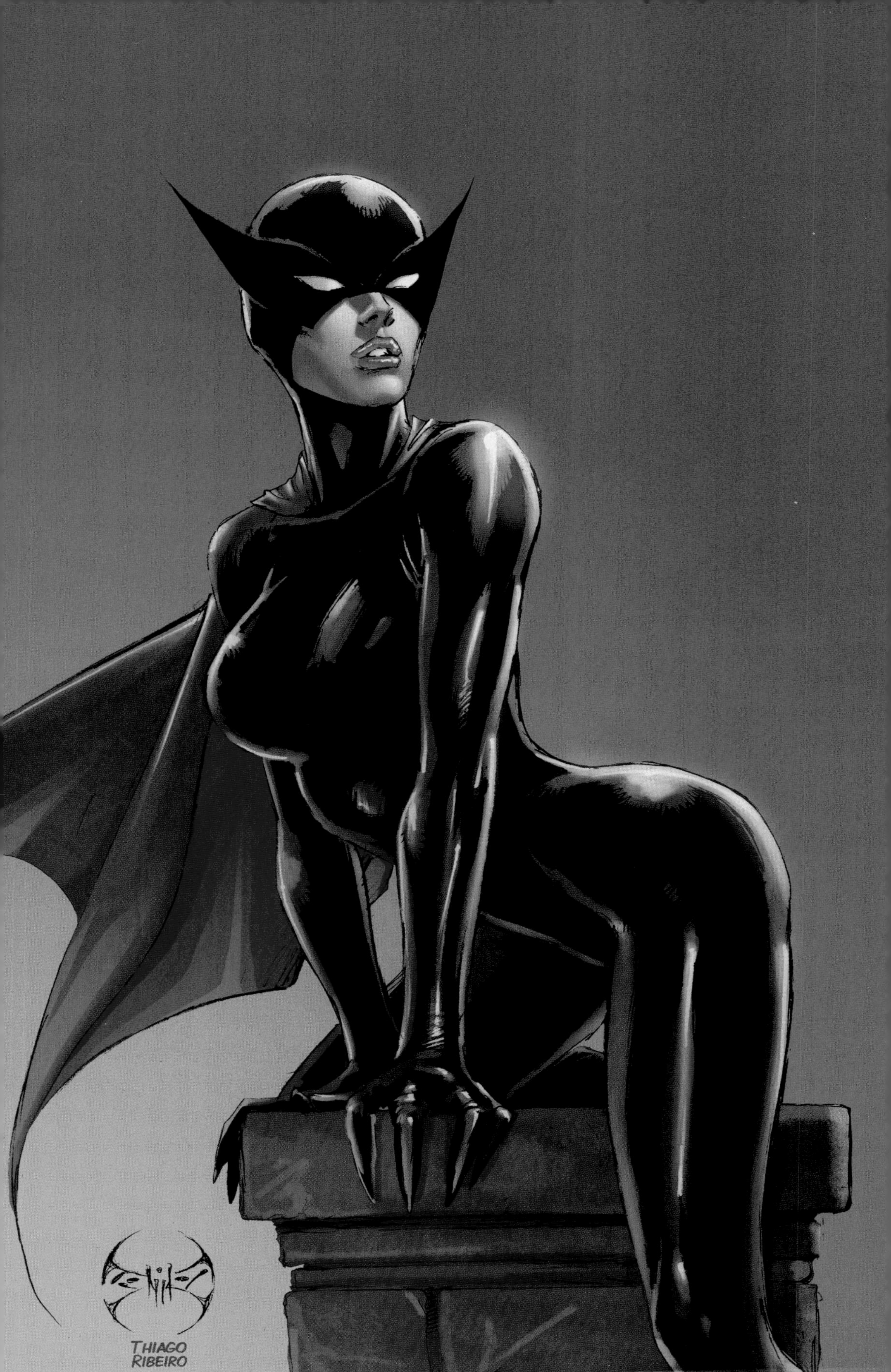
THIAGO
RIBEIRO

issue #3 cover by JOE BENITEZ

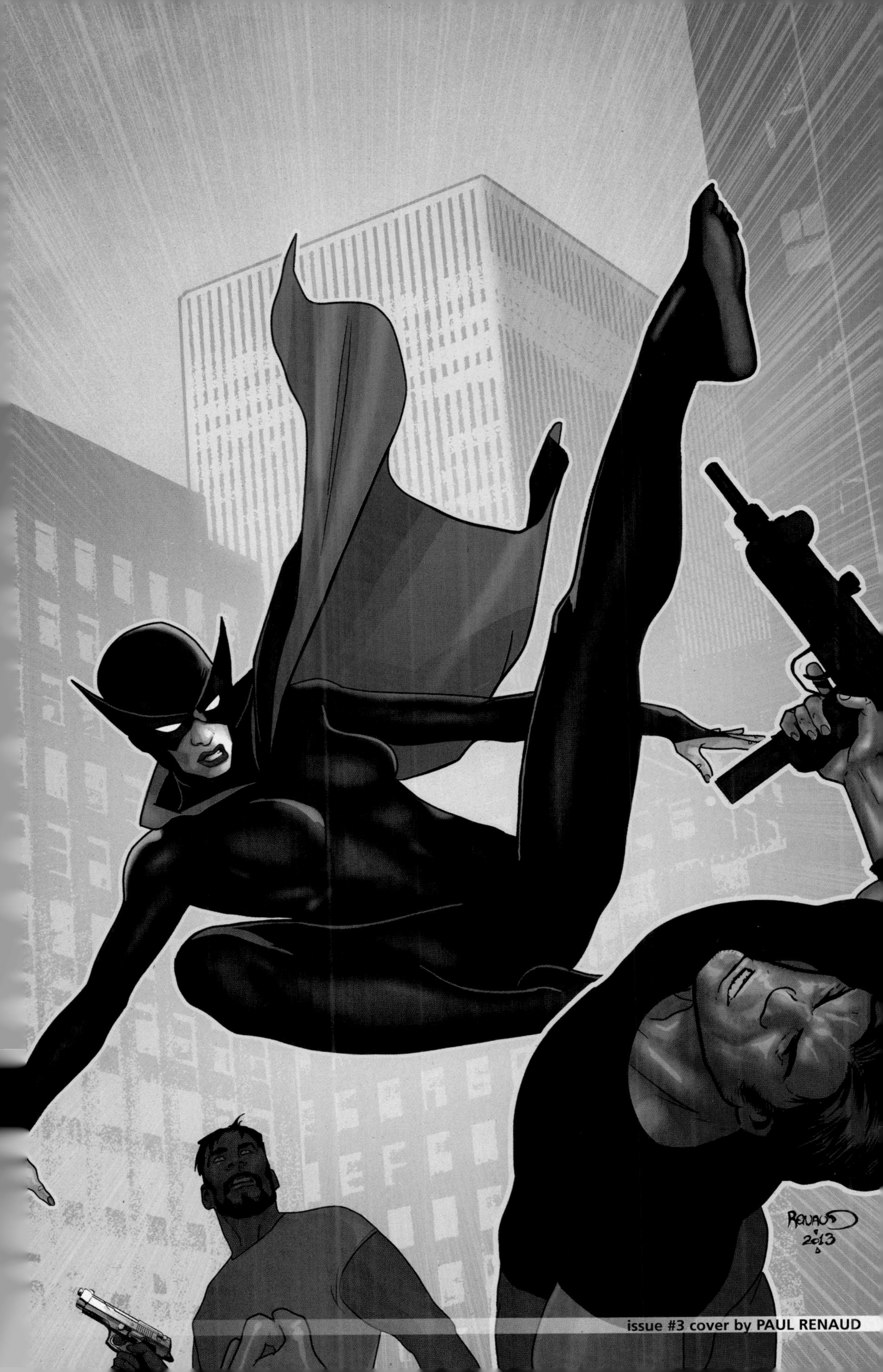
RENAUD
2013

issue #3 cover by PAUL RENAUD

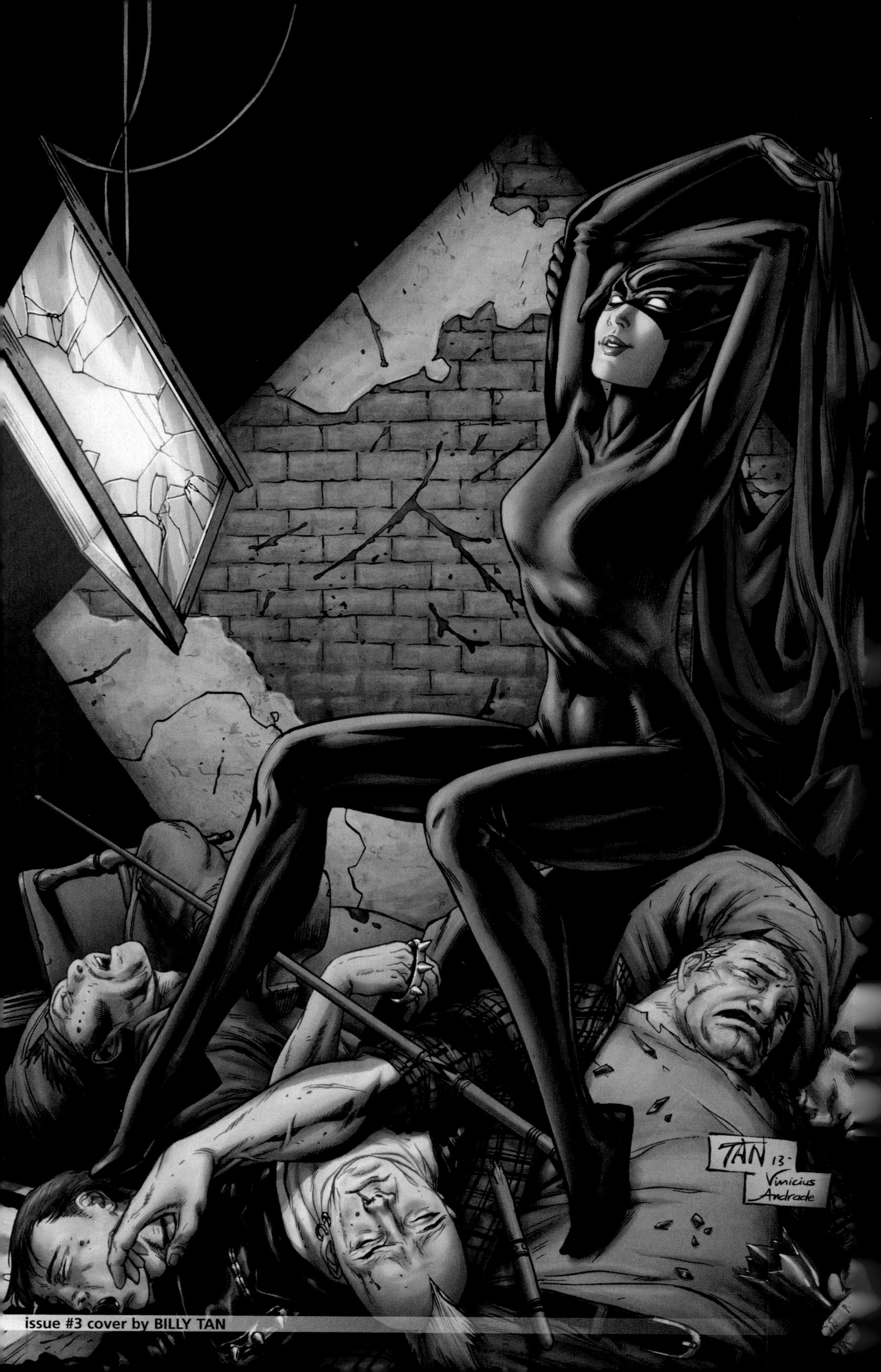
TAN 13
Vinicius
Andrade
issue #3 cover by BILLY TAN

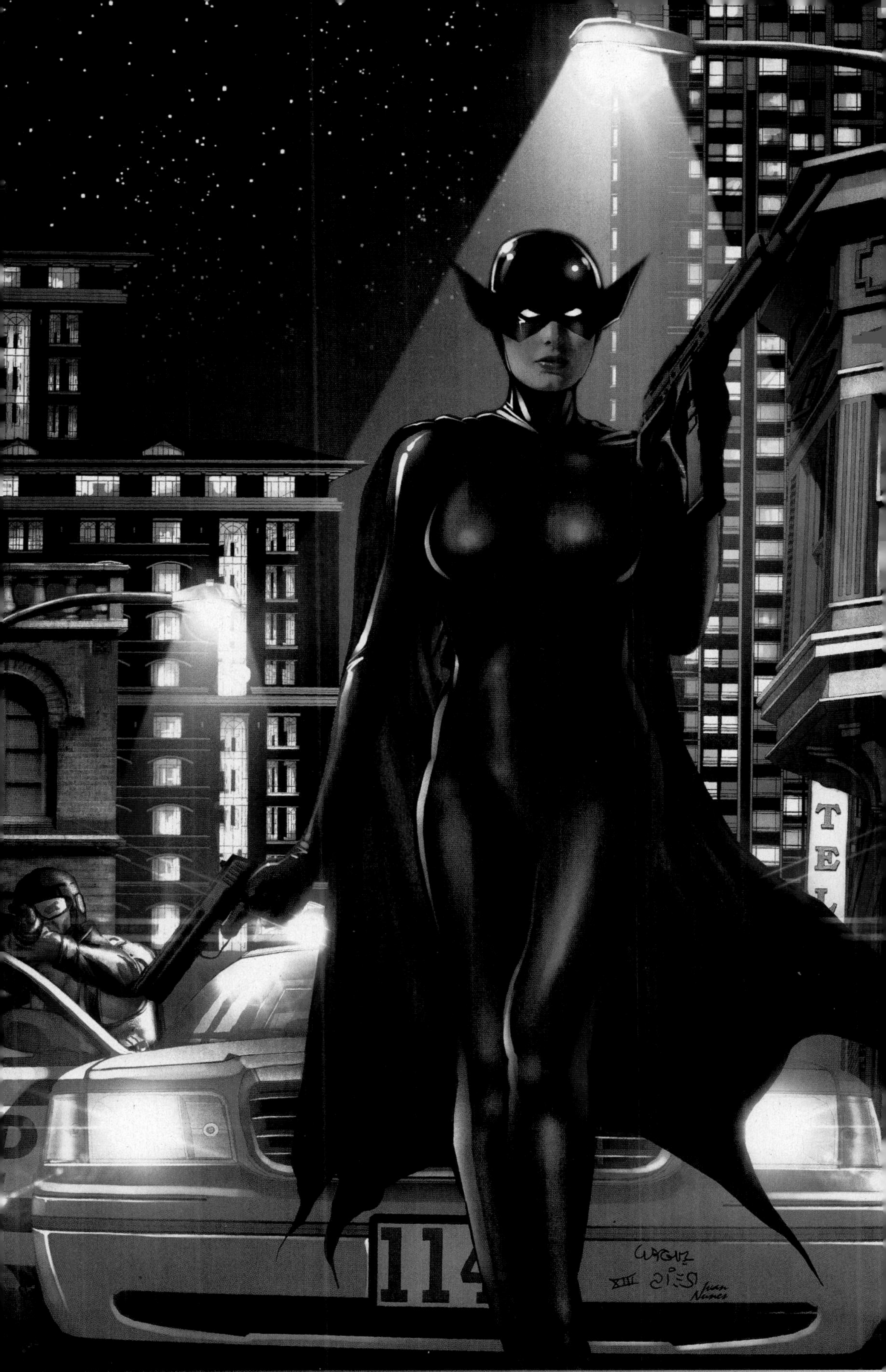
TEL
114

issue #3 cover by WAGNER REIS

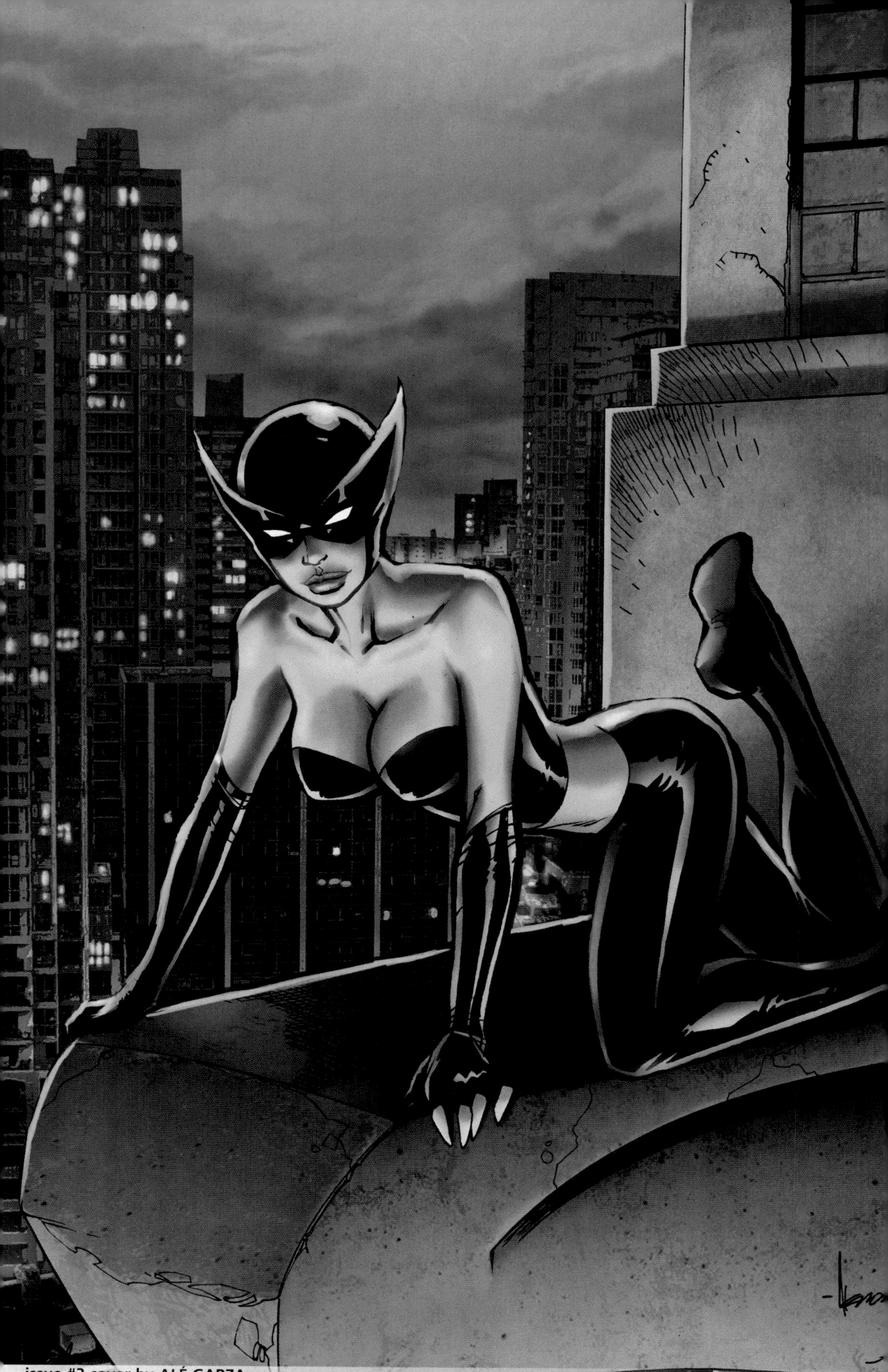

issue #3 cover by ALÉ GARZA

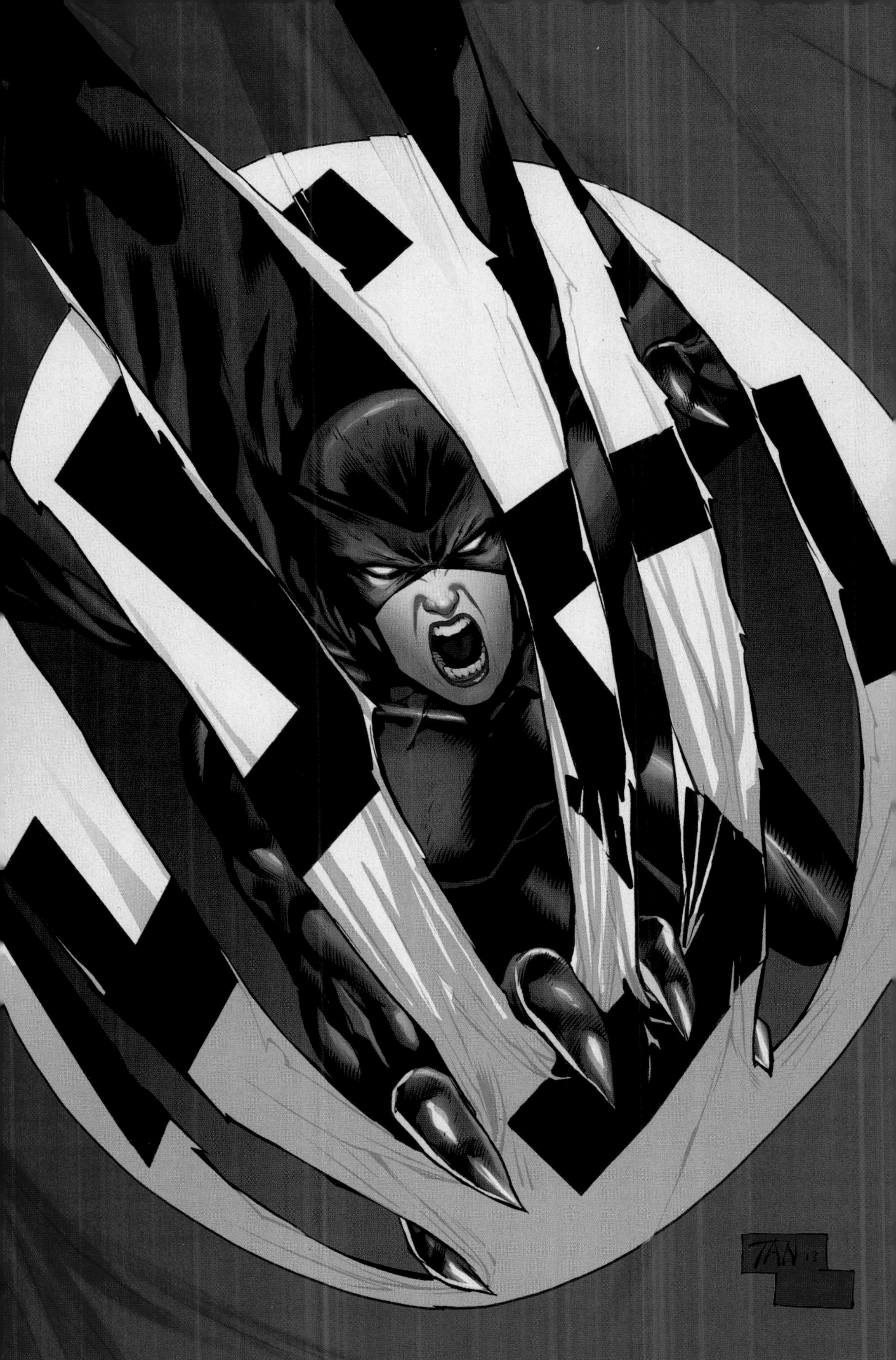
TAN 13

issue #4 cover by BILLY TAN

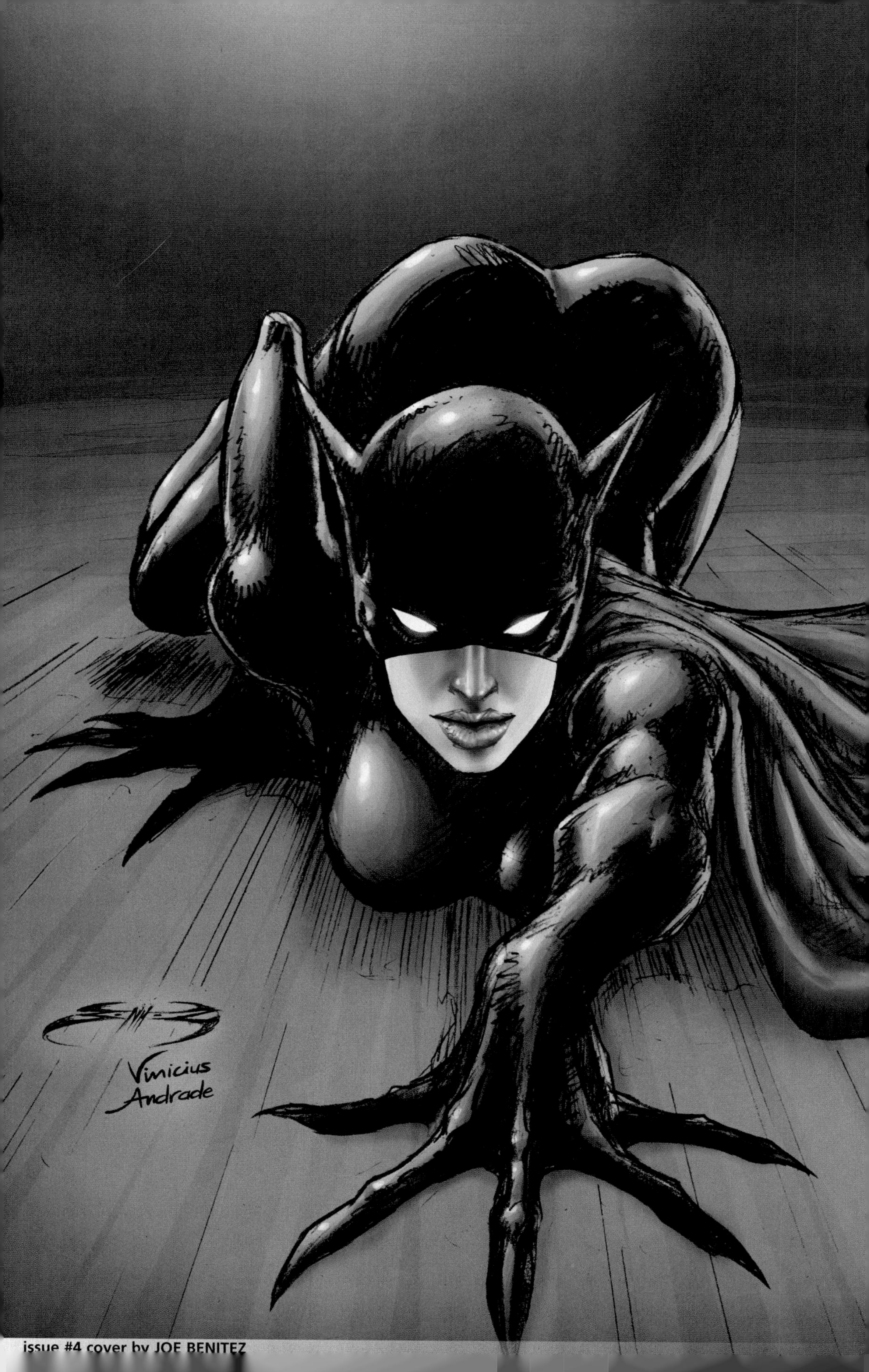
Vinicius
Andrade

issue #4 cover by JOE BENITEZ

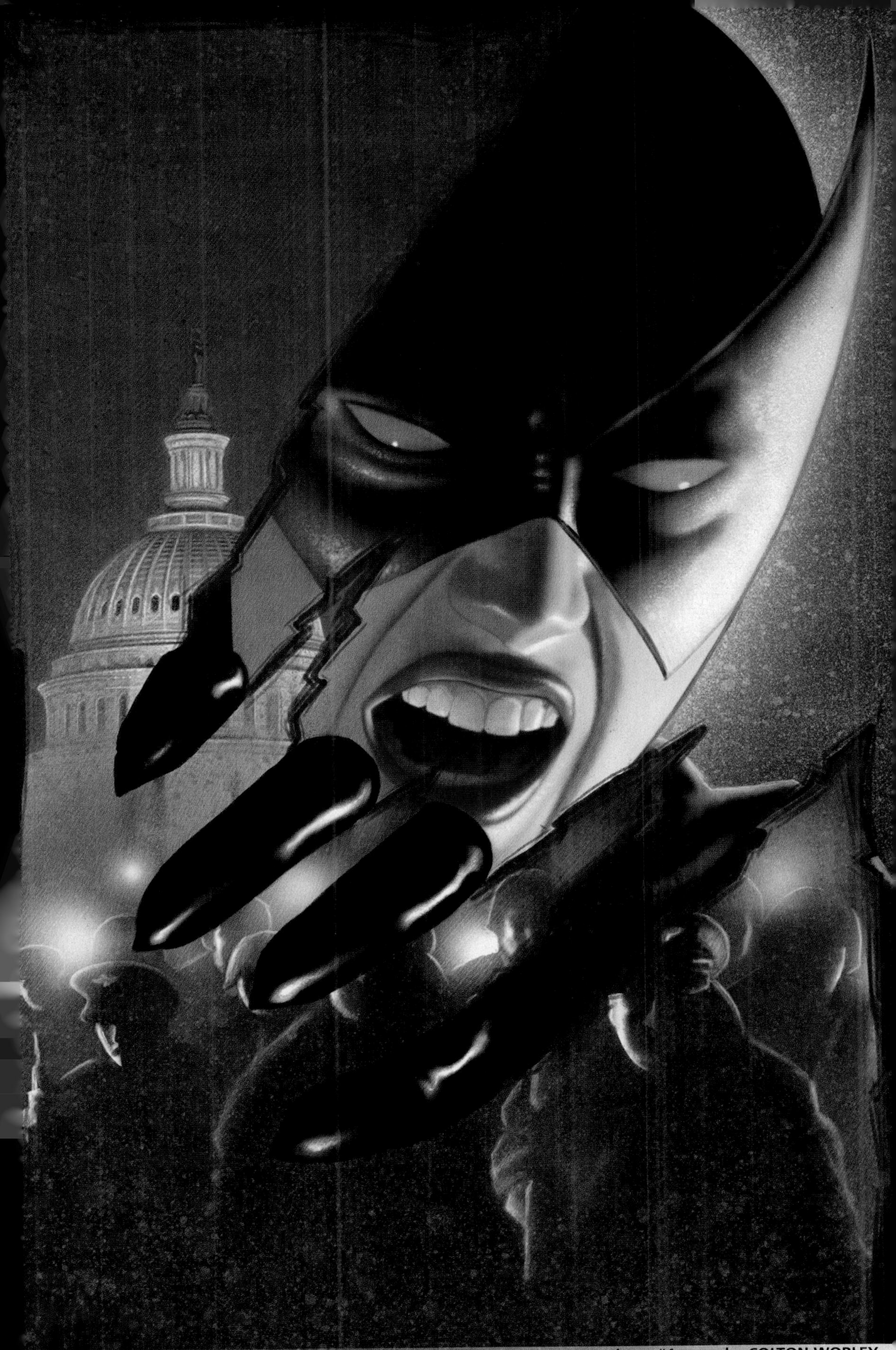

issue #4 cover by COLTON WORLEY

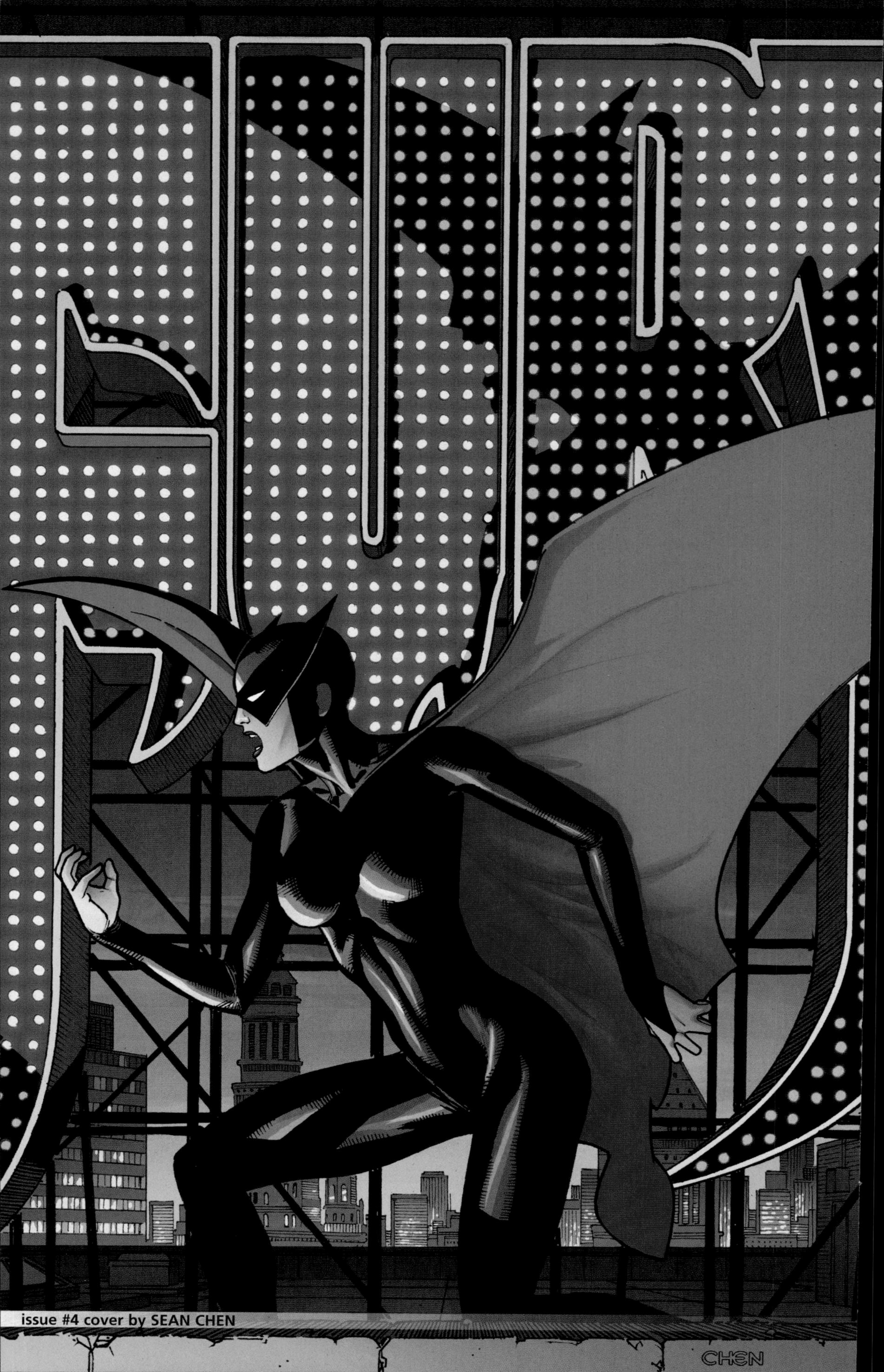
CHEN

issue #4 cover by SEAN CHEN

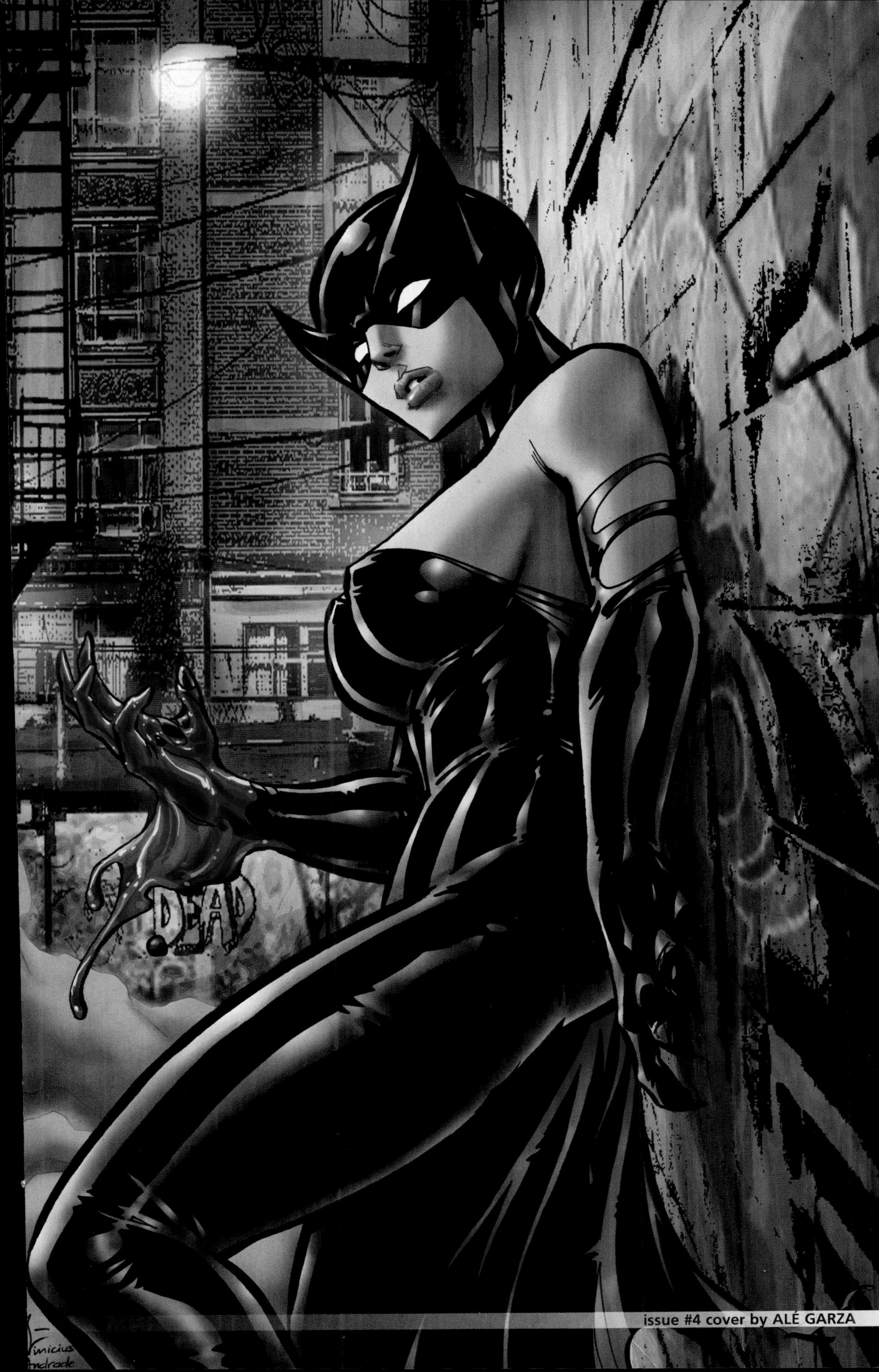
DEAD

issue #4 cover by ALÉ GARZA

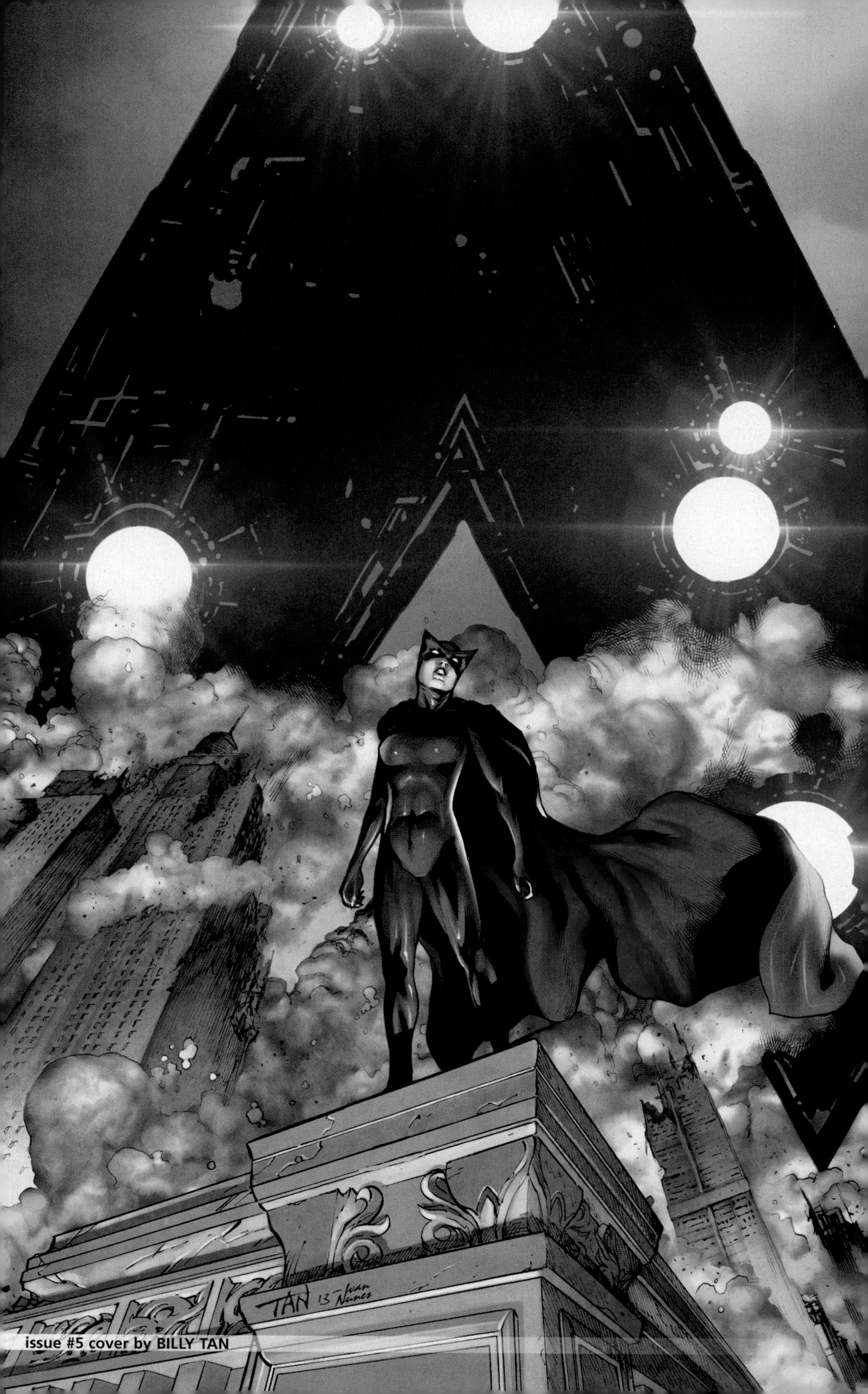
TAN 13 Ivan Nunes

issue #5 cover by BILLY TAN

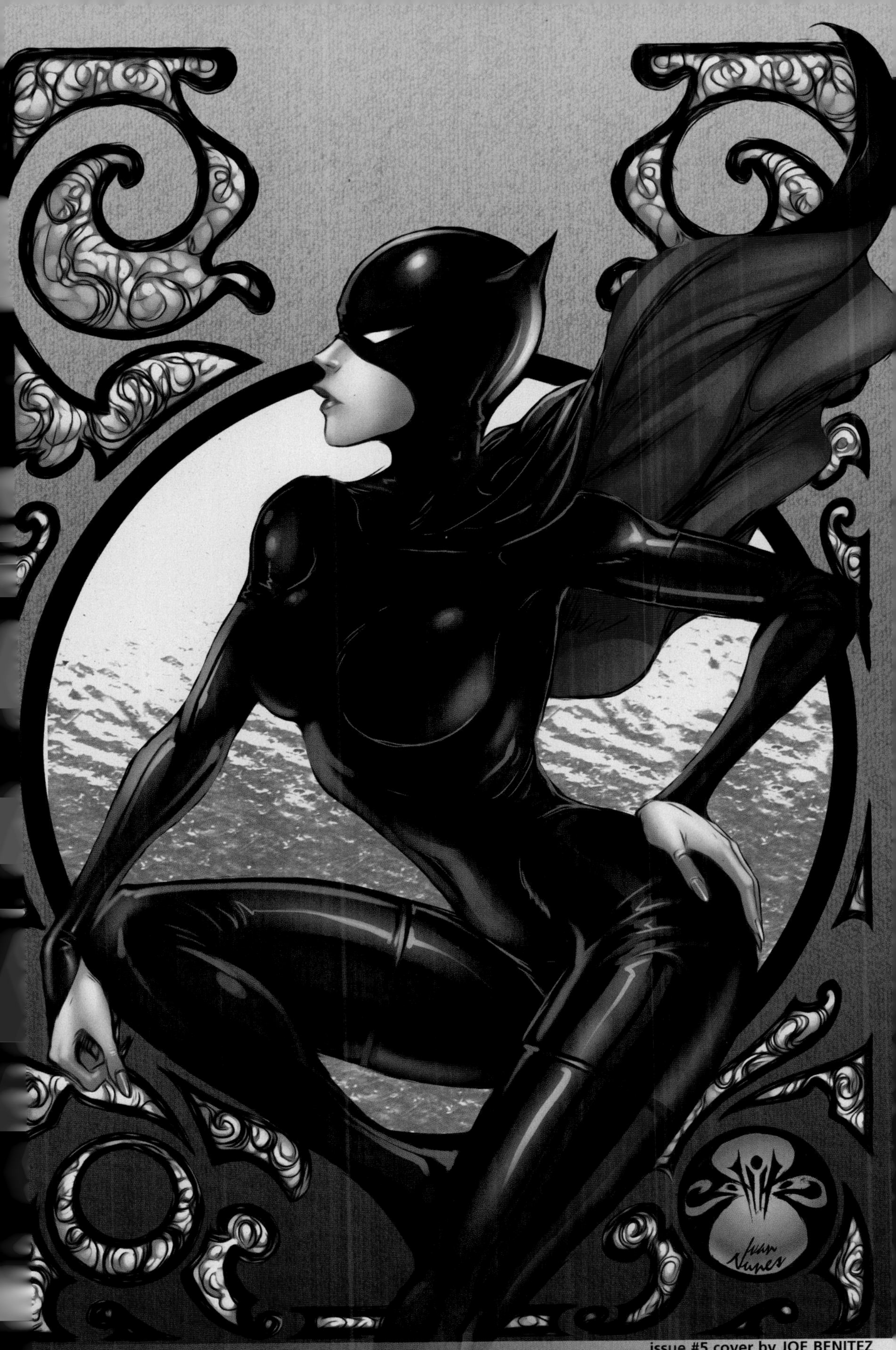

issue #5 cover by JOE BENITEZ

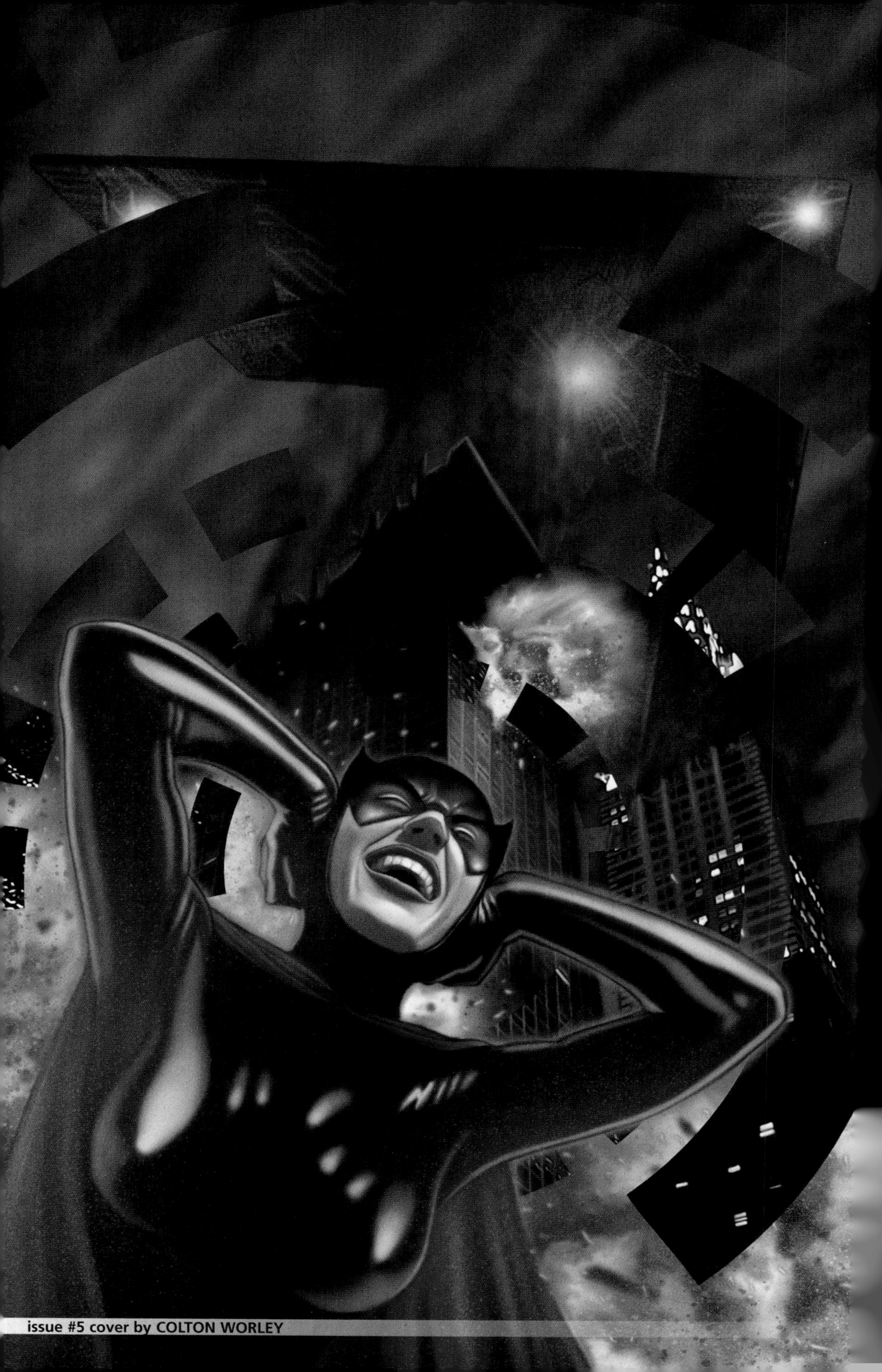

issue #5 cover by COLTON WORLEY

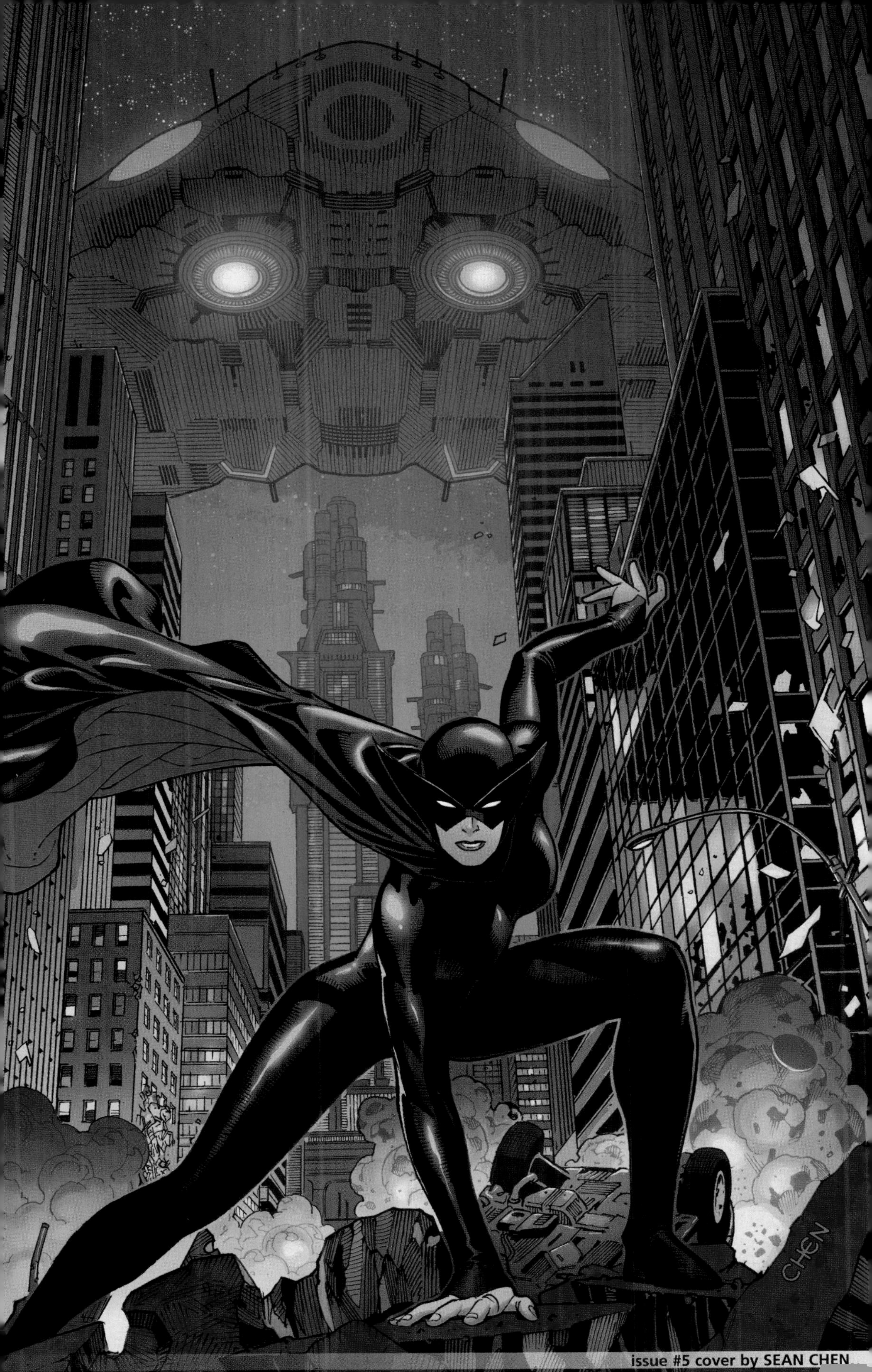
CHEN

issue #5 cover by **SEAN CHEN**

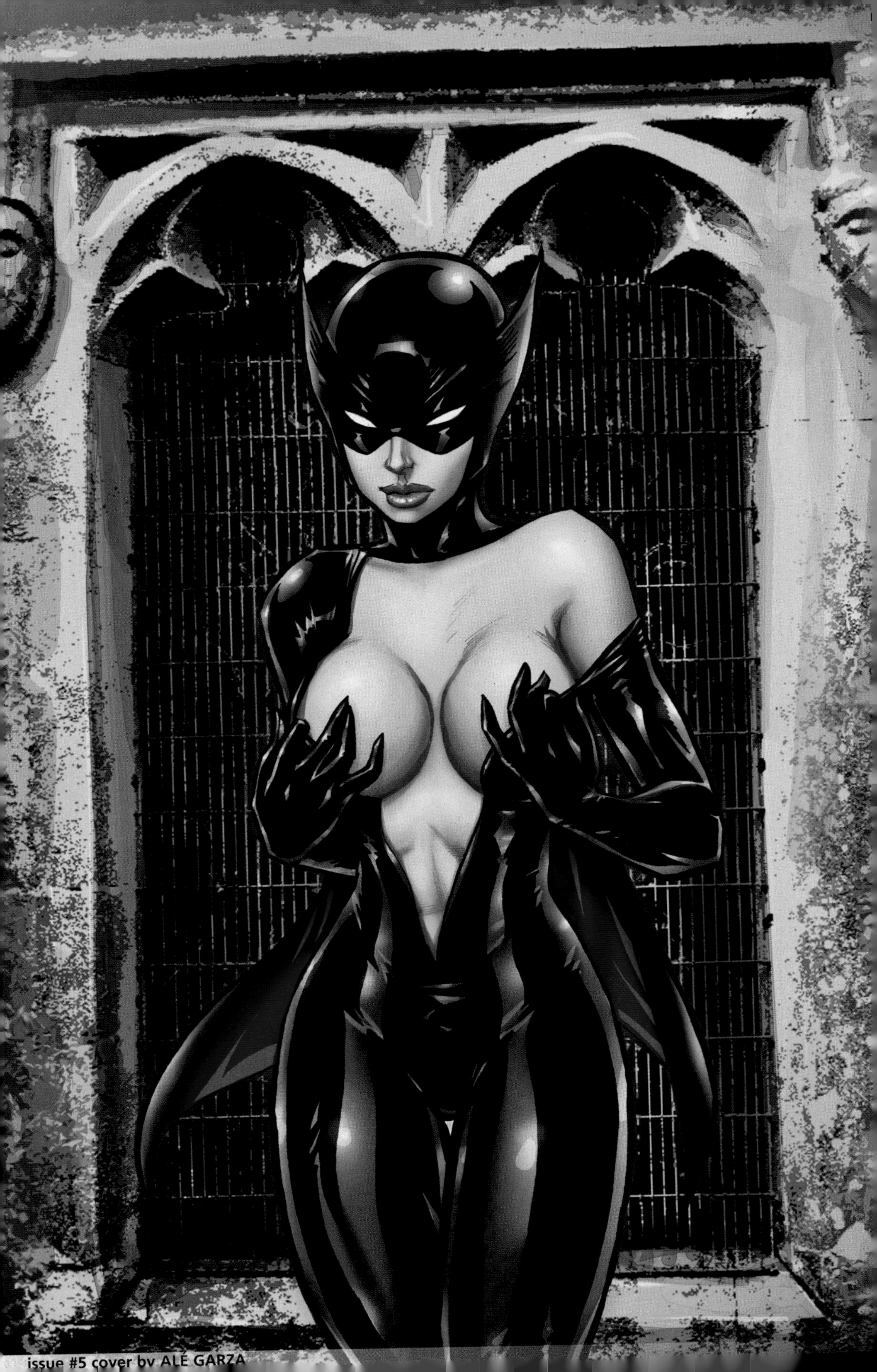
issue #5 cover by ALÉ GARZA

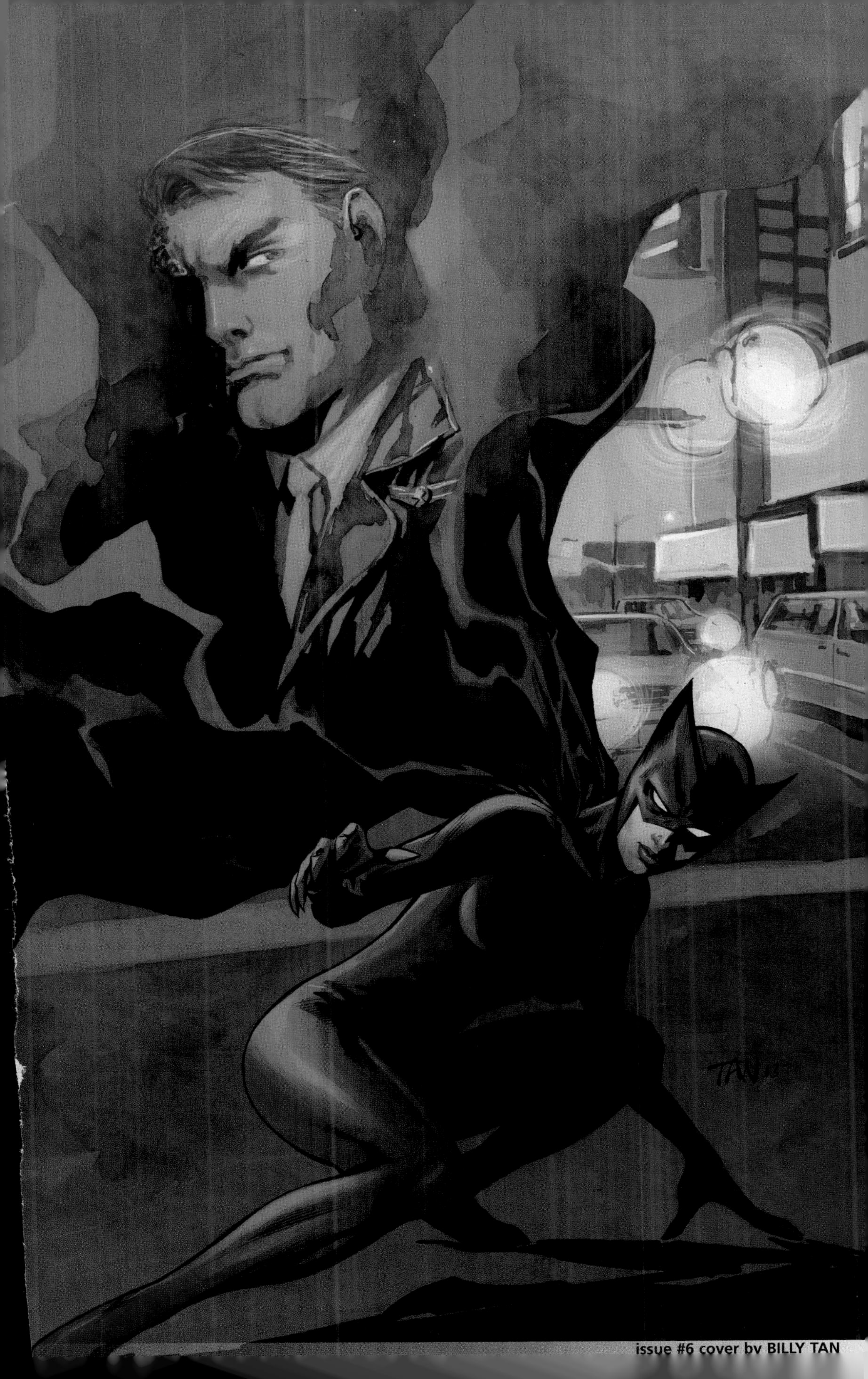
TAN

issue #6 cover by BILLY TAN

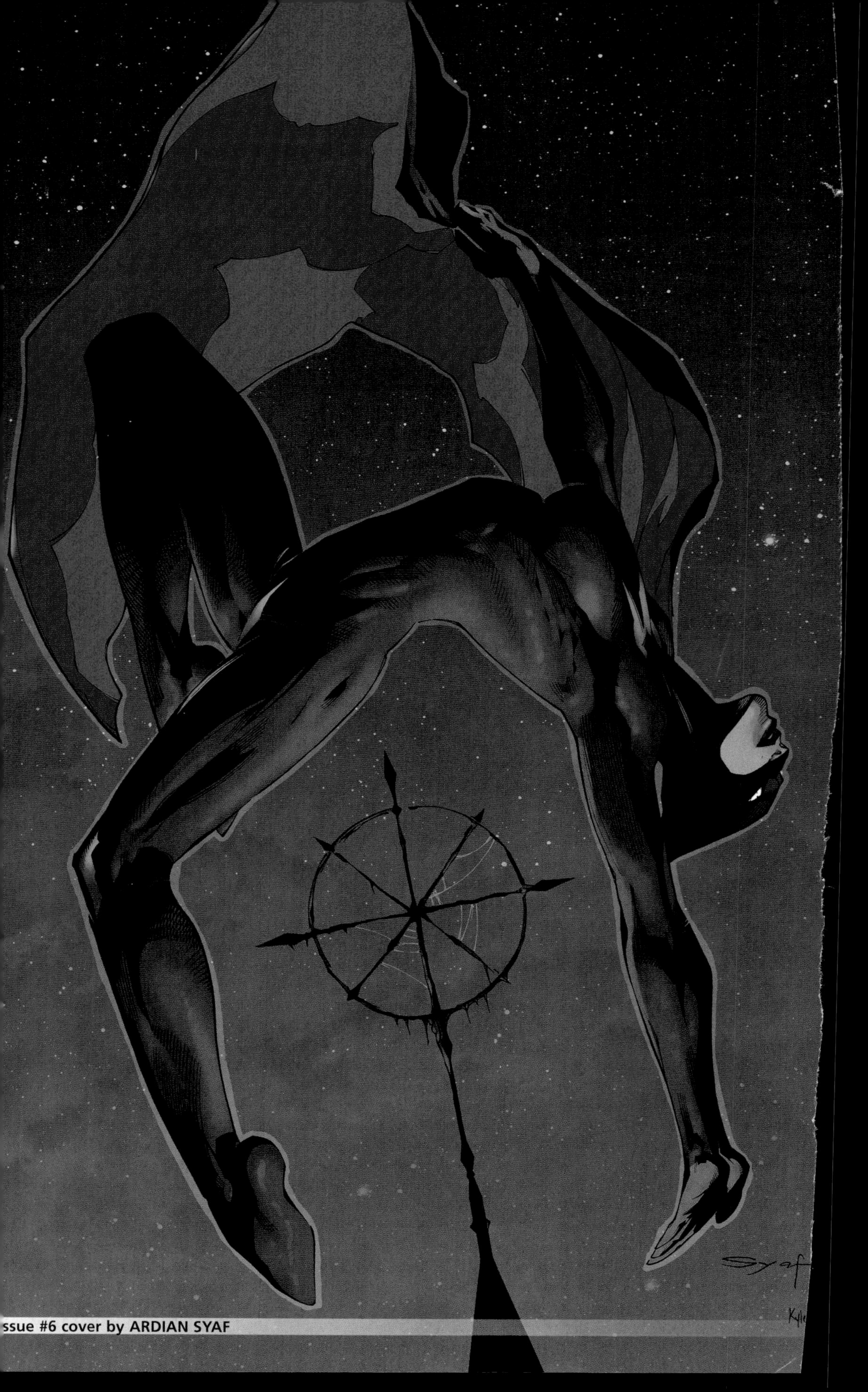
Syaf

ssue #6 cover by ARDIAN SYAF

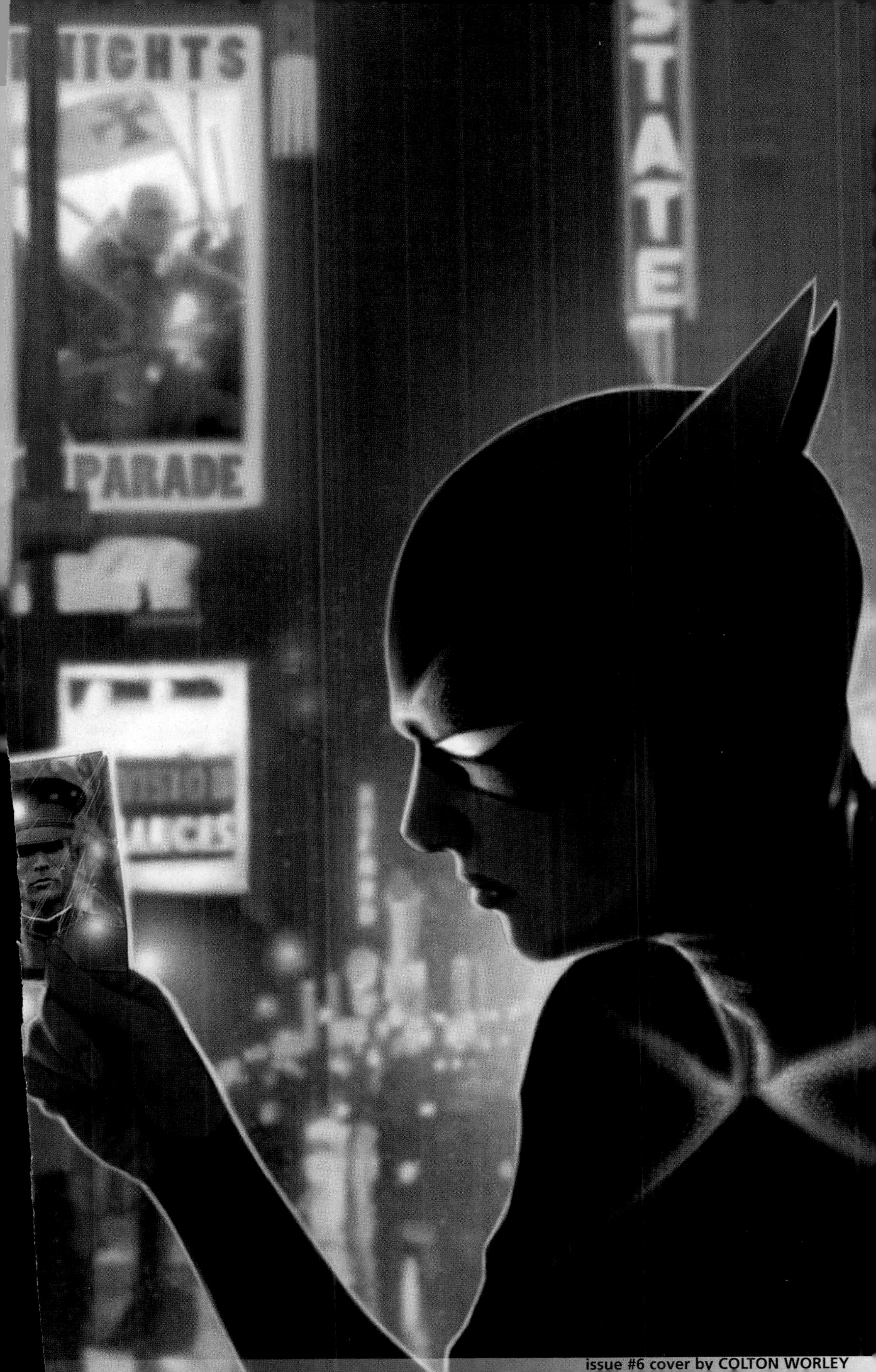
NIGHTS
PARADE
STATE

issue #6 cover by COLTON WORLEY

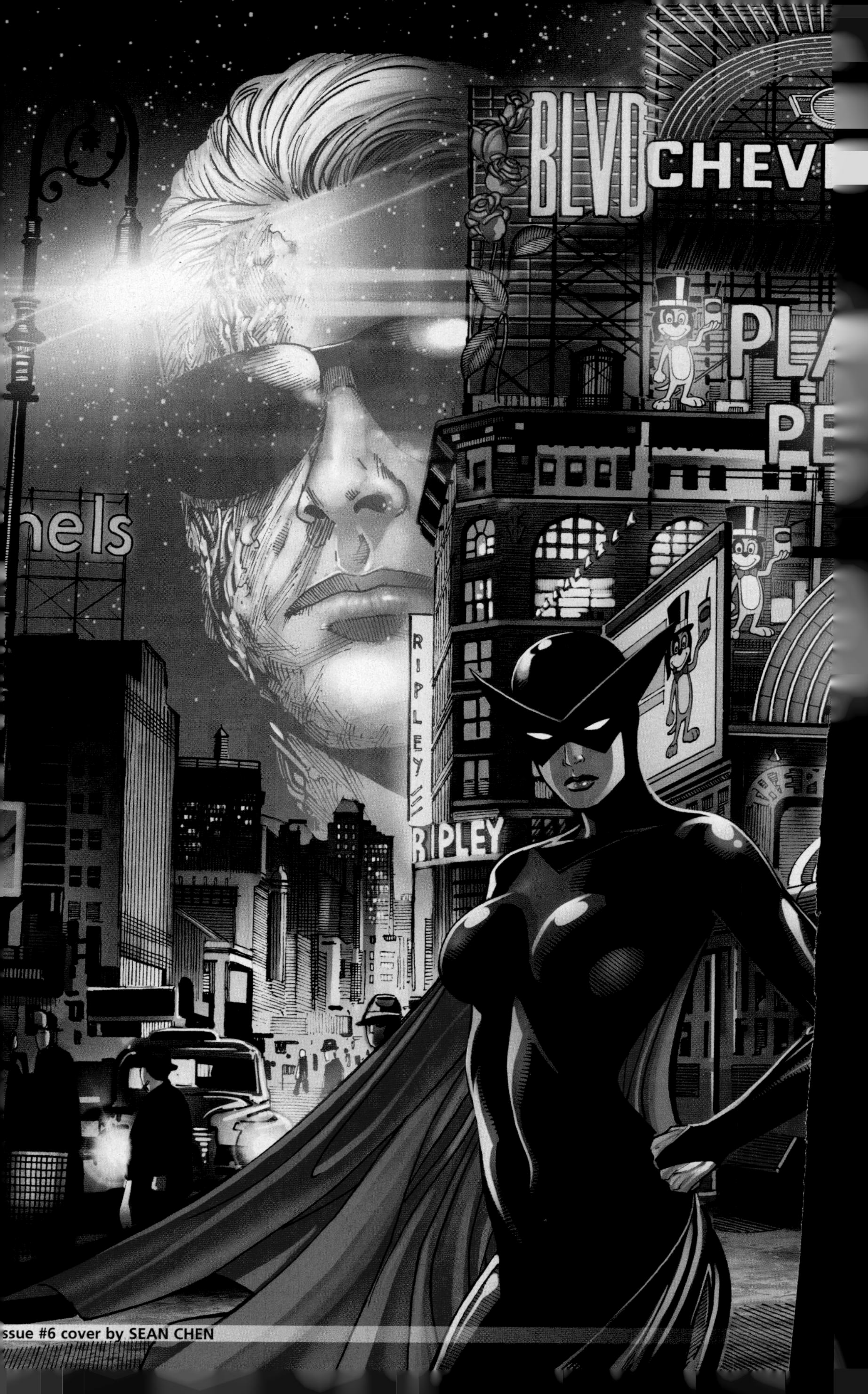
BLVD
CHEV
nels
PLA
PE
RIPLEY
RIPLEY
ssue #6 cover by SEAN CHEN

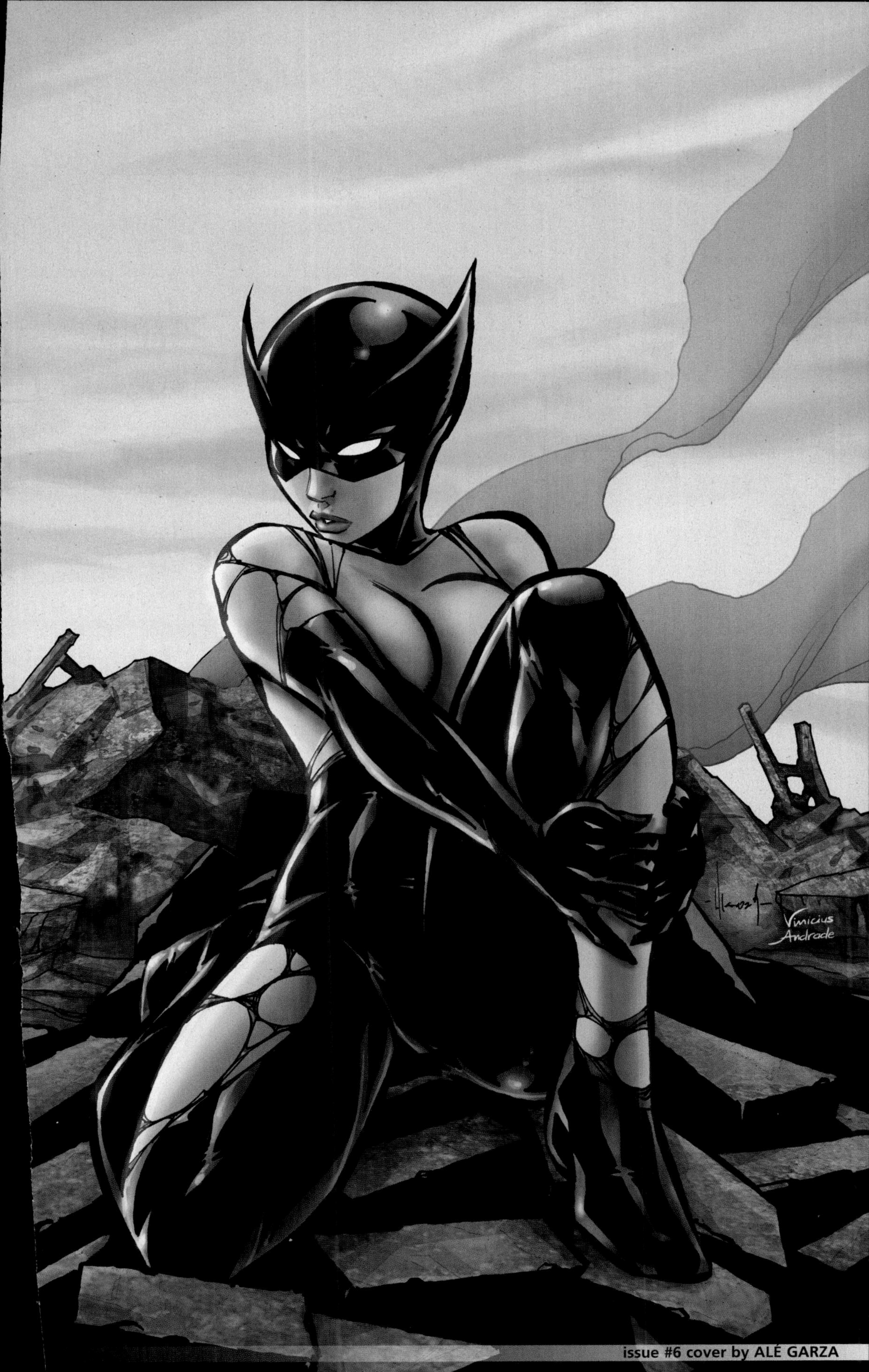
Vinicius
Andrade

issue #6 cover by ALÉ GARZA

"Waid is clearly on top of his game"
– NEWSARAM[A]

"Complete fun from start to finish"
– READ COMIC BOO[KS]

"You can't go wrong"
– DEN OF GE[EK]

"It's a fun ride from st[art]
to finish." – I[GN]

"Waid has crafted a great story"
– COMIC BOOK THERA[PY]

"A remarkable tribute to the fam[ous]
pulp hero." – MAJOR SPOIL[ERS]

The GREEN HORNET

Volume One: Bully Pulpit Trade Pap[erback]
By Mark Waid, Daniel Indro, and Ronilso[n Freire]
Collecting issues 1-6 of the acclaime[d series]
Collection in stores November 2013 - Ongoing series in stor[es]

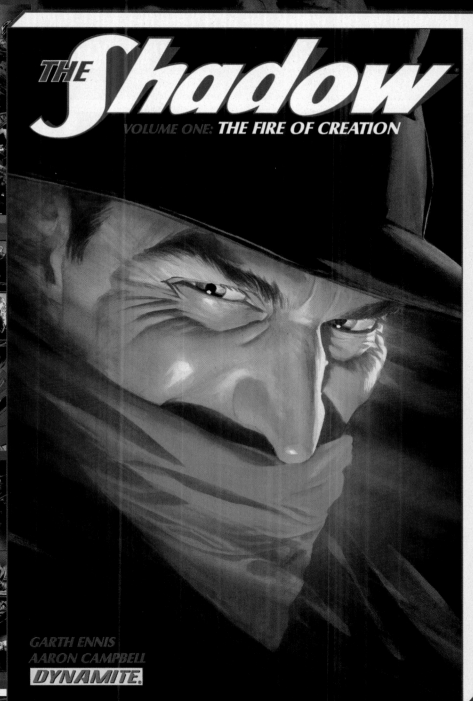

# THE SHADOW VOL. 1:
## THE FIRE OF CREATION TRADE PAPERBACK
written by *GARTH ENNIS* art by *AARON CAMPBELL*
cover by *ALEX ROSS*

"The Shadow is powerful, scary and full of crazy new powers of which most people are probably unaware. And under Garth Ennis' crafty pen, he is intimidating and interesting, both in and out of costume. I look forward to reading about the evil lurking in the hearts of men, especially if this version of the Shadow is on the case"
– NEWSARAMA

Reprinting issues #1-6, along with a complete cover gallery & more!

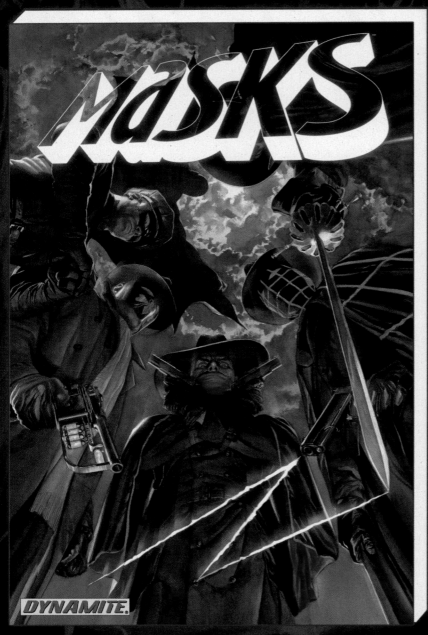

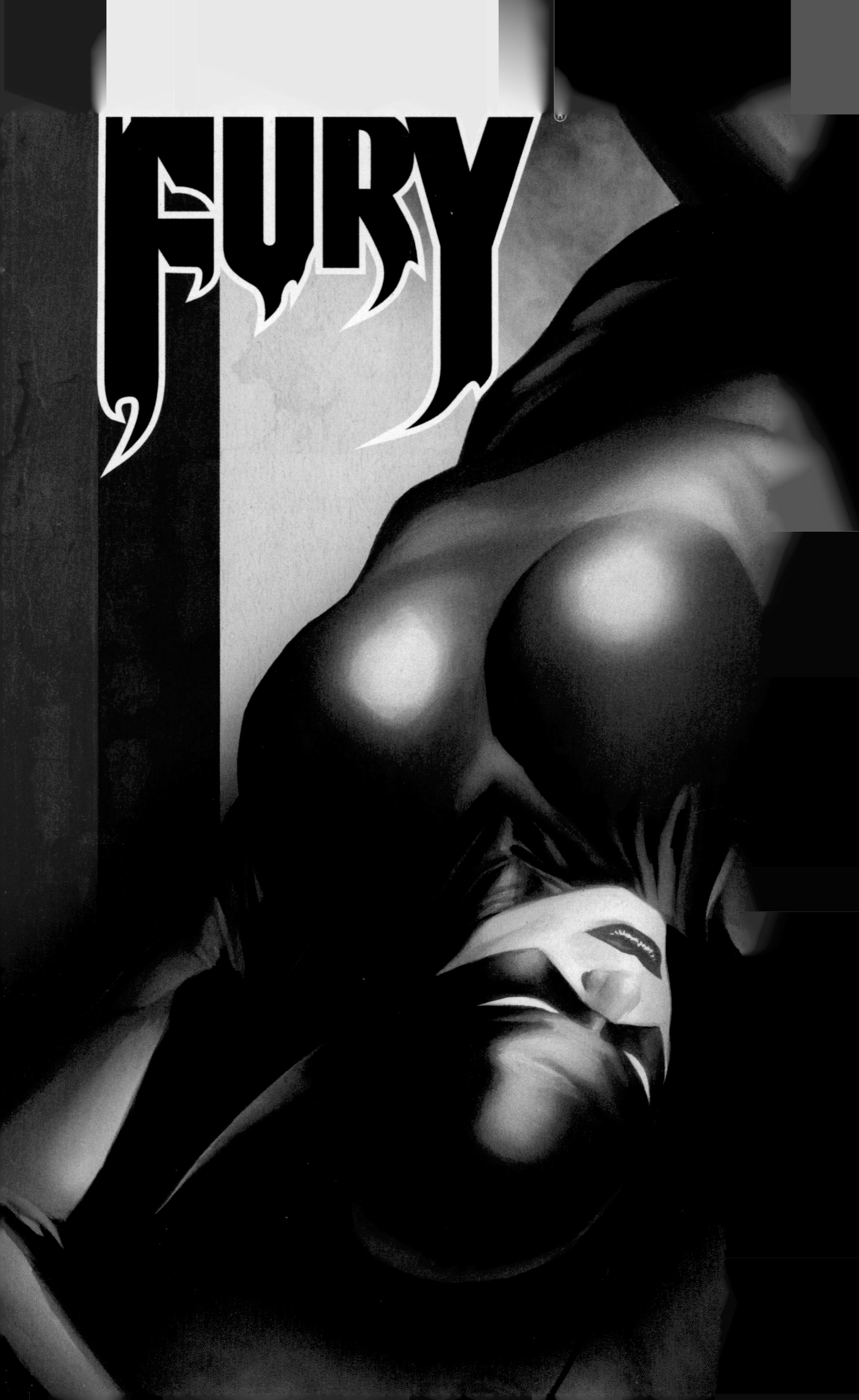
FURY